The Best of Mainly for Students

Volume Three

Edited by

Leslie Blake
and
Austen Imber

2004

EG BOOKS

A division of Reed Business Information
Estates Gazette, 151 Wardour Street, London W1F 8BN

First volume published 1993
Second volume published 1999
This volume published 2004

ISBN 0 7282 0422 3

©Estates Gazette 2004

Apart from any fair dealing for the purposes of research or private study, or criticism or review, as permitted under the UK Copyright Designs and Patents Act 1988, this publication may not be reproduced, stored, or transmitted, in any form or by any means, without the prior written permission of the Publishers, or in the case of reprographic reproduction, only in accordance with the terms of the licences issued by the Copyright Licensing Agency in the UK, or in accordance with the terms of licences issued by the appropriate Reproduction Rights Organisation outside the UK. Enquiries concerning reproduction outside the terms stated here should be sent to the Publishers.

The Publishers, editors and contributors make no representation, express or implied, with regard to the accuracy of the information contained in this publication and cannot accept any legal responsibility or liability for any errors or omissions.

The material contained in this publication constitutes general guidelines only and does not represent to be advice on any particular matter. No reader or purchaser should act on the basis of material contained in this publication without first taking professional advice appropriate to their particular circumstances. The Publishers expressly disclaim any liability to any person who acts in reliance on the contents of this publication. Readers of this publication should be aware that only Acts of Parliament and Statutory Instruments have the force of law and that only courts can authoritatively interpret the law.

Copying in any form (including all hard copy and electronic formats) is strictly forbidden without written permission from the Publishers, Estates Gazette, a division of Reed Business Information.

Typeset by Amy Boyle, Rochester, Kent
Printed in Great Britain by Bell & Bain Ltd., Glasgow

Contents

Foreword vii
Preface ix
Table of Cases xi
Table of Legislation xvii

Business Skills/Economics
1. Establishing your own practice 3
2. Business identity 9
3. Raising business finance 15
4. Business development/consultancy 25
5. Company accounts 30
6. Inflation 39
7. Negotiation skills 47

Commercial Law
8. Data protection 57
9. Self-employment and tax 62
10. Financial Services agency 68
11. *Force majeure* in contract law 73
12. Ratification and common mistake in contract law 79
13. Dealing with redundancies 85
14. Small print regulations 91

Construction and Dispute Resolution
15. Construction liability in contract and tort 99
16. The new scheme for adjudication under
    construction law 106
17. Partnering 111
18. Compensation for delay by contractors 117
19. International arbitration 123
20. Insurance against terrorism 128

Education and Training
21. Structured CPD training 137
22. Structured APC training 142
23. Lifelong learning 151

English Legal System
24. The definition of 'London' 159
25. The law of the calendar. 164
26. Denning's legal legacy. 169
27. Delegated legislation and the Human Rights Act 174
28. Famous cases: *R* v *Seddon* (1912) 179

Investment
29. Specialist property investment 187
30. Introduction to investment appraisal 196
31. High yield investment/business issues. 203

Landlord and Tenant/Estate Management
32. Introduction to Landlord and Tenant 213
33. Lease renewal. 223
34. Scottish/English Landlord and Tenant 231
35. Alienation 237
36. Dispute resolution – rent review. 247
37. Dispute resolution – other Landlord and Tenant. 255
38. Dilapidations (part 1) 264
39. Dilapidations (part 2) 272
40. Remedies for rent default 279
41. Peaceful re-entry. 288
42. Forfeiture and surrender of leases 293
43. Service charge disputes 299

Planning, Development and Environment
44. Water pollution and the law. 307
45. Human rights and the law of sewers 312
46. The law relating to waste disposal. 317
47. Public and private nuisance 322
48. Statutory nuisance 327
49. Noise nuisance and the doctrine of implied repeal. 332
50. Conservation areas and the law 337
51. Listed buildings. 343
52. Planning contravention notices 348
53. ISVA assignment submission/development scheme 352
54. Urban regeneration/RDAs 360

Procedure and Evidence
55. The rule against bias. 369
56. Expert witnesses (part 1). 375

57. Expert witnesses (part 2) 380
58. Similar fact evidence 385

Property Law and Trusts

59. Proprietary estoppel 395
60. Restrictive covenants on land 400
61. Secret trusts 406

Residential

62. Housing market 413
63. Residential lettings 418
64. Anti-social behaviour orders 427

Valuation

65. Introduction to investment valuation 435
66. Surrender and renewal valuations 444
67. Valuation of trading properties 450
68. Rating 456
69. Quarterly in advance 465
70. Rent-free periods 473
71. Telecoms valuation 480

Index 485

Foreword

'Mainly' is the operative word in the *Mainly for Students* articles that have appeared fortnightly in the *Estates Gazette* now since 1958. Research shows that these regular two or three page articles are as popular with property professionals born in the 50s and 60s as those born in the 70s and early 80s. Not only that, the same research shows that the articles that range from Establishing your own practice (chapter 1) to the Valuation of telecommunication installations (chapter 71) are just as well read as the weekly news.

Those that operate in the market need to acquire and maintain a deep knowledge of topics as diverse as International arbitration (p123) and the Law of waste disposal (p317). That knowledge needs to be constantly refreshed – and EG's *Mainly for Students* writers provide a clear and simple refreshing mechanism for both student and experienced practitioner alike.

But as the title of this third edition of *The Best of Mainly for Students* makes clear – this book is aimed more squarely at those entering the field who are seeking to gain a clear and simple understanding of the property profession. This carefully selected series of 71 articles that have appeared in *Estates Gazette* between 1998 and 2002 will, we hope, enable the reader to do just that.

Peter Bill
Editor
Estates Gazette

December 2003

Preface

Now in its 45th year, the *Mainly for Students* series continues to appeal to practitioners as well as university students.

This reflects the ongoing education of all property professionals, including accomplished specialists requiring an overview of other subjects.

The articles seek to combine business issues with mainstream areas of surveying practice, with comprehensive coverage also being made of legal aspects. Many of the articles cover the basic aspects of a subject, and also act as a platform for further study.

The selection of articles for this volume avoids those which have become outdated. In some cases, however, parts of articles may be affected by developments in case law, market practice, economic and property market conditions etc. since the original date of publication.

In *Estates Gazette*, the articles alternate on a two-weekly basis between the legal side, edited by Leslie, and the general practice side, edited by Austen.

Over the period 1998 to 2002, which makes up this third *Best of Mainly for Students*, the following have contributed to the legal side in addition to Leslie's many contributions.

Aviva Golden, freelance legal writer and author of *The Daily Telegraph Guide to Everyday Law*.

Silviu Klein, Barrister, Chief Executive, Specialist Engineering Contractors Group, London W2.

Janice Lambert, Formerly Standards Development Manager at the Financial Services Authority, London W4.

Adam Lominicki (died 11 July 2000), formerly Senior Lecturer in Law in the Department of Estate Management, South Bank University.

Rosalind Malcolm, Barrister, University Director in Law, Department of Law, University of Surrey.

Dr Alan Morris, Quantity Surveyor and Visiting Lecturer in Law, School of Surveying, Kingston University; South Bank University; and Surrey University.

Martin Moyes, Solicitor, London N1.

Gail Price, Barrister, Lecturer in Law, The College of Law, London.

Olivia Rahman, Visiting Lecturer in Law, University of Surrey.

Charles Ward, Solicitor, Chadwell Heath.

On the general practice side, many of the articles were contributed by Austen personally, having taken over as editor from Phil Askham in 1998. The following have either contributed articles or provided expert input within a number of articles.

Phil Askham, Senior Lecturer in Valuation at the School of Urban and Regional Studies, Sheffield Hallam University (and editor of *Mainly for Students*, 1988 to 1998).

Kerry Bourne, Partner, GVA Grimley.

Allyson Colby, Christopher Hancock and Suzanne Lloyd Holt, Wragge & Co LLP, solicitors, Birmingham.

Margaret Harris, CPD Policy Officer, Royal Institution of Chartered Surveyors.

David James, Northampton Valuation Office, and formerly Senior Lecturer at University of Central England.

Milan Khatri, Chief Economist, Royal Institution of Chartered Surveyors.

Thanks are also due on the general practice side to Howard Imber for proof reading, and to Mia Charlton for advice on suitability for students.

Support regarding education and training issues was provided by Scott Kind of GVA Grimley and Jacky Gutteridge of Birmingham Property Services.

For the ongoing series on regeneration, and also in view of their wider support of property educational initiatives, acknowledgements are due to Advantage West Midlands Regional Development Agency, in particular surveyors Honor Boyd, Yaseen Mohammed, Kitt Walker and Karen Yeomans.

The invaluable support provided by the main team at Estates Gazette includes editor, Peter Bill, and also Henry Everett, Alison Henry, Chris Moreton (since retired) and Adam Tinworth.

Particular thanks go also to former editor Phil Askham for the success of previous *Best of Mainly for Students*, and the consequent commissioning of this latest volume.

Leslie Blake and Austen Imber

December 2003

Table of Cases

Agip SpA v Navigazione Alta Italia SpA (The Nai Genova and
  The Nai Superba) [1984] 1 Lloyd's Rep 353 82

Bagot v Stevens Scanlon [1966] 1 QB 197 104
Beech v Secretary of State for the Environment [1993] EGCS
  214 348
Benjamin (VO) v Anston Properties Ltd [1998] 2 EGLR 147 457
Berger v Raymond Sun Ltd [1984] 1 WLR 625. 391
Billson v Residential Apartments Ltd [1992] 1 EGLR 43 . . . . 290, 295
Bishop Auckland Local Board v Bishop Auckland Iron Co (1882)
  10 QBD 138. 328
Blackwell v Blackwell [1929] AC 318 406
Botross v Hammersmith & Fulham London Borough Council [1995]
  Env LR 217 431
Butcher Robinson & Staples Ltd v London Regional Transport
  [1999] 3 EGLR 63 324

Cala Homes (South) Ltd v Alfred McAlpine Homes East Ltd
  (No 1) [1995] FSR 818 380
Cambridge Water Co Ltd v Eastern Counties Leather plc [1994]
  AC 264; [1994] 1 All ER 53. . . . . 308, 312, 323
Castle v St Augustine's Links (1922) 38 TLR 615 . . . . 322, 325
Central Estates (Belgravia) Ltd v Woolgar (No 2) [1972] 223
  EG 1273 290
Clay v AJ Crump & Sons Ltd [1963] 3 All ER 685 99
Cleaver dec'd, In re [1981] 1 WLR 939 409
Cleveland County Council v Springett [1985] IRLR 131 87
Clingham v Kensington & Chelsea Royal London Borough Council
  [2002] UKHL 39. 428
Collis Radio Ltd v Secretary of State for the Environment [1975]
  1 EGLR 146. 403
Conway v Crow Kelsey and Partners (1994) 39 Con LR 1 104
Co-operative Insurance Society Ltd v Centremoor (1983) 268
  EG 1027 83
Coular v Truefitt Ltd [1899] 2 Ch 309. 81
Coventry City Council v Cartwright [1975] 2 EGLR 112 331
Crane v Hegeman-Harris Co Inc [1939] 4 All ER 68, CA;
  [1939] 1 All ER 662 . . . . 81, 82

Dale dec'd, In re [1993] 4 All ER 129 409
Damiano v Topfer 105 Foro It 2285 (Cass 1982) 75

Danish Bacon Co Ltd Staff Pension Fund Trusts, Christensen, Re
  v Arnett [1971] 1 WLR 248................................. 408
Dean v Dean [1987] 1 FLR 517 429
Debenhams plc v Westminster City Council [1987] 1 EGR 248 344
Derry v Peek (1889) 14 App Cas 337........................... 351
Deutsche Schachbau und Tiefbohrgesellschaft mbH v R:As Al
  Khaimah National Oil Co [1987] 2 All ER 769................... 75
Dimes v Grand Junction Canal (1852) 3 HL Cas 759 .... 370, 372
Doe d Henniker v Watt (1828) 8 B&C 308 288
Donoghue v Stevenson (?) AC 562 404
Durham County Council v Peter Connors Industrial Services Ltd
  [1992] Crim LR 743 320
Dutton v Bognor Regis Urban District Council [1972]
  1 QB 373... 171
Dymond v Pearce [1972] 1 All ER 1142....................... 323

Ellen Street Estates Ltd v Minister of Health [1934] 1 KB 590 333
Etablissements Levy (Georges et Paul) v Adderley Navigation Co
  Panama SA (The Olympic Pride) [1980] 2 Lloyd's Rep 67.......... 83
Expert Clothing Service & Sales Ltd v Hillgate House Ltd [1985]
  2 EGLR 85.. 289
Express & Echo Publications Ltd v Tanton [1999] ICR 396........... 64

Fluor Daniel Properties Ltd v Shortlands Investments Ltd [2001]
  2 EGLR 103.. 300
Folkes v Chadd (1782) 3 Doug KB 157 374

Gateshead Metropolitan Borough Council v Secretary of State for
  the Environment [1994] 1 PLR 85........................... 317
Gillett v Holt [2000] 2 All ER 289 395
Gilje v Charlegrove Securities Ltd [2000] 3 EGLR 89 302
Glossop v Heston and Isleworth Local Board (1879) 12 ChD 102 ... 312
Godden v Hales (1686) 11 St Tr 1165 332
Gold v Hill [1999] 1 FLR 54.................................. 407
Goldman v Hargrave [1967] 1 AC 645 313
Grand Metropolitan plc v William Hill Group Ltd [1997] 1 BCLC 390 .. 82
Great Western Railway Co v Bishop (1872) 7 LR QB 550.......... 329

H (Minors) (Sexual Abuse Standard of Proof) Re [1996] AC 563..... 429
Hadley v Baxendale (1854) 9 Ex 341 119
Haringey Borough Council v Jowett [1999] EGCS 64.......... 334, 335
Henderson v Merrett Syndicates Ltd [1995] 2 AC 145 104
Hill v Secretary of State for the Environment [1993] JPL 158 348
Hinz v Berry [1970] 2 QB 40 170
Hirji Muiji v Cheong Yue Steamship Co Ltd [1926] AC 497 76

Table of Cases

Holding & Management Ltd v Property Holding & Investment Trust
  plc [1990] 1 All ER 938. 301
Hornal v Neuberger Products [1957] 1 QB 427 429
Hunter v Canary Wharf Ltd [1997] 2 All ER 426 . . . . 324, 325, 327
Hussey v Palmer [1972] 1 WLR 1286. 406

Intertradex SA v Lesieur-liJrteaux Sari [1978] 2 Lloyd's Rep 509 77
Inwards v Baker [1965] 2 QB 29 397
Ives (ER) Investment Ltd v High [1967] 2 QB 379. 397

Joscelyne v Nissen [1970] 2 QB 86 80

Kasperbauer v Griffith, unreported November 21 1997 409

Large v Mainprize [1989] Crim LR 213. 351
Lauritzen AS v Wijsmuller BV (The Super Servant Two) [1989]
  1 Lloyd's Rep 148 . . . . 74, 78
Leakey v National Trust for Places of Historical Interest or Natural
  Beauty [1980] 2 WLR 65 313
Lebeaupin v Richard Crispin & Co [1920] 2 KB 714. 74
Liverpool Roman Catholic Archdiocesan Trustees Inc v Goldberg
  (No 2) The Times, 9 March 2001 383
Lomax Leisure Ltd, Re [1999] 2 EGLR 37 291
London & Leeds Estates Ltd v Paribas Ltd (No 2) [1995] 1 EGLR
  102 . . . . 375, 378
Lonsdale & Thompson Ltd v Black Arrow Group plc [1993]
  1 EGLR 87. 160
Lovell & Christmas Ltd v Wall (1911) 104 LT 84 80

Mackenzie v Coulson (1869) LR8 Eq 368. 80
Magor and St Mellons Rural District Council v Newport Borough
  Council [1951] 2 All ER 839 171
Malton Board of Health v Malton Manure Co (1879) 4 Exch D 302. . . 328
Marcic v Thames Water Utilities Ltd [2002] EWCA Civ 64; [2002]
  07 EG (CS) 122; [2004] 1 All ER 135 . . . . 312, 314, 315, 316
Matharu v Matharu (1994) 68 P&CR 93 397
Metropolitan Asylum District v Hill (1881) 6 App Cas 193. 160
Metropolitan Board of Works v McCarthy (1874) LR 7 HL 243. 159
Metropolitan Properties v Lannon [1968] 1 QB 577 369
Montgomery v Johnson Underwood Ltd [2001] EWCA Civ 318;
  [2001] ICR 819. 63
Mood Music Publishing Co v De Wolfe [1976] Ch 119 391
Murphy v Brentwood District Council [1991] 1 AC 378;
  [1990] 2 All ER 908. . . . . 102, 104, 171, 316
Murray v Parker (1834) 19 Bear 305 82

National Coal Board v Neath Borough Council [1976] 2 All ER 478 . . 330
National Justice Campania Naviera SA v Prudential Assurance
  Co Ltd (The Ikarian Reefer) [1993] 2 EGLR 183 . . . . 375, 379
Navrom v Callitis Ship Management SA [1987] 2 Lloyd's Rep 276 75
Norsolor SA v Palbalk Ticaret Ltd (1983) YBComArb 362 75

Oceanic Village Ltd v Shirayama Shokusan Co Ltd [1999] EGCS 83 . . 82

Paal Wilson & Co AS v Partenreederei Hannah Blumenthal (The
  Hannah Blumenthal) [1983] 1 Lloyd's Rep 103 76
Parke v Daily News [1962] Ch 927 86
Palmiero, Re (debtor 3666 of 1999) [1999] 3 EGLR 27 291
Pemberton v Southwark London Borough Council [2000]
  2 EGLR 33 326
Porter v Honey [1989] 1 EGLR 189 172
Pritchard v Clwyd County Council The Times 16 July 1992 314
Pugh v Arton (1869) LR 8 Eq 626 291

R v Bolsover DC ex p Paterson [2000] EGCS 83 345
R v Bow Street Metropolitan Magistrates, ex parte Pinochet
  [1998] 4 All ER 897 370
R v Bow Street Metropolitan Stipendary Magistrates, ex parte
  Pinochet (No 2) [1999] 2 WLR 272 371
R v Bristol City Council ex parte Everett [1999] 2 AllER 193 . . . . 328, 331
R v Carrick District Council ex parte Shelley [1996] Env LR 273 330
R v Courvoisier (1840) 9 C&P 362 383
R v Deal Corporation and Justices, ex parte Curling (1881)
  46 JP 71 372
R v Falmouth and Truro Port Health Authority ex parte South West
  Water Ltd [2000] 3 AllER 306 328
R v Leominster District Council, ex parte Antique Country Buildings
  Ltd [1988] 2 PLR 23 346
R v Palmer (1856) Notable British Trials Series 382
R v Pittwood (1902) 19 TLR 37 101
R v Rouse (1931) Notable British Trials Series 375
R v Seddon (1912) Notable British Trials Series 179
R v Sharrock [1993] 3 All ER 917 322
R v Smith (1915) Notable British Trials Series 390
R v Sussex Justices, ex parte McCarthy [1924] 1 KB 256 . . . . . 370, 373
R v Teignbridge District Council, ex parte Teignmouth Quay Co Ltd
  [1995] 2 PLR 1 349
R v Westminster City Council, ex parte Leicester Square Coventry
  Street Association Ltd [1989] EGLS 38 402
R (on the application of Anglian Water Services Ltd) v Environment
  Agency [2002] 06EG155 (CS) 314

R (on the application of Bono) v Harlow District Council [2002]
    EWHC 423. 176
R (on the application of McCann) v Manchester Crown Court [2002]
    UKHL 39 428
R (on the application of Professional Contractors Group Ltd) v
    Inland Revenue Commissioners [2002] STC 165 66
Ramsden v Dyson (1866) LR 1HL 129. 399
Ready Mixed Concrete (South East) Ltd v Minister of Pensions
    and National Insurance [1968] 2QB 497. 63
Rimmer v Liverpool City Council [1984] 1 EGLR 23 331
Rochefoucauld v Bousted [1897] 1 Ch196. 409
Rugby School v Tannahill [1935] 1 KB 87 289
Rylands v Fletcher (1868) LR 3 HL 330 312

Salford City Council v McNally [1975] 2 EGLR 28. . . . . 328, 329, 330
Sedleigh Denfield v O'Callaghan [1940] 3 All ER 340 (HL) 322
Shimizu (UK) Ltd v Westminster City Council [1996] 3 PLR 89. 339
Shipley Urban District Council v Bradford Corporation [1936]
    Ch 375 81
Skerritts of Nottingham Ltd v Secretary of State for Transport and
    the Regions [1999] 2 PLR 109 344
Snaith and Dolding's Application, Re (1995) 71 P&CR 104. 403
Snowden dec'd, In re [1979] 2 WLR 654 . . . . 407, 409
Sonat Offshore SA v Amerada Hess Development Ltd [1988]
    1 Lloyd's Rep 145 74
South Lakeland District Council v Secretary of State for the
    Environment [1992] 1 PLR 143. 338
Southwark London Borough Council v Ince (1989) 21
    HLR 504 . . . . 334, 335
Sparham-Souter v Town & Country Developments (Essex) Ltd
    [1977] 1 EGLR 61 172
Sykes v Secretary of State for the Environment [1981] 1 EGLR 137. . 349

Targett v Torfaen Borough Council [1992] 1 EGLR 275. 331
Tarry v Ashton [1876] LR 1 QB 314 324
Tate & Lyle Food and Distribution Ltd v Greater London Council
    [1983] 1 All ER 1159 (HL). 324
Taylors Fashion Ltd v Liverpool Victoria Trustees Co Ltd [1982]
    QB 133 398
Templiss Properties Ltd v Hyams [1999] EGCS 60. 80
Tennent v Earl of Glasgow (1864) 2 Macph HL (22) 73
Tombesi [1997] 3 CMLR 673. 319
Trafford Metropolitan Borough Council v Secretary of State for
    Transport and the Regions [2000] PLSCS 118 338
Tulk v Moxhay (1848) 2 Ph 774 400

University of Westminster, In re [1998] EGCS 118 402

Vauxhall Estates Ltd v Liverpool Corporation [1932] 1 KB 733...... 333
Vessoso and Zanetti [1990] 1 ECR 146; 2 LMELR 133............ 319

Waste Incineration Services and Jacob v Dudley Metropolitan
 Borough Council [1992] 4 LMELR 200...................... 320
Weston's Settlements, Re [1968] 3 All ER 338.................. 170
Willmott v Barber (1880) 15 ChD 96 399
Wivenhoe Port v Colchester Borough Council [1985] JPL 175...... 330

Table of Legislation

Statutes
Access to Neighbouring Land Act 1992. 271
Acquisition of Land (Assessment of Compensation) Act 1919 333
Administration of Justice Act 1960 428
Arbitration Act 1996. . . . . 125, 249

Bill of Rights 1688. 177

Calendar (New Style) Act 1750 166
Civil Evidence Act 1995. 250
Crime and Disorder Act 1998. . . . . 427, 430
Criminal Law Act 1977. . . . . 289, 291
Criminal Procedure Act 1865. 378

Data Protection Act 1998 57
Defective Premises Act 1972. . . . . 103, 172

Employment Protection Act 1975 86
Employment Protection (Consolidation) Act 1978 86
Environmental Protection Act 1990 . . . . 319, 327, 334, 431

Finance Act 2000 296
Financial Services and Markets Acts 2000 68
Fires Prevention (Metropolis) Act 1774 160
Food Safety Act 1990 431

Health and Safety at Work Act 1974 431
Housing Act 1925 333
Housing Act 1930 332
Housing Act 1985 . . . . 333, 431
Housing Act 1988 423
Housing Act 1996 423
Housing Grants, Construction, and Regeneration Act 1996 . . . . 106, 112
Human Rights Act 1998. . . . . 176, 313

Industrial Relations Acts 1971. 86

Landlord and Tenant Act 1927 . . . . 230, 238, 239, 272
Landlord and Tenant Act 1954. . . . . 216, 223, 288
Landlord and Tenant Act 1985. . . . . 301, 423
Landlord and Tenant Act 1988. 245

Landlord and Tenant (Covenants) Act 1995 . . . . 220, 239, 270
Lands Tribunal Act 1949 402
Latent Damage Act 1986. . . . . 103, 173
Law of Property Act 1925 . . . . 268, 281, 289, 294, 403, 407
Law of Property Act 1969 404
Law Reform (Contributory Negligence) Act 1945 100
Law Reform (Frustrated Contracts) Act 1943. 76
Leasehold Property (Repairs) Act 1938. . . . . 268, 276, 289, 295
Local Government and Finance Act 1988 456
Local Government and Housing Act 1985 333
London Building Acts 1930–1939 161
London Government Act 1963 161

Magna Carta 1297 177
Metropolitan Management Act 1855 159
Metropolitan Paving Act 1817 159
Metropolitan Police Act 1829 159
Metropolitan Poor Act 1867. 159

Noise and Statutory Nuisance Act 1993 334

Party Walls Act 1996. 271
Planning and Compensation Act 1991. 349
Planning (Listed Buildings and Conservation Areas) Act 1990
. . . . 337, 339, 341, 343, 345
Protection from Eviction Act 1977 . . . . 288, 292, 295
Public Health Act 1936 . . . . 328, 334

Rating (Valuation) Act 1999 458
Redundancy Payments Act 1965 86
Rent Act 1977. 423

Short Titles Act 1896. 166

Telecommunications Act 1984. 481
Town and Country Planning Act 1971 349
Town and Country Planning Act 1990 349
Trade Union and Labour Relations (Consolidation) Act 1992 87

Unfair Contract Terms Act 1977 105

War Damage Acts 1941–1949. 129
Water Industry Act 1991 314

Statutory Instruments
Collective Redundancy and Transfer of Undertakings (Protection
  of Employment) (Amendment) Regulations 1995 87
Housing Benefit (General) Regulations 1971 176
Magistrates' Courts (Hearsay Evidence in Civil Proceedings)
  Rules 1999 430
Regulated Activities Order 2001 69
Transfer of Undertakings (Protection of Employment) Regulations
  1981 87
Unfair Terms in Consumer Contracts Regulations 1999 91

Business Skills/Economics

1. Establishing your own practice 3
2. Business identity. 9
3. Raising business finance. 15
4. Business development/consultancy 25
5. Company accounts. 30
6. Inflation. 39
7. Negotiation skills. 47

CHAPTER 1

Establishing your own practice

Published as 'Leader of the pack', 13 November 1999

The rewards of running your own business can be many – but so can the pressures and pitfalls. We look at what to consider in going it alone

Being your own boss may seem attractive, particularly when other employment offers limited career prospects or lesser financial rewards. Yet, as well as having the necessary expertise, surveyors need to ensure that the business proposition is viable and will be administered effectively.

Initial considerations

The personal qualities required to establish and run a business include initiative, determination, enthusiasm, confidence, commitment, resilience and organisational skills. Practitioners require management skills, leadership skills, the ability to make decisions, the ability to get on with clients and employees and an appetite for hard work over long hours. This may mean limited holidays and working through illness.

The effect on private and family life should also be considered. Families need to be supportive of the proposed venture. The financial risks should be evaluated. Even remote risks could induce concern, which can affect the success of a business.

Where a partnership is proposed, partners should consider what commitment they can each offer, and structure pay and other benefits accordingly. Conflicts may arise when partners are not equally dedicated.

Discussions could take place with contacts who already run their own businesses. Guidance could be sought from the RICS, or from organisations such as the Chamber of Commerce. The major banks produce guides for prospective businesses.

A business plan needs to be formulated, setting out the nature of the proposed venture and its financial projections. The lender will require a business plan if finance is being sought. The plan can subsequently be used to monitor performance and ensure that the original strategy is being adhered to.

Research and preparatory work can be done while in other employment. It may be possible to do certain work on a part-time basis in order to create a platform for the business to develop, or to establish whether the venture would be viable full-time.

Nature of the business

Some new businesses may start with a client base that has been developed elsewhere, and may immediately be successful. Others may be established more speculatively, relying on the reputation of an individual or partners to generate instructions.

A sole practitioner may wish to specialise in a narrow field, based on the expertise developed in previous employment, for example, in rating, in compulsory purchase compensation claims or in a particular line of investment consultancy. Expertise and reputation may result in a better-quality service than multi-skilled firms can offer.

Provided that sufficient business can be generated, special services may command higher fees than multi-skilled operations. Marketing could be better targeted and be more cost-effective. If instructions in a relatively narrow field dry up, the business could expand into other areas in due course.

The range of services to be offered by a practice should be determined when formulating the business plan. Regard needs to be given to whether the market has a requirement for the proposed services, and whether that market is growing or declining. Consideration should be given to the state of the economy and the property market, both locally and nationally.

An evaluation should be made of the other firms already operating in the particular market. Competition will vary between geographical areas and between the type of work undertaken. There may be scope to offer services which are not currently available or could be attractively differentiated from those already provided.

An assessment should be made of:

- who prospective clients might be;
- the volume of work that is likely to be generated; and
- the level of fees that could be commanded.

The geographical area that the practice intends to cover will depend on the nature of the practice, on the type of services being offered and on the requirements of clients.

If a practice purports to be able to offer a wide range of services, a certain level of expertise is required in all those areas. Value has to be added for clients. Clients are a source of repeat instructions, and may also introduce new clients. Clients could let others know if they are dissatisfied, resulting in a poor reputation being established.

Another partner, or a consultant, could be taken on in order to provide the practice with complementary skills. Surveying staff may need to be recruited. But once the practice expands beyond the resources of the principals, the operation of a businesses can change dramatically.

Principals may require training in business and management skills, or in basic accountancy and credit control.

Press releases and promotional material will be required. The name of the practice, letterheads, business cards, marketing particulars and other material should project the right image.

A profile as a sole practitioner or partnership may be considered more favourable than a limited company.

Accommodation

A sole practitioner may be able to work cost-effectively from home. Secretarial support may be available within the family.

However, running a business from home is not straightforward. Planning permission may be required. There may be restrictions on use within the title to the property, particularly for leasehold dwellings. The property may attract business rates. Mortgage arrangements or home insurance may be affected. Although it may be possible to set some expenses against tax, there could be a liability for capital gains tax if the property is sold.

Working from home requires a different method of operation and greater discipline than travelling to an office each day. A home atmosphere may not be attractive to clients. Accommodation could be taken in another firm's offices where secretarial services may also be available. Larger practices may require the profile provided by town or city centre accommodation which is accessible and attractive to clients.

Banking and financial requirements

A business plan should be formulated to enable a lender to assess the viability of the proposed venture. This need not be identical to that established for the benefit of the principals of the business. The lender will determine the amount of the loan that they are prepared to grant, and the rate of interest payable. Several lenders could be approached in order to secure the most favourable terms. It may be necessary for a home to be provided as security.

The business plan should set out the background, qualifications and experience of the individuals concerned. In addition to outlining factors such as the nature of the business, financial projections will have to be made.

Regard will be given to the level of fee income likely to be earned by the practice, to the costs incurred in employing other staff and to expenditure on items such as cars, office equipment and IT facilities (the internet and e-mail being essential). An assessment will be made of overheads such as rent, rates, service charges, insurance and utilities, and of items such as advertising and promotional expenditure.

The business plan should evaluate the risks that could result in projections not being realised, and should also outline opportunities that may be available to exceed the projections. The plan should consider how price-sensitive the market is for the proposed services.

It may be necessary to secure an overdraft facility to guard against cash-flow difficulties as the business develops. Partners may be able to inject additional cash. The business will require banking facilities, and possibly client accounts. A commercial mortgage may be needed if accommodation is being purchased. Leasing and hire purchase facilities may also be required.

Set-up costs and cash flow are important considerations. A new business may not be able to secure credit facilities, and have to purchase some items outright. Initial marketing expenditure may be substantial. Property transactions can take time to complete and delay the receipt of fee income. Valuation work can assist cash flow, but it is increasingly difficult for small, and particularly new, practices to secure major contracts/panel appointments.

Professional assistance

Legal advice is likely to be required to prepare partnership agreements or to establish a limited company. Practitioners should be familiar with data protection, copyright, misrepresentation, money laundering and, possibly, consumer credit and financial services legislation.

The name of the practice, stationery, invoices, letterheads, logos and advertising must meet certain requirements.

Letterheads and other material should correctly represent the status of the members of the firm. An employee could, for example, be held out to be partner if a letterhead does not distinguish between partners and staff.

Staff contracts may have to be prepared. The practice may need to be protected against staff leaving after a short period of time, or at short notice. Staff may have to be prevented from working for another practice in the area, and from taking the firm's clients with them. The firm may require the flexibility to shed staff cost-effectively.

Advice may have to be taken on matters such as annual leave policies, sick leave policies, or the need to arrange accident and illness insurance cover for principals or employees. Assistance may be required with other employment issues, such as health and safety, employees' entitlements, or ensuring that staff recruitment has regard to race and sex discrimination legislation.

An accountant is likely to be required to prepare the practice accounts and deal with VAT, income tax, general taxation issues, national insurance and pensions. An accountant can also assist with the financial projections for the business plan.

What the RICS requires

The practice must comply with the requirements of the RICS, some of which are as follows.

- Professional indemnity insurance. It is compulsory for surveyors to hold professional indemnity insurance, even if they are undertaking only a small amount of part-time work as a sole practitioner, or as a consultant. Surveyors acting as consultants to their former employer may, however, be covered by the firm's policy. Insurance is also required if surveyors undertake casual work outside their principal position of employment.
- Clients' money. If the practice intends to hold amounts such as rent, service charges or deposits on behalf of clients, the money should be paid into a separate bank account or 'client account'. The institution requires confirmation that clients' money has been administered properly.
- Rules of conduct. Surveyors should be familiar with the institution's rules of conduct. The rules cover matters such as

acting in the best interests of the client, being competent to do so, client confidentiality, standards of behaviour expected of chartered surveyors, advertising and attracting business, the relationship with the rest of the profession, disclosing conflicts of interest (which may involve declining to take instructions), involvement in connected businesses, the basis of fee quotes and taking fees for introducing business elsewhere.

Certain information has to be periodically provided to the institution, and surveyors have to undertake continuing professional development training. The institution, as well as the Inland Revenue, should be advised that a new business has been established.

Letters of instruction to clients need to meet the institution's requirements. Valuation report formats need to satisfy the provisions of the Red Book. Site boards must meet certain regulations. A complaints procedure will be required.

Conclusion

Running your own practice can provide personal, professional and financial rewards, but it has its pressures and risks. Prospective practitioners should ensure that there is a sustainable requirement for the services that they intend to offer. Administrative matters should be given early attention, so that once the practice is established, it can focus on fee-earning opportunities.

Contributed by Austen Imber

CHAPTER 2

Business identity

Published as 'What's in a name', 18 March 2000

The three main legal forms by which a smaller business can operate are as sole trader, partnership or limited company.

Choosing the right form is important for a business's image. An individual providing professional services could operate well as a principal, chartered surveyor, consultant or adviser. A one-man manufacturing or contracting concern will usually have greater credibility with suppliers and trade customers if it operates as a limited company.

Tradesmen dealing directly with the public could benefit from the personal touch associated with their name, such as 'Robert Evans, Electrician'. Names such as AA Plumbing will secure an early alphabetical appearance in Yellow Pages, but can sometimes appear disreputable.

The most suitable approach depends on the nature of the business and the market for its services – whether, for example, it is in a market town or a city.

A partnership, especially in professional services, offers the added prestige of an array of experts whose specialised knowledge could be attractive to clients.

The ability to transfer ownership of the business, and the retention of business names or brand names on sale – perhaps to help develop a new business, or to be sold elsewhere – depend upon the business type.

Although business names can be traded, individual names are not easily transferable. It should be noted that leases taken in the name of an individual may not be assignable, whereas a limited company, including its lease, could be sold – although the liability of any guarantors would continue.

Name selection is also important. Use of Millennium, for example, can appear unoriginal and tired. Carphone Warehouse could appear out of date with mobile phone technology. A relatively nondescript name can underpin a strong brand that stands the test of time.

Various trade names and branding could be used, with the true business identity not being apparent to customers – although it may be to suppliers.

Dixons, Currys and PC World are all owned by Dixons, for example. Smaller firms may take a similar approach, although stationery and other material must still indicate the true identity and legal basis of the business.

Searches on a limited company can establish the scale of its operation, but the size and solvency of a sole trader's venture or a partnership is difficult to establish.

Financial liability

The liability of the sole trader is unlimited. Business debts may have to be met by personal assets which, if insufficient, could result in bankruptcy. The same applies to a partnership, but each partner is jointly and severally liable for the business debts of the other(s).

The liability of shareholders within a limited company is limited to the amount of capital subscribed for the shares – which is issued share capital as opposed to authorised share capital – or to uncalled capital – issued share capital which is partly paid. However, directors may have to give personal guarantees to banks, suppliers, landlords and so on, particularly in the case of smaller companies, which would otherwise be sole traders or small partnerships.

Directors may not escape personal liability if fraudulent trading has taken place. Insolvency or financial wrongdoing could result in disqualification from holding company directorships for up to 15 years. Directors, like sole traders and partners, could also be personally liable for breaching health and safety laws or other legislation.

Legal requirements

The easiest means of starting in business is to operate as a sole trader.

A partnership would be started similarly, with a written partnership agreement being advisable, although not mandatory. This will deal with matters such as the share of profits, work responsibilities, expenses and taxation, together with provisions in respect of the change of partners.

A private limited company, which would have Limited after its name, requires only a single director and a secretary. A public limited company, which would have plc after its name, has more stringent requirements in respect of the number and nature of directors/secretary, capital subscribed and audit. A plc also tends to carry greater credibility.

It will be necessary for a company with limited liability to draw up a memorandum of association to include the name, the address of the registered office and the objects of the company.

Articles of association will also be required, setting out rules for managing the company. A limited company is usually formed afresh but, alternatively, an off-the-shelf or off-the-peg company could be bought, and the name changed if required.

Details of the various requirements affecting limited companies can be obtained from Companies House, or from solicitors or accountants. These include a registered office upon which notices can be served – but which need not be the trading address – and the filing of accounts.

Above a certain level of turnover, most limited trading companies have to carry an accounting certificate which, as turnover increases, extends to audit requirements.

Sole traders and partnerships do not need to do so, but individuals could have their accounts professionally prepared in order to assist in their dealings with the Inland Revenue, to help raise business finance or to secure domestic mortgages.

To finance the business, the sole trader is often reliant upon savings, investments, remortgaging a home, bank overdrafts, bank loans and so on. Funds can be injected into a partnership by taking in a new partner who has cash to contribute to goodwill and/or to the capital requirements needed to fund debts, effect work in progress and expand the concern.

Having more partners helps to raise finance by spreading liability. A limited company may be able to issue further shares, or raise venture capital.

Earnings and taxation

Income tax: A sole trader will pay income tax on the profits of the business, and any other income, calculated by reference to the personal allowances and tax rates stipulated by the Finance Acts which originate from the Chancellor's Budget. Partners will be taxed similarly in respect of their share of the profits.

A director of a limited company is an employee, with salary, income tax and expenses being broadly the same as other company staff. There are, however, special provisions relating to controlling directors – such as senior executives as opposed to divisional sales directors – and to participants – such as a majority shareholder who is not a director.

Corporation tax: This will be paid on the profits earned by limited companies. There may, therefore, be flexibility, first, as to the timing of director's salary payments between financial years and, second, as to whether a salary is actually taken. A director could be paying the personal tax rate of 40%, while the business pays a small companies corporation tax rate of 20%.

In drawing only an essential minimum salary, the tax liability can be minimised for the year, and more funds can be retained by the business for expansion or investment.

Shorter-term savings in personal and corporation tax liability could, of course, mean a relatively greater future liability. However, some gains could accrue as capital gains, for which individuals will have an annual exemption.

Tax losses: The position in respect of tax losses can vary depending on the legal form of the business, on whether profits are set against profits of previous, current or future years, and on the nature of the activity to which the losses relate.

A company can set losses against only the profits/capital gains of the company, and not against a director's other source of income. By contrast, a sole trader and partner can offset losses against any other personal or business – but not company – income earned.

Note that investment profits/losses are treated differently from trading profits/losses. Property income of companies, as well as individuals, can be classed as investment rather than trading, and usually result in a less favourable tax position.

National Insurance: National Insurance contributions are generally lower for a sole trader or partner – class 2 and possibly class 4 – than for a director of a limited company, who will effectively be a salaried employee – paying class 1 contributions.

A limited company also has to pay employers' NI contributions. Directors/employees, however, are likely to be entitled to more benefits than sole traders and partners, including redundancy payments.

Pensions: Opportunities to build a pension, including the ability to secure tax relief on contributions, are generally better with limited companies, with the company also able to make contributions on behalf of the employee/director.

Dividends: Although a company may pay dividends, these may represent double taxation in the case of salaried directors/owners because the dividends are payable after the company's taxation for the period, and are liable for personal income tax. Although dividend income is taxed initially at 10%, taxpayers will have subsequent liability if they are within the 40% tax band.

It is important that businesses take advice at the outset in respect of the finer details of financial, tax planning and accounting opportunities – all of which could be influenced by new legislation.

VAT pros and cons – the cost to your clients

It is compulsory to register for VAT above a certain level of taxable supplies, which is the level of sales subject to the addition of VAT, noting that VAT may not be imposed on all goods.

Businesses that are VAT-registered are able to recover the VAT paid on most costs and expenses, such as purchases of stock, raw materials, vehicle expenses, stationery and utility bills. VAT is added to rent if the landlord has elected to waive exemption.

Businesses should consider whether typical customers/clients are able to recover VAT. If not, the imposition of VAT will be a cost to them, thus making prices relatively higher, and goods and services less competitive.

Plumbers, electricians and other small tradesmen, for example, could benefit from not being VAT registered if they undertake work mainly for householders unable to recover VAT. They could benefit from VAT registration if undertaking commercial contracts, where the customer recovers the VAT on the contract price paid, and the tradesman recovers VAT on costs/expenses.

Regard is given to the proportion of turnover comprising costs/expenses that are subject to the imposition of VAT. This is likely to be low in the case of professional services, where principals charge for their time, and/or where costs are mainly salaries for other professional staff or secretaries. The same applies to other labour-intensive trades. The ability to recover VAT is less significant for companies enjoying high net profit margins.

Cashflow could be assisted when VAT is collected on a cash sale with suppliers being paid subsequently, but not when suppliers have to be paid first. Invoicing dates, payment dates, tax points and tax periods will also be relevant. Accounting for VAT is an administrative burden and a cost.

Applications for VAT registration can be made even if sales are below the limit for compulsory registration. This can help avoid companies being seen as operating in a small way.

Where all sales, or outputs, are exempt from the imposition of VAT, it will not be possible to register for VAT and recover VAT on inputs. Where items are zero-rated, VAT is not charged on outputs, but businesses can register for VAT and recover it on inputs.

Where sales are a combination of exempt and zero-rated outputs, VAT on inputs can be reclaimed on a pro rata basis.

Contributed by Austen Imber

CHAPTER 3

Raising business finance

Published as 'How to fuel the modern enterprise', 18 November 2000

Businesses can raise funding through a variety of mechanisms – and, as is demonstrated, each one has its own set of risks and benefits

Cash is king

The full potential of smaller businesses is often dependent on their ability to raise finance, with cash flow remaining essential for survival.

Most businesses are reliant on financing to some degree. The opportunities and risks associated with each source of funding need to be evaluated, together with the overall effect of borrowing on the business, and on owners' interests.

Factors affecting the ability to raise finance, and the suitability of individual sources, include the following:

- The nature and scale of the business, which could be a sole trader, a partnership, or a limited company. It is often easier for limited companies to raise external finance.
- The length of time the funds are required, such as to temporarily cover set-up costs and provide working capital, or to provide longer term support.
- The level of risk considered acceptable. Increased borrowing, or gearing, which is the proportion of borrowed funds to other funds, or equity, makes profitability more sensitive to variations in turnover, costs and interest rates. This can help successful companies expand relatively quickly, but can leave weaker companies exposed.

  An example of the effect of gearing is that an expanding company with £100,000 equity, earning 20% per year on 'capital employed', and not having borrowings, will earn £20,000. A company that additionally borrows £100,000 at 10% interest will earn 20% on the equity (£20,000), plus a net 10% (20%–10%) on the debt (£10,000), total £30,000,

producing a return of 30% on the £100,000 equity – debt helping raise profits by 50%. If returns fall below 10%, borrowing/gearing serves to compound any losses.
- Whether it is acceptable to reduce the level of ownership, and therefore, perhaps, control in a business. Taking on a partner or introducing new shareholders are examples.
- The reasons for requiring funds, such as for the purchase of stock, investment in more modern plant and machinery, acquisition of new premises for expansion, or for staving off creditors or meeting tax liabilities. The amount of funds required will also be relevant.
- The outlook for the business. Lenders such as banks and building societies, must be satisfied that interest repayments can be met, and funds eventually repaid.

Investors or shareholders will consider potential returns in addition to evaluating risk. A start-up business will be reliant on business plans and profit forecasts, whereas an established firm will also draw on a trading record, and relatively accurate accounting and financial information. Credibility has to be demonstrated to backers. Levels of risk will be reflected in the cost of finance/interest rate payable.

A company's longer-term prospects, and ability to raise finance on competitive terms, may be best served by cautious, more progressive growth, than by high gearing. A small company may improve its position by having its accounts audited despite being exempt from doing so, and quarterly management accounts may be produced for financiers. The level of management expertise within the company and the track-record of key personnel will strongly influence backers. Integrity is paramount.
- The ability of the business to grow, and its ability to cope with an increased scale of operation. New, and different, management skills may be required. New accounting controls may be needed. Investment in one area of a business, such as production, may necessitate expenditure in another, such as the acquisition of additional accommodation, or increased advertising and promotion. Production may already be near full capacity. Increased sales may reflect temporary demand. New products may not be as successful as established brands. There may be shortages of skilled labour.

The nature and fortunes of some businesses can change dramatically when they move beyond the involvement of the original proprietors and/or family. Businesses must always be alert to competition. They must plan for contingencies and evaluate worst-case scenarios, such as the loss of major contracts. The fortunes of all businesses will be influenced by changes in international, national and local economic conditions, and changes in technology, fashions and supply and demand. An entrepreneurial risk taker will approach business in a different way to proprietors of smaller companies with family responsibilities.

- The effect of initiatives for one part of a business on other parts. Businesses seeking to diversify into non-core areas, for example, may firstly be unsuccessful where they do not have the required expertise, and secondly may lose focus on the core areas. In other situations, complementary activities may add value through synergy.

Funds may be required to merely maintain a healthy cash flow position. Some firms may not be able to secure credit, and those who are able to, may pay cash to secure favourable levels of discount. Small businesses generally place a premium on cash flow. Indeed, companies can often go bust owing to a lack of cash rather than inherent unprofitability. Cash is king!

Smaller concerns

The finances of smaller businesses may be closely related to the personal finances of their principals.

Mortgage finance can be raised on a home through the usual homeowners' mortgage, or the property could be used as security for a business loan. Lower interest rates will usually be obtained with residential mortgages than with business loans, overdrafts and commercial mortgages. Discounted variable rates, fixed rates or capped rates may be helpful, and additional costs, such as arrangement fees, legal costs and valuation fees, will often be lower.

It may be possible to secure a loan-to-value ratio of up to 95%, or even 100%, on a home, but a loan against commercial property may be around 60–75% – with some not being mortgageable at all, owing to their age, condition, or specialist nature, for example. Banks and building societies may apply special criteria to the domestic mortgage arrangements of the self-employed and directors of small companies.

Owners of small business must give regard to their overall finances, which include cash and deposit account balances as well as borrowings. Private cash balances will earn lower rates of interest than rates usually repaid on residential mortgages. The difference between business account balances and commercial lending rates will typically be greater. Business interest repayments are tax deductible, but relief is not available on residential mortgage repayments (mortgage interest rate relief having now been fully phased out), unless the borrowing is used for business purposes.

Although bank and building society interest is taxed at 20%, recipients will have to account to the Inland Revenue at a higher rate if their total taxable income falls into the highest 40% band. With TESSAs and now ISAs, interest earned will be tax free, and usually at more favourable rates, but the money may not be easily accessible.

A medium- to long-term view has to be taken in shorter-term financial planning. Cash holdings and bank overdrafts will provide flexibility, but loans and mortgages will generally be longer-term arrangements.

Life, illness and other insurance policies may be taken out, and pension planning required. Unit trusts or individual equities may be held, and gilts/bonds may help to form a suitable personal investment portfolio – providing security for the family, a hedge against business risks and also an emergency source of funds. Sole traders and partners will be liable for business debts, and directors of small companies may have to provide personal guarantees for loan facilities.

When a business seeks funding in advance of its need, the negotiating strength of lenders/investors should not be as great as when the requirement is more pressurised, thus helping more competitive terms to be secured. Finance can take longer to raise than originally envisaged. It may sometimes, however, be wise to wait until up-to-date, year end, accounts are available.

It is also often easier to secure finance when individuals are committing their own funds to the business. Also, the more shareholders, the greater the stability of the business, and the lesser the perceived risks. It is unlikely in the small business scenario that a lender's funds will exceed those of the owners.

Creditors, including the Inland Revenue and Customs & Excise, can put pressure on a business, distracting its running as well as draining its funds. Desperate business people may obtain money from loan sharks, or even deceive associates, clients and family, or commit larger-scale fraud. Effective and honest management, accounting and advanced planning is vital.

Loans and overdrafts

Some businesses will require overdraft facilities to cover only periodic cash flow variations or temporary adversities, and/or to exploit particular opportunities (such as highly discounted bulk purchases). Other businesses will operate permanently with overdrafts.

Overdrafts will ensure that interest charges are incurred only when the facility is required, and will be more suitable as working capital (noting also that they could, in theory, be recalled at any time). Loans or 'term loans' will be more suitable for fixed assets and core borrowing, and will be of a set amount.

Loans will carry a fixed or variable rate of interest, or sometimes a managed rate reviewed, say, monthly by the lender. Although interest is payable on loans irrespective of the company's cash position, the benefit lies in the certainty of the availability and cost of finance. Repayment holidays or stepped repayment patterns may be negotiable. Loans cannot usually be recalled unless borrowers default on repayments. Repayment takes place usually throughout the term but sometimes at the end (that is, an interest-only loan).

Interest rates on loans and overdrafts will be set by banks or building societies at margins over their own 'base rate', which, in turn, will be set above the Bank of England base rate, and also reflect short-term market interest rates such as the London Interbank Offered Rate (LIBOR). The Bank of England base rate will be determined by the Bank's Monetary Policy Committee, having regard to the outlook for the economy, and particularly the need to control inflationary pressures. The margin required by the lender above their own bank/building society's base rate will reflect the nature and status of the borrower, and the overall evaluation of risk.

Overdrafts and loans secured on a home, a business' freehold premises, or even a property held separately as an investment tend to command lower rates of interest than 'unsecured' loans, again owing to the respective levels of risk to lenders.

Fresh equity

Sole traders and partnerships can raise finance by new partners committing funds to the business. Remuneration need not be proportionate to the level of funds committed.

Where a limited company is able to issue shares to new investors, unlike overdraft or loan borrowings, the funds do not carry the cost of interest payments. Although dividends may be payable to shareholders, this often need not be the case with smaller, expanding companies who wish to recycle profits for expansion.

The issue of shares to new shareholders does, however, erode the percentage ownership of the existing shareholders. Whether this is of benefit to shareholders depends on the returns being secured on the capital employed within the business, and on the suitability of other sources of finance (overdrafts and loans, for example, not influencing the share of equity).

In the case, for example, where a company is unable to borrow further funds from conventional banking sources, new equity capital may, firstly, improve the cash position, and ease any risk factors within the company. Secondly, new funds may comprise the element of equity upon which borrowing, and therefore expansion, is dependent (such as the 35% equity required for a property upon which a bank will lend only 65% of value).

The amount earned by the original owners on the new capital should be greater than the share of overall returns sacrificed to new investors. Director shareholders can, of course, redress any imbalance through salary levels, bonuses, share options and the like, but must be mindful of the impression this gives to investors, and of it being unlawful, in certain situations, to overpay themselves.

The dilution of the level of ownership can begin to affect the control of the company. The nature and objectives of new shareholders will need considering. Although ownership of at least 50% by one shareholder will technically guarantee full control, other shareholders may be able to exert undue influence on the management of the company. Certain resolutions can be blocked by holders of more than 25% of the shares, and minority shareholders can exercise rights through the courts.

'Golden' or 'management' shares may be introduced to increase the level of control disproportionately to the share of ownership, in order to secure the interests of minorities, but this could unnerve other investors.

It may be difficult to attract passive investors – or indeed any investors at all – for reasons including the risk of total loss and the difficulty in selling shares.

'Venture capital funds' seek well-managed, fast-growing companies operating in markets with strong potential. They provide funds, usually in exchange for ordinary shares, and may place their own director(s) on the board. They will often look to relinquish their interest after several years, with the company ideally having developed sufficiently to be floated on the stock market, or to be sold to another firm.

Business angels are high-wealth individuals looking to invest a personal stake in a business and apply their expertise to facilitate growth.

In a management buyout, a business is bought by its management, usually with a small part of the funding from their own equity, and the balance from financial backers. A management buy-in involves outside managers buying the business. Both could enable part of a company being sold to raise funds.

White knights are individuals or companies who rescue businesses from potential failure or from takeover by unsolicited bidders.

Bonds or 'corporate bonds' can be issued by a company, giving investors a fixed return, with the capital value varying to give the current yield (as with gilt-edged securities or 'gilts', which are government-backed bonds). A debenture is a fixed-interest loan secured against particular assets of the company. Loans could also be secured against all the assets of a business.

Smaller companies particularly may be able to benefit from grants, local authority support, initiatives such as the Small Firms Loan Guarantee Scheme or assistance from charities such as the Prince's Trust.

With all financial arrangements, proper advice should be taken, ranging from the local accountancy practice to the corporate finance adviser. Taxation planning is important, with tax savings and deferred liabilities effectively representing a source of funding. Companies may also benefit from initiatives such as the Enterprise Investment Scheme, which offers tax relief for investors in certain unquoted companies. Venture capital trusts are stock market-quoted companies also providing tax incentives to investors.

Raising funds through existing operations

It may be possible to realise funds from existing elements within a business before seeking fresh funding. This could include leasing rather than purchasing vehicles and equipment, negotiating more favourable credit arrangements with suppliers, running down/ carrying less stock – including improvements to stocking and distribution systems, pursuing debtors more concertedly, selling debts to recovery companies, laying off some staff and contracting out certain services.

Part of a business could be sold to raise finance for another part, or a whole business sold to pursue a new venture.

Property options include agreeing a revised rent repayment pattern with a landlord, selling or renting out surplus space, or relocating, with rent-free periods and other incentives helping cash flow provided they outweigh relocation costs.

A sale and leaseback arrangement could help raise funds. This could, however, be an expensive means of raising funds in situations where the market investment yield is relatively high, perhaps owing to the location, age, condition and use of the premises, and the covenant strength of the business/tenant. However, a good property, and strong covenant, may effectively help finance to be secured at relatively low initial investment yields (although the rent may increase at each rent review). Investment/sale value could be optimised by the grant of a sufficiently long lease, by other suitable lease terms and by improving the condition of the property.

Freehold ownership can utilise equity that could be better used for expansion. It can, however, help build value and secure goodwill in a business, as well as provide capital gains – upon which additional finance could be raised.

Increases in property values can be allocated to a company's re-valuation reserve in its accounts, increasing its shareholders' funds (which is its equity), reducing gearing, and improving its balance sheet strength and borrowing capacity (see Chapter 5 on interpreting company accounts).

The ability to borrow funds can be improved by the accounting policies and practices adopted, although some firms may undertake 'creative accounting', which may be unlawful.

Quoted companies: Raising finance through the stock market

The stock market is traditionally a source of finance for a company, but it also enables owners/shareholders to realise the value of their interests. The whole of a company's shares could be sold to the market, or the stock market 'listing' could be undertaken entirely for the purpose of raising new capital.

In the case of smaller companies, the retention of significant shareholdings by the key owners/personnel will be an important means by which investors are attracted; indeed, some owners/directors may be restricted from selling their shares for a period of time. There will still need to be a sufficient proportion of shares available to investors, as it will be important to create liquidity in the market for the shares (that is, a reasonable level of supply and demand and therefore trading in the shares).

One attraction to investors of shares in quoted companies is that they can be sold relatively easily (unlike holdings in most private limited companies). However, in the case of smaller companies particularly, lack of liquidity can mean a greater spread between the quoted buying ('offer') and selling ('bid') prices of the shares (known as the bid-offer spread, such as 100p–110p, which would require a 10% gain in the share price, before costs, to break even).

Lack of liquidity can also account for more volatile share price movements, which may not help endear the company to investors or lenders – but may attract the share speculator, and even the market manipulator. Another attraction to investors can be the prospect of takeover, but which may be remote where the majority share is with investors unlikely to wish to sell.

It will be mainly ordinary shares that are issued. These will provide dividends to investors, although the principal attraction is the prospect of capital gains. The company could also issue preference shares, which carry a fixed rate of return, preferential to dividends paid on ordinary shares, and preferential in the repayment of capital where funds are deficient.

As in the case of the limited company seeking new shareholders, equity finance may be cheaper to raise than debt finance, but it will dilute returns for existing shareholders. Although increased debt finance, and therefore higher gearing, can enhance earnings per share, it can lead to undue levels of risk. Financiers, investors and the financial markets generally will focus on the financial standing, or 'balance sheet strength', of the company. It may be then preferable to raise funds through the issue of new shares.

Typically this will be by way of a rights issue, where existing shareholders are offered a proportionate number of new shares, usually at a discounted price to the current share price. When funds are being raised by the issue of new shares, the higher the current share price, the cheaper the effective cost of the finance. Shares could, for example, be issued in the case of the acquisition of other companies. The exercise of share options, the take-up of new shares by employees and so on, may increase share capital, but usually in only a small way.

Where a company's cash position is strong, shares may actually be bought back by the company in order to enhance earnings per share for remaining shareholders – the best time being when the share price is low. Quoted companies will still make use of bank overdraft, loan and other sources of finance.

Contributed by Austen Imber

CHAPTER 4

Business development/consultancy

Published as 'The full service treatment', 23 March 2002

A chartered surveyor can develop business skills to provide strategic advice for a small property concern that is considering expansion

In response to the interest generated by our feature on the high returns available to effectively managed smaller property investment businesses (17 November 2001, p168 and Chapter 31), we now illustrate a simple form of business consultancy role that surveyors may take.

The illustration concerns a company operating within a mid-market area of a large UK city. Properties in their £8m portfolio range from £30,000 studio flats to £400,000 multi-let mixed residential-commercial interests, including student lettings. Gross rental income is £1.5m.

Family members are the only directors, and are also the majority shareholders of the company's £3m equity/shareholders' funds, with the remaining shareholdings also being family based. Full-time staff are mainly family members and management advice is provided by the consultant chartered surveyor.

Contributors to rapid expansion over recent years include the injection of fresh equity, equity released on remortgaging following increases in property values, the provision of bridging finance and other temporary loans, the support of three lenders and the effective management of high gearing and a sometimes precarious cash position. Strong profitability reflects the high-yield nature of the portfolio/sector, intensive management and family commitment.

The company needs to consider its options in respect of further expansion, bearing in mind that the current shareholders do not have any new equity to inject. The majority shareholders are apprehensive about a reduction in family control, but acknowledge that this now is a prerequisite for the next stage of growth, and for realising, at some stage, their original aspiration of stock market flotation. The principal two options available to the company may be outlined by the consultant surveyor as follows.

Option 1: manage and maintain existing portfolio

This confines the foreseeable future to the management of the current portfolio without seeking equity funds from new shareholders/investors. Although acquisitions will be possible from profits, growth will generally be slow. Furthermore, as lenders are generally reluctant to support relatively small single acquisitions, it may be necessary to progressively acquire properties individually for cash in order, in due course, to mortgage a package of properties.

Advantages of this option lie in the low risk profile, and the reassurance to the family shareholders that they have full control. Disadvantages lie in the loss of momentum to growth, reduced motivation and time commitment of current personnel brought about by the absence of new challenges and daily pressures, the lack of regular work to retain a predominantly in-house workforce of both skilled contractors and casual labour, and the difficulty in attracting good-quality professional support (from a consultant surveyor or other professionals looking to gain from a share of the equity, and share options, for example, in addition to fees).

Option 2: relatively rapid expansion, loss of majority shareholder/family control

If further rapid expansion is to take place, new sources of equity will be needed, which, given the current shareholders' lack of new funds, would have to be sought from other shareholders/investors, possibly including additional directors and external consultants. New staff would have to be attracted and key personnel offered satisfactory remuneration.

Advantages include the potential wealth that can be realised, extending beyond the retirement of the current shareholders/directors, who may otherwise be difficult to replace if the business took option 1 of mainly managing the current portfolio.

The company is now well positioned to enjoy further strong expansion, subject to a short-term improvement in its cash flow and profits position, and subject to minor refinements in its management systems. Such a move, from an essentially family enterprise to a company serving all shareholders equally, may, however, require too substantial a change in approach to be acceptable to the existing majority/family shareholders, especially as loss of majority family control would be likely.

Regard needs to be given to factors such as the extent to which majority shareholders are comfortable with the involvement and requirements of new shareholders/directors, the extent to which those other investors actually wish to risk committing equity to an essentially family business, and the overall aspirations of the company for growth. Future options include the sale of the company to a single investor, assembling smaller portfolios for sale, piecemeal sales of single properties or stock market flotation.

Another consideration is the possible buy-out by the main family shareholders/directors of the other family shareholders not involved in the business. This may be beneficial from a long term management and expansion perspective, despite any available funds possibly being better used for acquisitions in the short term.

The way forward

After the company decided to remain as a family-based enterprise for the near future, the consultant surveyor may have outlined some of the opportunities and the risks it faced, together with guidance on how these could best be managed.

The advice would have reflected the change of the company's investment profile from high gearing, and an often restricted cash position, to a lower-risk profile providing a more cautious approach to growth, with less reliance on external professional support for day-to-day matters. Key issues highlighted by the consultant may have included those listed on page 28.

Property-specific issues

The surveyor, as business consultant to a small property investment company, should be easily able to advise on property-specific issues, such as marketing methods and agency law, property management/IT systems, property purchases and sales, the terms of residential tenancies and commercial leases, rent reviews and lease renewals, minimising rates liabilities, administering service charges and rent collection, dealing with covenant breaches, complying with health and safety laws, ensuring planning consents are in place and arranging insurance.

This illustrates how business skills can be the route to wider fee-earning opportunities. Note also that although this feature has considered business consultancy to a property company, surveyors may advise non-property businesses as to the strategic role that property can play, having regard to their operational/trading requirements.

Strategic thinking: Key issues for the business

Investment and growth strategy

As mentioned before, acquisitions, with limited new equity, will be gradual and growth generally slow. There are nevertheless some properties within the portfolio which could be re-mortgaged, thus releasing equity for new acquisitions. In carrying properties at less than full value, however, a further cushion is provided against risk and adversities.

In acquiring new properties, regard needs to be given to the usual factors such as property type, percentage rental returns, management issues, extent of refurbishment expenditure, location, geographical diversity, scope for short-term capital gains (occasionally for sale but mainly for re-financing) and balance within the portfolio.

Acquisitions, refurbishment and maintenance need to be timed in relation to the regular on-going employment of any retained in-house workforce, and to the overall cash position. A vacant property requiring refurbishment is incurring interest repayments and works expenditure, while not receiving rent.

Economic and property market issues

A keen eye must be kept on economic and property market fortunes, internationally, nationally and locally – all of which can affect interest rates, rental demand, rental levels, capital values, profitability, and so on. Changes in landlord and tenant law, and planning legislation/guidance, can similarly have an impact.

Cash position

The company must aim to be in a positive cash position at all times, avoiding reliance on an overdraft facility. This will provide a cushion against periodic cash flow difficulties, as overdraft facilities will be drawn upon only in essential circumstances.

The student residential sector accounts for around 30% of the company's income. As most rents are received termly in advance, cash flow planning is vital. It is especially important to account for voids and half-rents during the summer months, noting that once termly cheques are received in April, full rents are not received until October.

The company must plan for interest and loan repayments due to lenders. Regard must be given to the point at which loan repayments are made on loans that are currently interest only, and to the point at which fixed-interest repayments for some properties revert to a possibly higher variable rate. The level of interest rates does, of course, need to be monitored, in terms of both the Bank of England base rate and the competitiveness of rates set by the company's lenders. It is essential to plan for other liabilities such as taxation and major works.

The personal finances of the majority family shareholders involved actively in the business as directors are also ideally structured to provide further guard against temporary adversities. Profitable businesses can still fail because of poor cash flow. If the company fails, losses would be likely to extend beyond the company to directors individually, owing to the personal guarantees provided to lenders and others.

Lenders and investors

It is important to work with a number of lenders, and therefore ensure that none can exert undue pressure in respect of interest rate and other charges, or the company's overall operation. New lending arrangements require structuring having regard to existing arrangements, portfolio issues and expansion plans. At all times, regard must be given to the effect of certain courses of action on the company's quarterly management and full year end accounts, which will be presented to lenders and any new investors in the future.

Personnel and professional

The company's in-house personnel, comprising family members, must have the requisite expertise for day-to-day matters, and must also recognise when external support is required.

(It should be noted that family enterprises are generally a specialist area of business consultancy owing, for example, to issues of maintaining family control, slowness to embrace change, problems with any poorly performing and/or dissenting family members, the attitude to outsiders, and the need to plan for succession.)

Contributed by Austen Imber

CHAPTER 5

Company accounts

Published as 'Called to accounts', 5 September 1998

Checking tenants' financial status is often a necessary part of a surveyor's work. We guide you through the jargon of company accounts

Surveyors may need to assess the financial strength of a company for several reasons. New tenants should be of an acceptable financial standing; until this is ascertained, it can be unwise to grant a reverse premium or other incentive. A particular tenant might enhance the overall investment profile of a property, but meanwhile another company's fortunes could be changing for the worse, and the tenant might not remain solvent.

The attractiveness of investment acquisitions and their associated risks may also need to be assessed and the sustainability of over-renting possibly considered. Covenant strength also affects investment valuations. It may be necessary to determine whether an application for assignment or subletting should be consented to, whether refusal could be proved reasonable or whether guarantors are required.

Surveyors may not bear the sole responsibility for interpreting company accounts. But they should be able to understand the accounts and any accountant's advice that is given.

Annual report

The company's annual report includes the chairman's statement and the directors' reports which summarise the year's trading and the company's future prospects. These are followed by the profit-and-loss account, the balance sheet and the cash-flow statement.

The notes to the accounts provide more detailed information, including the previous year's figures which enable year-on-year comparisons to be made.

The auditor's report judges whether the accounts meet legal

requirements and represent a 'true and fair view' of the company's trading year and its overall financial position.

A briefer interim report, which covers six months' trading, is also produced.

Accounting conventions vary, and annual reports can be presented in different formats. Although here we concentrate on the accounts of public limited companies, the same principles apply to smaller companies.

Accounts format

The first panel on page 38 shows a basic profit-and-loss account which represents trading during the financial year.

'Turnover' is sales income (excluding VAT). 'Cost of sales' includes the purchase of goods and raw materials, with adjustments made to reflect stock levels at each end of the financial period.

Expenses may be categorised as 'selling', 'distribution', 'financial' or 'other', and includes wages, rents, repairs and so on, together with non-cash items, such as depreciation or provisions for bad debts or other adversities.

'Operating profit' and 'profit before tax' are separated to allow for items that do not reflect normal trading operations. These could be reorganisation or redundancy costs; profits and losses from asset disposals; or investment income or interest payments.

'Profit after tax' is available to pay interim and final dividends to shareholders. 'Retained profit' is allocated to the reserves in the balance sheet.

The second panel on page 38 shows a balance sheet that represents the company's assets, liabilities and capital on the last day of the financial year.

'Fixed assets' include 'tangible assets' such as property, plant and machinery, and vehicles; and 'intangible assets' such as goodwill, trademarks and investments in group companies or other companies.

'Current assets' include stocks (raw materials, work in progress and goods for sale), debtors and cash balances.

'Current liabilities', sometimes just termed 'creditors', are debts generally required to be repaid within 12 months, including amounts owed to suppliers, tax payments due and bank overdrafts.

Current assets less current liabilities is called 'net current assets', and shows the company's working capital.

Fixed and current assets, less current liabilities, is known as 'net assets', which forms the top section of the balance sheet.

'Long-term debt/liabilities', also termed 'amounts falling due after one year', includes debentures or bank loans which may be secured or unsecured.

'Share capital' that has been issued is stated at its 'nominal' or 'par' value but does not reflect a company's capital value or 'market capitalisation'. Share capital includes preference shares which yield a fixed dividend, and ordinary shares which yield a dividend related to profits.

'Reserves' are retained profits that could be used for expansion or future liabilities. They could include sums for plant and machinery, for revaluation, or for profit and loss.

Share capital plus reserves is termed 'shareholders' funds'. Shareholders' funds plus long-term debt is called 'capital employed', which forms the bottom section of the balance sheet and, accordingly, equals net assets. Net assets can be considered as the items the company owns, and capital employed as the way the company is financed. Sometimes long-term debt is listed in the top half of the accounts and so, with net assets, equals shareholders' funds.

The accounts include a cash-flow statement which reconciles cash coming into the business with profits. This enables the treatment and effects of non-cash items, such as depreciation, to be assessed, and can also indicate whether any creative accounting might have taken place.

Interpretation

Establishing the financial standing, competitiveness, success and future prospects of a company involves considering profitability, liquidity/solvency, and gearing. The interpretation and comparison of these factors vary between industries and between accounting practices.

Profitability

Profitability can be measured by expressing gross profit, expenses or net profit as a percentage of turnover. A gross profit of £20m on a turnover of £200m produces a 'gross profit margin' of 10%.

Net profit generally means profit before interest and taxation, but a range of calculations can be undertaken to consider the effect of taxation, or of items that do not reflect normal trading operations, or of a particular capital structure.

Turnover should be considered with sales volume to establish whether growth is due to expansion or to reduced prices, which may decrease profits. Growth should be organic and not just a result of acquisitions. The effects of inflation also need to be considered. Improved profits and margins may result not from sales growth but from cost-cutting – a process that may not continue, and that may inhibit growth.

Very high margins invite competition, so the strength of barriers to entry to the industry – such as unique or well-patented products and services – should be considered. Falling margins may indicate that a company is losing its competitive advantage. Variable margin records may be due to periodic price wars or the cyclical nature of an industry's trade.

Low margins make profits sensitive to variations in turnover, costs and expenses. This is especially so where fixed costs, as opposed to variable costs, represent a relatively large proportion of total costs. Low margins add to risk, but can increase the potential to improve earnings substantially.

Profitability is also measured by the 'return on capital employed' (ROCE). 'Capital employed', as formulated above, is shareholders' funds (capital and reserves), plus long-term debt, which also equals net assets. Because capital employed equals net assets, ROCE can also be considered as the return made by the company on its assets.

ROCE is profit divided by capital employed, expressed as a percentage. The profit figure used should be profit before interest and tax, although combinations could again be used, and could be expressed in relation to total assets or shareholders' funds.

Levels of capital employed vary between industries, but ROCE can be used to make comparisons with similar companies and with other investments. The year-to-year trends of ROCE should also be considered.

Liquidity/solvency

Liquidity/solvency ratios are used to consider a company's ability to meet its financial obligations, and to avoid further financing or business failure.

The 'current ratio', sometimes termed the 'working capital ratio', is current assets divided by current liabilities. A high ratio, of 2 (200%) or more, may be a sign of financial strength while a low ratio, of 1.25 (125%) or less, may be a sign of financial weakness. A high ratio may, however, show poor investment policies or excessive stocks. A ratio of 1 confirms that liabilities could be met, but stock, for example, may not easily or profitably be turned into cash.

The 'liquid ratio', also termed the 'quick ratio' or sometimes the 'acid test ratio', is current assets less stocks, divided by current liabilities. Some literature excludes debtors from this ratio (current assets less debtors divided by liabilities).

The trend of the ratios should also be considered; comparisons should be made to sector averages and to similar companies. Particular regard should be given to factors such as the overdraft limit; whether the overdraft is secured or unsecured; whether an overdraft provides beneficial flexibility (even on a longer-term basis) that avoids the company carrying long-term debt; whether stocks have been run down near the year-end, thus improving the cash position; the extent of fixed assets, and the ability to use them as security to borrow for current liabilities or even expansion; whether investments are included and how marketable they are; and whether debtors and creditors incorporate parent/group/subsidiary debts and loans.

Activity ratios are used primarily to measure the efficiency of stocking processes and debt collection. They also indicate the speed at which stock and debtors can be turned into cash.

'Stock turnover days' is the number of days taken to turn stock into cash. This is calculated by dividing stock by the cost of sales, and multiplying by 365. The stock figure used should be the average of opening and closing stocks or, even better, the average of stock levels during the year.

Unused or unsold stock may incur losses through complete wastage, obsolescence or forced heavy discounting; excess stock holdings need to be financed. However, it is necessary to retain sufficient flexibility and capacity so as not to jeopardise production or forgo commercial opportunities such as capitalising on cheap raw materials and securing discounts for bulk purchases.

'Debtors' days' is the number of days taken for turnover to be turned into cash. This is calculated by dividing debtors (or average debtors) by turnover and multiplying by 365. Debts need to be financed, but a certain credit policy may boost sales and avoid the need to grant discounts.

Gearing

'Gearing' is the proportion of borrowed capital or long-term debt to other capital. If a company's capital structure includes £4m borrowings, £5m ordinary shares of £1 each and £3m reserves, then debt (£4m) divided by capital employed (£4m + £5m + £3m) produces gearing of 0.33 or 33%.

Alternatively, debt could be simply compared with shareholders' funds (£5m + £3m) to produce gearing of 0.5 or 50%. For quoted companies, gearing may be considered in relation to the market value of the equity capital, rather than in relation to the issued capital listed in the balance sheet.

The importance of gearing is the effect that borrowing has on profits. Borrowed capital incurs the commitment to pay interest, whereas shareholders need receive no dividend. If the investment of the debt produces a greater return than the cost of the debt, the shareholders should benefit. When businesses are recovering or expanding, high gearing can be beneficial. In tougher times, high gearing can cause serious problems. Borrowing can also be tax-efficient, because interest is allowable against tax but dividend payments are not.

For any company, a stage is reached where a certain level of borrowing induces higher risk, and an increased ability for interest payments to erode profits and compound any problems of reduced turnover or tighter margins. Whether high gearing is a problem, therefore, depends on the inherent level of profitability within the company. Regard must be given to profit margins, to the growth potential for earnings and cash flow, and to the return on capital employed. The trend of gearing will establish whether the debt structure is improving or deteriorating.

Interest cover indicates the extent to which profit covers interest payments. This is calculated by dividing profit (excluding interest payments) by interest payments. Low or deteriorating interest cover could lead to a fund-raising exercise or to business failure. Interest cover can also demonstrate the sensitivity of profits to variations in interest rates.

The borrowing capacity of different companies varies according to the timing, stability, and certainty of their earnings, to the amount of freehold property or other assets they can offer as security, and to their current level of gearing. Whether gearing levels are good or bad depends on a range of factors including the outlook for the economy, the prospect of higher interest rates, and the profitability and future prospects of the company.

Different practices' effects

Different accounting practices can produce different headline figures. During interpretation of company accounts and use of the various ratios, it is important that the components of the calculations are examined.

For gearing calculations, preference share capital should really be classed as long-term debt, but some companies may include it – together with ordinary share capital – as shareholders' funds to purport that gearing is lower. Financing by bank overdrafts, rather than by long-term debt, will make gearing and ROCE appear more favourable. However, it may make liquidity ratios appear worryingly low.

An intangible asset such as goodwill may not be listed in the accounts because it has been generated from within the company, but may be listed as an asset where it has been acquired.

Goodwill is the difference between the purchase price of a company and its net asset value. Some companies may write off goodwill completely or in part, immediately or over a period of time. Other companies may periodically revalue goodwill.

Its destination on immediate write-off would generally be reserves, whereas if progressively written off it would generally go to profits. Writing off goodwill to reserves reduces capital employed and increases the ROCE. Returns are then being considered in relation only to the tangible assets acquired, not to the whole acquisition cost. This flatters profits and exaggerates the success of acquisitions. Companies may see benefit in overstating goodwill by underestimating the value of the assets acquired.

However, it is likely that a new treatment and disclosure requirement will come into force shortly. This will provide that companies acquiring intangible assets will be unable to make an immediate write-off against reserves. The value of these intangible assets will be entered on the balance sheet and gradually charged against profits.

Creative accounting

Financial creativity is easier in some industries than others. It ranges from the desire to present a consistent growth record to the hiding of severe financial problems or fraud – although 'off balance-sheet finance' is now prohibited.

In assessing earnings, consideration needs to be given to whether items that do not reflect normal trading operations have been accounted for correctly, and whether amounts from trading operations have been included.

Profits can be affected by the timing of purchases and sales, or invoicing at either end of the financial year, by over-cautious provisions, by stock valuations or by depreciation methods and charges.

Interest is normally charged against profits, but during a construction project it might be added to the capital cost. This boosts the balance-sheet asset value as well as earnings and, possibly, reserves – particularly useful for over-geared companies. Reserves, and consequently borrowing capacity, could also be improved by property revaluations.

Tax losses may have been brought forward, even from an acquired company, and set against current profits, resulting in an abnormally low tax charge for the period.

Conclusion

When interpreting company accounts, it is important to:

- make year-to-year comparisons;
- consider the trend of the ratios and other measures and be aware of industry norms;
- understand the nature of the company's business;
- understand the company's accounting policies and the implications of any changes;
- examine the notes to the accounts;
- be aware of the overall company structure in terms of group or subsidiary companies;
- examine the auditor's report; and
- be alert to any creative accounting that may have taken place.

Accountants' advice should not be necessary for all the tasks that a surveyor may have to undertake, but surveyors should appreciate the limits of their expertise and seek accountants' advice where necessary.

Profit and Loss Account

    Turnover
−   Cost of sales
    Gross Profit
−   Expenses

    Operating profit
±   Items not reflecting
    normal trading operations

    Profit before tax
−   Taxation

    Profit available for distribution
−   Dividends

    Retained profit

Balance Sheet

    Fixed Assets
    Current Assets
−   Current liabilities

    Net assets

    Financed by:
    Share capital
    Reserves

    Shareholders' funds
    Long-term debt

    Capital employed

Contributed by Austen Imber

CHAPTER 6

Inflation

Published as 'Get a grip on inflation', 28 November 1998

The causes and effects of inflation are one of the primary concerns of any government. We look at how economic policies aim to control it

During 1998, as interest rates have risen in order to control inflation, some economists have mooted fears of deflation. More recently, however, interest rates have fallen.

Causes of inflation

Inflation can be induced by strong domestic activity and/or by rising cost pressures – more formally known as 'demand-pull' and 'cost-push' inflation.

Domestic/consumer activity

The main element of domestic activity that affects inflation is consumer demand (although growth in investment or even government spending can be inflationary in certain circumstances).

Consumer activity is influenced by spending power and confidence. The more direct influences on disposable income and potential levels of spending include earnings (overtime and bonuses as well as basic rates), the level of interest rates, taxation (including income tax, national insurance contributions and VAT) and one-off factors such as building society windfalls.

Wage rates, retail spending patterns, house prices, building society advances, new car registrations, and the savings ratio (the percentage of disposable income that is saved) all contribute to statistics which may provide an indication of consumer behaviour and prospective inflationary trends.

Economists also look at the money supply as a measure of retail spending on the high street. The narrow money aggregate (M0) mainly reflects the amount of notes and coins in circulation and, to some extent, mirrors trends in high street spending. Broader measures of the money supply, such as M4, provide evidence of the demand for credit for house purchases and general consumer borrowing as well as the corporate demand for loans.

Consumer confidence and the 'feel-good factor' result from the expectation and comfort of increased prosperity. Rises in the value of homes, shareholdings or other investments can increase households' propensity to consume.

There can often be an overconfidence that economic prosperity will continue, with relatively little thought being given to an often inevitable economic downturn, and possible recession. Indeed, consumer confidence, or lack of it, is partly responsible for the extent of booms and slumps in economic activity.

Trends in consumer spending are also very closely linked to other parts of the economy, such as business investment and exports.

Cost pressures

These include wage rates, prices of raw materials and commodities (particularly oil prices), any other input costs and manufacturers' output prices (which will be the input prices/costs of other manufacturers, wholesalers and retailers). Some of these costs will be imports.

Consumers and cost

The extent to which consumer demand and cost pressures can affect the rate of inflation depends on structural factors and on economic capacity (see page 44).

If the domestic economy does reach full capacity to serve domestic demand, additional demand can be met from imported goods and services. Moreover, an external shock, such as a rise in oil prices, can cause inflation to rise even when the economy is not at full capacity.

To lower unemployment, and raise output and economic capacity, government policy initiatives focus on increasing the flexibility of labour and products markets, and providing training and skills to the labour force that will match the needs of employers. Governments have abandoned attempts to lower employment through increased spending because this tends to lead to higher inflation in the medium to long term, rather than lower employment.

Another, albeit shorter-term, influence on economic capacity is inventory levels, in terms of the ability to release stocks to satisfy demand rather than increase production. Expectations play a part in that if, for example, stocks are built up in anticipation of a certain level of economic growth/retailing activity that does not fully materialise, the more gradual release of inventories will mean that output, relatively speaking, is lower. Conversely, if sales potential is under-estimated, accelerated production and supply shortages can be inflationary.

Generally, there will be a time lag before full economic capacity is reflected in an increased rate of inflation. This can account for inflation sometimes being perceived to be dead when, in reality, inflationary pressures are yet to be reflected in price levels.

Exchange rates

Inflation is also influenced by the value, or 'strength' of the pound. The pound strengthens, for example, when the exchange rate against the German mark increases from £1 = DM2.90 to £1 = DM3.

If the pound is strong, the price of UK exports will be relatively higher in overseas markets. In order to preserve competitiveness, maintain sales and retain a presence in foreign markets, prices (in pounds) are initially reduced, and profits are squeezed. At the same time, the strength of the pound results in cheaper imports, which displace and/or force price reductions in UK-produced goods. If the pound remains strong, in due course trade volumes are likely to fall. So, although a strong pound tends to have deflationary effects, it can also result in reduced output and increased unemployment.

Also, the competitive business climate which results from the strength of the pound, as with difficult trading conditions generally, tends to force companies to minimise costs and increase productivity. Similarly, recession can nurture more cautious and value-seeking attitudes by consumers to spending. Such characteristics often continue when economic fortunes improve.

A weak, or more 'competitive', pound would make exports cheaper and imports more expensive. This increases the volume of exports and reduces the volume of imports, leading to increased UK output and economic growth, but inducing inflationary pressures owing to increased consumer demand and imports being more expensive. For a very open economy, such as the UK, higher import prices tend to feed into higher overall inflation, unless domestic demand is sufficiently controlled.

Although manufactured goods account for the majority of the export trade, the service sector accounts for a substantial proportion of UK Gross Domestic Product – the total value of the output of all UK-produced goods and services. Manufacturing may, for example, be struggling if the value of the pound has remained strong for some time, while activity in the more domestically orientated services sector is causing concern about inflation.

One of the factors which can influence the strength of the pound is the level of UK interest rates. Higher interest rates and/or the expectation of higher interest rates will generally increase the strength of the pound as sterling deposits yield higher returns for investors.

Regard will therefore be given to the effects of the strength of sterling when interest rate rises are being set to curb inflationary pressures. Anti-inflationary policy cannot, however, become too dependent on the exchange rate owing to its relative unpredictability, and given that its main effects are on the manufacturing sector and traded goods. If the service sector is the main source of inflationary pressures, a rise in sterling will not bring inflation down unless a harsh downturn in manufacturing can be brought about.

Policy control of inflation

An almost continual rise in prices has been evident only since the second world war. Before then, prices tended to rise during booms and fall outright during periods of recession. This meant that the overall price level changed little over very long periods of time. Inflation has therefore become a real problem for governments only in recent decades.

In June 1997, the new Labour Chancellor passed the responsibility for setting interest rates to the Bank of England in the expectation that interest rates would be more stable in the longer term if set in the absence of political imperatives. Interest rates are set by the Bank of England's Monetary Policy Committee, having regard to the need to meet the government's inflation target – currently RPI-X of 2.5%.

If interest rates are not raised when necessary, once inflation begins to rise, relatively higher interest rate rises may be required at a later date to control inflation (and have a greater cost in terms of decreased output and employment). Expectations of inflation can result in prices being raised to allow for inflation and, with wage inflation, can cause inflation to spiral. If inflation reaches very high levels, it can sometimes be brought down only by a recession.

One of the difficulties in setting interest rates to control inflation is that, because of lag effects, regard has to be given to rates of inflation expected 18 to 24 months ahead. The accuracy and reliability of economic statistics will vary, and it may be difficult, for example, to judge the level of spare capacity within the economy.

Despite the attempts of government and central banks to control inflation and secure stable economic growth, economic activity will always be cyclical to some degree, and be influenced by the performance of other leading economies and possibly also by external shocks. Governments then need to minimise the extent of peaks and troughs in the economic cycle, and aim to ensure that, when economic fortunes deteriorate, there is a more gradual slowdown in economic activity (a soft landing), rather than a more immediate impact (a hard landing), which may be the beginning of a harsh recession.

Economic fortunes can deteriorate relatively quickly where the rate of inflation begins to increase as economic activity slows down. If, for example, the value of the pound remains high against the currencies of the UK's trading partners, and any other trade competitors, for a sufficient period (perhaps as a result of relatively higher interest rates), after initially having to reduce prices/profit margins, trade volumes and therefore the output of UK exporters falls.

Rising unemployment (and also reduced consumer and business confidence) begins to affect spending on goods and services. At the same time, the lagged effect of inflationary pressures (such as wage inflation) produces an increase in the rate of inflation. Also, falling production can increase unit costs.

Stagflation

'Stagflation' is where prices rise as the economy is weakening. A particularly severe recession could result where, despite interest rates typically being set with regard to economic activity and the rate of inflation expected over the next 18 to 24 months, concern over the current rate of inflation causes interest rates to be increased further. This can hit householders and businesses unnecessarily severely when the slowdown in economic activity would be adequate to ease price pressures. Generally, as the economy slows, there is often a tendency for interest rates to remain too high for too long.

Poor economic conditions could actually induce a sustained fall in the general price level of goods and services – a condition known as deflation. This is caused by a substantial contraction in demand conditions or if supply rises to a greater degree than the market can accommodate. Price declines in one particular sector or industry cannot be considered as deflation so long as prices rise elsewhere in the economy.

Consumer demand and cost pressure

Structural factors
These include:

- new technologies, improved working methods and other opportunities to increase productivity. Strong productivity growth (labour as well as technological) can, for example, offset the effects of wage inflation;
- labour legislation and the flexibility of labour: in terms of workers' rights, the coverage and generosity of social security benefits, the ability to shed and recruit staff, short-term contracts, part-time working etc. Labour insecurity can help to keep wage costs down;
- the power of trade unions, in terms of their ability to command wage increases and restrict productivity growth;
- the ability to vary wage differentials between different sectors of the economy. This would, for example, allow expanding industries to attract labour and declining industries to shed labour;
- the extent of any artificial controls on wages and prices;
- the ease of import penetration;
- export opportunities and free trade in general. An economy open to international competition puts pressure on domestic firms to be as productive as possible and, therefore, keep costs and prices down;
- the level of competitiveness within specific industries and between firms, in terms of the ability to expand profit margins by rising prices.

Economic capacity
Economic capacity, or the 'output gap', is a measure of the spare capacity in the economy which can be utilised to increase production. As resources within the economy become scarce, demand increasingly begins to exceed supply, leading to price rises. Economic capacity can be influenced by factors which include the following:

- levels of unemployment as, at a certain level of employment (known as the natural rate of unemployment), wage inflation begins to take off as

the contracting supply of labour enables workers to command higher wage settlements;
- skill levels, because not all the unemployed will have the necessary skills;
- asset bases, such as financial resources, premises, equipment and any other assets required to operate a business;
- previous levels of investment, both in the development of a skilled workforce, and in the investment in buildings, plant and machinery, technology and so on.

The effects of inflation
- a diminution in the real value of fixed incomes, savings and other forms of investment;
- a reduction in the real value of debt (and, as a result, the redistribution of wealth from debtors to creditors);
- increased uncertainty for businesses in terms of their pricing of goods and services;
- increased uncertainty as to the viability of investment;
- increased uncertainty and volatility in the financial markets;
- decreased international competitiveness owing to the increased cost of exports;
- the displacement of domestically produced goods by relatively cheaper imports from countries benefiting from lower levels of inflation; and
- higher interest rates as a means of controlling inflation. Rising interest rates increase household mortgage interest payments, reduce income available for other consumption, and thus depress the economy. Borrowing is more expensive, and the demand for credit is reduced. Falling demand for products and services reduces companies' profits and also their demand for labour. Overall, reduced output leads to unemployment and possibly recession.

While interest rates are likely to rise under high inflation, real interest rates (interest rate less inflation rate) are more important in analysing the consequences for households and the corporate sector. A rise in interest rates and debt payments in an inflationary climate may, for example, be offset by rising earnings growth and product prices.

Tell-tale signs of inflation
Inflation is measured by the Retail Price Index – a weighted basket of goods and services which is calculated monthly. The main measure of inflation, known as 'headline inflation', includes mortgage interest costs and taxation. Other measures are RPI-X, which excludes mortgage interest costs (and is known as 'underlying' or 'core' inflation), and RPI-Y, which excludes mortgage interest costs and tax.

Decisions to increase interest rates will have regard to the components of the RPI figures. Regard should, for example, be given to factors that force prices up temporarily, such as volatile food and energy prices. Import prices could be examined to establish whether cheap imports (which result from a strong pound) mask domestic price pressures that could make inflation higher at a later date, typically when the pound weakens. An increase in the price of oil may not result from increased consumer spending, but is nevertheless a cost pressure.

An example of how the RPI influences the government's ability to control inflation is that if interest rates are increased to curb inflationary pressures, the increase in mortgage costs will be reflected in a higher percentage rate for headline inflation, albeit temporarily. Wage bargainers will often give regard to current RPI figures and, particularly where the economy is nearing full capacity, wage rates may rise, causing nervousness about the prospect of wage-led (cost-push) inflation. Rises in indirect taxes such as VAT and duties can similarly increase the RPI.

The rate of inflation, as measured by the RPI, influences the level of government spending on pensions and other benefits (by index linking), public-sector pay, private-sector pay settlements, and the pricing policies of businesses.

Contributed by Austen Imber

CHAPTER 7

Negotiation skills

Published as 'Talk business', 18 April 1998

When surveyors are negotiating property transactions on behalf of clients, their company or themselves, their objective is to achieve the best settlement possible. Surveyors have a duty to secure the best deal for their client.

The approach taken to negotiations will reflect the personality, instincts, confidence and belief of the surveyor. The course of negotiations will be influenced by the respective characters of the parties. An intuitive approach, rather than a mechanistic approach, is therefore required.

The result of written, telephone and face-to-face negotiations is dependent on the balance of power between the parties. The balance of power which was perceived to exist at the start may have moved substantially by the time a settlement is concluded. Negotiating is a process of moving the balance of power in the desired direction. Some negotiators are able to move the balance further than others.

Perceptions of power

The parties' perceptions of their respective bargaining positions need to be realistic.

The surveyor who misjudges his bargaining strength and takes an overconfident, and possibly aggressive, approach could cause negotiations to deteriorate quickly and fail to secure a settlement which would be in the client's best interest. Over optimistic proposals for the renewal of a lease may, for example, prompt the property's current tenant to consider alternative premises, whereas a more realistic proposal may facilitate negotiations which retain the tenant, and uphold the property's investment value.

The negative surveyor, who mistakenly perceives his position to be weak, will not achieve the best deal. Comparable evidence presented by a landlord may appear to support a rent notice proposal. The surveyor with the tenacity and enthusiasm to research the evidence, and seek additional information, may find that the landlord's evidence reflects the desperation of a particular tenant for a property, and does not reflect the level of market rents in the area.

Selective details of transactions may have been presented. When evidence has been found to have been misrepresented, either deliberately or inadvertently, the balance of power between the parties can substantially alter.

Regard should always be given to the nature of the negotiations. A fallback option of being able to negotiate a letting with another party, for example, provides a greater bargaining strength than having to seek third-party determination if a settlement cannot be reached with a current tenant.

An experienced surveyor may well feel more powerful when negotiating against a less accomplished surveyor. An elder statesman may explore the possibility of reaching a settlement that is based on the relative ignorance of a junior surveyor. Younger surveyors can make it clear at the outset of negotiations that they have to apprise their superiors of the issues covered before they can secure authority to conclude a transaction. Generally, a requirement to 'refer back to the client', to 'take instructions' or to 'take legal advice' on the points raised avoids the dangers of being pressurised into a bad settlement.

Surveyors do not always negotiate with other surveyors. Where negotiations are undertaken directly with businesses, the surveyor may be subject to a particularly aggressive and intimidatory approach, which is constructed in the expectation that the surveyor will retreat, and accept a lesser settlement.

Threats may be made to approach the surveyor's superiors, possibly claiming that the surveyor has adopted an unreasonable attitude to negotiations. When surveyors are faced with such a situation, their resolve should not diminish. Managers should be fully supportive of their surveyor's actions, at least when in contact with the other party.

The ability to secure the best possible settlement can also be enhanced by being technically competent and knowledgeable, by preparing for negotiations, and by being able to provide documentary proof of any assertions that are made.

Some negotiators consider that they can enhance their position by adopting tactics such as providing particular seating arrangements, deliberately arriving too early or too late for a meeting or attending in convoy. Such initiatives tend to have little effect on the final settlement, and can be damaging when they are blatant and seen to be too clever.

Finer approaches that can be taken to negotiations include using and assessing body language, adopting particular tones of voice or choosing certain words.

Opening negotiations

The nature of most property transactions is that terms are negotiable. The initial proposals will invariably be rejected at some stage by the other party.

A proposal made by a landlord for a rent review could be optimistic, and provide a margin for negotiating with a tenant or for securing a favourable result if arbitration becomes necessary. An insupportable, and purely tactical, proposal may not form the best start to negotiations, and may not find favour with an arbitrator.

Similarly, tenants or purchasers should generally open negotiations at the lowest justifiable figure, and not discredit themselves and their case by adopting an unrealistic position.

Realistic terms may need to be quoted when marketing properties to attract interest and, subsequently, to establish the optimum bargaining position.

Price and other factors

Negotiations must consider factors beyond the price and any other terms of the transaction.

The aggressive private investor may be able to exploit a breach of covenant by a tenant by securing a higher rent as an alternative to seeking possession. A corporate landlord may have to be more conciliatory, and be aware of how adverse publicity could affect the relationship with existing and prospective tenants, and ultimately affect profitability.

Regard should be given to maintaining a good landlord and tenant relationship. It may not be appropriate, for example, to exploit the invalidity of a notice served by the other party, although it may be sensible to reserve the right to do so.

Delaying the conclusion of rent review or lease renewal negotiations may appear to benefit the tenant's cash flow position, but improved rental evidence may emerge that results in a higher rent having to be paid.

A settlement may be beneficial, or detrimental, to a transaction being undertaken on other properties. Once a property has been purchased, the goodwill of the vendor may subsequently be required.

Surveyors may also be responsible for agreeing a fee structure with clients, employing agents, negotiating contracts with staff, procuring the services of contractors or purchasing equipment or vehicles for the practice. The motivation and performance of agents, staff or trades people may be poor when they are disenchanted about the level of pay that they are forced to accept. The pursuit of a minimum price may not produce the maximum value.

Negotiations can, however, be undertaken relatively aggressively where regard does not need to be given to residual relationships between the parties.

In some situations, a ruthless approach may be required. A maximum rent may, for example, need to be aggressively sought to allow an investment property to be sold, or an uncompromising stance may need to be taken with the local authority or the district valuer. Surveyors who have to be mindful of their reputation and standing in an area, and of their relationships with fellow professionals, may not be comfortable handling such negotiations. Clients may prefer to instruct more remotely located surveyors in order to achieve their desired objectives.

Tactics

Each party will have different objectives. Some will be more valuable than others. A landlord may, for example, be indifferent to whether a five- or 10-year lease is granted, but the ability for the tenant to relocate an expanding business in five years' time may be of substantial value. A purchaser may be quietly assembling a development site, and be seeking to acquire properties cheaply.

Attempts should be made to ascertain the strengths, weaknesses, requirements and options of the other side. The more valuable the requirement, the more that can be secured in return. The true position of the other party may emerge progressively during negotiations.

When one party is attempting to work out the other's true position, it may be preferable to dismiss such enquiries as an irrelevance, rather than feeling forced to provide information that is best not divulged. In other situations, the questions may present an opportunity to enhance the balance of power between the parties by giving carefully crafted answers.

Surveyors should feel comfortable about asking any questions that may help their cause. Withholding information can be antagonistic, especially if the other party could secure it by alternative, if more inconvenient, means.

When there are breaks in conversation, care should be taken not to feel obliged to talk, and unnecessarily furnish the other side with information. Surveyors should guard against the initial exchange of pleasantries being shifted towards a probing for valuable information. Opinions made about the state of the market may, for example, weaken the strength of the arguments that were to be made once negotiations had begun.

In some situations, the parties will have to be open about their requirements because it is impossible to achieve their aspirations without disclosing them, or because their aspirations are likely to become obvious during negotiations and possibly be perceived by the other side to be more valuable that they would have been if raised more openly. If, for example, the landlord wishes to construct a deal to maximise investment value, he may be able to work with a tenant to realise value for both parties.

Common negotiating tips include not making concessions without seeking something in return, and not feeling obliged to make concessions when the other party does. However, this approach may not be cost-effective, especially if there are numerous contractual issues to consider.

In weak market conditions, it is likely that prospective tenants, or purchasers, may need to be made to feel that they have an exclusive opportunity to secure an acceptable deal. A position of subservience may be necessary to preserve the ability to conclude the deal.

In a stronger market, the other party could be requested to list all their requirements in advance, rather than addressing each requirement in turn. The acceptable requirements can be agreed, and a hard line can be taken on those which are not acceptable. Alternatively, the other party could be requested to confine their requirements to those which are a prerequisite of the transaction taking place, and advised that acceptance or rejection, but not negotiation, will follow. Clients will not, however, be impressed if a 'take it or leave it' approach results in a deal unnecessarily falling through.

Time should be taken to consider matters, and reach decisions. Decisions may not even have to be made. Surveyors should not be unnerved by periods of silence or by time delays promoted by the other party. Patience is required, although some individuals may need to be encouraged to move on from peripheral issues.

When time-scales are given to the other party for specific action to take place, the time-scale should be reasonable. The action to be taken in the event of non-performance should be formulated in advance, with a genuine intention that it will be carried out. If the other party lets the deadline pass without concern, the onus is then on the party imposing the deadline to act. Repeated, unactioned, threats can damage credibility and bring stalemate to negotiations. Similarly, although final positions may still be negotiable, they cannot be repeatedly so.

Surveyors should appear indifferent to threats made by the other party. Threats induced by the heat of negotiations may be ill-considered. Outlining the reasons why the threatened course of action is not feasible can destabilise the other party's position. A more subtle alternative is to set out the options that are available, and imply which course of action may need to be taken.

Surveyors must control their mood. Proposals should be reacted to objectively or impassively, but not with delight or gratitude. Negotiations can still be amicable where there is a lively exchange of views, provided the parties retain their professionalism. The other party should not be criticised or abused, but can be put under pressure by asking appropriate questions.

Surveyors should be alert to the tactics sometimes employed by purchasers. Some purchasers will offer a relatively high price in order to be the successful bidder, but with the intention of seeking reductions to the price once they perceive the vendor to be in a weaker position when the property is off the market. Surveyors should preserve the ability to negotiate with previously unsuccessful bidders. Repeated requests for variations or concessions should prompt consideration of whether refusal will jeopardise the deal, and whether a transaction should be allowed to proceed.

Tenants may have more to complain about when they are aware that a rent increase is imminent. They may wish to negotiate a revised rent payment pattern in the hope that they will be perceived to be in financial difficulty, and receive a favourable settlement.

Human factors

Negotiations should not be influenced by emotional or egotistical factors.

Surveyors should not dwell on previously unsuccessful negotiations that may have taken place with the other party, and should not be allowed to distract attention from the client's interests. Previous experiences may, however, warrant the need for an uncompromising approach.

Individuals need to feel that they command professional respect. Accepting defeat can be difficult. A desired result may not have been attainable.

Conversely, a relatively poor deal may be perceived to be acceptable because an astute negotiator has made the other party feel that they have obtained an attractive deal, letting them feel good about themselves. When surveyors have become embroiled in a case, it can sometimes be useful for a colleague to provide a more dispassionate opinion.

Prospective purchasers or tenants may think that they have secured a good deal. The surveyor may have created an illusion that they have. If an independent valuation suggests that the deal is less favourable than originally thought, the deal can fall through. Verbal acceptance to a deal may be withdrawn because the other party felt pressurised, or bullied into agreeing terms. Deals can also fall through because of disillusionment at the time taken to finalise a transaction. Vendors, landlords and their representatives should ensure that documentation is progressed quickly.

Surveyors may have to adapt their usual style of behaviour in order to endear themselves to the character of the other party, especially when they are not in a position of power. The onus is on the more vibrant character to tone down their natural exuberance. An aura of superiority may induce weakness in the other party, but can often result in obstinacy. Power dressing can intimidate, but may be seen for what it attempts to achieve, and cause resentment.

Some individuals are comfortable in adopting an unjustifiable or obstinate stance in writing or over the telephone, but will become more amenable once forced into face-to-face negotiations.

Conclusion

Negotiation is sometimes defined as a process of compromise, but whether it need be depends on whether it was intended to offer room for negotiation on the original proposal, on the respective positions of power of the parties and on whether those positions are sustainable. Negotiators can move the balance of power in the desired direction by having a good knowledge of the case and the subject area, by being well prepared, and by applying the skills which develop from both experience and education.

Contributed by Austen Imber

Commercial Law

8. Data protection 57
9. Self-employment and tax 62
10. Financial Services Agency. 68
11. *Force majeure* in contract law 73
12. Rectification and common mistake in contract law 79
13. Dealing with redundancies 85
14. Small print regulations. 91

CHAPTER 8

Data Protection

Published as 'Lock up your data', 14 October 2000

New legislation on data protection, aimed at protecting individuals, is especially important for the property professions

At the beginning of the 1980s, when video cassette recorders were new, there was a spate of burglaries from video-hire shops. The purpose was not to steal video tapes, but to obtain a list of the shop's customers. From this, the thieves obtained addresses of households that owned video recorders, and targeted future burglaries accordingly.

This provides a vivid example of the damage and distress that can follow when personal information falls into the wrong hands.

Since 1984, anyone holding and processing computer information about private individuals has had to register with the Data Protection Registrar (now known as the Data Protection Commissioner). They have also had to comply with a statutory code of practice governing the collection, processing, and disclosure of protected computer data. This has now been superseded and replaced by the Data Protection Act 1998 (DPA) and its associated regulations, which came into force on 1 March 2000.

The new legislation implements Europe-wide proposals contained in Directive 95/46/EC, which protects individuals with regard to the processing of personal data and the movement of such data. As holders of detailed information on properties, vendors, prospective purchasers and funders, data protection is important for the property professions, particularly where that information is stored on computer. It is even more important for firms that arrange mortgages or provide other financial services. Although the DPA applies only to personal information held on computer, such protection will, over the next few years, be extended to certain manual records.

What data?
The DPA covers computerised data about an identifiable living individual. It does not apply to information about companies or properties (so long as no living individual can be identified). Information about a person's racial or ethnic origin, political opinions, religious beliefs, trades union membership, physical or mental health, sexual life or alleged commission of any offence are regarded by the DPA as 'sensitive personal data' to which additional restrictions apply.

Principles
The DPA's principal requirement is that any organisation that processes protected computer data must register with the commissioner. Such registration must specify: the name and address of the person responsible for processing the data (the data controller); a description of the personal data to be processed; the purpose of the data; a description of any proposed recipient; and details of any non-EC countries to which that data may be directly, or indirectly, transferred. A fee of £35 is also payable. The data controller is also under a statutory duty to comply with the principles of data protection (see p61).

The data controller must demonstrate that the data subject has consented to the processing and that the data is necessary:

- for the performance of a contract;
- to comply with a legal obligation;
- to protect the interests of the data subject;
- for the administration of justice;
- for the legitimate interests of the data controller or the person to whom the information is to be transmitted.

Before sensitive data can be processed it is also necessary to comply with the additional statutory conditions applicable to sensitive data.

Rights of data subjects
As well as controlling the way in which personal data is collected, processed and disclosed, the DPA gives rights to data subjects. Individuals have a basic right to be informed by a data controller that data is being held and to be given details of that data, the purposes for which it is being processed and any recipients.

However, a data controller is only obliged to provide that information upon receipt of a written request accompanied by a fee of up to £10 (or £2 if the inquiry relates to a credit reference agency).

Individuals also have express rights to prevent their data being used for the purposes of direct marketing and to prevent a decision that significantly affects them being made by the automatic processing of personal data, without additional human input. Where, in the absence of such notification, this does happen, the individual concerned must be informed of the basis upon which the decision was taken, and be given 21 days to request a reconsideration of the decision by other means. These restrictions apply only to the evaluation of matters affecting an individual, such as their work performance, credit worthiness, reliability or conduct.

A data subject can also require the correction of any inaccurate data and the destruction of any opinion based upon inaccurate data.

Enforcement

Compliance with the DPA can be enforced by prosecution, statutory action by the commissioner or by an action for damages at the suit of any aggrieved data subject.

The prospect of prosecution will mainly arise when someone begins processing protected data without having registered under the DPA, or by collecting, processing, using or disclosing personal data other than for the purposes specified in that registration. There is no limit on the fines that can be imposed upon offenders, but criminal proceedings can normally be issued only by the commissioner.

If the commissioner believes that a data controller is contravening any of the statutory principles of data protection, he can serve the data controller with an 'enforcement notice', either requiring the controller to take, or to refrain from taking, any specified steps or to refrain from processing any personal data for a specified period. Before serving an enforcement notice, the commissioner must first consider whether the contravention has caused, or is likely to cause, the person involved any damage or distress. The notice must particularise the data protection principles that have been contravened, and must notify the recipient of the statutory grounds of appeal. A data subject may also request the commissioner to carry out an assessment to determine whether the DPA is being complied with in their case.

Upon receipt of such a request, or for any other reasonable purpose, the commissioner may serve an 'information notice' on the data controller requesting such information as the commissioner may reasonably require to ascertain whether the data protection principles are being complied with.

Non-compliance with either an enforcement notice or an information notice is an offence punishable by an unlimited fine. However, for all offences under the DPA, it is possible for anyone to use as a defence a demonstration that they have exercised all due diligence to comply with the DPA or the particular notice served. There is also a statutory right of appeal to the Data Protection Tribunal against either an enforcement notice or an information notice. The possible grounds of appeal can either be that the notice is legally defective or that the commissioner should, in any respect, have exercised his discretion differently. The general time-limit for appealing is 28 days from receipt of the notice. It is also the commissioner's duty to promote good practice by data controllers and to ensure their observance of the requirements of the DPA.

Any data subject who suffers damage as a result of an infringement may claim compensation, not only for any actual damage but also for any distress suffered as a result of the contravention. It is a defence for the data controller to demonstrate that he had taken such care as, in all the circumstances, was reasonably required to comply with the DPA.

Practicalities

As regards the practicalities of compliance, the first question for any business proprietor is whether he or she needs to register under the DPA.

This will depend, first, upon the nature of the information held (ie whether it relates to identifiable private individuals) and the manner in which that information is held. If registration is necessary under the DPA, the terms of that registration must be wide enough to cover every type of personal data that is likely to be processed, every purpose for which that data might be processed and any possible recipient of that data, so that there is no possibility for the data controller to process data beyond the scope of his or her registration particulars.

Data controllers must then review their procedures for collecting, processing, disclosing and destroying data records to ensure that they are consistent with the statutory principles of data protection, that is, they must identify any particular data that may be regarded as 'sensitive', and to which additional statutory restrictions will apply.

Last, and perhaps most important, is the need for proper and adequate security to avoid any possibility of protected data being misused or falling into the wrong hands.

Principles of data protection

The data controller must comply with the following:

- It must be processed fairly and lawfully.
- It must be obtained only for one or more specified and lawful purpose and not further processed in any manner incompatible with that purpose.
- It must be adequate, relevant and not excessive in relation to the specified purposes for which it is held.
- It must be accurate and up to date.
- It must not be kept longer than is necessary for the specified purpose.
- It must be processed in accordance with the rights of the individuals whom it concerns (ie the data subjects).
- It must not be transferred to any non-EC country or territory unless that country or territory ensures an equivalent level of protection for data subjects.

Contributed by VC Ward

CHAPTER 9

Self-employment and tax

Published as 'A few home truths on homeworking', 4 May 2002

If you work at home, are you an employee or are you self-employed? The answer will depend upon the specific conditions of your employment

Out of necessity or choice, more people are working from home. The advantages are clear for many who do so. Changes in technology, in the work place and in the way in which we do our work, are some of the most striking developments in the past few decades. No doubt there will be equally dramatic changes in the decades to come.

Employee or self-employed?

The question of status may be far from clear. When are homeworkers truly self-employed persons? Are they, in fact, employees in all but name? Another way of putting it is to pose the question: is there a 'contract of service' or is there a 'contract for services'.

However phrased, the difference is critical. We need to be categorised either as an 'employee' or as a 'self-employed person' in whatever job we are doing. It can be a vexed question. While, sometimes, the answer can be self-evident, at other times, it can be difficult to find, as we shall see.

Why it is important

Why is the categorisation so important? If we are employees, we are protected by the vast array of employment legislation that is intended to safeguard our rights in any number of situations: a falling out with an employer, a redundancy notice, discriminatory action, and so forth. We can receive sick pay and holiday pay, overtime or unemployment benefit. But none of this need cover the self-employed.

Of equal importance, the tax regime that applies to us is also dependent upon, and differs according to, our employment status (see below). Then again, liability in tort for negligent acts can be imposed upon an independent contractor, who will generally be held liable, while the employer can find himself vicariously liable for his or her employee's negligence. Other obligations, such as national insurance contributions, are also differentiated according to whether a worker is employed or self-employed.

Ignore the labels

It is important to remember that it is not a matter of what we may choose to call ourselves (or those who work for us). There are factors to be weighed in the balance that will assist in determining whether or not someone is employed or self-employed (see below). But, in the event, in the employment field a court will look at the situation in its entirety and in the light of all the facts. And the court's view will be decisive (in this, as in so much else), notwithstanding the label that either the employer or the employee will paste on, or paste over, their relationship.

The Inland Revenue has its own criteria, which overlap with those used in the employment field, but these two sets of criteria are not necessarily identical.

A question of control?

The standard starting point for ascertaining status was laid down in *Ready Mixed Concrete (South East) Ltd* v *Minister of Pensions and National Insurance* [1968] 2 QB 497, at p515. This test was recently reapplied in *Montgomery* v *Johnson Underwood Ltd* [2001] EWCA Civ 318; [2001] ICR 819. Today, of course, we no longer talk easily of master and servant relationships, but, clearly, the principle still holds good:

[The court] must now consider what is meant by a contract of service. A contract of service exists if these three conditions are fulfilled. (i) The servant agrees that, in consideration of a wage or other remuneration, he will provide his own work and skill in the performance of some service for his master. (ii) He agrees, expressly or impliedly, that in the performance of that service he will be subject to the other's control in a sufficient degree to make that other master. (iii) The other provisions of the contract are consistent with its being a contract of service.

Provided (i) and (ii) are present, then (iii) requires that all the terms of the agreement are to be considered before the question (whether there is a contract of service or a contract for services) can be answered.

Subcontracting
It is important to remember that if a person works for someone else but is not required to provide those services personally, as a matter of law the relationship between them cannot be treated as that of employee and employer.

In *Express & Echo Publications Ltd* v *Tanton* [1999] ICR 693, a driver was held not be an employee. This was because he had been taken on under a contract providing that, in the event of him being unable or unwilling to perform the services personally, he was to 'arrange at his own expense entirely for another suitable person to perform the services'.

Expert employees
Society provides many examples of professionals being used as employees, not as contractors. Surgeons, research scientists, technologists, and other experts are not usually subject to direct control by their employers. In many of these cases, the employer, or the controlling management, will have no more than a very general idea of how the work is done. They will have no inclination directly to interfere with it. None the less, the courts have reiterated the view that a sufficient framework of control must exist in such cases, if these professional persons are to be considered as employees, not self-employed contractors.

Other factors
Once the preconditions of a minimum mutual obligation (in respect of the work) and a degree of control (employer over employee) have been satisfied, certain other factors have been recognised as contributing to the picture as a whole (see p66). However, none of these other indicators are conclusive in themselves. The words 'self-employed' or 'employee' are not defined by statute, but have generally been dealt with through case law in a piecemeal fashion. In reaching a decision on the precise status of our working arrangements, all the relevant facts must be considered in detail. It is then a question of standing back and looking at the final picture.

An additional way of ascertaining status is to ask whether we are in business on our own account – so that success or failure depends upon ourselves, not others. But even taking this factor into account, the answer can sometimes be less than clear-cut: we can wear two hats. In other words, we can be an employee during the day, working for a surveyors' or architects' firm, and then, in our spare time, practise our profession on our own account – if our contract with our employer permits. This indicates the complexity of the various situations that can and do exist, as well as the fine lines that the courts have to tread and to draw. Moreover, exactly the same questions have to be weighed in the balance, notwithstanding that the work is only part-time or performed under a short-term contract.

Workers

Just to complicate further an already complex picture, even a self-employed person may be treated as a worker in certain circumstances, and there are extended statutory definitions of this term. A particular example can be found in section 13 of the Employment Relations Act 1999, which defines 'worker' to include an employee, a self-employed person, and, also, an agency worker.

Tax position

Employees are taxed under Schedule E, while the self-employed are responsible for their own tax under Schedule D.

However, the Revenue has been keen to deal with the rapidly expanding number of one-man companies in the 'knowledge-based' service industries, particularly those in the media and information technology fields. Highly skilled employees could resign one day and set up a one-man company the next, while still working for the same firm. Essentially, these were tax-avoidance schemes. Small salaries would be paid and the balance retained by the company, so that its profits became liable to corporation tax at a reduced rate.

The Revenue has taken steps to deal with schemes of this kind and to target the contract workers involved in them. It was necessary to do this in such a way that genuine self-employed activities would not be affected. But the Revenue wanted to ensure that an employee (in all but name) should be taxed as such, and that the money paid by the true employer (in all but name) should be treated as a salary, not as a contractor's fee. The fact that the money might be paid through an intermediary company can now be ignored.

This legislation, known as IR 35, has achieved 'unusual notoriety', according to Robert Walker LJ in *R (on the application of Professional Contractors Group Ltd)* v *Inland Revenue Commissioners* [2002] STC 165, a case that illustrated a failed attempt to brand the legislation as unlawful and contrary to EC law.

Further information

If after studying your position you are still not certain of your employment status, the Revenue can look at your contract to give a view. It also issues some helpful leaflets: for example, Employed or self-employed? (IR56). These are available free from local offices.

Further factors that can determine a person's work status

1.1 Guidance for the employee:
'you have to carry out the work personally
'someone else has the right to control what you do, even if such control is exercised infrequently or indirectly
'you work wholly or mainly for one firm or person
'work is generally carried out on the firm's premises
'none of your money is involved
'there is no possibility that you will suffer a financial loss
'you have no business set-up buying in stock or materials
'you do not engage employees or other assistants who answer to you personally
'you work set hours and receive a regular salary, eg by the week or the month
'there are disciplinary procedures in the event of a dispute
'you receive payment for overtime working, or when on vacation or sick leave.
1.2 Guidance for the self-employed:
'you can stipulate that if you cannot do the job, someone else can do the work in your stead
'no one has ultimate control over your operations
'you can work for several clients
'you supply the requisite materials or equipment necessary for fulfilling your contract
'you will bear any extra costs if you have underquoted for the task
'you have to accept other losses

'you are entitled to the profits
'you have a right to employ others and you pay them for the work in hand at your own expense
'you may be paid an agreed amount for the job regardless of how long it takes
'you are able to determine how and when the work will be done within your contractual framework
'you are responsible if something goes wrong, you have to correct the work in your own time, and, if need be, at your own cost.'

Contributed by Aviva Golden

CHAPTER 10

Financial Services Authority

Published as 'Act to tighten the financial screws', 29 June 2002

The Financial Services and Markets Act 2000 rationalises the regulation of the finance sector, but has it invested too much power in the FSA?

The Financial Services and Markets Act 2000 (FSMA) was introduced to parliament, as a Bill, in June 1999. It attracted more amendments (over 1,100) than any previous piece of legislation.

Regulation before the FSMA

The previous legal framework was primarily, but not exclusively, the Financial Services Act 1986. This established the following fragmented structure:

'Three self-regulatory organisations (SROs), supervised by the Securities and Investments Board (SIB), looked after different arms of the financial services market. In some cases, the SRO structure gave rise to dual regulation, where complex firms dealt with all three regulators. At the same time, however, there were gaps in the regulation.

'The Bank of England, as the central bank, was responsible for the prudential affairs of the banking system. Its "tea and cucumber sandwiches" style of supervision came under increasing pressure from the 1960s, following high-profile bank failures, such as Johnson Matthey and, more recently, BCCI.

'The insurance division of the Treasury was responsible for safeguards in the insurance industry. (This area is, of course, particularly crucial to pension provision.) The recent problems at Equitable Life mean that the Financial Services Authority (FSA) will, in future, put more resources into supervising the way in which insurance firms advertise, sell, and administer their products.

'Various mutual "grass-roots" organisations also existed. These offered financial services, but were usually established under their own legislation, often with their own commission supervising their business methods. Friendly societies, building societies and credit unions all followed this model of regulation. The government is very interested in these particular providers of financial services (which are often no more than the services of saving and borrowing) because they have a history of serving groups that are otherwise excluded from mainstream services.

From now on, all prior regulatory powers, in the form modified by the FSMA, are given over to the FSA. This means that some 10 disparate regulators have now been merged into the one regulatory authority.

Powers under the FSMA

The powers of regulation conferred upon the FSA are extensive. Firms (companies, partnerships or sole traders) must apply for authorisation to carry out certain activities. Their subsequent execution of such activities is then regulated, and any suspicion of breach can be investigated and the firms disciplined, if found guilty.

Parliament has charged the FSA to deliver four objectives, which are outlined in section 2 of the FSMA. The FSA must:

'maintain confidence in the UK financial system;

'promote public understanding of the financial system, including awareness of the benefits and risks associated with different kinds of investment;

'secure the appropriate degree of consumer protection (having regard to the different levels of risk in transactions and experience of consumers, together with the general principle that consumers should take responsibility for their decisions);

'reduce the extent to which it is possible for a business conducted by a regulated firm to be used for a purpose connected with financial crime.

It is stipulated that the powers may be exercised by the FSA only in a proportionate way and in line with the above objectives.

Secondary legislation

In addition to the main statute, there are a several pieces of secondary legislation. For example, the Regulated Activities Order 2001 replaces some insurance, banking and investment legislation, and defines certain activities as being within the scope of regulation. These range from accepting deposits (for example, a bank operating current and savings accounts for customers) to advising upon participation in syndicates at Lloyds, or even contributing to a prepaid funeral plan. The order also covers the same type of activities as those covered by the Financial Services Act 1986, such as giving investment advice, managing investments, or selling private pensions.

The scope of regulated business, and who is subject to regulation, has increased, even in the short time since the passing of the Act. Inevitably, any increase in scope fuels City concerns about the creation of a 'super regulator', but it is the Treasury that has initiated this extension. In December 2001, for example, it announced that both general insurance (not just investment products) and mortgages would be brought under FSA regulation over the next few years. (However, for the moment, the buy-to-let market remains outside the scope of these proposals.)

Other enterprises, previously subject to a different form of regulation, have also been incorporated. These late arrivals include listing authorities, exchanges and clearing houses, together with those professional firms – law firms, accountants, actuaries, and other professions – that offer investment business as a principal service to their clients.

Given its jurisdictional width, it is easy to conclude that the FSA has all-embracing powers over a wide range of activities, firms and individuals. It has regularly produced papers to explain how it intends to regulate and to fulfil its brief as an 'open and transparent regulator': see the FSA website at www.fsa.gov.uk for details.

How robust is the FSA?

There are three areas of concern:

1. The question of governance, namely concern about the combined role of the FSA's chair and chief executive and the (alleged) insufficient involvement of non-executive directors.
2. The potential for the FSA to act as judge, jury and executioner in the exercise of its powers. This is compounded by the dual aspects of the newly created offence of market abuse (which carries both civil and criminal implications). Concern has been voiced with regard to the fact that criminal intent does not have to be present in order for an offence to be committed, and that no legal aid is available until the case reaches a tribunal.
3. Fears have been voiced over the FSA's statutory immunity against actions for damages in negligence, and the lack of separation of powers (the FSA both makes secondary legislation and then enforces it).

However, all these points can be counter-argued.

1. Governance arguments over the role of a chair are more suited to public limited companies than to quasi-governmental bodies, and it has already been stated that when the current chair (Sir Howard Davies) moves on, a review will be undertaken.
2. The burden of proof for any charge that may be brought by the FSA lies with the FSA, and there is a right of appeal to an independent tribunal within the Lord Chancellor's remit. Moreover, statutory immunity is a feature of the Financial Services Act 1986, and has been enjoyed by previous regulators without comment. Any maladministration will be subject to independent investigation. The independent investigator, who will be appointed by a panel of practitioners and by a non-executive chair, is authorised to order compensation.

    Public accountability is reinforced by the requirement to report annually to parliament, via the Treasury, against agreed objectives.
3. With regard to the law-making process, the FSA is required to be 'open and transparent' with a number of practitioner panels and consumer panels, which must be consulted on major proposals. These panels have the power to review policy and decisions before final approval by the FSA board in its law-making capacity.

The legislation: Key elements of the FSMA

Approval
Firms wishing to undertake regulated financial services must obtain approval to do so. This is usually accompanied by certain 'permissions'. Approval requires applicants to submit evidence of certain 'qualifying conditions', such as the size of their resource (it is a general requirement that there must be sufficient resource for the risk) and that the applicant's senior management are fit and proper persons to transact such business.

Transacting or conducting the business
Once they gave been given the permissions to do certain activities, firms become subject to a large body of rules known as 'conduct of business' rules, which constrain the way in which they do business; how they collect information from a client; how they interact with that client; how they promote their products; how they keep their client money and so on.

These rules are largely subject to supervision, either in the form of desk-based monitoring from data sent in from firms, or in the form of visits.

Investigation and enforcement
The powers to investigate authorised firms are extensive. The FSA can make a public censure statement; impose a fine; and apply for injunctions to stop certain activities. Restitution is also available as a civil remedy in cases of market abuse. Money laundering and insider dealing are criminal offences, which can be prosecuted by the FSA under the Act. Administration and winding up can also be requested.

Contributed by Janice Lambert

CHAPTER 11

Force majeure in the Law of Contract

Published as 'An irresistible force', 6 April 2002

English courts have never provided an all-embracing definition of the concept of *force majeure*, but it forms an important part of contract law

As its name implies, *force majeure* has traditionally been treated by English courts as a foreign doctrine. The Roman law concept of *vis major* was originally seen as equivalent in English law to an act of God, which was finally defined by the House of Lords in *Tennent* v *Earl of Glasgow* (1864) 2 Macph HL (22) as:

a circumstance which no human foresight can provide against, and of which human prudence is not bound to recognise the possibility.

However, *force majeure* is now given a wider meaning by the English courts than *vis major* or act of God.

Force majeure in civil law jurisdictions

The modern English concept of *force majeure* derives from the Code Napoleon and, thence, the current French civil code. The expression is well known in all civil law jurisdictions. A failure of performance by a party to a contract governed by French law will be attributable to *force majeure* if, without any fault on the part of the party seeking to be excused performance, an event occurs that possesses the following characteristics:

- Irrésistibilité: The event must render performance of the obligation impossible, not merely more onerous.
- Imprévisibilité: The event must not be reasonably foreseeable because, if it had been, the party seeking to be excused ought to have taken steps to prevent it, or to avoid its consequences.
- Extériorité: The event must have occurred because of some external cause, that is, not from a cause within the responsibility of the party seeking to be excused performance.

Acceptance of *force majeure* by English courts

Although the English courts have never provided an all-embracing definition of *force majeure*, the wide definition in Goirand's *French Commercial Law* (2nd ed) at p854 was held, in *Lebeaupin* v *Richard Crispin & Co* [1920] 2 KB 714 at p719, to be a useful expression of the meaning of *force majeure* 'as used on the Continent of Europe and as often employed in contracts governed by English law':

Force Majeure: This term is used with reference to all circumstances independent of the will of man, and which it is not in his power to control, and such *Force Majeure* is sufficient to justify the non-execution of a contract. Thus war, inundations and epidemics are cases of *Force Majeure*; it has even been decided that a strike of workmen constitutes a case of *Force Majeure*.

However, it was also held in *Lebeaupin* that the *force majeure* clause in a contract should be construed in each case with close attention to the words that precede or follow it, and with due regard to the nature and general terms of the contract. Thus, the effect of the clause might vary with each instrument.

Although *force majeure* is not a term of art in English law, the following meaning is now generally accepted by the courts:

A party to a contract containing a *Force Majeure* clause is not liable for failure to perform (or perform punctually) any of his obligations under the contract insofar as he proves three things:

(i) Uncontrollability – that the failure was due to an impediment beyond his control; and
(ii) Unforeseeability – that he could not reasonably be expected to have taken into account when concluding the contract the impediment and its effects on his ability to perform his obligations under the contract; and
(iii) Unavoidability – that he could not reasonably have avoided or overcome the impediment (or at least its effects).

A party cannot rely upon his own act, negligence, omission, fault or default as an even of – see *Sonat Offshore SA* v *Amerada Hess Development Ltd* [1988] 1 Lloyd's Rep 145. According to Hobhouse J in *J Lauritzen AS* v *Wijsmuller BV (The Super Servant Two)* [1989] 1 Lloyd's Rep 148 at p160, 'fault' includes an event that the party relying upon it had the means and opportunity to prevent, but nevertheless caused or permitted to come about.

However, in *Navrom* v *Calliris Ship Management SA* [1987] 2

Lloyd's Rep 276 at p282, the English Commercial Court ruled that, in so far as the expression ' – ' had a general meaning in English law, the requirement of unforeseeability might not always be a necessary element. It held that a – clause would apply to excuse delay in berthing at Tripoli, despite the fact that Tripoli was known to be a port subject to extreme congestion. The foreseeability of congestion did not justify attaching an unusual or restricted meaning to the word 'hindrances' in the – clause.

The important question was whether the incidence of a particular peril, which could have been foreseen, could really be said to have caused one party's failure of performance. On appeal, the Court of Appeal agreed that the meaning of each individual cause of hindrance should not be limited just because the contract provision was headed ' – ', which was an omnibus provision.

Lex mercatoria

In the past 30 years, the law merchant, or *lex mercatoria*, is considered to have acquired the character of an autonomous legal system, or a universal trade usage. This is largely the creation of international arbitrators. The courts in a number of countries have recognised that it is admissible for parties and arbitrators to refer to the *lex mercatoria* as an autonomous legal system when determining the law governing a particular contract.

The French Cour de Cassation and the Austrian Oberste Gerichtsof recognised this, in 1982 and 1984 respectively, in *Norsolor SA* v *Palbalk Ticaret Ltd* 1983 YB Com Arb 362. In 1982, the Italian Corte di Cassazione also recognised it in *Damiano* v *Topfer* 105 Foro It 2285 (Cass 1982). The Court of Appeal, in *Deutsche Schachbau und Tiefbohrgeselschaft mbH* v *R:As al-Khaimah National Oil Co (No 2)* [1987] 2 All ER 769 at p779*, upheld the arbitrator's choice of a transnational law in the shape of 'a common denominator of principles underlying the laws of the various nations governing contractual relations'.

In spite of *Navrom*, which cast doubt on the concept of unforeseeability as a necessary ingredient of *force majeure*, both French and Greek law include it as such. It is not safe, therefore, when applying internationally accepted principles of commercial law, to assume that unforeseeability is not a necessary ingredient.

---

*   Reversed by the House of Lords on different grounds: [1988] 2 All ER 833.

Consequences of *force majeure*

If an event that causes delay to the performance of the contract falls within the contractual *force majeure* clause, no financial compensation would normally be payable by either party; there would only be an extension of time. Some contracts provide for unilateral or mutual termination if the event giving rise to *force majeure* persists beyond a fixed time.

Relationship between frustration and *force majeure*

There are two caregories of supervening events that may cause havoc with a contractual performance:

(1) A frustrating event: In *Paal Wilson 6-Co AS* v *Partenreederei Hannah Blumenthal (The Hannah Blumenthal)* [1983] 1 Lloyd's Rep 103 at p112, Lord Brandon identified two essential factors that must be present to frustrate a contract:
  (i) Some outside event or extraneous change of situation, not foreseen or provided for in the contract, that either makes it impossible for the contract to be performed at all, or at least renders its performance something radically different from what was intended by the parties.
  (ii) This outside factor or change must have occurred without the fault or default of either party.
  If frustration occurs, the contract is, under English law, automatically discharged by operation of law (see *Hirji Muiji* v *Cheong Yue Steamship Co Ltd* [1926] AC 497 at p505) and the financial consequences for the parties are then decided in accordance with statute: see the Law Reform (Frustrated Contracts) Act 1943.
(2) An event of *force majeure*: A supervening event that causes delay or otherwise makes performance more onerous, but which is not sufficiently fundamental to constitute frustration. Such an event must fall within the accepted meaning of *force majeure*.

Under Article 34 of the UN Industrial Development Organisation Model Form of Lump-Sum Contract for the Construction of a Fertiliser Plant, the normal categories of *force majeure* may include, but not be limited to, the following:

War or hostilities, any riot or civil commotion, any earthquake, flood, tempest, lightning, unusual weather or other natural physical disaster, impossibility in the use of any railway, port, airport, shipping service or other means of transportation or communication, any accident, fire or explosion, any strike, lock-out or concerted acts of workmen (except when it is in the power of the party invoking the *Force Majeure* provision to prevent such occurrence), shortage or unavailability of materials (compounded by the same shortage or unavailability from alternative sources).

Force majeure is always a matter of contract, while frustration occurs by operation of law. The contractual *force majeure* clause may also deal with frustrating events, such as war, which are then excluded as frustrating events by virtue of their inclusion in the contractual clause.

No *force majeure* clause?

The inclusion of a *force majeure* clause in the contract is to avoid protracted and expensive litigation and possible exposure to damages. But what if the contract contains no *force majeure* clause? If a supervening event were to occur, the affected party would, if possible, have to rely upon the common law doctrine of frustration.

Some events of *force majeure*, for example a period of bad weather that delays North Sea drilling operations, or a strike that causes delays on a construction project, would not normally meet the requirements of frustration. It will therefore ofren be difficult to invoke frustration as a substitute for a *force majeure* clause, which would have excused performance. If frustration does not apply, the party affected will be liable in damages.

When only one contract of two can be performed

A party may have agreed *force majeure* clauses in several contracts. If an event of *force majeure* were to occur, it might mean the performance of only one of two contracts, or only the partial performance of several such contracts. The party affected would be excused further performance if he were to perform one contract but not the other, or to allocate the available contract goods or services in a fair and reasonable manner between several contracts: see *Intertradex SA* v *Lesieur-liJrteaux Sari* [1978] 2 Lloyd's Rep 509.

Frustration, on the other hand, occurs by operation of law when a genuine frustrating event occurs. If the party affected then chooses to perform one contract and not another, or to perform several contracts only partially, the chain of causation is immediately broken.

The outcome cannot be an application of the doctrine of frustration, since the matter remains within the control of the party affected. In that situation, see, for example, *Lauritzen*, the party affected must perform his contract or be liable in damages.

Contributed by Martin Moyes

CHAPTER 12

Rectification and common mistake in contract law

Published as 'Write the wrongs', 19 October 2002

Although, for hundreds of years, the courts have applied the remedy of rectification to legal documents, they have been reluctant to extend this to contracts. How then can such instruments be rectified?

Background

Public policy requires certainty in the enforcement of contracts. The courts are reluctant to allow a party of full capacity who has signed a document, with the opportunity of inspection, afterwards to say that it was not what he meant.

How is it, then, that the remedy of rectification has been applied by courts of equity for hundreds of years? The answer is that the courts have applied rectification to documents, rather than to contracts. The purpose of rectification is to make the written record the true agreement of the parties.

Like all equitable remedies, rectification is discretionary. Relief may be refused if the parties have acquiesced in the situation, or, for example, if witnesses have died as a result of long delays (laches) in seeking the remedy.

Categories of documents that have been rectified include agreements, conveyances, deed polls, settlements, policies of life insurance, bills of exchange, leases, bonds, and company registers. In the majority of cases, rectification has been based upon a mistake of one or more of the parties to a document. This can take the form of 'unilateral', 'common', or 'mutual' mistake.

Rectification is not an appropriate remedy where the mistake relates to the transaction itself, rather than to the document that purports to record it.

Unilateral mistake
A unilateral mistake occurs where a party (A) executes a document under a mistake as to the provisions contained within it, while the other party (B) may be aware of the mistake but says nothing. It may then be unconscionable for B to be allowed to benefit by the mistake by objecting to rectification.

The party seeking rectification of a lease for unilateral mistake has to prove that the defendant knew of the claimant's mistake and took advantage of it: see *Templiss Properties Ltd* v *Hyams* [1999] EGCS 60. Lack of diligence on the part of the defendant or his agent, which led to them being unaware of the mistake, is not sufficient. It is essential that the defendant has acted unconscionably, that is, immorally, unscrupulously, unfairly etc. In other words, there has to be an element of 'sharp practice' by one party at the expense of another.

Common, or mutual, mistake
Common, or mutual, mistake occurs where all the parties to a document were under a mistake as to the terms set out within the document at the time of execution. In such cases, they would all have been under the misapprehension that the document recorded the terms of their prior agreement: but it did not do so. See p83 below for the usual constituents of common mistake.

The old heresy
In 1970, the Court of Appeal rejected the old heresy that, in every case, an antecedent-concluded agreement had to be proved, which the instrument to be rectified did not accurately record. Rectification can also be granted upon 'convincing proof' of a continuing common intention evidenced by 'some outward expression of accord': see *Joscelyne* v *Nissen* [1970] 2 QB 86.

Origin of the antecedent agreement heresy
In the earlier cases on rectification, weighty *dicta* established that the courts had no jurisdiction to rectify unless there was 'an actual concluded contract antecedent to the instrument which is sought to be rectified; and that such contract is inaccurately represented in the instrument': see *Mackenzie* v *Coulson* (1869) LR 8 Eq 368 at p375, *per* Sir WM James V-C. In *Lovell & Christmas Ltd* v *Wall* (1911) 104 LT 84, *dicta* in the Court of Appeal expressed the view

that there could be no rectification unless a pre-existing contract had been inaptly expressed in the final document.

Most early rectification cases had concerned the alteration of a final instrument, that is, a conveyance or a settlement, so as to make it accord with a previous instrument, such as a contract for sale or articles for a settlement. Moreover, cases where mutual mistake could be proved, in the absence of any previous written instrument, were very rare, because of the high standard of proof required by the court.

Thus, over time, the language used by the courts, in cases of rectification by reference to a previous instrument, had passed into the textbooks and had become authoritative in general terms. Such language was not strictly accurate in cases where rectification proceeded on proof of mutual mistake in recording the concurrent intention of the parties, at the moment of executing the instrument that it was seeking to rectify.

Now no need for a previous agreement

It was not until *Shipley Urban District Council* v *Bradford Corporation* [1936] Ch 375, a first-instance judgment, that the universal requirement for an antecedent-concluded agreement, written or oral, was questioned. It had long been established that the pre-existing contract could be a complete concluded oral contract.

For example, in *Coular* v *Truefitt Ltd* [1899] 2 Ch 309, a lease granted pursuant to an oral agreement was rectified so as to accord with that agreement. However, in *Shipley*, the parties were respectively a council and a corporation, neither of which could bind themselves legally otherwise than in a document under seal. It was therefore impossible to produce evidence of any binding agreement apart from the final document, which had been executed under seal. The court rejected (*obiter*) the requirement for proof of a previously existing legally binding agreement. The reality was that such proof was not usually available, because normally, even when the intentions of the parties coincided, nothing would be reduced to writing until the moment of executing the final written contract.

In *Crane* v *Hegeman-Harris Co Inc* [1939] 1 All ER 662, the court held that an actual prior agreement was not a requirement for rectification. Rectification could be granted upon proof, beyond all reasonable doubt, that the concluded instrument did not represent the common intention of the parties. Significantly, the court also made it clear that it was not sufficient to show that the written instrument did not represent the common intention of the parties, unless their perceived common intention could be positively demonstrated. On appeal, the Court of Appeal ([1939] 4 All ER 68) upheld the judgment at first instance, rejecting the requirement for any complete antecedent contract.

The 'outward expression of accord'

In *Joscelyne*, the Court of Appeal confirmed that an antecedent-concluded contract was not invariably required. Proof of a prior common intention represented an alternative route to rectification, albeit with the qualification that 'some outward expression of accord' would need to be forthcoming. The standard of proof that is now required is 'convincing proof', rather than proof 'beyond all reasonable doubt'.

This concept of 'some outward expression of accord' has been criticised; see Spry, *Equitable Remedies* (5th ed) 1997 p611. According to Spry:

It does not appear to be possible to find any basis in equitable principle for a requirement of this kind. The history and nature of the remedy of rectification are such that the validity of this suggested requirement should not be accepted, since the concern of courts of equity has always been with the actual intention of those concerned.

However, it is clear that the requirement for 'some outward expression of accord' (which was confirmed by the Court of Appeal in *Agip SpA* v *Navigazione Alta Italia SpA (The Nai Genova and The Nai Superba)* [1984] 1 Lloyd's Rep 353, *Grand Metropolitan plc* v *William Hill Group Ltd* [1997] 1 BCLC 390 and other cases) cannot be challenged at first instance.

Thus, in *Oceanic Village Ltd* v *Shirayama Shokusan Co Ltd* [2000] EGLR 148, rectification of a lease was refused in the absence of convincing proof of the necessary prior outward accord.

It remains unclear how the requirement of 'some outward expression of accord' is to be applied. Oral evidence of the parties' intentions and their state of mind has long been admissible: see *Murray* v *Parker* (1854) 19 Beav 305 at p308. In 1980, Mustill J held that the court must be sure of the mistake and of the existence of a prior agreement or common intention before granting the remedy. In the case of a common intention, this had to be objectively manifested. It was the words and acts of the parties demonstrating their intention, not the inward thoughts of the parties, that mattered: see *Etablissements Levy (Georges et Paul) v Adderley Navigation Co Panama SA (The Olympic Pride)* [1980] 2 Lloyd's Rep 67, at pp72–73.

In one case, a sub-underlease was rectified on appeal in a matter involving the financing, construction and operation of the Royal Scot Hotel at King's Cross (now known as the Islington Thistle). The Court of Appeal ruled that the party seeking rectification must show a common and continuing intention on the part of the parties, either outwardly expressed or communicated between them, that was not reflected in the concluded instrument that they had executed: see *Cooperative Insurance Society Ltd v Centremoor* [1983] 2 EGLR 52.

The practical approach may be to regard the 'outward expression of accord' more as a part of the requirement for convincing proof. The common intention must be demonstrated objectively by the words and conduct of the parties.

Elements of common mistake

1 All parties executed a document that purported to record a prior transaction.
2 The prior transaction consisted of either a concluded agreement or a common intention (which must have been demonstrated) continuing up to the time of execution of the document.
3 There must be evidence of some antecedent outward expression of accord between the parties.
4 The document, as executed, failed to record the prior transaction.
5 The document, as rectified, would record the prior transaction.

Cases referred to
Agip SpA v Navigazione Alta Italia SpA (The Nai Genova and The Nai Superba) [1984] 1 Lloyd's Rep 353
Cooperative Insurance Society Ltd v Centremoor (1983) 268 EG 1027
Coular v Truefitt Ltd [1899] 2 Ch 309
Crane v Hegeman-Harris Co Inc [1939] 1 All 662
Crane v Hegeman-Harris Co Inc [1939] 4 All ER 68
Etablissements Levy (Georges et Paul) v Adderley Navigation Co Panama SA (The Olympic Pride) [1980] 2 Lloyd's Rep 67
Grand Metropolitan plc v William Hill Group Ltd [1997] 1 BCLC 390
Joscelyne v Nissen [1970] 2 QB 86

Lovell & Christmas Ltd v *Wall* (1911) 104 LT 84
Mackenzie v *Coulson* (1869) LR 8 Eq 368
Murray v *Parker* (1854) 19 Beav 305
Oceanic Village Ltd v *Shirayama Shokusan Co Ltd* [1999] EGCS 83
Shipley Urban District Council v *Bradford Corporation* [1936] Ch 375
Templiss Properties Ltd v *Hyams* [1999] EGCS 60

Contributed by Martin Moyes

CHAPTER 13

Dealing with redundancies

Published as 'Downsize but don't demoralise', 7 March 1998

When managers must make redundancies, the staff should be consulted and alternatives sought – because swinging the axe can cut both ways

It has recently been reported that personnel managers implementing large-scale redundancies at a bank have been advised not to break the news to more than eight employees a day because of the adverse effect on their own morale. This raises the question of what responsible employers can do when a job, rather than the employee doing that job, is no longer needed.

The emergence of the European Union has meant that the UK has been compared (sometimes unfavourably) with its European neighbours in the way in which it treats its employees.

Changing patterns in the workforce have encouraged British employers to look at their personnel requirements in a different light. There has been an increasing trend towards a more flexible workforce in offices, supermarkets, financial institutions, factories and almost all other places of work.

At the same time, competition in the marketplace has become more keen. Trading barriers have come down within the European Union (and its associated free-trade area) – a trading zone which stretches from Norway's icy mountains to Polynesia's coral strand.

For all these reasons, British employers have looked towards 'downsizing' their workforces. They believe that shedding staff will allow them to take advantage of perceived gains in efficiency and to reduce their long-term costs.

The legalities

The tangled web of statutory provisions and case law makes it risky for employers to dismiss an employee if this might leave them open to claims of unfair dismissal and the lengthy (and often costly) tribunal hearings which go with such claims. (The rule that 'costs follow the event' does not automatically apply in tribunals, and employers usually have to pay their own legal costs even if they have successfully defended a claim for unfair dismissal.) For this reason, employers often think that it is easier to assert that employees are 'redundant', even if they have some other reason (good or bad) for dismissing them.

An employee will usually be entitled to compensation for dismissal on grounds of redundancy, but this will be a modest arithmetically computed sum, dependent upon the employee's age and his length of service. (A tribunal hearing will therefore be unnecessary in most cases.) Compensation for unfair dismissal, on the other hand, will exceed the amount which would have been payable for redundancy, and it will almost always need to be assessed by an industrial tribunal after a long and (usually) bitterly-contested dispute between the employer and his former employee.

The Redundancy Payments Act 1965 was the first attempt by parliament to address the problem of redundancy and to give employees 'property in their jobs' – a movement from contract to status. The law of 'unfair dismissal' was not invented by parliament until the Industrial Relations Act 1971 although, of course, in a minority of cases an employee might sue for breach of contract in the ordinary courts, eg if he was sacked without proper notice or before his fixed-term contract expired.

The Redundancy Payments Act 1965 was primarily intended to overrule the decision of the High Court in *Parke* v *Daily News* [1962] Ch 927. In that case it had been held that the directors of a company had no power to be generous to employees at the expense of the shareholders when selling the assets of the company and putting the employees out of work. The 1965 Act created a legal duty to pay compensation to redundant employees at the expense (if need be) of the company's shareholders and its unsecured creditors. The presumption that 'a man intends to be just before he affects to be generous' had therefore taken on a new meaning, namely that a redundancy payment was an act of justice, not an expression of generosity.

The 1965 Act was followed, not only by the Industrial Relations Act 1971, but also by the Employment Protection Act 1975 and the Employment Protection (Consolidation) Act 1978. These statutes included provisions about the proper procedures to be followed in a 'redundancy situation', including the vexed question of fair and unfair selection for redundancy. (Even if an employer was genuinely obliged to shed jobs, he might end up having to pay compensation for unfair dismissal if he unfairly selected an employee for dismissal on grounds of redundancy.)

European directives

The earlier statutes were later consolidated into Part IV of the Trade Union and Labour Relations (Consolidation) Act 1992. This Act gave rights of representation and consultation to trade unions, prior to a redundancy taking place, but the European Commission took the view that it did not go far enough. The commission commenced infraction proceedings against the UK because it felt that the British legislation did not properly implement the Collective Redundancies Directive and the Acquired Rights Directive (which was designed to safeguard the rights of employees in the event of a business transfer).

The commission argued that it was too easy for employers in the UK to make their employees redundant because the Transfer of Undertakings (Protection of Employment) Regulations 1981 (usually known as 'TUPE', and pronounced 'tuu-pee') required employers to consult with their employees through the 'recognised' trade unions (if any).

It was established law in England and Wales and also in Scotland (but not in Northern Ireland), that an employer had a right to refuse to recognise a trade union, however popular, responsible and eminent that particular trade union happened to be: *Cleveland County Council* v *Springett* [1985] IRLR 131.

The European Commission argued that the directives imposed a wider obligation on employers to consult with the 'representatives' of their employees, not just with officials of a 'recognised' trade union. The case was finally decided in June 1994 and the European Court of Justice found in favour of the European Commission.

As a result of the decision of the European Court of Justice, the UK introduced new regulations in 1995 – the Collective Redundancy and Transfer of Undertakings (Protection of Employment) (Amendment) Regulation. These new regulations seek to bring the UK into line with the rest of the European Community (see below).

The 1995 regulations do not require an employer to consult with individual employees about an impending redundancy. Nevertheless, case law and good working practice sometimes requires such a consultation to take place. However, for some redundancies (involving less that 20 employees) it would appear that employers in the UK may dismiss their staff without entering into the prolonged consultation process, provided that no actual unfairness in the selection process is perpetrated.

Last in, first out

Figures for redundancy in the UK fluctuate, showing that it is easier to dismiss employees for this reason when finances are needed in the short term and to hire new employees when this is no longer the case. In the period between the winter of 1994–1995 and the winter of 1996–1997 there was an increase of 106,000 in the number of redundancies in the UK. This took the total for the period December 1996 to February 1997 to 225,000. In addition, 58% of people making new claims for unemployment benefit between October 1995 and January 1996 had claimed the same benefit less than 12 months previously.

This shows two things: first, a lot of hiring and firing goes on in the UK; and, second, UK managers seem to be using methods of selection for redundancy which can be likened to 'LIFO' (last in, first out). This is usually accepted as a fair method of selection and it also has the advantage of minimising redundancy payments (and often avoiding such payments altogether).

From the point of view of an individual employee, who may prefer the security of status to the perils of contractual freedom, the law of the UK still compares unfavourably with some other European countries. In Germany an employer must agree with a 'team works council' before deciding to declare an employee's job redundant. If he failed to do this there would be an investigation by the Labour Court. Spanish law also requires agreement with regional labour authorities in an alleged redundancy situation. Possible alternatives have to be investigated and the fairness of the selection procedure has to be established.

From the management's point of view, the main problem that arises from large-scale staff cuts is that the workforce is demoralised. This loss of motivation will not be confined to those whose jobs have been declared to be redundant. The most valuable and employable workers go elsewhere. The remainder fear (like the conspirators in Julius Caesar) that 'high-sighted tyranny' will rage on until each man drops by lottery.

The insecurity which goes with an environment of downsizing, or with a fast turnover of labour, leads to stress. This, in turn, can lead to a severe dislocation of normal behaviour.

Can redundancy be prevented?

The first alternative is 'natural wastage', whereby the organisation loses staff naturally over a long period while stopping all or most recruitment in the meantime. The danger here is that the best and most up-to-date people leave (because they are employable elsewhere), and the less able and less up-to-date people stay.

Another method is to to terminate temporary contracts, reduce overtime and offer early retirement. This, however, will result in a certain level of insecurity and the loss of those employees who will find it easy to work elsewhere.

Retraining and redevelopment of employees is an attractive option, especially if (as it often will be) it is more cost-effective than paying the alternative expenses – compensation to dismissed employees, legal expenses (if there is a tribunal case), recruitment expenses and induction costs.

Good management of necessary redundancies is essential if the motivation and productivity of employees is to be sustained during and after redundancies. The management of redundancies has four stages:

- consulting staff, representatives and trade unions;
- taking avoiding action (mentioned above);
- selecting staff for redundancy;
- providing assistance and compensation.

When selecting staff for redundancy, employers use different methods. In addition to LIFO, employers also use such indicators as attendance records, disciplinary records, skills, competencies, qualifications, work experience and performance records. Although these are arguably fairer methods than LIFO, they are likely to provoke differences of opinion, resentment and allegations of injustice. Moreover, the matter is now fraught with problems about the rights of sick and disabled employees.

There is, therefore, no getting away from the fact that employers must engage in meaningful consultations about redundancies, and that they should be sympathetic and supporting in their counselling. Nevertheless, employees must recognise that the old saying 'a job for life' cannot any longer be true.

Collective Redundancy under 1995 Regulations

- An employer need only consult about a redundancy situation if he proposes to dismiss 20 or more employees at any one site.
- The consultation process must begin at least 90 days before the proposed dismissals if 100 or more employees are to be dismissed.
- The consultation process must begin at least 30 days before the proposed dismissals if less than 100 employees are to be dismissed.
- An employer must consult representatives of an independent and recognised trade union or the elected representatives of the employees.

Contributed by Olivia Rahman

CHAPTER 14

Small print regulations

Published as 'Read the small print', 24 March 2001

The 1999 'small print' Regulations were brought into force to protect consumers from being trapped by unfair standard terms in contracts

Many of us order goods that turn out to be shoddy, or enter into agreements for services that prove unsatisfactory. We may then find ourselves apparently trapped by a clause that appears in small print in our contract with the shop or supplier. Are our basic consumer rights being denied, and must big business always have the upper hand?

The answer may lie in the 'small print' Regulations. Implemented as a direct result of an EU directive on consumer protection, these regulations were brought into force in 1994 and updated in 1999. Their formal title is the Unfair Terms in Consumer Contracts Regulations 1999. They provide that consumers are not bound by a standard term in a contract if that term is unfair. So what is a standard term, and what would be considered unfair?

Scope of the regulations

It might be easier to discuss these issues by dealing with what is excluded from the ambit of the regulations.

First, core terms are excluded. A core term is one that determines the content of a contract and sets its price. For example, an insurance policy will cover certain risks and exclude others, and will set out the monthly or annual premium. However, it is important to note, even in this context, that a core term must be unambiguous and clearly expressed. Moreover, it must be drawn to the consumer's attention.

Terms that have been negotiated by the parties themselves are also excluded, as these constitute non-standard terms. Standard terms must form part of every contract a firm offers to its customers: for example, a standard form contract to rent a car or to buy and use a mobile phone.

It is important to remember that the regulations apply to consumer contracts. They do not apply, for example, to business-to-business contracts or to those between employers and their employees.

What is an unfair term?

The regulations require that all terms must be written in plain and intelligible language. Clearly, this requirement also applies to the core terms. Thus, the primary purpose of the regulations is to challenge those contractual terms that we may not read because, for example, they are printed on the back of an invoice or contract, appear in very small print, or are written in such a way as to confuse or mislead, rather than enlighten us.

The regulations describe an unfair term as being contrary to the requirement of good faith and causing a significant imbalance in the parties' rights, to the detriment of the consumer. The focus is therefore upon the parties' respective bargaining power.

A schedule to the regulations provides illustrations of standard terms that could be considered unfair. This list is not exhaustive, but examples include the following run-of-the-mill pitfalls:

'a term that allows the supplier – but not the consumer – to cancel the contract;

'a term that unfairly penalises the consumer if he or she cancels the contract;

'a term that allows the supplier to vary the terms after agreement, for example by allowing it to raise the price unilaterally.

It is important to note that consumers do not have to rely exclusively upon the regulations; they supplement all other consumer protection remedies.

Who can take action and what type of action?

The Director General of Fair Trading, along with other regulatory and consumer bodies (ie the Consumers' Association, the Financial Services Authority, trading standards officers, regulators for gas, electricity, water, etc, and the Data Protection Registrar) can act to prevent businesses from putting into their standard contracts terms that are unfair to customers.

Once it has received notification of their intention to take action, the Office of Fair Trading (OFT) co-ordinates all the bodies involved in enforcing the regulations. The Director General of the OFT publishes any information, including undertakings, in its bulletins, as it does with all the cases under its consideration. Once the OFT has received a complaint, it is under an obligation to investigate it. Rather than resorting to court action, which is rare, it usually seeks an undertaking from the business to the effect that the term will no longer be used, or will be reworded so that it is no longer unfair.

However, this may not be the final word. Even if the OFT receives a formal, or informal, undertaking, the courts can still be called upon to make the definitive ruling.

Thus, in cases where undertakings are insufficient – or are being breached – the OFT (or other regulatory body) can seek the intervention of the courts: the county courts as well as the High Court.

In one case, involving a consumer credit contract, a borrower had got into financial difficulties and was ordered by the court to pay off his arrears by instalments. However, a term in the contract allowed the finance house to continue to charge interest at the contractual rate and the borrower found that he still owed a large sum. The company refused to alter the term and was duly taken to court by the Director General. The court found in favour of the borrower, and struck down the clause as unfair.

What is covered?

The OFT publishes bulletins detailing the complaints it has dealt with, which make for illuminating reading. As a result of its intervention, businesses and organisations have been obliged to vary their contracts by giving formal or informal undertakings. Terms that have fallen foul of the regulations range from those relating to package holidays, the supply of cable TV, and the purchase of second-hand cars. Unfair terms in contracts covering services have included those imposed by: a dating agency; the provider of a savings plan; a will-making service; and an internet service provider. Vocational training contracts have also been subsumed under the consumer umbrella. Home improvement contracts and mobile phone contracts, needless to say, are high on the 'hit list'.

Interestingly enough, domestic care, nursery, and educational contracts have also come under scrutiny, particularly where they contain terms insisting upon prepayments, or conditions that will disallow a refund if the contract is cancelled, or fine print clauses that deal with price increases.

Following an investigation last year, the OFT was responsible for the significant changes that were introduced into the IATA contract terms. These changes were aimed at making the purchase and transfer of airline tickets a fairer deal for consumers – both for independent travellers and for those whose flights are incorporated into package holidays. (The principal changes are reported in the OFT's Unfair Contract Terms Case Report Bulletin issued in November 2000.)

Contracts relating to land

After some initial uncertainty, it is now beyond doubt that the regulations apply to contracts relating to interests in land. This point has been clarified by the definitions of 'seller' and 'supplier' in the 1999 Regulations, which conform more closely to the wording of the Directive than the text contained in the 1994 Regulations. In fact, the OFT had already dealt with cases involving land before the changes were made in 1999.

Thus, agreements provided by estate agents for residential tenants have been scutinised and and revised. A surveying firm was also obliged to reword its contract to conform to the regulations, and mortgage agreements allowing banks and building societies to charge retrospective redemption penalties have also been struck down.

Two cases concerning letting agencies

In one case, two clauses were withdrawn and an undertaking was given that the general tenancy conditions, which were deemed unfair, would not be used in future. One of the clauses had contained a financial penalty of £5 per day whenever the tenant was in arrears with his rent. The forfeiture clause in the same agreement was designated by the OFT as (a) onerous and (b) not in plain language.

In the other case, involving a residential letting agency, a clause was partially revised to explain the purpose of the 'holding deposit' and the circumstances in which that deposit would be refunded.

Surveyors

A firm of surveyors was taken to task over its general conditions of engagement. Three clauses were subsequently deleted from its contract. One of these had dealt with the exclusion of liability for consequential loss; it also gave an unclear indication of the client's statutory rights. The second had concerned the potential exclusion of liability for oral statements, and the third had allowed the firm to substitute another supplier for a telephone hotline service, thus binding the consumer to the substitute firm's new terms and conditions. It also had to revise the penalty clause and the clause covering the price to be agreed in advance. The clause whereby the firm purported to exclude liability for failure to perform the contract was rewritten, so that if a property proved unsuitable for the level of inspection required, the firm would stop the inspection and discuss future action with its client.

All in all, it pays to mind the small print!

Contributed by Aviva Golden

Construction and Dispute Resolution

15. Concurrent liability in contract and tort 99
16. The new scheme for adjudication under
    construction law 106
17. Partnering 111
18. Compensation for delay by contractors 117
19. International arbitration 123
20. Insurance against terrorism 128

CHAPTER 15

Concurrent liability in contract and tort

Published as 'Double trouble', 30 May 1998

Be aware, UK law allows for concurrent liability, namely that professionals can be sued for torts of negligence as well as breaches of contract

Concurrent liability means that a person can be sued for committing a tort as well as a breach of contract. Lawyers, valuers, surveyors, architects, engineers and other professional persons therefore find the concept worrying. Concurrent liability means that they are exposed to greater legal liability in the UK (and in the Republic of Ireland) than they would be in many of the other states of the European Union.

An example of concurrent liability is provided by *Clay* v *AJ Crump & Sons Ltd* [1963] 3 All ER 687. In that case, an architect and a demolition contractor consulted with each other and negligently came to the conclusion that a retaining wall on a building site was safe. The architect therefore allowed the wall to remain in position and for a building contractor to build a hut in its lee. The wall subsequently collapsed, killing two of the building contractor's workers and injuring another.

The Court of Appeal held that, for the purposes of the tort of negligence, both the architect and the demolition contractor owed a duty of care to the workers, even though their contractual duties were owed to the employer (the owner of the site), not to the building contractor or to his workers.

The Court of Appeal went on to hold that the building contractor should share some of the blame. He owed a contractual duty to his workers and he also owed them a concurrent duty of care not to be negligent. As the employer of the men, he owed them a duty (both in contract and tort) to provide a safe place of work, a safe system of work and safe fellow workers to work with.

Joint and several liability

Clay v *AJ Crump & Sons Ltd* also provides an example of joint and several liability and a 'right of contribution' between joint tortfeasors. (A 'tortfeasor' is a person who commits a tort – in this case, the tort of negligence.)

The Court of Appeal upheld the decision of the trial judge to apportion liability between the defendants as follows: architect 42%; demolition contractor 38%; and building contractor 20%. This apportionment meant that the plaintiff (the injured workman) had the right to enforce his judgment, in full, against all or any of the defendants – even against the defendant who was least to blame. Nevertheless, the defendants had a 'right of contribution' between themselves.

If all three defendants were solvent or adequately insured against claims, the damages would be paid in the shares stipulated by the trial judge. If, however, one or more of the defendants was not solvent and not adequately insured, the remaining defendant or defendants would have to pay additional money in order to satisfy the judgment of the court.

A right of contribution therefore only benefits a defendant if he is able to show that some other person (worth suing) was also responsible for the loss or damage caused to the plaintiff. It is a different concept from 'contributory negligence', which is an allegation that the plaintiff himself was partly to blame for his own misfortune.

The right of a defendant or judgment-debtor to make a claim for 'contribution' against another person is now governed by the Civil Liability (Contribution) Act 1978. The right of a defendant to reduce his financial liability by proving 'contributory negligence' on the part of the plaintiff was created by the Law Reform (Contributory Negligence) Act 1945.

Criminal prosecutions

In certain circumstances, a person's contractual duty to another person may give rise to a duty under the criminal law, whether or not it gives rise to a duty in the law of tort.

This is particularly true in the case of the relationship of employer and employee, because the employer will be answerable to the criminal courts under the Health and Safety at Work Act 1974 if he fails to take reasonable care for the health, safety or welfare of his employees.

In exceptional circumstances, an employer and/or an employee may even be prosecuted for manslaughter. In *R* v *Pittwood* (1902) 19 TLR 37, a level-crossing keeper working for a railway company went home early, leaving the gates unattended. This was a breach of his contract of employment.

Some time afterwards a train collided with a cart on the crossing and a man was killed. It was held that, although the gate keeper's contractual duty was to the railway company, he also owed a duty, at common law, to the users of the level crossing. He was therefore guilty of manslaughter, contrary to common law, when a fatal accident resulted from his gross neglect of this duty.

Self-evidently, the gate keeper would also have been liable to pay damages for the tort of negligence but, because he was an employee (not an independent contractor), any such claims would have been made against the railway company. The right to make such a claim is known as the law of 'vicarious liability' or, as it is sometimes called, 'the search for the solvent defendant'.

Limitation of actions

When a defendant owes a duty of care in the law of tort, as well as a contractual duty to the same person, that person may be able to take advantage of the more generous limitation periods which apply in the law of tort. In other words, he may be able to sue a professional person for negligence, even if the limitation period for a contractual claim against that defendant has expired.

The limitation period for breach of contract is six years from the date of the breach. If the contract was executed as a deed, this period will be 12 years. In the case of a claim against an architect, surveyor, engineer, contractor, etc, a claim for breach of contract will have to be brought within six years (or 12 years) of the date of practical or substantial completion of the project.

If a claim is brought for negligence (eg for damage to furniture, works of art, etc, caused by defective building work) the limitation period will be six years from the date of the damage. This may, of course, be several years after the building work was completed.

If damage is caused but is not immediately noticeable, the Latent Damage Act 1986 gives an alternative to the plaintiff. He may sue within three years of the 'discoverability date' – the date on which the damage in question would have been discovered by a reasonably diligent person.

In order to put some limit on how far into the future this might be (and therefore to give professional people some relief in the making of their insurance arrangements) the 1986 Act creates a 'long-stop' period of 15 years from the date of the negligent workmanship.

Again, this 15-year period is likely to commence with the practical or substantial completion of the work because, prior to that time, the defendant will have had the opportunity to put right what was previously done wrong.

The 15-year long-stop means that the victim of newly-discovered defects may find that he or she has less than three years in which to sue the culprit, because the last day of the 15-year deadline might be only a few months or weeks away. Indeed, that period could have elapsed already, leaving him or her with no remedy for negligence at all and (of course) no remedy for breach of contract either.

In such a case, he or she can only proceed with a claim if there is strong evidence of fraud on the part of the defendant. There is no 15-year 'long-stop' for actions for fraud. (The claim would then be for the tort of deceit and the six-year limitations period would start to run from the date on which the fraud became discoverable.)

'Pure economic loss'

The decision of the House of Lords in *Murphy* v *Brentwood District Council* [1991] 1 AC 378 had the effect of rendering the Latent Damage Act 1986 useless for most purposes. Indeed, it can be argued that the *Murphy* case was wrongly decided because of its failure to give effect to the obvious intentions of parliament as expressed in the 1986 Act.

The House of Lords held in *Murphy* v *Brentwood District Council* that latent defects in buildings (for example, defective foundations) were a form of 'pure economic loss'.

Essentially, the purchaser or lessee of the property was complaining that he had paid too much money for the building because he did not know the true situation. His complaint was not to be equated with that of a landowner who complained about physical damage to his property (eg damage caused by the collapse of a neighbouring building or the impact of a negligently driven vehicle).

Having categorised latent defects as 'pure economic loss', the House of Lords went on to promulgate a general rule that the tort of negligence should not be used to enable plaintiffs to recover damages for such a loss. Clearly, the House of Lords could not deny that there were, and would continue to be, certain exceptions to this general rule (claims for negligent misstatement, for example).

Nevertheless, their lordships were not prepared to recognise latent defects in buildings as one of these exceptions – not even if the building in question was the plaintiff's home, the largest consumer purchase in his life, and the place where he eats, sleeps and has his being.

This being the case, it has now become very difficult to think of a situation where the Latent Damage Act 1986 would operate to give a plaintiff three years in which to sue from 'discoverability date' (up to a maximum of 15 years from the date of the construction work).

If a defect in a building causes damage to furniture or to other personal property, the damage in question is likely to be obvious (patent), not latent, and the plaintiff will have six years in which to sue, starting from the date on which that furniture, etc, was damaged. (If he suffers personal injuries, he will have three years from the date of the accident or, in the case of a latent disease, three years from the date when he ought reasonably to have discovered the injuries.)

If the plaintiff is seeking to claim recompense for the cost of repairing his own defective building, or for the diminution in its market value, this will be categorised as a claim for 'pure economic loss' and an action for negligence will be struck out.

Leaving aside questions of fraud, this will leave the plaintiff with only two possibilities. He may, perhaps, have a claim for breach of contract, if that shorter time-limit has not yet expired.

He may also have a claim against the builder or developer or architect, etc, under the Defective Premises Act 1972 – but only if the building in question is a 'dwelling' and, even then, only if the work in question was done within the previous six years.

Is there a choice of remedies?

In those cases where an action for tort can be pursued, the damages will be calculated in a different way from the measure of damages in the law of contract. Damages for breach of contract will usually be greater than damages for the tort of negligence.

This is because the law of contract allows plaintiffs to sue for 'loss of bargain', whereas the law of negligence merely allows plaintiffs to claim a sum of money which reinstates the position as it used to be before the tort was committed, in so far as money can ever do that.

Nevertheless, in certain circumstances, the damages awarded for the tort of negligence may exceed the damages which would have been awarded for breach of contract as, for example, where the market is falling rather than rising.

It used to be thought that a professional person, such as a surveyor or architect, could only be sued (by his client) for breach of contract, not for the tort of negligence: see *Bagot* v *Stevens Scanlon* [1966] 1 QB 197. Indeed (because of the *Murphy* case), this may still be the case if the claim for negligence is a claim for 'pure economic loss' – unless this loss was caused by negligent misstatement.

In *Conway* v *Crow Kelsey & Partners* (1994) 39 Con LR 1, a house had been damaged because of the removal of a tree. The owners engaged a firm of engineers to prepare a report and to supervise the necessary remedial works. The recommended works were not successful and so the owners sued the firm of engineers for the tort of negligence: the limitation period for a contractual claim had already expired.

The engineers claimed that they could not be sued in the law of tort because their relationship with the owners of the house had been a contractual one. The High Court had no hesitation in finding the engineers were liable in tort.

There was no rule against the concurrent liability, and if (as here) the limitation period for a tort action was still unexpired, the clients were entitled to take advantage of that cause of action. (It is interesting to note that the court treated this claim as a claim for negligent misstatement rather than as a claim for negligent workmanship, thus allowing a 'pure economic loss' claim to slip through the defences erected by the *Murphy* case.)

In *Henderson* v *Merrett Syndicates Ltd* [1995] 2 AC 145, the House of Lords had to deal with one of the actions brought by disappointed Lloyd's underwriters against their financial advisers. Lord Goff said, at pp532–533:

> The common law is not antipathetic to concurrent liability, and ... there is no sound basis for a rule which automatically restricts the claimant to either a tortious or a contractual remedy. The result may be untidy: but, given that the tortious duty is imposed by the general law, and the contractual duty is attributable to the will of the parties, I do not find it objectionable that the claimant may be entitled to take advantage of the remedy which is most advantageous to him, subject only to ascertaining whether the tortious duty is so inconsistent with the applicable contract that, in accordance with ordinary principle, the parties must be taken to have agreed that the tortious remedy is to be limited or excluded.

Lord Goff has offered a way out to surveyors, engineers and other professional advisers – namely to exclude (in the contract) any right of the client to sue for the tort of negligence. But this, in turn, may lead to an argument about whether such a clause would contravene the Unfair Contract Terms Act 1977. That, of course, is another story.

Contributed by Silviu Klein

CHAPTER 16

The new scheme for adjudication under construction law

Published as 'New scheme of things', 27 June 1998

On May 30 1998 key aspects of the new construction contract legislation were reviewed; here we take a closer look at its innovatory scheme for the adjudication of disputes

The Housing Grants, Construction, and Regeneration Act 1996 came into force on May 1 1998. Part II applies to construction contracts entered into or after that date. It requires them to incorporate certain provisions on adjudication and payment. If this is not done, a statutory 'scheme for construction contracts' will provide a fall-back mechanism.

This legislation may be regarded as an innovation in legislative drafting. It is relatively easy for parliament to declare contractual provisions to be void or unenforcable. For example, the Unfair Contract Terms Act 1977 invalidates any contractual term or non-contractual notice which purports to exclude liability for death or personal injuries caused by negligence.

By contrast, it is much more difficult for parliament to require certain matters to be included in contracts. What could the sanction be for failing to do so?

The Scheme

The Scheme for Construction Contracts overcomes this problem by automatically becoming part of any contract which falls foul of Part II of the 1996 Act.

Parliament is acting like a rather benevolent ruffian on the stair. If the scheme was not mentioned in the room where the bargain was made, the parties will be taken to one side, before they can leave the building and be persuaded of the wisdom of the 1996 Act.

There is a significant difference between the scheme's provisions on adjudication and those on payment. If the contract does not provide for adjudication (or if its procedures are not in accordance with the Act) the scheme's provisions on adjudication will take effect. By contrast, the scheme's provisions as to payment adopt a 'menu approach'.

These provisions do not transfer wholesale into a non-compliance contract unless, in contravention of the Act, there is a 'pay-when-paid' clause (and the parties have not been able to agree alternative payment arrangements) or the entire payment provisions contravene the Act*.

Adjudication

The scheme requires the party who is intending to refer a dispute to adjudication to give written notice of this intention. This notice must briefly set out:

- the nature of the dispute;
- a brief description of the dispute;
- the parties involved;
- when and where the dispute arose;
- the nature of the redress sought;
- names and addresses of the parties to the contract.

The scheme recognises the possibility that the parties could have named an adjudicator in their terms of appointment. That person should be formally requested to act as adjudicator in the dispute and the request should be accompanied by a copy of the above notice.

If there is not a named person (or the named person is unwilling or unable to act) but the terms of appointment have named a nominating body, that body should be requested to select the adjudicator. If the contract is silent, so that there is no named adjudicator or named nominating body, the party referring the dispute can request an adjudicator nominating body (ANB) to select the adjudicator. An ANB is defined as a body which 'holds itself out publicly as a body which will select an adjudicator when requested to do so by a referring party'.

Adjudicators must be individuals acting in their own personal capacity. Needless to say, they should not be employed by any of

---

* For a discussion of the provisions relating to payment see *The Best of Mainly for Students*, Volume 2, Chapter 7.

the parties and should declare any interest they might have in any matter relating to the dispute.

Adjudicator's decision

The scheme follows the Act in requiring the adjudicator to reach his decision within 28 days. If the referring party agrees, the adjudicator can have an extra 14 days or a longer period as may be agreed by both parties. He is not required to give reasons for his decision unless requested to do so by one of the parties to the dispute.

The adjudicator is required to deliver a copy of his decision to the parties as soon as possible after he has reached it. Unless he states differently, compliance with his decision must be immediate on delivery of the decision.

Adjudicators are entitled to be paid a reasonable amount by way of fees and expenses. The parties are responsible for payment both jointly and severally. This means that the adjudicator can pursue one or both of the parties for his fees. However, he can apportion payment of his fees between the parties. The adjudicator should have a contract with both parties so that he has a contractual basis for the recovery of these fees.

Enforcement

Enforcement is the key to the success of adjudication. The lack of effective means of enforcement will undermine the process. In conformity with the Act, the scheme makes it clear that the adjudicator's decision shall continue to be binding until the dispute is finally determined by agreement between the parties, arbitration or legal proceedings.

What happens if one party fails to abide by the adjudicator's decision? First, the enforcement process is dependent upon the adjudicator, in his decision, ordering a party to comply 'peremptorily' with his decision.

This will then 'trigger' the power of the court to require a party to comply with the adjudicator's decision. The scheme does this by adopting section 42 of the Arbitration Act 1996 with some amendments. This gives the court the power to order compliance with the adjudicator's decision, failing which it can use the sanctions available to it for breach of a court order. These include fines and, possibly, imprisonment for contempt of court.

However, there are flaws in this process. The court has discretion about whether to make such an order. Also, section 42 commences with the words 'Unless otherwise agreed by the parties, the court may make an order...' There is scope here for stronger parties to impose upon the weaker parties a requirement that the court shall not have the power to make orders in this context.

The scheme's adjudication provisions are likely to create benchmarks for the entire construction industry. In fact, it is highly probable that many in the industry will simply adopt the scheme's provisions rather than drafting their own. Contracting parties will find that their decisions will become increasingly subject to the scrutiny of adjudicators.

The powers of adjudication

The adjudicator has substantial powers to investigate the dispute and come to a decision. He has been given inquisitorial powers, and overriding authority to take the initiative, ascertain the facts and law and decide on the procedure. Some of the powers are listed.

Of particular significance is the right to 'make such site visits and inspections as he considers appropriate, whether accompanied by the parties or not'. A contractor diligently working at his desk should not be surprised to discover an adjudicator looking over his shoulder.

The adjudicator can seek help from technical experts or lawyers, provided that he has the consent of the parties and avoids incurring unnecessary expense. Moreover, the 'parties shall comply with any request or direction of the adjudicator in relation to the adjudication'. Failure to comply will not, however, obstruct the course of the adjudication.

There is scope for disputes under different contracts to be joined and decided by one adjudicator. Provided that the parties to the various disputes agree, the adjudicator can decide to adjudicate on disputes under different contracts, provided that they are related.

One of the more contentious provisions in the scheme is that it permits one or both parties to be represented by lawyers. While lawyers may be helpful in advising on procedure and in drawing up the necessary documentation, it is questionable whether their involvement before the adjudicator will necessarily be beneficial.

Contractors will, no doubt, claim that the adjudication will be undermined and could even go the way of arbitration. However, the involvement of lawyers is unlikely to be that great since legal costs will not be recoverable from the ultimate loser.

How parties can refer to an adjudicator

The referring party has seven days from the date on which he notified his intention to the other party to go to adjudication to refer the dispute to the adjudicator. Such referral should be accompanied by relevant extracts from the contract and any other document which the referring party intends to rely upon (eg correspondence).

All the documents sent to the adjudicator should be copied to the other party.

There is no requirement for the other party to submit any formal response to the paperwork sent by the referring party to the adjudicator. It would, of course, be in the adjudicator's interest to require the non-referring party to respond.

Under both the Act and the scheme, the adjudicator is required to act impartially. He cannot listen to one side without hearing the other. Once the referring party has initiated the adjudication, the adjudicator takes over the proceedings.

Contributed by Silviu Klein

CHAPTER 17

Partnering

Published as 'Building partnerships', 6 October 2001

It is recognised that a new collaborative approach to construction procurement is required, but will partnering come up trumps?

Of all government construction projects, 70% are delivered late and 73% are over budget. These sad statistics are contained in the National Audit Office report *Modernising Construction*, which was published on 11 January, and relates to the general performance of government construction projects. Add to this, poor-quality buildings, unhappy clients, and costly disputes, and you have an idea of the problems facing a UK construction industry that, in 1999–2000, had an estimated annual turnover of £65bn.

The report suggests that construction costs could be slashed by up to 30% if the industry, together with its clients, adopted a more collaborative approach to construction procurement. It explains why the government is so keen to encourage partnering, whereby clients and contractors establish long-term collaborative relationships for their mutual benefit. Partnering requires the client and the contractor to work together to improve building design changes, identify (and drive out) inefficiency in the construction process, replicate good practise learned from earlier projects and reduce the risk of disputes. It should not be confused with the government's programme for public/private partnerships, which has received much recent criticism.

Traditional procurement

Partnering contrasts strongly with traditional construction procurement, which is, by its nature, adversarial, ie one party's gain is someone else's loss (or reduced profit). Under traditional procurement, someone wishing to commission the erection of a building will invite construction firms to tender for the work to be carried out, according to a detailed design provided by the client.

This design work may itself have been the subject of a previous tendering exercise among firms of architects. Of course, there are variations. A single construction company might be invited to design and build, or, in the case of the government's Private Finance Initiative (PFI), be responsible for designing, building, financing, and operating the project throughout the lifetime of a contract extending for 25 years or more. But however the project is tendered, and all other things being equal, the lowest bid will usually win the work.

The problem with this approach is that it forces contractors, if they are to succeed in the bidding process, to work to uncomfortably low profit margins. The only way in which the contractor can then increase the profit margin is by way of subsequent contract cost variations, often arising from a client's wish to change the original design. The lowest-bid approach also takes little account of the whole-life cost of a development project, meaning the projected future cost of maintaining, repairing, and operating a development throughout its expected life.

As stated above, the traditional construction contract can also be regarded as adversarial, requiring slavish adherence to a fixed design and a strict completion timetable, and incurring fierce penalty clauses against any contractor who fails to deliver a satisfactory product on time. Within such contracts, contractors have little incentive to seek improvements beyond the original design or to identify mutual cost savings. There is, moreover, too much scope for disputes and litigation if defects become apparent or if costs overrun.

Legislation
It was the perceived unfairness of the traditional construction contract towards contractors that prompted the last Conservative government to enact Part II of the Housing Grants, Construction and Regeneration Act 1996. This provides for the swift adjudication of disputes that arise during the course of construction; a right to stage payments; and restrictions on the right of a commercial client to withhold payments from a contractor without good reason, and only then if the relevant legislative procedure have been followed. For more information on this legislation, see Silviu Klein's Mainly for Students articles published in volume 2 of *The Best of Mainly for Students*, Chapter 7 and Chapter 16 in this book.

Partnering v traditional procurement

To illustrate the difference between partnering and traditional procurement, imagine that a plumber is needed to repair a central-heating system. A house owner might seek quotes from several plumbing firms, but these are likely to be high and relate not so much to the work to be carried out as what the market will bear. If the house owner were to adopt a different approach, however, he could procure a better deal.

Instead of seeking competitive quotes, the house owner could sit down with a plumber whom he trusted. He could ask him about his daily rates and how much he expected to earn from this project. He could ask him where he would obtain his materials and how much he would pay for them. Did he know of any more cost-effective ways of dealing with the problem or achieving cost savings? Only then would the householder be in a position to agree terms that remunerate the plumber fairly for his work and give the householder value for money. This is the essence of partnering.

Its core characteristic is the formation, at the outset, of a team to see the project through to completion, and possibly for many years beyond. The project team will comprise representatives from all those involved in the project, including: client; end-user; architect; quantity surveyor; main contractor; subcontractors, and component suppliers. The basis of the relationship between each of these partners is mutual trust and a willingness to work together to achieve a win-win situation for all parties. They will seek a reasonable profit margin for everyone within the team who is providing a product or service and the best outcome for the client or end-user. A partnership charter will incorporate mutual objectives, and problems will be identified and resolved collaboratively by the team, rather than being made the responsibility of one party.

Government initiatives

The concept grew out of Sir Michael Lithium's 1994 report *Constructing the Team*. This said that the client should be at the core of the construction process and that client satisfaction was to be achieved through teamwork and co-operation. This was followed by Sir John Egan's 1998 report, *Rethinking Construction*, which said that effective projects require a clear process, of which partnering was a vital part. It added that while creative design was important, the overall process involved stripping out waste and inefficiency. This was necessary to meet client aspirations for a harmonious building or civil engineering project that worked.

Central government departments, which jointly account for £7.5bn worth of construction business each year, are also promoting partnering. Government initiatives include the movement for innovation, a housing forum, which aims to promote innovation through demonstration projects (of which there were 171 by 31 July) and the 'achieving excellence' programme to improve the performance of government departments as purchasers of construction services. The Office of Government Commerce (OGC) has also issued useful guidance.

Personalities

The ultimate success of a partnering arrangement will be dependent upon the personalities of each member of the project team and their ability to work together. Extreme care must be therefore be taken when selecting a team: anyone who may be unsuited to team work or who is not prepared to listen and to learn from others should be excluded. Each team member will then sign up to the partnering charter, which will: identify the common goals for success; set out procedures for reaching decisions and solving problems; identify measurable performance targets, and set gain share and pain share incentives. This charter will be more like a statement of intent than a legally binding document and will not replace formal construction contracts.

Prime contracting

But if partnering is essentially about changing attitudes, prime contracting will increasingly achieve the delivery of projects. This is important because the Treasury and the OGC have issued a joint directive that, as from 1 June 2000, all central government clients should have limited their procurement strategies to PFI, and, as from 1 June 2002, these procurement strategies should be applied to all refurbishment and maintenance contracts. Traditional non-integrated strategies will rarely be used, and only then if it can be demonstrated that they offer the best value for money.

A prime contractor can be defined as a single organisation having overall responsibility for the management and delivery of a project, including co-ordinating and integrating the activities of a number of subcontractors to meet the overall specification, effectively, economically, and on time. This differs from simple design-and-build, in that, when tendering for the project, the prime contractor must identify membership of the supply chain (i.e. provide details of all subcontractors and other suppliers of goods and services whom the prime contractor will use in association with the project) and provide an assurance that this chain, and best practise, will remain in place throughout the life of the contract.

For more information
The internet provides one of the best sources of free information about partnering and prime contracting. This is particularly so of government department websites. Among the most detailed, is the Defence Estate web site, which includes full-length specimen prime contracts for both stand-alone projects and for regional prime contracts where a prime contractor is required to design, construct and maintain sites in a region. However, both partnering and prime contracting are still largely in their experimental stages and it remains to be seen whether they will solve the problems of the construction industry.

Traditional procurement and partnering – Comparisons between the two concepts

Traditional	Partnering
Adversarial relationships	Collaborative work
Arms-length relationship	Trust
Rigid design specifications	Flexibility – encouraging innovations
Arbitrator or litigation	Disputes procedure
Lowest tender	Whole-life cost
Apportion for blame for problems	Team approach to problem solving
Commercial secrecy	Open-book accounting

The main characteristics of prime contracting – What the concept will mean in practice

- Collaborative working (ie partnering).
- Open-book accounting: the contractor must operate an accounting regime that provides the client with sufficient financial information to: monitor, among other things, the actual costs incurred against target costs; substantiate claims for payments; agree changes to the target

costs to reflect any additions/deletions from the scope of the contract; access final costing; and consider the impact of innovative proposals.
- An output specification setting out what the client wants to achieve, but without the detail of traditional construction procurement. It will then be for the prime contractor to find the most efficient and cost-effective way to meet client requirements.
- Innovative solutions: where prime contractors are encouraged to think of innovative ways of delivering client requirements, which demonstrate value for money and continuous improvement.
- Value engineering through life costs: this will embrace industry best practise so as to demonstrate what really provides value for money over the lifetime of the project.
- A dispute review board: this will normally comprise three persons, one of which will be appointed by the prime contractor, one by the client, and the third to be a joint appointment.

Contributed by VC Ward

CHAPTER 18

Compensation for delay by contractors

Published as 'Constructive foresight', 19 August 2000

The inherent risks involved in construction mean that compensation schemes are an essential part of the contract, but how are they assessed?

A remarkable but usual feature of construction contracts is their express provision for the parties to compensate each other, if the circumstances arise, thereby avoiding the need to use the dispute resolution process. Such provision is subsumed under a number of terms. For property developers, the most familiar will be loss and expense, and liquidated damages.

A further noteworthy feature is that the basis of compensation is different for each party: ie the builder (often referred to as the contractor), on the one hand, and the developer (often called the employer) on the other hand. At first sight, this may be a matter for surprise, but there is good reason for it. The compensation arrangements in these contracts are carefully worked out, and take into account the interests of both parties.

In context, the developer enters into a contract with the builder to obtain a finished building on or before a particular date. He has undertaken to provide the builder with all the information necessary to complete the building on time. The provisions for compensation, agreed between the parties, are a response to the difficulty of keeping to contractual time-limits.

In any business contract parties will invariably consider compensation as soon as something goes wrong. However, in the construction sphere this amounts to something completely different. Here, when entering into the contract, the parties are agreeing compensation for a potential, not an actual, catastrophe.

Basis of compensation
The parties agree that compensation:
(i) is to be paid by the guilty party;

(ii) is to cover or mitigate the loss to be caused, or reckoned in advance to be caused.

The reason for agreeing to pay compensation is mainly due to the risky nature of construction projects. The parties make promises that they may not always be able to fulfil.

Consider the following scenario. A developer has promised to provide 'design information' as and when the builder requires it to enable him to finish the proposed building on time. Late one afternoon, soon after work on the site has started, a large hole in the ground is discovered in the course of constructing the foundations. The foundations therefore need to be redesigned, which is expected to take at least three days. The builder's work is brought to a halt. If he is unable to divert his resources while waiting, he will suffer unavoidable loss. The builder is then entitled to look to the developer for compensation.

The builder may also find himself in default. For instance, he may be unable to complete the building on time. The developer will then be the one to suffer loss. Perhaps the builder has been let down by his supplier. If materials are not delivered on time, the builder (if he is unable to make up the lost time) will suffer a delay in completing the building.

Under these circumstances, the developer will be required to hire alternative accommodation while waiting for the building to be completed. He will be entitled to look to the builder for compensation.

In either case, the parties will consider their respective positions with regard to compensation.

The basis of compensation agreed by the parties, and which is different for each party, follows a well-established pattern.

Compensation payable to the builder

The compensation payable to the builder under the contract, known as loss and expense, is very close to what may be obtained in an action for damages in the courts.

In order to obtain compensation, the builder must satisfy three criteria: cause, effect and amount of loss, which, again, is the same as in an action for damages.

Cause In construction contracts, this would be a particular event that is stated expressly in the contract, such as late information on the part of the developer.

Effect This would include delay or disruption to the use of the developer's resource.

Loss This must be shown to have followed from the previous two events.

The recoverable amount is assessed in the same way as damages for breach of contract at common law. These were explained in the case of *Hadley* v *Baxendale* (1854) 9 Ex 341:

Where two parties have made a contract which one of them has broken, the damages which the other party ought to receive in respect of such breach of contract should be such as may fairly and reasonably be considered either (1) arising naturally, ie according to the usual course of things from such breach of contract itself, or (2) such as may reasonably have been supposed to have been in the contemplation of both parties at the time they made the contract, as the probable result of the breach of it.

Compensation payable to the developer

The pre-assessed amount of compensation payable to the developer is called liquidated damages. The amount of the loss does not have to be proved; it is an amount agreed in the contract between the parties. Why is this basis preferred? Let us take a look at the builder's position.

The late completion of the building is an expensive risk faced by the builder. One way or another, he would be liable to the developer if this were to happen. The liability would, of course, be in addition to the loss suffered by himself.

Any loss due to late completion may, of course, severely affect all parties, and, although the developer may suffer disproportionately, if his loss were to be met in full by the builder, the latter could actually lose money on the project.

Prudence does not permit the builder to agree to terms such as these. He cannot afford to carry the developer's loss in full.

For example, if (because of delayed completion) the developer is forced to find a replacement office building, the cost within one year could be twice as much as the contract sum in the original building contract. The builder's profit might only be 5% of this contract sum, and, of course, he will also remain responsible for costs relating to his own workforce.

The developer will suffer loss of production because his own employees will have been denied occupancy of the proposed new building, or (if the building were intended for letting) he will suffer the loss of potential rental income.

To summarise, therefore, the losses caused by the builder's

default will far exceed any profit he could have made by finishing the work on time: see table on pp121–122.

So, what can be done? The developer, naturally, would like to receive compensation for his entire loss. The builder, however, must have a figure he can manage, and one that is agreed and contractually binding from the outset.

The developer must accept the builder's position. If the developer wishes to see his building, the builder must have an acceptable basis upon which to contract, in the same way that shipping companies and airlines limit their own liability when undertaking the risks of carrying passengers.

The liquidated damages agreed between the parties may say more about the builder's profit forecast than about the loss likely to be caused to the developer if he has to wait for his building.

For the developer, there is some consolation in having the amount of compensation agreed. It will not have to prove its loss – unlike the builder in the converse position. The developer's path to entitlement is easier; it is limited to the amount agreed.

Extension of time

Extension of time is an everyday feature in the world of construction management. So far as the contract conditions provide, time must be extended in certain pre-agreed circumstances. This would, of course, ease the date for the completion of the building. The device sustains liquidated damages as a workable arrangement within the contract, and, by this means, the developer will free himself, wiping his hands clean of any cause of delay. It will also help the developer to satisfy the courts when making any claim in liquidated damages.

Conclusion

The agreed scheme of compensation in construction contracts is an essential arrangement for avoiding disputes in an area where risks abound and the inherent uncertainties encourage dispute.

A balance is achieved, and the manner of paying and receiving compensation, which, in these circumstances, need not be delayed for either party, helps to accommodate their different circumstances and needs. The builder, on the one hand, is protected from paying compensation out of all proportion to his contemplated profit. The developer, on the other hand, although receiving a restricted amount of compensation, is nevertheless advantaged in being relieved of lengthy legal procedures.

Liquidated damages – Role of the Courts

The courts adopt a somewhat cautious approach when interpreting agreements for liquidated damages. In effect, the agreement bypasses the courts' usual function of deciding compensation for breach of contract, but they will not recognise the agreement unless it meets certain preconditions.

The agreed figure must not be a penalty (ie a financial punishment on the builder, not compensation to the developer). It must represent a bona fide estimate of expected loss. This is to be judged in the light of the facts as they were at the time the contract was entered into.

The amount agreed by way of liquidated damages should not be more than the loss that was reasonably foreseeable at the date of the contract.

What about the builder, negotiating a reduction in the compensation to be paid to the developer? The courts' concern is with excess; there is no objection to negotiating down.

The courts also enforce a further precondition before they will support a claim for liquidated damages. The claimant party must not be guilty of the very thing of which it complains. For example, a developer claiming in liquidated damages against the builder for a delay in the completion of a building must not have caused some of the delay itself. A maxim comes to mind (even though we are dealing with common law concepts):

'He who comes to equity must come with clean hands.'

However, a party can seldom, if ever, be entirely untainted in this matter. Perhaps, therefore, this further precondition could render unworkable the agreement for liquidated damages?

How may the agreement then be sustained? A device recognised by the courts could provide the answer: express contractual provision for extension of time.

Comparison of employer's loss due to delay and builder's profit

(Illustrative figures only)

Office: building cost per m^2 of floor area	£2,000
Total building cost (for 1,000m^2)	£2,000,000
Builder's profit for constructing the building, say 5% of building cost	£100,000
Cost of employing office worker (pa)	£40,000
Each office worker occupies 10m^2 of floor area (includes a proportion of circulation space)	
Building accommodates 100 office workers (100 × 10 = 1,000); at an annual cost of	£4,000,000

Added value to employer: say 0.25 of cost (£4,000,000 × 25%)	£1,000,000
Total value to employer (pa)	£5,000,000
Total value to employer (per week)	£100,000
Loss of productivity of office workers occasioned by late delivery of the building	say 20%
Loss in value to employer occasioned by late delivery of the building (per week)	£20,000
Employer's loss over only a few weeks of delay (5 × £20,000) equates to the whole of the builder's profit for constructing the building	£100,000

Contributed by Alan Morris

CHAPTER 19

International arbitration

Published as 'International relations, 11 August 2001

Arbitration is not a pleasant experience at the best of times, but when it crosses national boundaries it can raise further, specific difficulties

As anyone with experience of it knows, arbitration is best avoided. This is especially so in the case of international arbitration (see p126). International arbitration is likely to present specific difficulties, for example: obtaining evidence that may be located in another country; or enforcing the award, if the assets (out of which the award should be paid) are located in a different country. Even the law that is applied in the arbitration – the applicable law – may cause surprises and bring the process to a halt.

Advantages and disadvantages

Once in motion, the parties must decide where the arbitration is to be held. For one of the parties, at least, a foreign country and a foreign legal system will be involved: a considerable disadvantage. The parties may agree to equalise on the point and insist that the arbitration takes place in a country foreign to them both. Thus, there may be a foreign law, a foreign language, a foreign arbitrator – foreign to both parties. For example, in a dispute between a firm located in Belgrade and another in Helsinki, Austrian law was agreed upon and Vienna was chosen as the venue.

Dependence upon law

The concern uppermost in the parties' minds when choosing the location will be the stance taken by the courts in that country towards arbitration. The help of these courts may have to be sought if, for example, the arbitrator needs to be removed on grounds of bias, or a party requires a decision following objections made by the other side. Thus, the parties must carefully consider both the courts and the law of the country in which the arbitration is to take place. They must also make a careful study of the law of the country in which the assets are located, if this is different, with a view to securing the enforcement of the award.

Three points should be considered when deciding upon the location:

- **'Is the subject matter recognised as "arbitrable" in the country in question?'**

This is a matter of public policy for that country. Different countries, and their legal systems, come up with different answers to this question. Arbitration derogates from the state's power to oversee disputes. There are differences of opinion across nations as to which aspects of life may be taken out of the supervision of the state. Is it right for disputes concerning the rights of third parties in an insolvency, or disputes between employer and employee, to be taken out of the state's supervision? Not all countries are of the same mind with regard to these issues.

- **'Is the country a suitable location for the arbitration?'**

This raises the following questions:

Is the country a convenient venue? Is its arbitration law adequately developed? Is the culture compatible? Are the courts independent of both parties? Will the judgment be recognised in the country where the respondent's assets are located?

These points are for the parties to decide. The existence of a model law, model sets of arbitration rules and some international conventions should be noted. Each of these may serve the purpose of increasing the suitability of a particular country as the location for the arbitration process.

- **'What law or laws will the country apply?'**

The courts of each country will decide which law to apply when considering any matter arising from international arbitrations. Almost all countries are willing to apply the law of another country where it is appropriate to do so. But this raises the question of which law will apply, and, here, countries will apply their own norms. For one country, the law of the country in which the contract was made will be the basis referred to, while elsewhere the law of the country in which the contract was carried out will provide the basis.

However, most countries' courts will agree that where the parties have decided upon the law to be applied, it will be treated as decisive, provided the choice is reasonable. The question of which law applies penetrates the whole arbitration process (see p127).

Promulgated model law

In England we are used to a well-developed body of arbitration law. In many countries, however, this is still not the case. The United Nations Commission on International Trade Law has attempted to redress this position. In 1985 it promulgated the UNCITRAL model law on international commercial arbitration.

The purpose of this model law is to provide a body of well-thought-out arbitration law for incorporation into the law of any country that lacks such a provision. It can be incorporated whole as it stands, or it may be departed from, if this should be considered necessary by the country concerned. The model law has been influential in the development of arbitration law throughout the world. It may be noted that the (English) Arbitration Act 1996 incorporates many elements of the UNCITRAL model.

Clearly, in those cases where a country has incorporated the model law in its entirety, one may at least have confidence in that aspect of the country's suitability.

Model arbitration rules

The function of arbitration rules is to provide a structure for the efficient conduct of arbitration, from start to finish, concluding with the making of an enforceable award. Such rules provide a means by which the parties may agree a reliable basis for the conduct of their arbitration.

Thus, just as there is a UNCITRAL model of law, so, also, are there UNCITRAL rules. By adopting these rules, the parties will have a well-tried foundation for their arbitration.

International conventions

A number of international conventions have been entered into, in which one country undertakes to enforce certain agreements and decisions made according to the law of another country in the course of arbitration proceedings. The New York Convention of 1958 (New York Convention on the Recognition and Enforcement of Foreign Arbitral Awards (1958)) is the most universally recognised of these. This touches upon:

' the enforceability of the arbitration agreement; and

' the enforceability of the arbitration award.'

When contracting into such conventions, nation states incorporate their terms into their domestic law. It may be possible to incorporate partial exclusions and reservations (for example, a reservation as to reciprocity) as part of the convention. By doing so, countries can participate in the convention on a less-than-entire basis, where, otherwise, they would not feel able to participate at all.

The above measures enable a country to host international arbitrations. However, it will also be necessary for parties to arbitration to carry out exhaustive checks on other counts. For instance, some countries still forbid non-nationals from sitting as arbitrators or acting as advocates. In other countries, the courts can still interfere to an excessive degree.

There can be no substitute for properly assessing the suitability of the country in which it is proposed an arbitration should take place.

Institutional arbitration

It is clear, from the foregoing, that international arbitration is not for the unwary. Skilled advice is required at all stages of the proceedings.

The parties can opt to use the services of an arbitration institution. Although this can be expensive, it should be considered where any risk of difficulty is present; conducting an arbitration under the authority of an institution may greatly assist to alleviate problems. Most institutions take a hand in ensuring that: the arbitrator is appointed; the basis of the arbitrator's remuneration is established; advance payments are made in respect of the arbitrator's fees and expenses; and time-limits for the appointment of the arbitrator are observed.

Advice

It has to be remembered that an arbitration that is valid in one country may not be valid in another. The key issue and the key decision, perhaps, with regard to international arbitration, concerns the country in which it is due to take place.

Another key factor will be the enforcement of the award. It may be prudent to locate the arbitration proceedings in the country in which the debtor's assets are based, or, alternatively, in a country that is linked by a convention for the enforcement of awards to the country in which these assets are located.

Whichever course is taken, it should be decided upon early and is best concluded before any dispute between the parties has arisen. Negotiation will often be necessary. Agreement between the parties is best entered into at the start of the project.

International arbitration – Main definitions

International arbitration: arbitration that involves: 'parties that have their places of business in different countries'; and deals with disputes arising out of obligations 'to be performed in a country different from the place of business of at least one of the parties' or with disputes 'connected with subject matter in a country different from the place of business of at least one of the parties'. [UNCITRAL Model Law on International Commercial Arbitration]

Different elements and laws – Applicable law

Part of the difficulty with international arbitration is that a number if different elements are present, and each element is potentially different as to it applicable law.

There is arbitration agreement, which contains two elements:

(i) the capacity of the parties to enter into the arbitration agreement; and
(ii) the law applicable to the arbitration agreement (the New York Convention may be of help here). Other elements include: the arbitration proceedings; the content of the dispute; the validity of the award (again, the New York Convention may be of help).

To ensure that the arbitration will not founder, it is important to know which law will be applicable, in each of the above aspects, in respect of the country that is being considered as the host in the arbitration proceedings and, also, the country in which the enforcement of the award will take place.

Contributed by Alan Morris

CHAPTER 20

Insurance against terrorism

Published as 'Take over against terrorism', 3 November 2001

In the light of recent events the property industry is taking a close look at terrorism insurance cover, we consider the Pool Reinsurance scheme

The devastating events in New York have alerted minds afresh to the fearful possibilities consequent upon terrorism, which is now of a scale not previously envisaged. Precautions of all kinds are being considered. Property holders and those engaged in property development, should review the arrangements for compensation against their property (and property developments) being damaged or destroyed by a terrorist attack.

The recent devastation is not entirely new. It has been seen in the past in conventional warfare. Indeed, there was something of it in the terrorist bombs of the 1990s in the City of London and Manchester. Provision for compensation, sufficient for the occasion and moulded by opinion, has developed over recent years. There is, therefore, in place provision against the present threat; provision extending not only to finished buildings, but also to buildings in the course of construction.

Two schemes of compensation

It is important to appreciate that the United Kingdom already has two separate schemes that provide compensation for property and works in the aftermath of a terrorist attack. One applies to Northern Ireland, the other to mainland Britain. Public funds are involved in both of these arrangements, although the involvement differs markedly between the two, both in nature and extent.

The scheme for Northern Ireland closely resembles a scheme of compensation that was set up by the government in the second world war. The mainland scheme, which was set up in the last decade, adopts a novel approach.

Northern Ireland

When the second world war started in September 1939, it was clear that bombardment from marauding aeroplanes would feature prominently in the conflict. The damage and destruction that was envisaged – correctly envisaged, as experience would soon show – was too great to be dealt with by the insurance market. It was necessary for the government to provide for compensation. This was arranged through the War Damage Acts.

The term 'war damage' became part of common parlance: it attached to compensation provided by the government where damage occurred as a result of the hostilities. A small contribution towards the cost was required, but, in the main, compensation for the destruction that ensued throughout the country came from government funds. The insurance market played no part in the scheme.

The concept that 'the government will pay' in regard to such compensation found common acceptance, and it persisted in the context of more localised damage ('war damage' now becoming 'criminal damage'). This perception has applied to the troubles in Ireland, now stretching over 30 years or more. Over the course of those years, the cost to the Exchequer has been considerable.

Mainland

The City of London has lived with terrorism of one kind or another for decades. Since the 1990s insurers excluded terrorism from the cover afforded by them. Alternative provision was urgently required, because only in Northern Ireland was there already in place specific compensation for damage to buildings caused by terrorism.

The government was unwilling to extend 'criminal damage' (the basis of the provision operating in Ireland) to other parts of the United Kingdom. Its view in this respect was that the insurance market should take the strain, with the government itself playing only a supportive role. Following prolonged negotiations, a scheme (the Retrocession Agreement) was agreed. The insurance market would once more provide cover; the government role would be no more than that of a long-stop – reinsurer of last resort – if there should ever be a shortfall of funds. By means of paying an additional premium, cover for damage caused by terrorism could be 'bought back'. A mutual insurance pool was created – pool reinsurance, or Pool Re for short.

Pool Re

Pool Re was dedicated to providing for damage to property caused by terrorism. Premium money paid for terrorism cover, by 'buying back', would be fed into the pool. In turn, claims for terrorism would be paid from it.

The government has reserved a right of withdrawal from the above arrangements, in the terms shown below (p133).

Understandably the government does not wish to bind itself in perpetuity to the agreement with Pool Re . It is hoped that in time circumstances will be such that the insurance market will be able to discontinue its limitation of cover for damage brought about by terrorism. It would seem that the government's intention is to remain involved until such time as the insurance market is so ready. The government could hardly desert the arrangements, leaving property owners high and dry.

In the case of building development sites, there is a special consideration: that a contract will already be in place with a building contractor. Under an ordinary building contract, there is provision made for taking out cover for fire and explosion, however caused. Either the builder or the employer will have this obligation. But the government has the right of withdrawal (even if it is very unlikely that this right would ever be exercised, without there being an alternative source of cover available).

Were the government to withdraw, however, cover for fire and explosion caused by terrorism might not be obtainable. Hence, it is possible that the contractor or the employer might find itself in breach of contract, with no means available of remedying this position. It is normal, therefore, for special provision to be made covering this contingency in a building contract: that upon the government withdrawing from its agreement, responsibility as between employer and contractor, regarding damage caused by terrorist attack, shall always be vested, solely, in the employer, and that various options will be available to the employer, including a right to discontinue the project (see, for example, the Standard Form of Building Contract – JCT 98 issued by the Joint Contracts Tribunal).

There are some unusual features to this scheme of buying back terrorism cover. All insurers charge the same premiums. Payments of premium go to Pool Re without deduction, not even for commission.

The entire claim is not paid from the pool. The first £100,000 of every head of cover must be borne by the insurer. There are four heads of cover: (i) buildings and completed structures; (ii) other property (including contents, engineering, contractors (sic) and computers); (iii) business interruption; and (iv) book debts.

The £100,000 retention, referred to above, to be paid by the insurer, applies to each of those heads of cover. This amounts to no easy road for the insurer to travel, bearing in mind that premiums paid by clients for buying back cover are passed on by the insurer, in their entirety, to Pool Re (see p133).

The government – the reinsurer of last resort in the terrorist arrangements – tops up the fund, should an underwriting year result in a loss to Pool Re Ltd. But here again, there is a snag for the insurer: before the government's obligation to pay kicks in, each insurer must itself make a further payment into Pool Re. The amount payable is up to 10% of premium passed on to Pool Re, by the insurer, for the then current year. Fortunately for the government, no government support has been needed for the scheme. Property owners, builders, developers, and insurers have, together, borne the cost involved.

Buying back cover is not available as a stand-alone provision. For it to become an option, ordinary insurance against fire and explosion must be taken out first. Then terrorism cover is offered. The insured has 30 days from the making of the offer in which to take it up.

Questions

'What if I overlook obtaining the terrorism cover until the 30 days have passed?' Terrorism cover can still be obtained, but a full year's premium will have to be paid in return for less than the full year's cover.

'Must I buy back cover for all my buildings? Some of my buildings (and development sites too) are in locations in which the risk is not great. I might be best suited not to insure them for terrorism: take the risk and save some money...?' Such an approach is not permitted under the terrorism scheme: the insurers have a rule to put an end to such thinking. It is called the 'all or nothing' rule. If you require cover, then you must have it throughout – existing properties, buildings and works. Or else you will not be able to obtain cover at all. There is not much scope for being selective (see p133).

Housing
The scheme does not apply to every kind of building. Housing in private ownership is excluded, since cover for damage caused by terrorism is still provided by ordinary insurance policies. But flats and houses owned by companies, and all housing sites under construction, are within the scheme, although special considerations apply.

Premium charge – Pool Re
The premium levied by Pool Re Ltd is closely related to the incidence of claims, and the outlook for the future. Typically, premium is payable in two tranches: a deposit premium, payable at the beginning of the year of insurance (perhaps 60% of the total premium); and a balancing payment to 100% payable within 30 days from the end of the year. In years devoid of acts of terrorism leading to claims, the balancing payment (or, possibly, part of it) may be waived.

Government
HM Treasury, on behalf of the government, exercises a controlling role: no changes in any of the arrangements for the scheme may be made without obtaining Treasury approval. The Treasury also has a particular interest, since there is a premium that will be payable to the government by Pool Re if ever its surplus exceeds £1bn.

Present and future
Pool Re continues to ensure that terrorism cover for the full sum insured remains available should the need arise. Already, it has covered a substantial part of the claims resulting from the Bishopsgate bomb (1993), the Israeli Embassy bomb (1993), the South Quay bomb (1996) and the Manchester bomb (1996). The procedures for settling claims are the same as those adopted in the insurance industry.

Importantly for the taxpayer, the arrangements for Northern Ireland, involving substantial payments from the government, have not been found necessary on the mainland. It may be hoped that this will continue. Indeed, it may be hoped that terrorism itself will be assigned to the past throughout the UK.

Terrorism cover – Points to bear in mind:

The government's right of withdrawal from the Pool Reinsurance scheme

[Pool Reinsurance] is of indefinite duration, but may be terminated with effect from midnight 31 December in any year by either party giving at least 120 days' notice in writing...

Terrorism rates

The material damage terrorism rates are divided into rating zones. The highest rate applies to Zone A – the central London postal districts. Zone B, set at 50% of the Zone A rate, covers broadly the remainder of inner London and central business areas in the rest of the country. Zone C and Zone D (at much lower rates) take up the balance of the country.

Excluding properties

1 The scope for excluding properties from terrorism cover is limited to properties whose values fall completely within a large decuctible under the standard policy cover. The minimum deductible for this to be the case is £250,000.
2 It is also permissible for an insured not to purchase terrorism cover for business interruption if it chooses.

Contributed by Alan Morris

Education and Training

21. Structured CPD training 137
22. Structured APC training 142
23. Lifelong learning 151

CHAPTER 21

Structured CPD training

Published as 'Top fees go to the specialist', 16 September 2001

Surveyors can gain an edge in their markets and further their careers by developing areas of expertise gained from structured training

Surveyors' salaries and careers are influenced by their experience, and aptitude for the job. But personal advancement can be accelerated by the acquisition of knowledge and skills gained through structured training.

During rent review negotiations, for example, the ability to promote third-party determination may see a swift and successful settlement reached against a surveyor of lesser expertise.

The under-trained surveyor may be left struggling to account to clients, and being held in low regard by colleagues. Training, as well as experience, in third-party procedures, relevant legislation and case law, the use of Calderbank letters and so on, therefore, does make a difference. With increased expertise and confidence, rent review and other transactions can be progressed more expediently, and therefore more profitably.

A surveyor regularly undertaking rent reviews may wish to specialise in the subject, aware that special expertise often carries premium value through higher pay. The ability to progress cases through to arbitration, for example, may be attractive to new employers, especially when other surveyors may lack such capability.

Surveyors may wish to train to become arbitrators. This would provide a new source of income if acting as an arbitrator, but also raise credibility as a rent review specialist, serving the surveyor well during negotiations, and enabling larger instructions to be secured.

A public sector surveyor may complement an involvement in CPO work with wider private study, and develop an expertise that enables promotion, or a position in private practice, to be secured as a CPO specialist.

Job prospects can often be influenced by snippets on a CV. Surveyors can gain an edge with an ability to state special expertise and/or particular achievements among wider skills. Career and pay opportunities can therefore be dependent on the energies devoted to training.

In-house opportunities

The most effective training programmes are those which reflect the nature of an organisation and the roles of individual personnel. A local authority or other in-house property team, for example, may see individual surveyors covering rent reviews, lease renewals and other landlord and tenant cases, as well as sales and lettings work, together with involvement in areas such as rating or asset valuation.

Surveyors in smaller private practices may cover a similar range of work, but surveyors with the larger firms may have relatively specialised roles – and therefore have very different training requirements.

Most organisations possess a level of expertise among their surveyors which can help develop the skills of others without the expense of formal training events. Surveyors' involvement in training could range from the day-to-day support provided for junior staff to the devising and delivery of training of qualified colleagues. Clients could be invited to talks, as could surveyors from other firms.

A company's solicitors could be encouraged to deliver seminars. Many already see the commercial benefit of doing so, and surveying practices could do more in this respect.

The organisation's provision of refreshments can be an effective way of ensuring that some training events take place outside fee-earning hours, with surrounding social activity adding interest.

Training sessions conducted on a suitable group basis can also enable team-building skills and morale to be improved. This includes support staff and younger surveyors, for example, being seen as a more valued part of the team. Indeed, the ability for support staff to deal with basic property cases, following training, can present cost and resource flexibility to an organisation.

Softer subjects, such as negotiation, report writing and coping with change, are also important, but tend to be given lesser priority to topics that are more fee related.

When work pressures tend to take priority over the arranging of training activities, it is important that the organisation designates personnel with specific responsibility for ensuring that training does take place.

Structured training

To most qualified surveyors, structured training means much more than undertaking 20 hours per year of continuing professional development in accordance with the RICS requirements. 'Structured' means that training activities stem from pre-identified requirements as part of an ongoing programme, as opposed to occurring on an *ad hoc* basis.

For individual surveyors, structured training involves identifying training requirements through the RICS Personal Development Planner. Attention is focused on strengths and weaknesses, and on how training can aid personal development, along with business opportunities.

For organisations, structured training involves ensuring that surveyors, and also support staff, enjoy the best opportunity to develop their skills.

Private study

RICS CPD works on the basis of self-assessment. Surveyors determine the suitability of the training initiatives themselves, and record the activities undertaken, together with the number of hours devoted.

Structured private study can qualify for up to two-thirds of the RICS minimum CPD requirement. This can be a particularly effective form of study, especially as surveyors have a differing knowledge and training requirements.

Private study should generally be structured around specific subjects, or be part of wider learning initiatives. Simply reading *Estates Gazette*, would not, for example, be satisfactory, but the study of particular articles therein may be.

Articles do not require a 'CPD' or 'distance learning' type of designation, or the need to obtain certification from the provider, to count as CPD. When providers state the number of hours available, this must be regarded as indicative, with the recorded number of hours being determined by surveyors themselves.

Private study could also comprise preliminary research, and/or subsequent study around a course or seminar.

Surveyors attending courses should disseminate the information to colleagues, and can also arrange discussion groups. These can consider the various issues in relation to the work in which the organisation's surveyors are usually involved.

Training events and training providers

Courses and seminars are particularly useful for specialist requirements, and also where it is necessary to be informed of new legislation, case law, market practice and so on. Many of these courses are useful because they cover many topics within a single day.

The quality, content and suitability of training events can sometimes be difficult to determine in advance of attendance, especially with a large number of training providers in the market. Most commercial property training companies are in business because of an established demand for the quality of training they offer.

Where to find quality CPD events

Some universities run highly regarded CPD events, but others operate only in a small way. Providers with 'trust' status may be providing genuine support and funding for training, but some may use the term to mask commercial motives.

Courses also provide the opportunity to meet other surveyors specialising in similar areas. Indeed, some courses are renowned for the pulling power of champagne lunches and networking opportunities.

Some companies unfortunately require training to be undertaken by staff at their own expense, in their own time. The non-fee-earning nature of training time can sometimes be cited as a ground for its avoidance. 'Investors in People' type accreditation can remain a marketing cosmetic, and not reach the staff it is designed to support.

Surveyors should pro-actively ensure that their requirements are being met. Enquiries could, for example, be made about a company's training initiatives when employment is being sought.

The RICS assesses the records of individual members as part of its rolling programme of spot checks. Guidance and support is always available for those who struggle to meet the minimum requirements.

Companies should consider the image presented if future strategy sees all surveyors requested to provide CPD records, and if non-compliance and poor standards are reported in the property press.

And it is not just the RICS taking a keen interest in the surveyors' commitment to training. When appointing agents, local authorities and major clients of the profession are increasingly inquiring about surveyors' skill levels – as evidenced by training structures as well as by the experience of individuals and the reputation of their practice.

Taking responsibility

The decision for individual surveyors to develop themselves through structured training initiatives depends on their professionalism, and their aspirations for promotion, salary increases and job opportunities.

For organisations, vision is required as to how training can raise expertise, improve job performance, expand client bases, increase profitability and, consequently, be seen as a net return investment. Effective training will always separate success from underachievement.

The RICS too, is raising standards through training programmes for its employees. It is increasingly aware it is judged by members' dealings with the organisation, as customers, and that service levels must match those portrayed by promotional efforts.

Contributed by Margaret Harris and Austen Imber

CHAPTER 22

Structured APC training

Published as 'Work don't swot', 12 January 2002

As the final part of APC assessment looms, candidates who have applied themselves consistently to study will find the interview more straightforward than those who try to learn it all at the last minute

Following previous *Mainly for Students* features on the Assessment of Professional Competence (APC), candidates have raised a number of queries. The common theme is how to give themselves the best chance of success, and whether some of the horror stories they have heard about the final assessment interview can safely be ignored.

Commencing training

On becoming professionally employed, candidates need to register for the APC with the RICS in order to formally commence their training period of at least 24 months. Delays could result in final assessment interviews having to be undertaken later than planned.

With their APC 'supervisor' and 'counsellor', candidates initially consider RICS APC requirements, and determine the areas of work in which they are likely to be involved. Work experience is recorded against 'competencies' in an APC diary and logbook, and summarised at both interim and final assessment. Competencies relate to APC routes and now also to the new faculties/surveying specialisms such as commercial practice or valuation. 'Core' competencies are compulsory, and 'optional' competencies are selected in relation to the type of work expected to be undertaken.

Competency selection

At the final assessment interview, a detailed knowledge is required of the main competency areas, and a more general awareness is required of other areas of surveying (see later). Competency selection must accurately anticipate the type of work in which candidates are likely to be involved and, from a more tactical perspective, reflect how certain competencies and their combinations influence the final assessment interview.

For example, if a candidate chooses optional competencies of property marketing, landlord and tenant and estate management because they will be involved in lettings and landlord and tenant work, the three areas more easily interrelate than may be the case if, for example, a fourth competency such as local taxation (rating) or planning was added. Some candidates gain little experience in such additional areas, and present themselves with considerable learning and revision efforts near to final assessment, when it is too late to change competencies.

Care needs to be taken with competency selection, noting, for example, that general practice surveyors sometimes select 'property development and acquisition' because it appears to sound appropriate, but is actually a competency for building surveyors.

Competency levels

General practice and commercial practice/valuation candidates select a minimum of three optional competencies to level 3, or two at level 3 plus two at level 2. Level 3 involves a more detailed knowledge than level 2, and as the depth of APC interview questioning will reflect this, the selection of four competencies rather than three should limit the level of knowledge required in two of them. However, it may be considered easier to build from level 2 to level 3 within a particular competency, than to have to introduce another.

Recording experience

Some candidates record experience in many more than their minimum three or four optional competencies. Although this may be necessary where a change of employer, department or caseload brings different areas of experience, the selection of numerous competencies may lead ultimately to a wider range of interview questioning, and to unnecessarily increased learning and revision efforts. This may particularly be the case where competencies are taken to level 2, but difficulties are unlikely to arise for any additional optional competencies recorded only to level 1.

Diary entries
The purpose of the diary is to serve as a representative record of the experience gained, rather than as a precise match of activities with dates. It is acceptable for candidates to make daily notes and then suitably complete their diary at the end of each month. This avoids the need to record occasional administrative duties and isolated work beyond the main competency areas, and enables the recorded experience to focus on the quality work being undertaken.

Professional development
Professional development/CPD is another important contributor to APC success. Candidates with a quality record that exceeds the minimum 48 hours per year present themselves to the interview panel as conscientious and committed. This is in contrast to candidates who view professional development simply as a compliance requirement, and submit records showing little effort, and sometimes also non-qualifying activities.

For further guidance, including illustrations of qualifying activities, see Chapter 21.

Interim assessment
Within one month of completing their first 12 months' experience, candidates need to complete an 'interim assessment'. This operates on the basis of self-assessment with the candidate's supervisor and counsellor. Random checks are made by the RICS, and assessments should be completed on time so as not to risk deferment of the final assessment interview, or giving the assessors an unfavourable impression (noting that interim assessment records form part of final assessment submissions).

Final assessment
Final assessment submissions include a copy of the interim report/assessment, a summary of the experience gained since the interim stage, logbook, record of progress, professional development record, a critical analysis and, in the case of referred candidates, a 500-word report explaining how previous deficiencies have been addressed. The diary is not submitted, but may subsequently be requested.

Candidates state a specialist area on their application forms, such as valuation, property marketing and acquisition or property investment. This helps to ensure that the assessors' respective areas of experience are consistent with those of the candidate, and that the interview can focus mainly on a candidate's competencies. Candidates must still be alert to issues outside their competencies that still reflect the work undertaken within their competencies. An understanding of planning issues, for example, may be required for marketing, valuation and development appraisal work. And rates liabilities, as an overhead, affect many areas of work.

It is essential that candidates understand professional ethics. They should also be familiar with current issues affecting the work in which they are involved and the profession generally.

The critical analysis is a detailed examination of a particular case in which candidates have been involved. Candidates can help themselves by ensuring that their specialist area, main competencies and the subject of critical analysis are consistent. As part of an hour-long final assessment interview with three assessors, candidates provide a 10-minute presentation on their critical analysis.

Candidate responsibility

Candidates' requirements may differ. They may have commenced training at different dates, are taking the experience-based route, are operating under a different faculty/specialism or have been referred – hence the need for candidates to study RICS guides in detail themselves, and generally take personal responsibility throughout the training period for meeting the requirements. APC expertise within firms inevitably varies, and supervisors and counsellors are not expected to learn all the technical minutiae.

When the RICS makes changes to the system, candidates may be affected by transition arrangements which are not possible to cover in RICS guides. These include the introduction of faculties/specialisms, and changes to interim assessment which also lead to variations for final assessment. The precise requirements placed on candidates will be notified in the documentation sent to them by the RICS. Guidance in respect of matters such as the differences between faculties/specialisms, changing competencies midway through the training period, or selecting competencies from other faculties/specialisms, is set out in RICS guides, with RICS practice qualifications staff able to provide additional help if need be.

Tough times at the interview

Seemingly unsatisfactory situations occasionally arise in an interview-based assessment process such as the APC, but candidates should not be distracted by the reported experiences of others. It is difficult for candidates to be fully aware of the extent of their knowledge in relation to that required to succeed at interview, and it can also be human instinct to direct blame elsewhere (noting, for example, a tendency for candidates to report obscure interview questions that did not affect their result, rather than the mainstream questioning, which would have).

Candidates sometimes consider that assessors have adopted an over-assertive approach. Although assessors should aim to get the best out of candidates by easing their nerves and helping them to settle, as well as avoiding an impatient tone during questioning, the style of some assessors may be to create a more lively momentum. Candidates should not correlate the manner adopted by any assessors with their chance of success, and should still maintain their temperament and confidence – bearing in mind that they would likewise have to perform in practice if involved in uncomfortable negotiations on behalf of clients.

Also, a candidate's view of what constitutes an assertive approach is formed under the anxious conditions of the APC interview – where candidates can sometimes be over-sensitive to the effect of minor issues that have no bearing on their chances of success.

It is, however, worth highlighting just a few potential sources of frustration for assessors, which also serve as further guidance to candidates.

- Candidates not following RICS requirements, and/or submitting poor-quality submissions, which imply a lack of effort and conscientiousness. Assessors may conclude that service to clients will be of a similarly poor standard.
- Candidates not having undertaken sufficient experience to be ready for final assessment, and/or being signed off by employers as meeting competency levels when they clearly fall short.
- Candidates not having recorded professional development/ CPD honestly, as possibly evidenced by their inability to answer simple questions on areas they purport to have studied.
- Candidates deliberately providing long-winded answers to

questions as a tactical attempt to talk out time and limit the number of questions being asked. Assessors are also alert to some candidates' strategic attempts to trigger certain questions from the critical analysis and presentation, for example.
- Candidates regularly failing to listen properly to the interview question, latching on to a few key words, and assessors being forced to halt the candidate's inevitable off-track answer and repeat the specific elements of the question that were initially missed.

After the disappointment of referral, candidates tend to reflect only on their interview performance, whereas the cause often lies in the approach taken to learning and development over the full two-year training period (as well as poor-quality written submissions). The APC is not about two months of revision – candidates who seek to learn late in the process are more likely to have gaps in their knowledge and understanding exposed at the interview.

Support from employers throughout the training period is, of course, essential. Furthermore, organisations such as GVA Grimley, the UK's largest recruiter of general practice graduates in 2001, and Birmingham Property Services, the UK's largest in-house local authority property consultancy, have secured considerable commercial gain from their training achievements (see pages 148–150).

Whether to appeal if it goes wrong

Candidates who genuinely feel aggrieved as to the way their interview was conducted and/or to the grounds stated for referral, have a right to appeal which will lead to a re-sit shortly afterwards, if upheld.

There are no grounds of appeal formally specified by the RICS, but reasons could include the panel focusing too heavily on areas outside the candidate's main competencies, a candidate's specialisms not being reflected in panel composition, the panel making critical comment on a candidate's written submissions which on closer inspection are invalid, an assessor being known to the candidate and having a conflict in view of negotiations in which they had been involved, an assessor taking an unnecessarily hostile approach or the candidate suffering from RICS procedural or administrative faults.

What does not constitute a ground for appeal is the candidate's and/or employer's view (or any others who can be persuaded to lend their weight) that the candidate is considered to be good enough in practice, and really ought to have passed. Interview questioning can, of course, reveal certain deficiencies not yet highlighted in the workplace, and candidates may simply have a bad day at the interview, especially if they have not been best prepared.

Although not suitable grounds for appeal in their own right, disruptions, such as the need to leave the room for 10 minutes as a result of a fire alarm, may add to the overall problems. Any family, health or other personal difficulties should have been made known to the RICS in advance or at the start of the interview.

Genuinely aggrieved candidates should not be deterred by comments from colleagues (often those who know nothing about the APC) that they may in some way be rocking the boat if they appeal. Rather than being out to rebuke the candidate, the panel conducting an appeal respects the candidate's situation in the knowledge that the RICS does not uphold appeals lightly, and there must be very good reason if it does.

Training support

The starting point for candidates is the official RICS guides, currently edition 5 of APC candidates and employers guide and APC requirements and competencies. In addition to the RICS staff, regional training advisers provide a source of guidance as well as a monitoring role, and APC doctors also provide support.

At final assessment, evening sessions, half-day and full-day courses are run by some universities, commercial training providers and local RICS groups. Midlands Property Training Centre is a facilitator of training for general practice surveyors, and provides independent advice in respect of structured training, suitable training providers and so on.

Training and business: making the links at GVA Grimley

Candidates at the largest national practices sometimes report that APC training and wider career prospects promised as part of graduate recruitment do not always materialise. Their disappointment can soon spread to other graduates and students, and begin to affect their firm's recruitment initiatives as well as staff retention. And some candidates' motivation for the APC becomes the chance to move on to better things elsewhere.

At the commencement of their training period at GVA Grimley, candidates work with APC supervisors and other managers to plan a two-year training programme embracing work in several departments (including, for example, valuation and industrial agency). This enables detailed experience to be gained in the main competencies, thus equipping candidates well for the final assessment interview. The usual three-monthly reviews and interim assessment requirements help to fine-tune candidates' progress, and include consideration of how professional development/CPD initiatives can further aid their development.

Professional development initiatives include the facilitating of study groups for candidates, which take place within each office or region for the main subject areas, and on a national basis for specialised areas. Candidates also help with the research and writing of articles for professional journals, and are generally encouraged in their development of any special areas of interest. Throughout the training period, a central source of specialist general practice APC advice is available to candidates.

At final assessment, intensive in-house training sessions comprise a half-day written submissions event, a one-day interview, presentation and professional ethics event and a one-day APC interview questions-and-answers event. Mock interviews then put candidates through their paces for the APC interview and, in addition to up to 10 days' study leave, GVA Grimley's qualified surveyors support revision workshops and help with general queries.

Since Scott Kind, GVA Grimley UK training and development manager, initiated the structured training programme last year, the interest from the next round of graduates in joining the firm has increased sharply, and the training has already helped with the internal career development of successful candidates beyond the APC.

Structuring the training period: drawing on IT at BPS

One of the key contributors to APC success is ensuring that work experience is recorded appropriately, and that the diary, logbook and record of progress are consistent with candidates' stated levels of attainment for each competency. This is not always easy, as some areas of work can cover several competencies, such as a rent review involving competencies of landlord and tenant, valuation and property inspection.

Another key factor is the regular monitoring of the weighting of experience gained in competency areas. This is a laborious task, often not undertaken if the totalling of days' experience is undertaken manually, with some candidates discovering an imbalance only on completing their records close to submission deadlines.

In order to avoid such problems and to structure his and his colleagues' training effectively, Barrington Maye, an APC candidate at Birmingham Property Services, the in-house property consultancy of Birmingham city council, developed a computer programme containing the following features:

- Diary entry facility, describing work experience undertaken, and logging against competencies appearing as columns (rather than allocating only a competency reference).
- Running monthly and grand totals of days' experience gained in each competency together with target levels.
- Automatic entry and totalling of days' experience to the logbook.
- Prompt facility at three-monthly intervals for review with supervisor and counsellor, including interim assessment requirements.
- Pop-up boxes providing information such as an explanation of the type of work falling under a particular competency area (helping to allocate competencies accurately), the criteria by which levels (1, 2, 3) can be signed off, and a reminder of supervisors' and counsellors' responsibilities.
- Automatic completion of final submission documentation to RICS template requirements.

The up-to-date overview of the balance of experience against competencies also helps candidates to demonstrate to their employer any new areas of casework required – noting also that a forward-planning element is now an important element of interim assessment. Moreover, the programme helps to ensure that the APC operates as a training period of two years or more, rather than as crash learning for the interview.

Since Jacky Gutteridge, BPS training and development manager, initiated the structured training programme in 1999, all nine of BPS's candidates have passed at their first attempt

Contributed by Austen Imber

CHAPTER 23

Lifelong learning

Published as 'Arrive via training', 13 July 2002

The combination of performance in practice and a commitment to learning can bring rich rewards. Here we examine how a culture of lifelong learning is developing within the surveying profession

Lifelong learning involves surveyors realising their personal and business development potential at all stages of their career. It means that the professionally qualified surveyor complements work in practice with suitable study, raising performance, pay and promotion prospects, and bringing wider career and lifestyle options.

RICS education and training initiatives

Initiatives being undertaken by the RICS in respect of education and training include:

- promoting the profession to schools;
- developing partnerships with approved/accredited universities, ensuring that entry standards and course content attract the right recruits, and equip them to contribute effectively once beginning work in practice;
- creating opportunities for property support staff, in particular through NVQs, and by developing technical membership, known as TechRICS, through the Assessment of Technical Competence (ATC);
- providing non-cognate and experience-based routes into the profession;
- ensuring that the Assessment of Professional Competence (APC) provides graduates with a strong professional training period, maintains high standards, and remains up to date with market changes;
- maintaining standards for clients, and for the profession more

generally, through continuing professional development (CPD) requirements placed on all members.

Lifelong learning brings these initiatives together, enabling the RICS to further develop the profession's knowledge and skills base, following the introduction of mandatory CPD in 1981.

RICS lifelong learning/CPD initiatives are led by the institution's education and training division, based in Coventry. This includes supporting the 16 RICS faculties, other industry groups and forums, partnership/accredited universities, surveying firms and individual members to ensure that high-quality, affordable training is available within the profession.

RICS members are being consulted on the format of an enhanced system to identify learning objectives, how to meet them and how evaluation and further objectives can best be planned. A questionnaire will be posted on the RICS's website.

Training links with business

CPD monitoring exercises have discovered relatively few examples of non-compliance, with salary and business surveys continuing to highlight a strong relationship between attitudes to CPD and business success.

Indeed, many firms are increasingly recognising the link between training and business development, and winning new business on the back of a commitment to training. Some firms, however, remain unaware of how public-sector clients, in particular, consider the training and development achievements of those pitching for business – often by more subtle judgment than direct questions on application or tender forms.

Raising the profession's profile

Corporate initiatives being undertaken by the RICS include:

- raising the profile and status of the chartered surveyor within the UK by providing guidance to small businesses and promoting to the corporate sector the contribution property makes to business – in both cases stressing the value that chartered surveyors can add;
- marketing the RICS and the chartered surveyor worldwide, and generally positioning the institution as the lead global governing body for property;

- providing opportunities for surveyors to develop business skills;
- developing the membership, such as through mergers with other institutions.

All the above initiatives aim to raise the fee-earning and salary potential of all members and ensure that some of the roles of the chartered surveyor are not eroded by other professions and institutions. Although some elements are not always palatable to all members, the RICS continues to focus on the net gain it considers can be achieved.

Business skills

The RICS Agenda for Change highlighted the need for surveyors to gain better business acumen. In May 2002, through its journal, *CSM*, the RICS stated:

In drawing primarily on technical skills, surveyors do not tend to possess a natural instinct in the fields of business and management. RICS education and training initiatives, together with related corporate strategies, therefore seek to raise the profile and earning capacity of the profession through the development of business skills. What this means for individual members depends on their area of work, interest in business issues and overall career aspirations.

The ability to understand a client's business objectives not only ensures that a high-quality service is provided in individual cases, but can also lead to securing consultancy roles. In gaining new clients through a successful consultancy arm, instructions in mainstream casework may follow.

As well as advising such non-property companies on the strategic role that property can play, surveyors may help drive a property-related business forward, such as an investment, development or contracting company – or indeed a surveying practice. In fact, surveyors' detailed knowledge of their industry/market, combined with a basic appreciation of marketing and business development techniques, usually puts them a long way ahead of business and marketing consultants from non-property backgrounds.

Business skills encompass an understanding of economic and property market trends and, at a more advanced level, a knowledge of finance and accounting techniques. An up-to-date awareness of developments in information technology, including websites, e-mail and mobile communication, helps surveyors keep a step ahead of the competition, and for those with a keen business eye, also helps new opportunities to be exploited.

Effective management creates internal efficiencies in both the private and public sectors, and good interpersonal skills and presentation technique are essential for all professionals.

To help surveyors develop the required business skills, the RICS is working with partnership universities, business schools and other training providers to make post-graduate business and management qualifications available. This includes a certificate in management studies, which would count towards surveyors' CPD requirements, and may also lead to a diploma in management studies or an MBA for surveyors wishing to develop their skills further.

Degree courses will continue to provide an introduction to business areas, and some universities are making business skills a greater component in suitably tailored courses than has traditionally been the case.

Qualifying learning activities

Note that while simply reading *Estates Gazette* does not count as CPD, 'private structured study' of particular articles does, as do discussion/workshop sessions between colleagues/companies on the issues raised in articles.

It is worth noting also that private study can count towards two-thirds of surveyors' CPD requirement, with courses and seminars – including talks given internally by colleagues – making up the rest. The RICS requires students to undertake 60 hours of CPD over any three-year period. However, it stresses that certification is on the basis of self-assessment, with the relevance and quality of study activities being more important than the mere logging of hours.

CPD can now be recorded on line at www.rics.org/careers/cpd/online_recording, and includes the identification of personal and business development aims, and related learning objectives.

Lifelong learning: putting it all into practice

As an example of how career progression can be accelerated through a pro-active approach to lifelong learning, a young surveyor may have found a particular interest in landlord and tenant issues while at university, and identified the subject for particularly concerted study, seeking to gain an edge for job interviews as well as examinations.

Consequently taken on by a landlord and tenant team of a major national practice, through the APC and beyond, the surveyor draws on the latest case law and market practice in rent review and lease renewal work, including third-party dispute resolution processes. This helps secure expedient and successful settlements on behalf of clients.

For the firm, strong fee levels and profitability are achieved in relation to the time spent, and pitches for new business can be made competitively, thus also maximising instructions received.

Through writing articles in journals, and contributing to training events for others, the surveyor's profile is raised. Together with the increasing ability to undertake higher-value transactions, this further increases fee/salary/bonus earning capacity.

The firm continues to expand its landlord and tenant team, and, in due course, the surveyor's lifelong learning efforts turns partly to business and management topics in order for the surveyor to realise aspirations of setting up his or her own practice.

Later, in mid-career, learning options include qualification as an arbitrator and/or independent expert. Later-career interest is provided by training and work in practice in respect of rent review and also valuation practice for new and specialist property types, helping to lead the field in some areas, and picking up further instructions in other areas, through cross-selling, for an ever-expanding practice.

Contributed by Austen Imber

English Legal System

24. The definition of 'London' 159
25. The law of the calendar. 164
26. Denning's legal legacy. 169
27. Delegated legislation and the Human Rights Act 174
28. Famous cases 179

CHAPTER 24

The definition of 'London'

Published as 'Capital appreciation', 8 April 2000

Now that a Mayor for London and a London Assembly are to be elected, the age-old question once again arises: what constitutes London?

At the time Dr Johnson paid his famous tribute, 'When a man is tired of London, he is tired of life', there could well have been doubts in the minds of his listeners as to whether Chelsea, Kennington or Stepney were a part of London, let alone Islington, Bayswater or Bow. Even Westminster would still have had the characteristics of a separate city, in much the same way as Kingston-upon-Thames still looks like a separate market town and county town of Surrey 35 years after becoming a London borough.

In 1801, when Henry Addington followed William Pitt the Younger as prime minister, the witticism that quickly went round was that 'Pitt is to Addington as London is to Paddington': Paddington was then a village, not the site of a major railway terminus, which, within 40 years, it was to become.

Metropolis

By the 19th century, the urban conurbation of London extended far beyond the legal boundaries of the ancient City of London, reaching into the counties of Middlesex, Essex, Surrey and Kent. Parliament therefore tended to use the word 'metropolis' (or 'metropolitan') in Acts of Parliament that were intended to regulate this growing urban sprawl. Examples of this legislative extension are to be found in the Metropolitan Paving Act 1817; the Metropolitan Police Act 1829; the Metropolitan Management Act 1855;and the Metropolitan Poor Act 1867.

The Metropolitan Management Act 1855 created the Metropolitan Board of Works. This 'creature of statute' is still remembered in such case law as *Metropolitan Board of Works* v *McCarthy* (1874) LR 7 HL 243, which was the well-spring of the famous 'McCarthy rules' to be found in the law of injurious affection.

The Metropolitan Poor Act 1867 became a precedent in the law of nuisance: see *Metropolitan Asylum District* v *Hill* (1881) 6 App Cas 193, a case relating to the proposed building of a smallpox hospital in the residential area of Hampstead.

Those studying the law of tort will be familiar with the Fires Prevention (Metropolis) Act 1774, sections 83 and 86 of which are still in force. The Act contains a preamble stating that it applies to:

the Cities of London and Westminster and the Liberties thereof, and, other, the Parishes, Precincts, and Places within the Weekly Bills of Mortality, the Parishes of Saint Mary-le-bon, Paddington, Saint Pancras, and Saint Luke at Chelsea, in the County of Middlesex.

The 'Places within the Bills of Mortality' were those parishes neighbouring the City of London that produced statistical returns of the deaths occurring within their boundaries: a practice pre-dating the Great Plague of London, but more stringently enforced since then.

This Act applies not only to the London area but also generally throughout England and Wales. Thus, in *Lonsdale & Thompson Ltd* v *Black Arrow Group plc* [1993] 1 EGLR 87, a dispute about a fire insurance policy taken out by a lessor for the benefit of his lessee was dealt with under section 83 of the 1774 Act, even though the premises were situated in Liverpool.

The Metropolitan Police Act 1829, known, in its day, as Peel's Police Act, created a Metropolitan Police District that covered a radius of seven miles from Charing Cross, excluding the one-square mile of the ancient City of London, which had (and still has) its own police force. This area now covers about 700 square miles, with a radius of approximately 15 miles from Charing Cross. It is therefore one of the last surviving 'metropolitan' authorities to extend beyond the legal boundaries of Greater London.

However, with the introduction of an elected Mayor for London (and certain responsibilities for policing he will be given), the boundaries of the Metropolitan Police District will be made coterminous with the boundaries of Greater London. Thus, for example, the policing of Epsom, and, with it, Derby Day on Epsom Racecourse, will no longer be the responsibility of the Metropolitan Police, but will become the responsibility of the Surrey Police.

London County Council

The London County Council was established in 1888, when the Local Government Act of that year established elected administrative county councils throughout England and Wales. Thus, the counties of Middlesex, Surrey and Kent lost territory to the new County of London (a term that continued to exclude the ancient City of London).

The new County of London was divided into 28 metropolitan boroughs, although Westminster retained the title of City of Westminster. Yet, ordinary London streets continued to mark (or would soon come to mark) the boundaries between the County of London and the adjoining boroughs in other counties, for example Hornsey, Ealing, Hounslow, and Brentford in Middlesex; Leyton, East Ham and West Ham in Essex; Wimbledon and Croydon in Surrey; and Bromley and Beckenham in Kent.

The expansion of the legal boundaries of London to their present metes and bounds came about on 1 April 1965, this being the date upon which the London Government Act 1963 came into force. In addition to creating the administrative county of Greater London, the 1963 Act abolished the 28 metropolitan boroughs and created 32 much larger London boroughs by the amalgamation of existing metropolitan boroughs and other outer-London local authorities and/or the redrawing of interior boundaries.

One of the anomalies that continued for some years after 1965 was that the London Building Acts 1930-1939 applied to the old London County Council area, but they did not apply to the outer-London boroughs, which still retained their own building byelaws under the Public Health Act 1936.

The second-tier authority for Greater London, known as the Greater London Council, was abolished on 1 April 1986: see the Local Government Act 1985, which also abolished other metropolitan county councils, such as Merseyside.

City of London

London was already almost 1,000 years old when William the Conqueror recognised the ancient customs and the internal government of the city in order to secure his throne. The City can therefore claim to be a corporation by prescription, pre-dating the 'year of legal memory', ie 1189 AD. Royal Charters did not create the City of London, they merely recognised and affirmed its existing rights.

Indeed, Magna Carta, which was signed in 1215, contains a clause that 'the City of London shall have its liberties'. Thus, the Local Government Act 1972 did not affect the ancient electoral system used in the one square mile that constitutes the City of London, nor can the Boundary Commission do any more than simply adjust the boundaries of the City – it cannot greatly enlarge or reduce its area.

The City of London is not a local authority but a corporation by way of immemorial prescription. It comprises the Lord Mayor (the first person to hold that office seems to have been in or about 1189), the commonalty and the citizens. Together, these persons are known as 'the Commune of the City'. The commonalty are the members of the livery companies; there are 12 great livery companies and more than 90 more modern ones, including the Chartered Surveyors Company. The citizens are those 'freemen of the City', who are not members of a livery company.

The commune of the City acts through various assemblies: the Court of Common Council; the Court of Common Hall; and the Court of Aldermen.

Commune of the City

The Court of Common Council has been given the functions exercised by local authorities elsewhere in England and Wales. It consists of the Lord Mayor, 24 (other) aldermen, and common councilmen. There are 25 electoral wards each of which elects one alderman (the Mayor being one of them), and a certain number of common councilmen. Common councilmen have to be re-elected every year. Aldermen used to be elected until retirement (at the age of 70), but they are now elected for a period of six years, and, if they are under 70, they are eligible for re-election.

There are only about 5,500 residential voters in the City of London, most of whom live in the Barbican. Although the City of London has residential tenants in many housing estates beyond the City boundaries, these tenants do not have the right to vote in City elections – they are eligible to vote only in the local authority area in which they live.

The City of London is unique within the United Kingdom for retaining voting rights based on membership of livery companies, and also upon the freehold or leasehold ownership of business property. Sole traders who hold freehold or leasehold business property in the City may vote in the elections for aldermen and for common councilmen.

Partners in firms practising in the City may also vote in those elections, but many professions now allow their members to practice as limited companies, and many trading enterprises are, in any event, incorporated as companies.

For this reason, the City of London (Ward Elections) Bill – which is currently before parliament – seeks to give votes to the one or more representatives of each limited company holding freehold or leasehold premises in the City, according to a formula based upon the rateable value of those premises.

The distinct and exceptional nature of the electoral system pertaining to the City of London is based upon the fact that the City is now principally a place where people work, and no longer a place where people make their homes.

Contributed by Leslie Blake

CHAPTER 25

The law of the calendar

Published as 'It's all a matter of time', 8 January 2000

Time is not fixed, but has been subject to manipulation over the centuries. However, the legal calendar has its foundations in the law of nature

Why, as a matter of English law, does this edition of *Estates Gazette* bear the date 8 January 2000?

This is a two-part question: (1) why is this year called the year 2000?; and (2) why did it begin on 1 January? Why, for example, does the calendar year begin on 1 January, but the tax year not begin until 6 April?

The solar year

In what we know as the pre-Christian year of 45 BC, Julius Caesar reformed the Roman calendar. This had been numbered from the legendary foundation of the city of Rome by Romulus and Remus in 753 BC. The length of the year was based upon a combination of the cycles of the moon and the sun.

Caesar replaced this calendar with one that was based solely upon the sun. In the Northern hemisphere, the sun reaches its zenith at the summer solstice, which takes place around 21 June, and reaches its lowest point in the sky at the winter solstice, around 21 December. The word 'solstice' derives from the Latin; the 'sun' being made to 'stand still'.

The sun makes its northern stand at the Tropic of Cancer in June, returning to the south, to make its southern stand at the Tropic of Capricorn, in December. Between these two points, there is equal night and day on (about) 21 March and (about) 23 September: the vernal equinox and the autumnal equinox. Thus, the practice of dividing the year into four legal 'quarter days' has its basis in the law of nature.

The Julian calendar

The Julian calendar, the calendar of Julius Caesar, was based upon the calculation that the period from one winter solstice to the next is 365 days and 6 hours. The leap year is, of course, intended to account for this fraction of a day, but, unknown to Caesar, the rotation of the earth is a little slower than the projected 365.25 days*.

Because the pre-Julian calendar had incorporated the moon's cycle into the annual reckonings, Caesar reluctantly agreed to commence his new calendar year on the first new moon following the winter solstice of the year 45BC. That is why December still extends beyond the winter solstice and why, as far as the solar year is concerned, the month of January retains its delayed start.

The quarter days

In 325 AD, a date that would not, of course, have been used at that time, the Council of Nicea – a council of the Christian church – adopted quarter days that accommodated the festivals of the Church and spurned the pagan worship of the sun. These days were:

- the Feast of the Nativity of Christ – Christmas Day, 25 December;
- the Feast of the Annunciation of the Blessed Virgin Mary – Lady Day, 25 March;
- the Feast of the Nativity of John the Baptist, 24 June; and
- the Feast of St Michael and all the Angels – Michaelmas Day, 29 September.

Of course, these dates fell close to the solstices and equinoxes of the solar year, but, as they were fixed dates, and as the Julian calendar was not accurate in its measurement of the solar year, a divergence became increasingly apparent. For instance, by 1750, the vernal equinox was occurring on or about 9 March in England, whereas it had occurred on or about 21 March in the year of the Council of Nicea.

---

* Caesar's astronomers were also in error when they believed that 235 lunar months would be exactly equal to 19 solar years.

Numbering the years

Until recently, the usual method of identifying years in legal documents was by way of 'regnal years'. Hence, popes would date their documents according to whether they were in the first, second, third (and so on) year of their pontificate. Kings, princes and other temporal rulers would do likewise, according to the length of their respective reigns. Thus, the Council of Nicea had been held in the 12th year of the pontificate of Pope Sylvester I and in the 15th year of the reign of the Roman Emperor Constantine I. (Regnal years for British Acts of Parliament were not entirely abolished until 1963.)

In 527 AD a monk called Dionysius Exiguus published his calculations concerning the date of the birth of Christ. The celebration of the new millennium is a repeated reminder that his suggested date was probably incorrect by approximately four years; the actual birth occurring earlier. He also followed the practice of popes and kings, in that the first year of the life of Christ was called 'year one' (AD). Thus, the notional first birthday of Christ would have been held in 2 AD. Nevertheless, Dionysius' chronology was gradually accepted throughout the Christian world. In England, it was adopted by the Synod of Chelsea in 816 AD.

The Gregorian calendar

In 1578 Pope Gregory XIII reformed the Julian calendar to bring it more in line with the actual length of the solar year. Scotland adopted this calendar, and so did many other countries in Western Europe. However, Protestant England was slow to do so. By 1750, England was using a calendar that was 11 days behind the Gregorian calendar, and, therefore, 11 days behind the Scottish calendar, even though Scotland and England had shared the same line of monarchs since 1603 and had been one nation since 1707. Thus, Mary II died in December 1694 by English reckoning, but in January 1695 by Scottish reckoning.

In 1750 parliament passed the Calendar (New Style) Act 1750 – a title that did not attach to it until the Short Titles Act 1896. This provided that, in England and Wales, the next natural day following 2 September 1752 should be 14 September 1752. (It was not until 1781 that parliament confirmed that the Act applied also to Ireland.) The Act also provided for the adoption of the Gregorian calendar by omitting leap years in 1800, 1900, 2100, 2200, 2300 'and any other hundredth year of our Lord which shall happen in time to come', while retaining those leap years falling in the year 2000 and all other years divisible by 400.

Because of the loss of 11 days from the calendar of 1752, parliament had to allow rents, annuities, debts, etc, to be paid 11 days later than the apparent contractual date, although, of course, no actual delay would have occurred: see section 6 of the Act of 1750. Thus, until old leases and contracts had run their course, rents were payable on quarter days that fell 11 days later than those laid down by the Council of Nicea. Eleven days after Lady Day is 5 April.

The beginning of the year

Dionysius appears to have dated the incarnation of Christ from the date of His conception, rather than from the date of His birth. Thus, Lady Day (25 March) has always laid claim to be the beginning of the Christian year. In 12th-century England, this date was chosen in preference to Caesar's date of 1 January. The practice of dating the new year from 25th March was continued by English settlers and colonists in various parts of the world, and it was used as the tax year for such annual taxes as land tax.

There was no income tax in 1750. Annual taxes, such as taxes on land, windows, servants, clocks and other indicators of wealth, were paid on one of the four quarter days, postponed by 11 days following the calendar reforms of 1752: 5 April, 5 July, 10 October and 5 January.

One reform brought about by the 'new style' calendar was the adoption of 1 January as the beginning of the calendar year. Thus, the Bill of Rights, passed in February, takes the date 1688, according to the old method of numbering years, and 1689, according to the method now in use.

Income tax resulted from the financial cost to Britain of the wars against Napoleon. Existing taxes had been increased with effect 'from and after' 5 April 1798, and income tax followed after one year, on 6 April 1799. So, a new tax came into effect on the first day after the next quarter day used for tax purposes, a day that had itself arisen from the need to add 11 days to Lady Day in 1752.

Lady Day still stands as a quarter day in the law of landlord and tenant, and, as there can be very few leases now in existence that were created before 1752, there is no need to add 11 days to that rent day. However, the law of taxation, and the financial year that it uses, still dances to a different music of time.

The calendar year 2000

The solar year: Winter solstice (22 December 1999); Vernal equinox (20 March 2000); Summer solstice (21 June 2000); Autumnal equinox (22 September 2000); Winter solstice (21 December 2000).

The lunar year – Dates of the new moons: 7 December 1999; 6 January 2000; 5 February 2000; 6 March 2000; 4 April 2000; 4 May 2000; 2 June 2000; 1 July 2000; 31 July 2000; 29 August 2000; 27 September 2000; 27 October 2000; 25 November 2000; 25 December 2000.

The legal quarter days: Christmas Day (25 December 1999); Lady Day (25 March 2000); Midsummer Day (24 June 2000); Michaelmas Day (29 September 2000); Christmas Day (25 December 2000).

Note: No year can include the same day twice. Hence, in law, a person attains a certain age on the day before his or her birthday (in the same way that a season ticket runs out on the day before the anniversary of its purchase). 'The law takes no account of part of a day'.

Contributed by Leslie Blake

CHAPTER 26

Denning's legal legacy

Published as 'Denning's legal legacy', 15 May 1999

We look back on the career of Britain's most admired judge, who championed the cause of the common man and courted controversy

Lord Denning's death at the age of 100 was briefly noted in this column on 20 March. No other judge could more aptly be described as a judge who was 'mainly for students'.

Alfred Thompson Denning was born in Whitchurch, Hampshire, on 23 January 1899. He died on 5 March 1999. He was appointed to the High Court in 1946 and to the Court of Appeal in 1949. He was promoted to the House of Lords as a Lord of Appeal in Ordinary in 1957. In 1962 he was appointed to high judicial office, returning to the Court of Appeal to preside over it as Master of the Rolls, a title dating back to the time when court records were stored as scrolls.

Having been appointed to the bench before 1959, he was therefore exempt from the compulsory retirement age of 75, introduced that year, which has recently been reduced to 70. He continued to serve as Master of the Rolls until he retired in 1982.

Proper words in proper places

Lord Denning was living disproof of the argument that to be understandable the law must be codified. He came from the great tradition of Victorian judges who could define a complex concept such as 'interest' as 'payment by time for the use of money', or such a mysterious thing as marriage as 'the voluntary union of one man with one woman, for life, to the exclusion of all others'.

In 1968 the Court of Appeal had to decide whether it was for the benefit of children (born and yet to be born) to vary a trust so that the money and the family could be transferred to Jersey, to save tax. Lord Denning's response was memorable and terse: 'Many a child has been ruined by being given too much. The avoidance of tax may be lawful, but it is not yet a virtue': *Re Weston's Settlements* [1968] 3 All ER 338 at p342. He then added a final comment:

> There is one thing more. I cannot help wondering how long these young people will stay in Jersey. It may be to their financial interest at present to make their home there permanently, but will they remain there once the capital gains are safely in their hands, clear of tax? They may well change their minds! Are they to be wanderers over the face of the earth, moving from this country to that, according to where they can best avoid tax? I cannot believe that to be right. Children are like trees: they grow stronger with firm roots.

A teller of tales

When Robert Louis Stephenson went to live in Samoa the local people called him 'tusitala', which means 'the teller of tales'. Lord Denning was our 'tusitala'. He had the ability to express complicated concepts in simple language, but he was not unique in this. His uniqueness lay in his understanding that man is a story-telling animal, and that he learns more from solving problems that have already arisen than from trying to predict those contingencies that may happen in the future.

The strength of the common law is the fact that it arises out of the problems and disputes of ordinary people. The weakness of codified law is that it tries to lay down, in advance, a set of propositions against which all future experience must be judged. But, like the dinosaurs in *Jurassic Park*, life always finds a way to escape from any mechanism intended to confine it. More than any other judge Lord Denning understood the educational value of case law. Continental lawyers boast that their cheap and available codes create a system where 'who may run, may read'. however, in truth, the reader of these codes comes away with a batch of platitudes and very little access to the 'preparatory works' that continental lawyers and judges habitually consult. No one ever came away from reading a judgment of Denning without enlightenment.

The law as explained by Lord Denning reads like a story, not like a dry legal text. For example, he contributed one of the most memorable openings to a judgment in an early case on nervous shock: *Hinz* v *Berry* [1970] 2 QB 40:

> It happened on April 19, 1964. It was bluebell time in Kent. Mr and Mrs Hinz had been married some 10 years, and they had four children, all aged nine and under. The youngest was one. Mrs Hinz was a remarkable

woman. In addition to her own four, she was foster-mother to four other children. To add to it, she was two months pregnant with her fifth child.

Here also is the beginning of his judgment in *Dutton* v *Bognor Regis Urban District Council* [1972] 1 QB 373:

In Bognor Regis there was years ago a rubbish tip. It was filled in and the ground made up so that it looked like the land next to it. You would not have known there had ever been a rubbish tip there.

Later in the judgment, Lord Denning referred to the fact that the local authority's building inspector had failed to detect that the builder had used inadequate foundations when building a house on that land:

[Mrs Dutton] alleged that [the] building inspector was negligent in passing the foundations. The council did not call any evidence to deny this. The building inspector had left and had gone to Australia. The trial judge found that the council's inspector was negligent. He said: 'The distinction between building a house on rock and building a house on sand has been widely known for many centuries.' The judge gave judgment in favour of Mrs Dutton. The council appeal to this court. Never before has an action of this kind been brought before our courts.

Denning and parliament

In *Dutton* v *Bognor Regis*, Lord Denning agreed with the trial judge that the local authority should pay damages to Mrs Dutton for the negligence of their building inspector. He also indicated that a claim against the builder was justified, under the tort of negligence, even though there had never been any privity of contract between Mrs Dutton and the builder. In 1990 this decision was criticised by the House of Lords: see *Murphy* v *Brentwood District Council* [1990] 2 All ER 908. In effect, the Court of Appeal was accused of judicial law-making. But Lord Denning was never afraid of such criticisms. For example, one of his dissenting judgments was once criticised by Lord Simonds (in the House of Lords) as 'a naked usurpation of the legislative function under the thin disguise of interpretation': *Magor and St Mellons Regional District Council* v *Newport Borough Corporation* [1951] 2 All ER 839 at p841.

Ahead of his time

It is arguable that Lord Denning was ahead of his time in that case, predicting a method of statutory interpretation whereby the judges would 'fill in the gaps' if it appeared that Parliament had not foreseen a particular eventuality. It is certainly the case that the House of Lords has now gone further than merely 'filling in the gaps' when a defect is found in secondary legislation, such as the Control of Advertisement Regulations: see *Porter* v *Honey* [1989] 1 EGLR 189.

Dutton v *Bognor Regis* showed Lord Denning at his best. In upholding the right of a house purchaser to sue the local authority for negligence, and, indeed, the original builder also, he was asserting the principle that the absence of legislation on a particular topic does not necessarily mean that parliament wants that topic to be left alone by the courts. In other words, just because parliament is supreme in what it chooses to do, this should not be taken to mean that it wants to assert a monopoly over law reform or to be taken as supreme in what it chooses to leave undone.

Later, in *Sparham-Souter* v *Town & Country Developments (Essex) Ltd* [1977] 1 EGLR 61, Lord Denning reflected on the fact that parliament had enacted the Defective Premises Act 1972 in an effort to give some statutory protection to the purchasers of houses, flats and other dwellings. His criticisms of the shortcomings of that Act could be usefully quoted by examination students in the law of tort to this day:

Section 6(2) of the 1972 Act says this: Any duty imposed by or enforceable by virtue of any provision of this Act is in addition to any duty a person may owe apart from that provision. I would quite agree that, in that provision, parliament did nothing to recognise *Dutton*'s case as good law. But if it be good law – and our present decision is good law – it has several advantages for the ordinary man... the Act makes the cause of action run from the time when the house was 'completed', whereas under our present decision it runs from the time when the purchaser knew, or ought to have know, of the defects. [Also] *Dutton*'s case, if correct, gives a remedy against a local authority whose inspector is negligent or turns a blind eye; but it is doubtful if the Act gives a remedy. It depends on whether he is 'taking on work ... in connection with' the provision of the house.

Lord Denning's decision in *Sparham-Souter* was that the common law right to sue for negligence, established in *Dutton*, was in addition to, and had not been replaced by, the substandard remedies given by parliament in the Defective Premises Act 1972.

Denning vindicated
The decision to pass the Latent Damage Act 1986 was seen, at the

time, as a vindication of Lord Denning's approach, because that Act gave a more realistic limitation period (for actions for negligence involving latent damage) than the short limitation period in the Defective Premises Act 1972. The 1986 Act was clearly passed on the assumption that house purchasers were entitled to sue builders and local authorities at common law, and were not obliged to sue within six years of the 'completion' of the house (under the 1972 Act).

Sad to say, when the House of Lords criticised *Dutton* in 1990 they turned a blind eye to the Latent Damage Act 1986: see *Murphy* v *Brentwood District Council*. Their lordships decided that *Dutton*, and all the cases following it, including at least one decision of the House of Lords, had been wrongly decided.

The reasoning behind this decision was twofold: (i) that it is inappropriate for the courts to be more generous than parliament – 'parliament' for these purposes was taken to be the parliament that had passed the Defective Premises Act 1972; and (ii) that latent defects in a house were not a form of damage to property, but nothing more than 'pure economic loss' – a type of claim more suitable for the law of contract than for the law of tort.

It comes hard to a purchaser of a dwelling – the place where he intends to eat, sleep and to have his being – to learn that building defects are a form of 'pure economic loss', outside the concern of the law of negligence. Not for the first time, Lord Denning was ahead of his time.

Contributed by Leslie Blake

CHAPTER 27

Delegated legislation and the Human Rights Act

Published as 'Problematic pronouns', 8 June 2002

Attaining elegance in the drafting of legal documents can be a tall order, and nothing is more troublesome than the pronoun – the little substitute for the noun

There is a respectable legal argument that President George W Bush is not (as recent reference books inevitably claim) the 43rd president of the United States, but only the 39th. This argument has got nothing to do with the fact that the presidential election of 2000 was a disputed one. Rather, it has to do with what Sir Ernest Gowers, in *The Complete Plain Words*, called 'Troubles with Pronouns': troubles, in this case, arising from the wording of the US constitution.

'The use of pronouns,' said William Cobbett, 'is to prevent the repetition of nouns, and to make speaking and writing more rapid and less encumbered with words.' The word 'it' in the last sentence of the preceding paragraph is a pronoun, avoiding the need for the writer to use the phrase 'this argument' once again, when this particular thought ought to have been (so he hopes) recently in the readers' minds.

Mr Tyler's unopened letters

Article II of the United States Constitution contains the following provision:

> In Case of the Removal of the President from Office, or of his Death Resignation, or Inability to discharge the Powers and Duties of the said Office, the Same shall devolve on the Vice President...

This provision illustrates the trouble that can arise when a pronoun seeks to serve (or appears to serve) two masters. ('If the baby does not thrive on raw milk, boil it,' is a particularly nasty example, which

Sir Ernest Gowers quotes.) In the provision Article II of the US Constitution, the phrase 'the Same' is being used as a substitute for 'it' or 'they' (it is not clear which). These words are, of course, pronouns. Thus, it is not clear whether it is the 'Powers and Duties' of the president's office that 'devolve on the Vice President' when (for example) the president dies, or whether it is the office itself.

This problem did not arise in practice until 4 April 1841, when president William H Harrison died in office, from pneumonia caught at his inauguration ceremony. His vice-president was John Tyler. Mr Tyler promptly took the oath 'to faithfully execute the Office of President,' and throughout the remaining term (to which Harrison had been elected) he insisted upon using the title 'president'. He returned, unopened, any letters addressed to him as 'acting president Tyler'. This precedent was afterwards followed by every vice-president who succeeded to the office of a deceased president, as, indeed, happened in 1850, 1865, 1881, 1901, 1923, 1945 and 1963. The legal position was not finally clarified (at least for the future) until 1967, when section 1 of the 25th Amendment to the US Constitution confirmed John Tyler's approach to the problem:

In case of the removal of the President from office or of his death or resignation, the vice-president shall become president.

John Tyler, and three of the other vice-presidents who followed his example, were not afterwards elected to the office of president in their own right. Thus, they could be viewed as acting presidents only if (as may well have been the case) the founding fathers of the US Constitution intended the phrase 'the Same' to refer only to the 'Powers and Duties of the said Office', not to the office of president itself.

Can legal draftsmen hope for elegance?

Sir Ernest Gowers, who more than any other writer is the guide and inspiration for those who contribute to the *Mainly for Students* series, recognised one exception to his campaign 'to rescue the English language from slipshod use, not least from jargon': *Chambers Biographical Dictionary*. In 'A Digression on Legal English' in chapter II of *The Complete Plain Words*, he observed that:

The drafter of authoritative texts must aim at certainty and cannot hope for elegance.

Anyone who has ever read or drafted a lease will understand the wisdom of this statement, and, in particular, of Sir Ernest's *caveat* that:

> drafting is more a science than an art; it lies in the province of mathematics than of literature, and its practice needs long apprenticeship.

Nevertheless, some legal texts do succeed in attaining elegance, especially if their purpose is to inspire respect for common law principles, older than the legislation itself (see p177). Such provisions are not intended to be literally interpreted, but to enshrine enduring values. As the American jurist Oliver Wendell Holmes put it:

> A word is not a crystal, transparent and unchanging, but the skin of a living thought.

Troubles with the Human Rights Act

Although the European Convention on Human Rights (ECHR) can make some claim to elegance, no one would suggest that the Human Rights Act 1998 (HRA) succeeds in attaining that standard, or that it seeks to do so. Rather, it has the purpose of precisely telling judges when the Convention is to prevail over UK laws and when it is not. By now, every law student probably knows that, unlike European Community law, the ECHR does *not* prevail over UK primary legislation if that legislation cannot, with the best will in the world, be read so as to be 'compliant' with that Convention. But what is the situation if *delegated legislation* (eg a statutory instrument) cannot be read so as to be compliant with the Convention?

In *R (on the application of Bono)* v *Harlow District Council* [2002] EWHC 423; [2000] NPC 46, Mr and Mrs Bono appealed against Harlow Council's decision that they were not entitled to receive housing benefit for a certain number of weeks in 1998 to 1999. Under the law as it then stood, they had to appeal to a district housing review board, which consisted of councillors of Harlow Council. The Bonos were unsuccessful, and they claimed that this drumhead right of appeal infringed their rights to a hearing by 'an independent and impartial tribunal' under Article 6 of the ECHR. The council argued that they had no alternative but to set up, and operate appeals, in this way because of provisions in the Housing Benefit (General) Regulations 1971.

Richards J held that the provisions of this statutory instrument infringed Article 6. He also held that there was no need for them to have done so, because the primary legislation under which those regulations were made did not compel such a procedure to be used.

Harlow Council argued that Article 6 could not apply if the delegated legislation was legislation 'which' could not be read or effected in a way so as to be compatible with the Convention: see section 6(2)(b) of the HRA.

In *Harlow*, the judge held that the word 'which' in section 6(2)(b) referred only to the primary legislation. If that legislation could be read compatibly with the Convention, it was no excuse for a local authority to say that they were acting in accordance with delegated legislation made under that statute. Accordingly, Harlow Council had no defence to the Bonos' claim that their rights under Article 6 had been infringed.

Whatever problems public authorities expected to face with the HRA, pronouns were not, perhaps, among them. But authorities are now placed in the unenviable position of having to second-guess the legal status of delegated legislation more than they have ever had to do before.

Texts that, through elegance, evoke common law principles (These are not intended to be interpreted narrowly or literally)

No freeman shall be taken or imprisoned, or be disseised of his freehold, or liberties, or free customs, or be outlawed, or exiled, or any other wise destroyed; nor will we not pass upon him, nor condemn him but by lawful judgement of his peers, or by the law of the land. To no man will we sell, or deny, or defer right or justice.

(Chapter 29 of the Magna Carta, 1297 version)

freedom of speech and debates or proceedings in Parliament ought not to be impeached or questioned in any court or place out of Parliament... excessive bail ought not to be required nor excessive fines imposed nor cruel and unusual punishments inflicted.

Bill of Rights, 1688

nor shall any person be subject for the same offence to be twice put in jeopardy of life or limb; nor shall be compelled in any criminal case to be a witness against himself, nor be deprived of life, liberty, or property without due process of law; nor shall private property be taken for public use, without just compensation.

5th Amendment to the US Constitution, 1791

Note: The entire US Bill of Rights – the first 10 Amendments to the Constitution consist of only 413 words.

In the determination of his civil rights and obligations or of any criminal charge against him, everyone is entitled to a fair and public hearing within a reasonable time by an independent and impartial tribunal established by law... Everyone charged with a criminal offence shall be presumed innocent until proved guilty according to law...

Article 6 of European Convention on Human Rights

Note: Section 6(2) Human Rights Act 1998 provides that it is unlawful for a public authority to act in a way which is incompatible with the ECHR unless:
(a) as a result of primary legislation the authority could not have acted differently, or
(b) 'provisions of, or made under, primary legislation **which** cannot be read ... in a way which is compatible' with the ECHR required the authority to act in this way.

Contributed by Leslie Blake

CHAPTER 28

Famous cases: *R* v *Seddon* (1912)

Published as 'No getting away with murder', 29 April 2000

There is a public house called the Buck's Head close to Camden market on the Regent's Canal. Many visitors probably use the pub, but few will know the story behind it. It is the story of a lease, and of human greed, and of the difference between a personal obligation and security for a debt.

'Security' is one of those words that translators call a 'false friend'; it means different things in different languages. The same dangers exist when a word means one thing in common parlance, but an entirely different thing in the mouth of a lawyer. To a property lawyer or financial consultant the word 'security' refers to a very particular type of safety for an investment or a debt.

A secured creditor has the benefit of a mortgage, debenture or some other legal 'charge'. He has a claim against specific, identifiable property, and he, or a receiver or trustee acting on his behalf, will be entitled to sell that property if the debtor defaults.

Conversely, other creditors of the same debtor will have no right to stop that sale or to share in the proceeds, unless there is an excess after the debt has been repaid. Even 'preferential creditors', such as the Inland Revenue, have to wait until after the secured creditors have enforced their rights against the 'security' in question.

Secured creditors only lose out if they lend more money on the security than they are able to realise when it is sold. They then become 'unsecured creditors' for the balance of their debt, ranking behind 'preferential creditors' and sharing any remaining assets with tradesmen, customers, suppliers, and all the other unsecured creditors. This is why the *Estates Gazette* often reports claims for alleged professional negligence against valuers who have advised investors about the value of land on which they are proposing to lend money.

Personal promises

One of those who misunderstood the difference between 'security' for a debt and a personal promise to pay that debt was the leasehold owner of the Buck's Head public house in 1910. This was part and parcel of a fatal misunderstanding on her part about the trustworthiness of the person to whom she assigned that lease, Frederick Henry Seddon.

Seddon was the district superintendent for the Islington district of London & Manchester Insurance Co. He lived at 63 Tollington Park, in a part of Islington that we now know as Finsbury Park. In 1910 it was declining from the previously prosperous residential district settled by wealthy merchants, most of whom had taken advantage of the railway to leave London.

Seddon worked diligently for his employers, but he also did many deals on his own account. Lord Birkett, the famous judge (and even more famous murder trial advocate) summed up the position, as it had stood in 1910, when he made a radio broadcast about Seddon's case in 1961:

Seddon was a most intelligent man but he was a miser and avaricious in the extreme. Fate so decreed that he took into his house as a lodger a sick and slightly mad old lady who was as avaricious and miserly as himself. She was also the possessor of a few thousand pounds' worth of property. When she died, only a year or so later, all her property was found to be in the hands of Seddon.

This lady was Eliza Mary Barrow. Among her property was the lease of the Buck's Head, together with the barber's shop next door. The brewers Truman Hanbury & Co held a sublease of the pub and paid Miss Barrow a rent of £105 pa. She also received £50 pa from the tenant of the barber's shop. Her own rent for the entire premises, payable to her landlord, was £20 pa. Her lease was not due to expire until 1929: there would have been no statutory right to hold over after 1929 or to apply for a new lease, as this right was not created until 1954. This future loss of rental income worried Miss Barrow, as she wished to live beyond 1929.

Miss Barrow also owned £1,600 in India stock, which, according to Seddon, brought her in a 'trifle over £1 per week'. She had £200 in a savings bank and, again according to Seddon, about £30 to £35 in gold coins, together with jewellery and other personal possessions.

Between October and December 1910 Miss Barrow transferred the lease of the Buck's Head and all her investments to Seddon in return for an annuity of £2 8s (£2.40) per week and the right to continue living rent free in Seddon's house. Her rent had been 12s (60p) per week. Miss Barrow died on 14 September 1911 aged 49.

Annuities

An annuity dies with the recipient. The fact that Miss Barrow had transferred her investments and assigned the lease of the Buck's Head to Seddon less than one year earlier meant that he was able to write to her relatives that 'she has simply left furniture, jewellery, and clothing'.

Her relatives' suspicions were aroused. These were fuelled when it afterwards transpired that Seddon had given Miss Barrow the cheapest possible funeral and had extracted a commission from the undertaker. The relatives conveyed their suspicions to the police. Miss Barrow's body was exhumed and she was found to have died from arsenical poisoning.

Seddon and his wife were charged with murder. They both took advantage of a new statutory procedure introduced by the Criminal Evidence Act 1898, by choosing to give evidence in their own defence, a procedure that had not been generally available before the 1898 Act.

In Seddon's case, this proved to be a mixed blessing, because the right to give evidence in one's own defence carries with it the obligation to be cross-examined by the prosecution.

Seddon was cross-examined by the Attorney General, Sir Rufus Isaacs, who was courteous, quiet, painstaking and relentless. His questioning wrong-footed Seddon by underlining the human dimension in the relationship of landlord and tenant (especially when they are living under the same roof):

Q: Miss Barrow lived with you from 26 July 1910 till the morning of 14 September 1911? A: Yes.
Q: Did you like her? A: Did I like her?
Q: Yes, that is the question. A: She was not a woman you could be in love with, but I deeply sympathised with her

Isaacs' cross-examination slowly revealed Seddon's character to be one so dominated by financial calculation that he would no more show 'deep sympathy' for anyone else than would an unreformed Scrooge. He boasted about the profit he had made by using Miss Barrow's property for more financially rewarding investments: see p183.

Seddon showed indignation and lack of control at one point only in his cross-examination. Isaacs put it to him that he had been seen, in his office, counting out Miss Barrow's gold coins shortly after she had died. He replied that this was 'absurd':

I am not a degenerate. That would make it out that I was a greedy, inhuman monster.

Seddon was shouting at this point and, when pressed by the prosecution, continued:

That I am a greedy, inhuman monster, or something with a very degenerate mind, to commit a vile crime such as the prosecution suggest, and then bringing the dead woman's money down and counting it in the presence of my two assistants and flouting it like that...

Edward Marjoribanks, a commentator on the trial, wrote that Seddon did himself more good by this angry outburst than by all his cool cleverness, but he subsequently ruined the effect by adding, with a sarcastic smile: 'I would have all day to count the money.' Lord Birkett's comment was succinct: this was a comment by Seddon that 'visibly tightened the coils about him'.

Verdict

The cross-examination of Seddon, carried out with an accountant's rigour, revealed a man who was capable of committing a murder for money. Mrs Seddon, however, came across as a down-trodden woman, who was capable of kindness towards her lodger. The jury therefore felt justified in convicting Seddon of murder and acquitting his wife.

Seddon was sentenced to death, which reduced the judge almost to tears because Seddon and he were both freemasons, and Seddon had sworn 'by the Great Architect of the Universe' that he was innocent.

Security for Miss Barrow's annuity would not, in itself, have prolonged her life, but she ought to have been more suspicious of someone who was offering her such a deal without any security attached.

Mean though he undoubtedly was, one must always be left wondering whether the real reason Seddon poisoned his tenant was to rid himself of 'the sick and slightly mad old lady who was as avaricious and as miserly as himself'.

Seddon was cross-examined with an accountant's rigour

Sir Rufus Isaacs' cross-examination slowly revealed a character that was perfectly capable of murder for greed

Q You had got the property on condition that you were to pay out the annuity?
A Yes, exactly, which I did.
Q You had sold the India Stock...?
A For a better investment.
Q You had bought the property in Coutts Road with that?
A Yes.
Q The fourteen houses which we have heard of ?
A Which brought me in £4 a week against her £1–£4 a week profit against her £1 per week.
Q You had got that property ?
A Yes, exactly; it was good security for her too.
Q What I am putting to you is that when she died it is clear you had no longer to pay out money to her... Certainly not; that is the basis on which an annuity is granted.
Q That I agree. It is very important, of course, in the purchase of an annuity to have security that the money would be paid?
A Yes.
Q Would you tell me what security you gave her...?
A Yes, she had 12s a week saved in rent...and I gave her an annuity certificate...
Q Where is it ?
A I do not know where the original is...
Q ... the security was the obligation on you to pay ?
A I am bound legally to pay.
Q Oh, I know, but do you mean to say you do not know the difference between security and a personal obligation on you to pay after your years of experience in business?
A I had 5 to 1 on security.
Q I am not asking about you; I have no doubt that you had sufficient security?
A I intended to carry out my obligations. I have never been known to break them...
Q I put to you a very definite question, and I want you to answer it. You were dealing with this woman who was living in your house, and who had certainly, as regards this matter, no other advice ?
A That was her fault...
Q Do you wish the jury to believe that you do not know the difference between making an obligation to pay the money and giving security for the payment of it?

A But isn't a legally drawn up certificate security on my estate?
Q Do you not know that that is only a personal obligation on you?
A I understand that it is recoverable by law.
Q Well, I have given you an opportunity of dealing with it...

Contributed by Leslie Blake

Investment

29. Specialist property investment 187
30. Introduction to investment appraisal 196
31. High yield investment/business issues 203

CHAPTER 29

Specialist property investment

Published as 'Making more of money', 7 April 2001

Want to be a property investment specialist? University can be the starting point, or relevant work experience may prompt a career move

In the investment sector, surveyors interact with a range of other professionals, and substantial funds are often at stake. Investors range from the major institutions and property companies to high-wealth individuals.

Some investors look for long-term returns and others for quick profits, depending on their investment strategy. Investment surveyors need to be fully aware of developments in capital markets, and understand the transmission mechanisms between the bond, equity and commercial property sectors. The rapid expansion of the securitisation and derivative markets, for example, has led to some innovative forms of financing and investment within property.

Institutional investors

Institutional investors such as insurance companies and pension funds generally hold multi-asset portfolios: equities/shares, bonds/gilts, cash and property.

The mix of assets is determined by the investor's liability profile and his risk and return requirements. Investors adjust their portfolios according to their expectations of relative future performance. If they believe a particular asset type will perform well, they increase its weighting, subject to overall portfolio risk. Performance is measured usually by total return, combining income and capital returns.

Insurance companies and pension funds are some of the traditional long-term owners of commercial property. The bigger insurance companies and the very large pension funds have extensive property expertise and, as well as acquiring and managing completed investment properties, are capable of undertaking major developments.

Property companies
Property companies include the major investment and development companies – some quoted on the stock market and others in private ownership, and smaller traders and dealers. Institutional investors are significant shareholders of property companies, illustrating the close inter-linkages and overlaps in the sector.

The quoted property sector includes over 100 property companies, accounting for around 1.25% of the stock market's total value. Many have a value, or 'market capitalisation', of less than £100m.

The larger companies such as Land Securities, British Land and Slough Estates have been established for some time, but many of the traders and dealers are newer ventures, funding their operations extensively by bank finance.

Other investors
Overseas buyers have had a greater influence on the UK market since the late 1980s, when they began making substantial purchases, concentrating on prime central London sites. This first wave of Japanese, Scandinavian and American investors suffered badly in the crash that followed, and withdrew from the market. They have since been replaced by German open-ended funds and European investors. The Americans have, however, recently returned.

Wealthy UK and overseas private individuals are also active, buying some of the larger interests, as well as the more usual smaller auction lots. The distinction between the individual and the company is blurred, with many entrepreneurs and investors operating through a company vehicle. Charities are also significant investors in property. Overall, about 45%, by value, of the UK's commercial property is held by investors.

Property as an investment
Property is held as an investment because of its current rental income, expected rental growth, potential for capital gains and diversification benefits within a portfolio, as well as providing a hedge against inflation in certain economic conditions.

The income and capital elements create an asset which can be financed, and also allow property to be valued and analysed in a similar way to other investments. Income returns are relatively stable, and total returns generally lie between those from equities and gilts. On the downside, property is relatively illiquid, suffering also from relatively high acquisition and management costs.

The Office for National Statistics estimates the total value of UK property at £250bn, separated into commercial buildings, industrial buildings, residential, agricultural/forestry, and other buildings. Property in an investment context relates exclusively to commercial property, including offices, retail, warehouses and industrial, all of which account for around 10% of the total net wealth of the UK economy. Residential property, at 41% of net wealth and worth over twice as much as all other categories of property, is not part of the mainstream property investment market – although attitudes to it as an investment are changing.

Development options

An example of institutional investors undertaking development can be seen at Green Park, south of Reading. In 1997, after a decade of site assembly and the finalising of planning consent for a 47.8ha (118-acre) office park, Prudential Life Fund retained the risk of being sole developer of the 165,360m^2 (1.78m sq ft) of lettable space.

The development appraisal in 1997 indicated market rents of about £258 per m^2 (£24 per sq ft), a yield of 7% and a development period of 12 years. By 2000, rental levels in the area were up to £301 per m^2 (£28 per sq ft) – some £50m per year, improving by nearly 17% – and yields had dropped to 6.25% (improving by nearly 11%). All the lettable space had been put under option or offer to tenants earlier than envisaged, with Cisco committing to 1.26m sq ft in the biggest-ever deal outside London.

End value was improved by £250m, while the shorter than expected development period also reduced interest charges.

One reason for investors accepting the increased risk of development is to achieve higher returns. Indeed, property's relative long term under-performance against other assets accounts partly for the decline in institutional investors' exposure to the sector.

Investment strategies

The investment approach adopted by institutional investors may be very different to that of smaller property companies.

A prime institutional grade investment may, for example, be producing a full market rent from a 'blue chip' covenant on a long unexpired lease term. This may provide little, if any, scope to add value, other than at the next rent review, based largely on general market changes.

In other situations, value can be added by improving a property's condition and/or its leasing/investment profile. Where a property is purchased having imminent lease expiries or tenant's break clauses, for example, the uncertainty as to which tenants will renew and which will vacate will be reflected in the price paid, providing considerable scope for value to be added through letting and management initiatives.

Another strategy could be to negotiate a lease surrender with a tenant in order to refurbish and relet the space at a higher rent, and perhaps securing a better tenant on improved terms, thus also reducing the yield and increasing capital/investment value. Innovative landlords are increasingly adding value from their existing tenant base by supplying certain services and providing flexible lease formats.

The role of the surveyor

Because there is no central market for property and because no two properties are alike, the surveyor has an important function in advising on investment characteristics and in matching buyers and sellers. The specialist investment surveyor tends to be a general practice commercial property surveyor whose agency work typically includes:

Investment appraisal and acquisition – evaluating the merits of an investment opportunity, and advising clients, having regard to their specific investment objectives.

A purchase report and valuation is prepared for the client, and the transaction negotiated through to completion, working closely with the lawyers. The acquisition process could include identifying the tenant's occupational needs, accurate cost planning, gathering an in-depth knowledge of local planning policy and market conditions, and carefully evaluating exit values.

A detailed strategy will be supported by precise cash flows, demonstrating both the cash returns and internal rates of return. A good agent will also pro-actively put deals together, rather than merely react to clients' instructions.

Disposal – assessing the most effective means of disposal in order to achieve best value.

A marketing report is prepared for the client, detailing price, timescales for disposal and marketing strategy. A detailed analysis is made of the bids received, including the price, the bidders' profiles, their ability to raise finance and other any risks of non-performance.

Recommendations are made to the client, and the transaction followed through to completion. Most major property transactions are negotiated by private treaty, but auctions may be used for secondary and tertiary property and for smaller lots. Some properties are sold off-market to specifically targeted investors.

Asset/portfolio advice – reviewing property portfolios and providing strategic investment advice having regard to local and national investment market conditions, and research in respect of the performance of specific markets.

The investment agent must have a good understanding of landlord and tenant issues to take account of how lease terms, and the ability to secure growth through rent reviews can affect rental returns and investment value. It is essential that the agent can price property correctly.

Agents develop a strong knowledge of market trends and property values through being involved in a large number of transactions. This is one of their strongest assets, given the lack of a central and visible market for property.

Similar work is undertaken by specialist investment surveyors employed on an in-house basis with institutional investors or property companies, for example.

Investment-related work undertaken by surveyors in other areas includes:

Lettings – securing tenants who help to optimise the investment profile and value of the property.

Particular regard will be given to the financial standing, or 'covenant strength', of the tenant, and to the length of lease achievable. For retail investments, tenant mix may be especially important.

Development advice – as developments will become standing investments once complete and fully let.

Landlord and tenant work – undertaking rent reviews and lease renewals, and advising on lettings, assignments, sublettings, surrender and renewal transactions, and other landlord and tenant issues such as dilapidations liability and break clauses.

Management – dealing with service charge management, rent collection, facilities management and buildings maintenance.

Valuation – for company accounts, loan security, takeovers, prospectuses etc, as well as in connection with acquisition, disposal and portfolio management.

Legal and accountancy

A lawyer specialising in commercial property has a good understanding of the relevant law, ensuring that the client's objectives are met, working closely with other professional advisers, and advising on the consequences of any proposed action – including factors which could impact on investment value.

On an acquisition, an investment property must have good title, free from adverse matters such as covenants restricting its use or compulsory purchase orders. The lawyer also ensures that the terms contained in leases accurately reflect the information on which the client has made his bid. Leases should provide for full recovery of service charge costs, and contain adequate provisions to deal with rent default or tenants' breach of any other covenants.

On existing properties, the lawyer drafts and negotiates leases, and advises on management issues. Landlord and tenant law is a minefield for the unwary – for example, a seemingly simple consent by the landlord allowing the tenant to carry out alterations may result in a guarantor being released from their liabilities unless the guarantor is joined as a party to a formal licence.

The commercial property lawyer works with other specialist lawyers, advising on corporate, tax, planning, environmental, construction and litigation issues.

The larger City firms of solicitors also take a lead role in setting up new forms of property ownership, and work with merchant banks and accountants on the forms of financial engineering associated with property, such as structured finance securitisation, private finance initiatives and special purpose vehicles.

Accountancy advice will be required in connection with company accounts, prospectuses and takeover documents. Accountants also advise on the tax implications of property investment and development, as well as structuring property vehicles such as limited partnerships, and providing tax planning advice.

Financing

Investors and property companies often need to raise finance. This not only enables additional funds to the investor's own equity to be utilised but can also help higher total returns to be made (with a profit margin being earned on debt as well as equity). An increased proportion of debt to equity, known as 'gearing', does, however, bring higher risk.

Corporate finance is available to those owning or undertaking a venture, and is structured as a corporate investment or debt. Project finance is available on a specific project and is structured as a project investment or debt.

Debt finance is structured as a loan, secured by way of a charge over the property, which may be supported by a corporate or personal guarantee. The lender of debt finance is entitled to receive interest on the loan, and the right to be repaid capital at preset intervals. Debt finance involves ownership rights only where the borrower defaults, and repossession is required to recover any sums owing.

Investment/equity finance provides the lender with partial ownership, including the right to income and capital growth, but sharing the related risks.

The debt providers for UK property investment comprise mainly UK and foreign banks, building societies and life insurance companies. The equity providers are mainly life insurance companies, pension funds, venture capital funds and participants in the global capital markets.

In project finance, a distinction needs to be made between lenders who provide 'senior debt' (the lowest risk part of the loan), and those who take more risk in return for higher interest rates and profit share (through 'mezzanine finance'). Mezzanine financing requires more property expertise than senior debt lending, and is undertaken by merchant banks, some senior banks and a few specialist lenders.

The primary concern of banks providing senior debt for investment property is the certainty of loan and interest repayments. The maximum amount a bank will lend is determined by the 'loan to value' ratio (LTV). An initial valuation enables the lender to satisfy itself that there is sufficient security in the asset to repay the loan. Account should also be taken of obsolescence, which erodes asset value over the term of the loan (notwithstanding any general growth in property market values).

The LTV ratio does not operate in isolation because interest cover, which is the extent to which rental income on the property covers interest on the loan, usually influences the amount of the loan. These are relatively traditional ratios in debt financing, and more sophisticated measures of risk analysis are increasingly being used.

Banks will make an assessment of the borrower and of the property to determine their lending basis. They need to know to whom their money is being lent, and the purpose of the loan. Is it wanted to acquire a new property or to refinance an existing loan? They will also seek to establish a relationship with the borrower. For loans on secondary and/or actively managed interests, they will need to be satisfied that the borrower has the expertise and experience to deliver the enhanced product.

Bank lending without recourse to the borrower or its parent company is not uncommon. Loans are often structured via single asset/special purpose vehicle companies, whereby the property forms the sole asset of the borrowing company. Here, because the form of security for the loan is paramount, lenders will give increased weight to the assessment of the property.

More overseas participants are now seeking exposure to the risks and rewards of an expanding finance market for UK property. And some are prepared to experiment with new financial structures in a changing environment.

Fund management

The role of the property fund manager (PFM) in a property investment management organisation is to organise the structure and assets of the property fund or portfolio, and optimise potential returns against a particular benchmark, and within a defined risk tolerance agreed with the client.

PFMs will typically have a property investment or asset management background. They will usually have a broad understanding of a wide range of investment issues (rather than specialist knowledge in a particular area), and need to have strengths in financial analysis and interpretation.

The equity analyst is another player in the investment market, but will usually have a financial background. He will rarely be a qualified surveyor.

Research

The major investors and their advisers have research departments who identify trends in the occupier and investment markets, and forecast expected future performance in sub-markets.

Some publish indices of past performance and stock figures on supply and demand of different types of property in different regions. There are also specialist organisations who provide independent research and advice on most aspects of property investment and development.

Investment Property Forum

The Investment Property Forum (IPF) was established 11 years ago as an ideas and information exchange group for investment surveyors, and has developed into an influential force for the property investment industry.

The forum has an active educational role, which includes its Advanced Education Programme. This is jointly delivered by City University Business School and Cambridge International Land Institute, mainly to surveyors working in practice but also to postgraduate students. A series of two four-day modules can be taken individually or as a complete programme, leading to the Investment Property Forum Diploma. The seven modules, which illustrate the skills required by the property investment specialist, are: Accounting and Taxation for Property Investors, Introduction to Portfolio Management, Financial Instruments and Investment Markets, Property as an Asset Class, Advanced Property Investment Appraisal, Advanced Property Finance and Advanced Portfolio Management.

The IPF also co-ordinates CPD lectures and workshop sessions ranging from fundamental investment theory to complex current issues. It also has an active research programme.

As a non-profit-making organisation, the IPF currently has around 1,300 members, including investment surveyors, fund managers, academics, bankers, lawyers, actuaries and related professionals. Historically, only senior professionals have joined, but the IPF is keen to recruit younger members with at least three years' experience in property investment.

Automatic membership is available to those who have completed either an MSc in Property Investment at City University, an RICS Diploma in Property Investment at the College of Estate Management or all seven modules of the IPF's Advanced Education Programme.

Contributed by Investment Property Forum and Austen Imber

CHAPTER 30

Investment appraisal

Published as 'How much will I make', 10 August 2002

Finding out how much a property is worth, and how much it is likely to earn, is the essence of investment appraisal. Here we look at the basics

This introduction to investment appraisal for first and second year university students outlines the basic workings of net present value and internal rate of return. It assumes that students are familiar with investment valuation fundamentals, including the use of years' purchase (YP) and present value (PV), as outlined in *Mainly for Students*, Introduction to Investment Valuation, 18 September 1999, p164 (and Chapter 65).

The specific investor

Investment appraisal involves the concept of 'worth', in addition to the more familiar terms 'price' and 'market value'.

Price is sale price achieved for a property. Market value (MV), also known as open market value (OMV), is an estimate of the price that should be achieved if the property were exposed to the market. This is established by undertaking a 'valuation'.

Worth or 'investment worth' is the value to an individual investor, reflecting factors including unique circumstances, perceptions, investment objectives/strategy, financial and tax status, the ability to secure funding, portfolio issues, alternative investment opportunities and required rates of return. This is established by undertaking an 'appraisal', or 'investment appraisal', known also as a 'calculation of worth'.

An investment appraisal is most commonly undertaken to establish whether a new investment should be purchased, and what price the individual investor is prepared to pay. Sometimes this may be considerably less than the asking price, indicating that other investors' individual circumstances are more suited to the property. In other situations, such as where an investor has existing properties nearby, the property may still represent a good acquisition if having to be purchased some way above the asking price. Even so, the investor will still look to negotiate a purchase as cheaply as possible.

Rate of return

Each investor has a required 'rate of return' from a particular investment. This is known as the 'target rate', 'hurdle rate' or 'discount rate'. In some cases, all of an investor's projects/properties will have to secure a minimum rate of return whereas, in other cases, acquisition criteria may be more flexible, depending on the overall qualities of the investment and also wider business issues.

Market yields

It is important to note at this stage that a market yield, such as 6% from a £100,000 property producing a market rent of £6,000 pa, is not a rate of return. Market, all risks, equivalent and certain other yields are essentially means of comparison of income yielded by an investment, whereas the rate of return considered in investment appraisal is the total return over the life of the investment. This combines rental income and increases – or decreases – in capital value, expressed on an annualised percentage basis.

NPV and IRR

The principal types of investment appraisal studied at this level are net present value (NPV) and internal rate of return (IRR).

Net present value

If, for example, an investor has the opportunity to invest £10,000 now to secure an income over three years of £3,000 (year 1), £4,000 (year 2), and £5,000 (year 3), and has a target rate of return of 8%, the viability of the investment can be considered by the use of a discounted cash flow table as shown in Table 1.

Internal rate of return

The IRR is the rate at which the present value of the cash inflows equals the present value of the original outlay and, therefore, the point at which NPV = £nil (and is the total return). In the above

1. Non-property investment
Establishing the rate of return

Year	Cash flow	PV £1 at 8%	NPV
0		1	**(10,000)**
1	3,000	0.926	2,778
2	4,000	0.857	3,428
3	5,000	0.794	3,970
			10,176
			NPV + £176

- The investment is viable because the NPV is positive at £176.
- The investor would be prepared to pay up to £10,176 to secure the required return of 8% – so although available at £10,000, the investment is 'worth' £10,176 to this specific investor.
- As the NPV is in excess of £nil, the rate of return on the investment of £10,000 must be greater than 8%. See main text.

example, had the NPV been £nil, the investor's return on the capital outlay of £10,000 would have been exactly 8% (the target rate of return).

Although computerised methods are available, students are usually required to calculate the IRR by trial and error. A trial target rate of 9% as well as 8% could be applied to the cash flow table above to produce NPVs of +£176 (8%) and -£21 (9%) respectively. The IRR can be calculated by apportioning the difference between the two trial rates: 8% + 176 ÷ (176 + 21) = 8.934, say 8.9%. Alternatively, the IRR could be calculated by linear interpolation.

IRR on property investments

The income flow produced from property is potentially more complex than the cash flow evaluated above, with account usually having to be taken of the potential for growth in both rental values and capital values.

It may, for example, be necessary to calculate the IRR on a property investment available at £100,000 which produces a rent passing of £5,000 pa during a five-year term, followed by a reversion to a market rent of £7,500.

2. Property investment
Calculating the NPV

Year	Cash flow	YP 6.75%	PV 6.75%	Net present value
0				**(100,000)**
1–5	5,000	4.128		20,640
6–perp	7,500	14.815	0.721	80,112
				100,752
				NPV + £752

The IRR can be calculated from tables, but requires preliminary calculations to be undertaken to find the 'initial yield' and the 'rental factor'. The initial yield = rent passing (£5,000) ÷ price (£100,000) = 5%. The rental factor = market rental value (£7,500) ÷ rent passing (£5,000) = 1.5.

No expectation of rental growth

On the basis that there is no expectation of rental growth, and the market rent as well as the rent passing is fixed, reference can be made to 'internal rate of return – with no projected rental growth' tables in Parry's Valuation and Investment Tables. For 'initial yield 5%', 'rental factor 1.5', 'five years to review/reversion', the IRR is listed at 6.8%. The same results could have been obtained by using trial rates in a cash flow table, such as above, for a trial rate of 6.75%. A slightly higher trial rate would produce the NPV of £nil. This is, in fact, 6.8% (which also has been derived from tables).

Expectation of rental growth

On the basis that rental growth is expected up to the reversion, reference is made to 'internal rate of return – reflecting projected growth in full rental value to next review/ reversion' tables. If, say, 5% pa growth is expected, the 5% initial yield, 1.5% rental factor and five-year term to reversion are the same, and the internal rate of return is 8.1%.

As expected, the internal rate of return from an investment with growth potential (8.1%) is greater than the internal rate of return from an investment producing a fixed return (6.8%).

3. Accounting for rental and capital growth
Raising the rate of return

Year	Rent	Am £1 5%	Inflated rent	YP 11%	PV 11%	NPV
0						(100,000)
1–5	5,000		5,000	3.696		18,480
6–10	7,500	1.276	9,570	3.696	0.593	20,975
11–15	7,500	1.629	12,218	3.696	0.352	15,896
16–perp	7,500	2.079	15,593	12.5 (8%)	0.209	40,736
						96,087
					NPV	−£3,913

The IRR could also be calculated by trial/target rates in a cash flow table similar to table 2, with the market rent of £7,500 at year six being uplifted at 5% pa over five years (by amount £1, five years at 5% = 1.276) to £9,750 – such methodology being illustrated in the above example.

In the previous example, growth was accounted for up to the reversion and not into perpetuity, as would be the case with most property investments. Although arguably unrealistic, students are required to go through examples such as the above in order to progressively build an understanding.

Examples would also be studied where the period to the next rent review/reversion would be, say, three years, rather than five, thus highlighting the effect of differently profiled investments on rates of return. The effect of 'quarterly in advance' tables would also be considered (the calculations in this article being on the annually in arrears basis).

In order to calculate the IRR on the basis that rental growth is realised beyond the reversion, the market rent could continue to be uplifted for each successive five-year period (assuming rent reviews are five yearly). In using a trial rate of 11%, in the table above, the NPV for 11% is −£3,913. For 10%, the NPV is +£5,895. The IRR is calculated at 10.6% as per the same methodology in the first non-property IRR illustration (Table 1).

The IRR could also be determined more precisely by computer calculation (noting the range of valuation/appraisal software available).

An 8% yield, known here as an 'exit yield', appears in the appraisal as the property is assumed to be sold after 15 years – at the market yield of 8% – reflecting the potential for income and capital growth in the normal way (noting that this element of the appraisal is market based, as the property is being sold on the open market).

The difference between the IRRs calculated above demonstrates the need to accurately account for the potential for rental growth within investment appraisals and investment valuations.

Investment decisions

Having established the IRR, the decision to invest will have regard to the cost of capital, in terms of the interest return available on cash holdings, the cost of borrowing and/or the opportunity cost of capital (the return available on the next-best investment).

The cash flows adopted to establish the IRR are assumed to represent guaranteed income. Uncertainty, risk and any other characteristics of the investment are accounted for when the IRR is being compared to the cost of capital and to the returns available on other investments. Investors may, for example, be exposed to an increase in interest rates, to the projected level of income not materialising (because of tenant default or rental voids, for example) and to the projected rate of growth being too optimistic – risks which may mean that the project is not considered viable (despite the IRR exceeding the cost of finance). Because of such risks, investors consequently require a relatively higher rate of return.

The further that an investment moves away from being a guaranteed cash flow, and the more diverse the range of investment opportunities that are available, the greater is the need for intuitive judgments. IRR analysis may not, therefore, always be an ideal appraisal tool. As demonstrated above, the IRR is particularly sensitive to assumptions made in respect of the potential for rental growth.

Students will also have to consider the factors which affect the decision to invest in one of a number, or 'mutually exclusive' projects, as well as being able to evaluate the merits and criticism of NPV and IRR generally. As investors will give regard to the balance of a portfolio and the extent to which risk is diversified, portfolio and risk analysis techniques will also be covered. At a more advanced level, investment appraisal may, for example, have to account for situations where investments are financed partly from debt and partly from equity, and/or where different cash flows are financed at different rates.

Contributed by David James and Austen Imber

CHAPTER 31

High yield investment/business issues

Published as 'Profiting from property', 17 November 2001

Investment returns underpin property values, but richer rewards than valuation practice can imply are available – especially to smaller investors

If an institutional investor, such as a pension fund, has cash to invest, and acquires a prime investment property for £10m, producing a market rent of £600,000 pa, the yield is 6% (£600,000 divided by £10m).

Other types of investor, in order to acquire more properties and/or higher-value interests than are possible from committing only their own funds, or 'equity', seek finance. If 75% of the market value of a property is borrowed (known as the 'loan-to-value ratio' or 'LTV') £250,000 equity could, for example, be utilised to acquire a single tenant high street retail investment for £1m. If this produces a market rent of £80,000, the yield, as analysed by the valuer as comparable evidence, is 8% (£80,000 divided by £1m). The profitability to the investor, however, if a rate of interest of 6.5% is paid on the loan/debt element, is shown on page 208.

In securing a 1.5% profit on the debt element in addition to the 8% on the equity element, the overall return on equity is increased by more than 50% from 8% to 12.5%.

Higher yielding investments

The 8% retail investment may provide relatively secure income, but other investors seek higher-yielding interests which include the scope to enhance returns through active management – including new lettings and also rent reviews and lease renewals typically among a number of different tenants.

A property investment company acquiring mainly industrial investments may, for example, secure finance at 7% on an LTV of 65%, and acquire an industrial estate for £2m, producing a market rental of £240,000. The market yield is 12% (£240,000 divided by

£2m), but the return on the equity element is just over 21% (£700,000 equity earning 12% + £1.3m debt earning 5% profit (12% – 7%) = £149,000 divided by £700,000).

Also active in the property market are much smaller investors, often operating on a local or regional basis, and more easily able to exploit special situations as a result.

For example, an investor acquiring mainly residential interests, letting usually to students and young professionals, may secure a yield of 20% or more on some properties – particularly those acquired, and priced, as a home and then let on a multi-unit, room by room, basis, either as a single letting to a group of students, or as individual studio or one-bedroom type lettings following conversion/refurbishment. A 20% yield, LTV ratio of 75% and finance cost of 8%, produces a rental return on equity of 56% pa.

To further illustrate the returns available, a residential property worth £100,000 may be acquired for, say, £95,000, with vacant possession, because the buyer is paying cash and completing quickly. There is an immediate £5,000 capital gain, but also, once let, an investment profile is created which may further increase value above the vacant possession basis – to, say, £115,000.

It is this investment valuation figure against which finance may be then raised – 75% of which is £86,250, leaving the investor's equity contribution at £8,750. If a rental of £20,000 (20% of the initial £100,000 market value) is secured, the return on equity is 150% pa (£20,000 less £6,900 (8% interest on £86,250) = £13,100 divided by £8,750).

The above examples may appear simplistic and do not yet take account of other aspects, but there can be both costs which reduce profitability, and factors which actually enhance profitability further.

Legal fees, stamp duty (for acquisitions above £60,000), and a proportion of the investor's operating costs/professional fees will be incurred on acquisitions. Some initial refurbishment/conversion expenditure may be required, with planning consent sometimes having to be obtained.

Management will be relatively intensive for investments able to secure returns of 20% or more, and there may also be rental voids, and ongoing repair and maintenance expenditure.

Not every property in the portfolio will secure yields of 20% plus, otherwise the investor could be over-exposed to a particular property type and sub-market, such as the student sector.

Obtaining funding

In the above residential example, cash may have been required initially to secure such favourable acquisition terms, and mortgaged soon after. Some commercial lenders will not, however, deal in such small amounts, and require investors to assemble a number of properties which can be mortgaged as a package. Not all lenders will accept a LTV ratio as high as 75% (although some will accept more). Lenders' arrangement fees, valuation fees and further legal and management fees may also be incurred.

Funding may be harder to obtain for private individuals and smaller companies, although it becomes easier as a track record develops, and expansion takes place. Because an equity element is always required for acquisitions, the availability of funds, and the commitment of lenders, are therefore essential to property investment. The availability of bridging finance from specialist lenders or director's/private investor's own resources can be invaluable (enabling properties to effectively be acquired for cash, and subsequently mortgaged). For private investors, buy-to-let finance can be helpful initially, and be cheaper than commercial finance, but lenders may impose restrictions on the number of properties that can be acquired, and also on the type of lettings undertaken, including the multi-occupational situations that can command particularly high yields.

Further sources of value

Increases in rental values over time add to profits which can be ploughed back into the business for further acquisitions. Increases in capital values will usually facilitate re-mortgaging, thus raising further finance, but will sometimes enable sales to take place at relatively low yields, releasing equity that can be put to better-yielding, higher-profit opportunities (after allowing for capital gains tax, fees etc.). Indeed, the opportunity to trade on a property once an investment profile has been created, and a capital increase achieved, is another source of profitability – noting how such capital gains can be achieved relatively early after acquisition, and that the funds realised from the sale can be used to repeat the exercise.

High yields provide a greater cushion against adverse interest rate movements and other market factors, especially in multi-let situations and in terms of an overall portfolio. Smaller investors may, however, be more exposed to localised variations in supply and demand. To further reduce risk, finance could be secured at a fixed rate of interest, rather than at a variable rate, and a lower LTV may also be wise. Loans can be taken on an interest-only basis – cash flow otherwise being impeded by the repayment of the loan element.

Note that whereas commercial investment property values are determined mainly by rent and yield, with rental increases and other improvements to the investment profile sometimes producing substantial increases in capital value, residential investment property values are usually influenced strongly by vacant possession values. This limits the extent to which the investment valuation may exceed the vacant possession valuation for residential property, but for the type of residential investment situation above, allows relatively high yields to be maintained, which help protect against risk and generate profits for expansion.

Building businesses

To build a property investment business, an effective overall strategy is essential. Consideration must always be given to the effect of individual acquisitions on the whole portfolio. A suitable balance may be required between acquisitions providing relatively immediate income and those requiring more extensive repair/refurbishment, and/or requiring tenants to be found. This enables income-generating properties to cover interest repayments, refurbishment/repair costs and other expenses on other properties. Regard must also be given to factors such as the need to keep in-house contractors in work, and the need to trade in a way that ensures year-end accounts present a favourable view to backers.

The minimisation of tax liability, and indeed all cost savings, are effectively a further source of funding that helps optimise long-term profitability. Although improvement expenditure has to be capitalised to the company's balance sheet as fixed assets, repair/reinstatement expenditure, including that for properties acquired in disrepair, can generally be set against profits, thus reducing income/corporation tax liability – as well as still helping increase capital value to facilitate re-mortgaging.

Another technique is to make a reasonable apportionment of the purchase price between the property itself and its fixtures and fittings. Firstly, fixtures and fittings can be depreciated against profits, and, secondly, the acquisition price of the property itself, compared to mortgage valuation, can demonstrate a particularly prudent acquisition strategy to lenders and others (noting that the cost of acquisition may be carried in a 'for management purposes only' section of the company's accounts alongside the year-end valuations for each property).

Both of the above approaches may effectively create a higher ultimate liability for capital gains tax on the sale of the property, but they are still likely to be beneficial, especially to the longer-term investor who may also gain from certain allowances and reliefs.

As a company expands, in-house letting and management functions become more efficient. In a localised market, a reputation as a good landlord helps create a brand which sees tenants introducing other tenants (minimising reliance on advertising), low tenant turnover and minimal voids. The above illustration concerned residential property, but the investor may also have an exposure to commercial property, including secondary shops with flats above, or other mixed use interests.

The local investor may also develop bolt-on businesses such as a small building firm, property maintenance company or letting agency, which add to profitability – provided they do not distract focus from the core property investment function of the business, and also that they generate funds for the investment side, as opposed to utilising its capital which could be more profitably spent on property investment.

From valuer to business consultant

This feature demonstrates the opportunities available to surveyors with wider business skills in advising or managing property companies. In addition to underlying property expertise, a broad working knowledge is required of areas such as economics, accountancy, finance, taxation, company law, business management, growth strategies, equity and other financial markets, marketing and also people management.

Surveyors also advise non-property businesses in relation to the strategic role that property can play from both an operational and corporate perspective. Business skills are also applied in areas such as corporate and personal insolvency, LPA receivership (which involves taking responsibility for property management, letting, disposal etc in distress situations) and turnaround management (which involves reversing the fortunes of struggling companies).

Management consultancy is sometimes seen as the work undertaken by the larger practices for the corporate sector, but the subject really incorporates the scope for all surveyors to provide a wider range of business consultancy services to smaller businesses.

The following illustrations were also provided in the article.

The benefit of borrowing: Raising the return on equity

Equity element
£250,000 at 8% return £20,000

Debt element
£750,000 at 8% return £60,000
less £750,000 at 6.5% interest £48,750 £11,250

£31,250

£31,250/£250,000 = 12.5% return on equity

The use of debt together with equity is known as 'gearing' (or sometimes 'leverage'). Although this can bring increased returns, especially in favourable property market and economic conditions, it creates increased risk. Consider, for example, the 8% retail property mentioned above, securing a 12.5% return on equity with finance at 6.5% on an LTV of 75%. If interest rates rise by 1/2% to 7% or £70,000 pa, and rental income falls from £80,000 pa to £70,000 pa as a tenant departs, assuming now that the property was multi-let, the investment only breaks even. If the position worsens, the investor has to find funds from elsewhere to meet interest repayments – and is in a particularly precarious position in the case of a single tenant who goes bust or vacates at lease expiry.

The tighter the margins between the cost of finance and the rate of rental return, and the higher the debt element/gearing, the greater will be the risk – subject, of course, to the range of factors influencing returns and risk to property investment generally, and to the solvency of investors/property companies.

Another effect of gearing is that falls in capital value create larger losses. If, for example, rental income remains at £80,000 but market yields rise 1% from 8% to 9%, capital value falls from £1m to £888,888, representing a loss of nearly 50% on the initial equity commitment of £250,000.

High gearing brings pitfalls for the unwary. Problems could arise, for example, when a smaller investor expands beyond a strong equity and cash position, and the change in gearing sees interest repayments and related financing costs, as well as all other expenditure, quickly drain cash and profitability. All businesses should evaluate worst-case scenarios, including the effects, for example, of changes in interest rates, economic and property market fortunes, planning policy, legislation and local factors influencing supply and demand. Cashflow difficulties, rather than profitability, can be the downfall of small businesses who over-trade. Low gearing, and too much new equity/cash, on the other hand, can dilute earnings for existing shareholders.

Acquisition, letting, financing

As an illustration of the returns available in certain situations, examples of acquisitions made by a small West Midlands-based investment company in a mid-market residential area are as follows:

Investment: Mixed retail/residential property, acquired November 1999, cash, £38,000, vacant possession.

Refurbishment: Cost £4,000 (total cost therefore £42,000).

Letting: Shop £4,300 pa, first-floor flat £5,000, rear storage £1,500, total £10,800 (investment profile created).

Mortgage valuation: April 2000, £55,000.

Investment analysis: Approximately 25% gross rental return on £42,000 cost, and 20% gross return on £55,000 valuation.

Funding: 70% LTV (£38,500 debt out of £55,000).

Net equity input: £3,500 (after mortgaging). Add, say, £1,000 for acquisition/mortgaging fees = £4,500.

Rental return: At 8% interest, repayment on £38,500, gross rental return on initial equity = £10,800 rent less £3,080 interest = £7,720 divided by £4,500 = approximately 170% per annum. Allow, say, 20% for external repairs, management and buildings insurance = net annual return on net equity input of approximately 125%.

Capital returns: £13,000 – 30% on acquisition cost, created by physical improvements, and creation of investment profile and modest market increase.

The key features here were the unattractiveness to the market at large because of the poor physical appearance of the property, the ability to optimise the potential of three areas of the property (which owner-occupiers especially would be unlikely to achieve) and the finding of a good commercial tenant (which is not always easy within secondary retail parades). Although percentage returns are illustrated above, including a 125% pa rental return on net equity input (including management costs, excluding voids, if any), property as an investment has really become a product and an enterprise.

VP-related residential – creating profits for growth

Investment: Two vacant residential properties, acquired January 1995 for £100,000

Refurbishment/repair cost: £10,000.

Income: Multi-let, net £52,000 pa.

Re-mortgaging: April 2000, £175,000.

Valuation pegged to vacant possession. 30% yield on valuation, 100% on equity. Profits facilitating new acquisitions.

Yield-driven commercial – creating equity for growth
Investment: Vacant retail, offices, residential, acquired May 1998 for £90,000.
Refurbishment/repair cost: £30,000.
Income: Cafe, shop, workshop and student lettings, net rental income £50,000 pa.
Re-mortgaging: April 2000, £325,000. £289,000 new equity; £950,000 new acquisitions facilitated (70% LTV).

Contributed by Austen Imber

Landlord and Tenant/ Estate Management

32. Introduction to Landlord and Tenant 213
33. Lease renewal 223
34. Scottish/English Landlord and Tenant 231
35. Alienation 237
36. Dispute resolution – rent review. 247
37. Dispute resolution – other Landlord and Tenant. 255
38. Dilapidations (part 1) 264
39. Dilapidations (part 2) 272
40. Remedies for rent default 279
41. Peaceful re-entry 288
42. Forfeiture and surrender of leases 293
43. Service charge disputes 299

CHAPTER 32

Introduction to Landlord and Tenant

Published as 'Tenants, reviews and rent', 20 October 2001

An understanding of landlord and tenant is not a requirement of management surveyors alone. This introduction discusses the basics

Landlord and tenant work broadly comprises rent reviews and lease renewals, together, for example, with assignments and sublettings, user provisions and repair/dilapidations. A basic introduction is provided here mainly for students, but also for property support staff who may become involved in the more straightforward case work traditionally undertaken by the surveyor.

Leases, tenancies and licences – types of agreement for landlords and tenants

The term 'lease' is used to denote the contract by which a tenant holds its 'leasehold' interest in property. The terms 'lease' and 'tenancy' are often used interchangeably. Leases for more than three years must be granted by deed. Leases for lesser periods, where the tenant takes immediate possession and pays a full open market for the property, and periodic tenancies, need not comply with this requirement.

The traditional 'institutional lease' favoured by institutional investors was 25 years, but leases of 10 or 15 years are increasingly common, owing mainly to changes in economic and property market conditions and developments in landlord and tenant and other legislation.

A commercial periodic tenancy will continue indefinitely until determined by one of the parties, typically at six months' notice expiring at any time. This is more commonly granted by local authorities or other large in-house property teams, but also smaller landlords, for properties at the lower end of the market where tenants require flexible terms.

A 'contracted out' lease/tenancy is one in which the parties exclude the security of tenure protection afforded by the Landlord and Tenant Act 1954. At lease expiry, the landlord may choose to grant the tenant a further lease without having to undergo the statutory lease renewal process – but noting that a tenant's absence of rights may place them in a precarious position, owing to the negotiating strength that therefore rests with the landlord being able to require them to vacate.

Licences are granted in respect of rights, for example, to park a vehicle, obtain access or use a storage facility. As a general rule, however, if exclusive possession is granted of a defined area, the agreement may, in fact, constitute a tenancy, thus providing security of tenure.

A tenancy at will, however, does not afford protection. This is a personal relationship between the original landlord and tenant, and is determinable at the will of either of them. The use of the words 'tenant at will' in an agreement will not create a tenancy at will if there is any suggestion that the tenant will be entitled to possession for a definite period. The documentation should not therefore make reference to rent being payable in advance, as this would suggest that the tenant has a right to occupy for that period. The agreement must make it clear that the landlord is, at all times, entitled to ask the tenant to leave. This is generally unacceptable to tenants, because it offers no certainty.

Landlords must take care not to inadvertently afford security of tenure to tenants, such as by entering into an agreement which could ultimately be construed as a tenancy, by incorrectly administering a tenancy at will, or by accepting rent beyond a short term or contracted out tenancy. This could be particularly costly in the case where tenants are situated within potential development opportunities.

Rent review

The purpose of rent review is to maintain the rental value of a property, helping keep the rent in line with inflation and the general rise in property values. This also helps to maintain the capital value of property, also known as investment value, bearing in mind that the general objective of landlords is to secure growth in rental and capital values in order to maximise profitability.

At rent review, the landlord and tenant seek to establish a new 'market rent', known also as the 'rack rent'. The lease contains a range of assumptions and disregards relating to a 'hypothetical' letting. This ensures that the valuer assesses the amount of rent that the property would expect to achieve if exposed to the market, seeking to attract a tenant on the basis that the property is vacant – and therefore ignoring the presence of the current tenant.

This 'open market' basis is the most common means of review, but rent may alternatively be increased by reference, for example, to the retail price index (RPI), to a tenant's turnover/sales, to sublease rents, or to pre-agreed/stepped increases.

In most leases, rent reviews take place every three or five years, although in older leases in particular, reviews may, for example, take place at seven-, 14-, or 21-yearly intervals, or not at all.

Factors for the landlord to consider at the start of the rent review process include:

- the 'effective date' of the rent review, which is the date that the revised rent will commence;
- the current level of rent, known as the 'rent passing';
- the likely level of the new rent, that is, the market rent – enabling an initial assessment to be made as to whether there is a prospect of a rental increase;
- whether the rent review clauses in the lease provide that the rent can go upwards only or could actually go down – although most leases have upward-only reviews;
- the provisions in respect of the service of notices – such as the 'rent notice' typically required to be served on the tenant to instigate the review, and the 'counter-notice', usually served subsequently by the tenant on the landlord, objecting to the level of rent required, and seeking to negotiate. Some modern leases may, however, dispense with such formal notice procedures.

Many factors can influence the rental value of property, and therefore the negotiations which take place between the surveyors acting against each other on behalf of the landlord and the tenant.

Surveyors examine evidence of other rental transactions, which are known as 'comparable evidence' and include lettings, rent reviews and lease renewals. For most property types, including retail, offices and industrial, comparison is made of the rates per m^2/per sq ft obtained, with adjustments being made between various factors affecting value in order to determine the value of the subject property. Alternative valuation methods may be used for other properties, such as a profits basis for licensed and leisure interests.

Straightforward factors affecting value could include the location or size of the property. More technical factors affecting value could include the length of the unexpired term of the lease. If, for example, a rent review was taking place with effect from 2000, of office accommodation held on a 25-year lease commencing in 1980, the tenant may argue that the unexpired term of five years is so short that there would not be any tenants in the market for such a facility. The tenant would suggest that prospective tenants would require a lease term of, say, 15 years, and that, therefore, a significant discount should apply to a rent based on a five-year term. In order for a landlord to avoid such a problem, there may be 'hypothetical' rent review provisions in the lease which provide, for example, that the unexpired lease term shall at each review be assumed to be 15 years. In other situations, short leases will command higher rents, owing in particular to their greater flexibility for tenants.

If the landlord and tenant cannot agree a revised rent, there are usually provisions in the lease whereby an arbitrator or an independent expert can be appointed.

Once the rent is agreed, the parties usually need to sign a rent review memorandum. The new rent will also need to be entered into the computer/management system in order to generate rent demands/invoices.

Lease renewal

The process of lease renewal takes place at the expiry of a lease. This provides an opportunity for the landlord and tenant to consider their aspirations for the property. The possibilities include:

- the tenant wishes to vacate the property and relocate the business;
- the tenant wishes to take a new lease on suitable terms that will help the business develop;
- the landlord wishes to secure possession from the tenant in order to redevelop the property or to occupy the property themselves, or because the tenant is in default of certain obligations contained in the lease;
- the landlord wishes to grant the tenant a new lease at a market rent, and on other terms, which will help optimise the investment value of the property.

Under the Landlord and Tenant Act 1954, tenants have 'security of tenure'. This means that at the end of their lease, they have the right to a new lease, subject to the ability of the landlord to establish a ground for possession. Compensation for disturbance is due under some grounds, and compensation for improvements may also be payable.

Not all business leases are afforded the protection of the 1954 Act, with exceptions including fixed-term tenancies for less than six months (with no right to renew or extend the term, and where the tenant has not been in possession for more than 12 months), tenancies at will and contracted out tenancies. Licences are also excluded.

There are notices that need to be served in order to bring the lease to an end and commence the renewal process, noting that the lease does not simply end because its expiry date has been reached. The landlord, for example, wishing to formally bring the lease to an end, to either grant a new lease or to secure possession, has to serve a 'section 25 notice'. The tenant wishing to end the lease, and request a new lease, has to serve a 'section 26 notice'.

One of the differences between rent review and lease renewal is that at rent review, the terms of the lease are fixed, whereas at lease renewal, the terms of the lease are renewed, and could therefore change. The general principle is that the terms of the existing lease should be incorporated into the new lease, and the party seeking any variation will need to justify the change.

Also, whereas the revised rent payable with effect from any rent review is fixed by reference to the terms of the lease, the rent payable on lease renewal is governed solely by reference to the provisions of the 1954 Act.

Another difference is that at rent review, the lease is most likely to provide that the rent can go upwards only, whereas at lease renewal there is no such provision. If, for example, the current rent/rent passing is £10,000, and the market rent is £8,000, the landlord would not try to increase the rent at rent review. At lease renewal, the rent would still be to market value, but would go down to £8,000. Also, whereas the effective date of an increase at rent review does not alter if negotiations are delayed, with lease renewal, the new rent commences from the eventual commencement date of the new lease. 'Interim rent' is payable in the meantime, but the 1954 Act does not contain any provision to enable tenants to apply for an interim rent if they are paying a rent above market value, and/or rental values are falling. If the parties cannot agree new lease terms between themselves, the matter is determined by the court.

Lease renewal is an area where surveyors often have to work closely with solicitors in respect of procedures, and the service of notices, in order to protect the interests of either the landlord or the tenant – noting that a business could have to relocate if it fails to apply to the court for a new lease within a set time scale. It is also an area where surveyors and finance staff have to follow laid-down procedures, and ensure that the rights of either the landlord and tenant are not, for example, prejudiced by neglecting to make the requisite computer inputs that affect the generation of rent demands. Once the new lease has been executed, details will need to be entered into the management/computer system largely as if it were a new letting.

User clause

The 'user clause' is a covenant within the lease which governs the use to which the property can be put by the tenant.

The lease may, for example, provide that 'the tenant shall not use the property other than for the purpose of a clothes shop'. This is an absolute prohibition against changing the use of the property – and termed an 'absolute' user clause. Here, if the tenant wishes to change the use of the property, the landlord could refuse outright, or could require a consideration from the tenant. The tenant could, for example, be required to sign a new lease, pay a higher rent, and/or give the landlord a lump sum in exchange for allowing the change of use.

Another lease may provide that 'the tenant shall not use the property for anything other than a clothes shop, without the consent of the landlord'. This is a 'qualified' user clause. Here, if the tenant wished to change the use of the property, the landlord could still refuse, but could not demand a consideration, such as an increased rent, for granting consent.

A further lease may provide that that 'the tenant shall not use the property for anything other than a clothes shop, without the consent of the landlord, such consent not to be unreasonably withheld'. This is a 'fully qualified' user clause. Here, the landlord would not be able to unreasonably withhold consent and would not be able to demand a consideration for granting consent.

In addition to the management issues surrounding user clauses, an important aspect is their effect on rental values. If there is a 'restrictive' user clause, such as being able to use a shop only for the purpose of selling clothes, then this would have a depressive affect on the level of rent that the property could command. This is because the market is effectively restricted to the demand from clothes retailers, when there may be a variety of retail users who could take the property.

The extent of the discount having to be applied for the restrictive user could be in the order of 15% – with the use as a clothes shop commanding £8,500 pa, for example, against £10,000 for a shop which could be used for any retail purpose. In other situations, the discount could be much more.

It is also worth noting that any other restrictive or onerous lease terms can limit the level of rent that can be achieved. Regard has to be given to all the other terms of the lease when considering the effect of an individual aspect – with the need to construe user and alienation provisions together being a good example – noting that it is likely to be a new tenant rather than an existing tenant that wishes to change the use, thus requiring consent for both user variation and assignment/subletting. The ability to end or 'break' during the term of the lease, may, for example, mitigate the effects of restrictive alienation or user provisions.

Alienation

Alienation provisions are included in a lease in order to allow the tenant to 'assign' the lease, or to 'sublet' the whole or part of their interest. If a tenant is committed to a number of years' occupation under the lease, it is only reasonable that they are allowed to relinquish such a liability by finding another occupier who will pay the rent and meet other obligations.

Landlords need to control the type of tenant in order to protect their investment but, as mentioned above, need to ensure that the alienation provisions are not unduly restrictive so as to have a detrimental effect on the ability to achieve rent increases.

Assignment involves selling the lease to a new tenant. A 'premium', really a purchase price, may be paid by the new tenant to the existing tenant, and would reflect the fact that the new tenant would benefit from a rent below the market rent until the next rent review or lease renewal. The current tenant may sometimes have to pay a new tenant to take over the lease. This is known as a 'reverse premium', and would apply, for example, where the current tenant pays a rent above market value and the property is 'overrented'. The reverse premium makes up for the fact that the new tenant could obtain a cheaper market rent elsewhere, such as taking a lease of a vacant property direct from a landlord as a 'letting'.

Tenants who assign their interest would no longer have any control over the property. But in subletting the whole or part of their interest, they would continue to be liable directly to the landlord for the rent and any other obligations, notwithstanding the obligations they may place on sub-tenants.

'Privity of contract' is a situation where the original tenant of a lease is liable for rent and the performance of other covenants for the duration of the lease, irrespective of the number of times that the lease may be assigned. If, for example, a tenant took a 20-year lease in 1985, and assigned the lease in 1988, they could still today be pursued for rent arrears that have resulted from the default of the current tenant – over whom the original tenant had no ability to choose, or control thereafter.

This potentially unfair system was remedied in part by the Landlord and Tenant (Covenants) Act 1995. For leases entered into on or after 1 January 1996, original tenants are liable only up to the point at which they lawfully assign the lease. However, the alienation provisions in these new leases may oblige the outgoing tenant to enter into an 'authorised guarantee agreement' (AGA) with the landlord on the assignment of any such lease – making the tenant (T1) liable for rent arrears or any other default of the next tenant (T2 – the 'assignee'). But T1 will cease to be liable under that agreement when T2 lawfully assigns to T3.

Privity of contract still applies to leases entered into prior to 1 January 1996. However, for all leases, for the landlord to be able to pursue original tenants, previous tenants, guarantors and so on for 'fixed charges' such as rent and service charges, those parties have to be advised of the amount claimed within six months of becoming due.

As with user provisions above, alienation and subletting provisions may be absolute, qualified or fully qualified. However, for the qualified covenant, the law implies that consent by the landlord should not be unreasonably withheld – unlike user clauses.

Most modern leases impose different controls in respect of assignment and subletting, and impose various restrictions – including, for example, restrictions on underletting at less than the open market rent and/or the passing rent and prohibiting the payment of a capital sum by or to the subtenant in respect of the subletting.

Repair

The tenant will require the repairing obligation within the lease to be fair having regard to the age and condition of the property, and to the other terms of the lease, including the length of the lease.

The landlord ideally places the responsibility for repairing a standalone property on the tenant, thus enabling a 'clear' income to be secured which helps optimise investment value. The landlord will, however, be mindful of imposing repair obligations on the tenant which are so onerous that they restrict the level of rent that can be secured.

In larger multi-occupied properties, the cost of repairs is typically covered by service charge contributions made by tenants.

If a property is not in an acceptable condition at the start of a tenancy, the tenant may include in the lease a 'schedule of condition', which records the condition of the property. This ensures, firstly, that the tenant will not be responsible for bringing the property up to a better condition and, secondly, that rent reviews will reflect the unimproved condition, rather than any improved condition which the tenant may have created at its own expense.

At the end of a lease, a tenant may be pursued by the landlord for damages in respect of the disrepair of the property. It is worth noting that the landlord's claim for damages is not necessarily the cost of undertaking the repairs to the property. The claim is either the cost of undertaking the repairs or the diminution in the value of the property which results from the state of disrepair – whichever is the lower. If, for example, at the end of a lease, an old vehicle repair garage would cost £5,000 to be brought to standard of repair required by the lease, but new tenants would only spend £1,000 owing to the fact that the property will soon return to the current condition, then the level of damages could be £1,000. Also, if, for example, the property were to be demolished at lease expiry for the purpose of redevelopment, then there would be no liability placed on the tenant in respect of disrepair.

Other areas

Landlord and tenant and estate management work often overlaps. In addition to the above areas, surveyors' work may include:

- dealing with tenants' rent default;
- dealing with breaches of other covenants, such as repair, user and alienation;

- granting consent to tenants for improvements and/or alterations;
- service charge administration;
- registering assignments and sublettings;
- establishing maintenance plans, arranging works and co-ordinating contractors;
- ensuring that the property is insured, either directly as the landlord's responsibility, or as either insurance rent paid by tenants, or within a service charge contribution;
- ensuring compliance with health and safety legislation;
- considering the effects of new legislation such as the Disability Discrimination Act, and the extent of compliance measures;
- minimising liability for rates, particularly for void areas, which may attract 'empty rates' charges;
- being alert to new income-producing opportunities such as telecoms facilities, short-term lettings, parking licences and advertising rights;
- periodically inspecting properties to ensure tenants are generally in compliance with covenants.

It is also important that agency surveyors have a good understanding of landlord and tenant, because the terms agreed at the initial letting determine the basis of rental value determined at subsequent rent reviews. Investment surveyors especially will have a keen eye on how lease terms affect income security, and the scope to achieve rental and capital growth. Valuers also need to be able to price the effect of certain lease terms.

Contributed by Austen Imber

CHAPTER 33

Lease renewal

Published as 'Taking notice', 8 August 1998

Lease renewal may be unattractive to landlord or tenant. Adequate notice needs to be given to ensure that agreement can be reached on conflicting interests

Lease expiry provides an opportunity for landlords to consider their future aspirations for the property and for tenants to consider the future of their business. The surveyor should be familiar with the process of lease renewal in order to determine an appropriate course of action that enables value to be enhanced on behalf of either the landlord or the tenant.

Surveyors involved in lease renewal may need to consider the principal issues covered below, but noting that, with such a basic overview, there may be qualifications, exceptions, related legislation and particular lease terms which warrant taking more detailed advice.

Parties' requirements

Tenants may wish to vacate the property at the expiration of the lease, or may require a new lease providing adequate security of tenure that enables them to develop the business, secure finance or sell their business in the future. Tenants may require flexible lease terms that consequently make the investment profile of the property unattractive for the landlord.

The landlord may wish to secure possession for redevelopment, or may wish to oppose renewal because of breaches of covenant by the tenant.

The balance of such potentially divergent requirements is struck between the parties under the provisions of Part 2 of the Landlord and Tenant Act 1954 (see references to sections, below), by noting the precedents established by case law, and by considering the likely approach of a court if the parties cannot reach agreement.

Procedures and notices

The lease can be ended on or after the 'expiry date' by the landlord serving a section 25 notice, either requesting or opposing renewal, or by the tenant serving a section 26 notice, requesting a new tenancy. Between six and 12 months' notice of the proposed 'termination date' can be given.

If the tenant wishes to vacate the property, he can serve a 'section 27 notice', giving at least three months' prior notice to quit at lease expiry. Beyond lease expiry, the three months' notice would have to expire on a quarter day. The possibility for the tenant to relinquish his interest by vacating the property at lease expiry, without having served notice, shows the need for the surveyor to be familiar with evolving case law. From time to time, certain provisions of lease renewal will be challenged or brought into doubt and will influence the way in which negotiations proceed.

After the expiry date, the lease automatically continues on the same terms and at the same rent passing by 'statutory continuation' (section 24) until the lease is terminated. Beyond the termination date, where an application has been made for a new tenancy, the lease continues by 'interim continuation' (section 64), again on the same terms, although interim rent may be payable.

After a section 25 or section 26 notice has been served, each party has additional responsibilities. The tenant requiring a new lease, for example, must serve a counternotice within two months of the giving of the landlord's section 25 notice, and apply to the court for a new tenancy within two to four months of same.

It may be necessary to determine the identity of landlords, tenants and subtenants to ensure that notices are served correctly. Section 40(1) notices can be served by landlords and section 40(2) notices by tenants no more than two years before lease expiry to secure the necessary information. To ensure that notices served and received are valid (section 44) a landlord must also be 'competent', ie a freeholder or a leaseholder whose lease will not end by expiry within 14 months. Because statutory renewal rights can be assumed, a business tenant/intermediate landlord is competent until he receives a section 25 notice or serves a section 26 notice.

The tenant is not entitled to a new tenancy of the whole or of part of the current demise where he is not in 'business occupation' (section 23), such as where the property is vacant or has been sublet (but noting that subtenants may have the right to take a new tenancy from the superior landlord). Changes of company name and occupation by group companies can cause difficulties for the tenant in establishing that they are in business occupation, but need not jeopardise the entitlement to a new lease.

Because of the potential complexities of the lease renewal process, it is vital that solicitors are fully involved. The position may be particularly complicated where there are subtenants.

Valuation date and interim rent

The valuation date adopted to determine the rent to be paid under the new lease is technically the date ordered by the court for the new tenancy (usually three months after the court disposes of the matter), but for practical purposes is the date of the court hearing.

Until the hearing is fixed, there is therefore a rolling valuation date, during which time market values and comparable evidence may change. Any subsequent appeal hearing would establish a new valuation date. The rolling valuation date contrasts with the situation at rent review where the valuation date would usually be the effective date of the review.

The rent payable under the new lease is the market value which, unlike most rent review situations, could be lower than the rent passing.

Interim rent is payable between the termination date of the lease (or the date of the landlord's application for interim rent if later) and the date ordered for the new tenancy. Only the landlord can apply to the court for interim rent.

The differential between full market value and interim rent depends on the type of property and the other terms of the lease, together with the assumption that the property is held on a tenancy from year to year.

As an approximate guide, interim rents may be at a discount of 10%–15% from the full market value. The award of interim rent is, however, at the court's discretion.

Where there is a large increase in rental value, the interim rent could, for example, be discounted at a large percentage from the new market rent under the 'cushion' principle – even though the tenant has had the previous benefit of a low rent and has known that a full rent would be payable at renewal.

Tactical considerations

The tactical approaches that landlords and tenants can employ are influenced by the time-scale for progressing the renewal process and the procedures for serving notices, by the level of the rent passing, the state of the market, envisaged movements in value, the availability and usefulness of comparable evidence and by the parties' particular aspirations for the property or their business.

The landlord may wish to renew the lease as soon as possible where the rent is below market value, or where a new lease would enhance the property's investment profile. The tenant may require an early renewal where the existing rent is above market value, or where he senses that the landlord has redevelopment aspirations but is not yet able to establish an intention to redevelop.

If the party requiring the earliest possible termination date does not serve a '12-month' notice to terminate the lease on the expiry date, the other party could, at a later date, serve a 12-month notice to prolong the existing lease.

Conversely, the landlord may wish to protect an over-rented situation or the tenant may wish to preserve a low rent. The party requiring the most distant termination date could delay serving a 12-month notice, but be pre-empted by the other party serving a six-month notice.

The parties may not have considered their options at least 12 months in advance of lease expiry. Care should be taken, for example, not to alert the other side by serving a section 40 notice. Tenants should avoid failing to pay rent or commit other breaches of covenant, which could attract attention.

Landlords could mitigate against loss by interim rent or could deter delay by tenants by providing for a rent review shortly before lease expiry, or even providing for a 'last-day review'. The valuation date for the review would be fixed and the review could still be progressed during statutory continuation or interim continuation. The landlord could therefore secure full rental value when he did not wish to begin renewal proceedings, knowing that a further rent increase could be secured at renewal. The tenant would be liable for the reviewed rent whether or not a new lease is eventually taken.

Terms of the new tenancy

For the new tenancy, the court can determine the extent of the demise or 'the holding' (section 32), the duration of the tenancy (section 33), the rent (section 34) and any other terms (section 35).

The holding Where the tenant is not in business occupation of parts of the property, the landlord can exclude those areas from the holding. The landlord can insist on areas being included to facilitate good estate management practice.

The term of the lease The length of the new term could reflect the length of the current lease, the tenant's business requirements and possible need for flexibility, and the landlord's requirement for a lease term which does not damage the value of his interest. The term could also reflect the landlord's future aspirations to redevelop or take occupation for his own use. The maximum term the court can grant is 14 years; either party could secure a break clause.

The rent The rent is determined having regard to comparable evidence, but will be strongly influenced by the terms that have been established for the new lease (owing to the 'presumption of reality'). Flexible terms for the tenant, for example, may warrant a higher rent.

The determination of the rent in accordance with section 34 does not assume vacant possession or that the property is let as a whole. Unlike most rent review provisions, therefore, the rent could be based on a number of lettings and could take account of subtenancies. The extent to which this enables a relatively higher rent to be achieved depends on the feasibility of letting the property in parts, the rental differentials for quantum and any allowances for newly created common areas or increased management costs or service charges.

The ability of the landlord to adjust the rent to take account of tenants' improvements provides an opportunity to substantially enhance value. The '21-year rule' provides that the value of improvements cannot be taken into account where they were undertaken during the current lease (which could have been more than 21 years ago), or where they were completed less than 21 years before the application for a new tenancy. The landlord may therefore benefit where a succession of shorter leases have been granted, or where the term of a new lease is scheduled to expire only a short time after 21 years from the date of the improvements.

The other terms These must primarily have regard to the terms of the current tenancy. The onus is on the party seeking change to justify it. It would not be possible, for example, for a landlord to widen a user clause in order to secure a higher rent.

The new terms should be fair and reasonable, and in accordance with the purpose of the Act – which is to protect tenants. New terms could reflect modern lease-drafting or changes in the law, or could be consistent with the terms on which neighbouring properties are held. New terms may facilitate the overall estate management of multi-occupational interests. Terms which are out of date and have ceased to serve a purpose may be excluded.

Changes are more likely to be supported by the court where they are effective only on tenant default, where the tenant's security of tenure is not diminished or where he can be compensated by way of an adjustment to the rent or other terms. The frequency of rent reviews (or indeed the length of the lease) could be reduced to reflect current market practice as evidenced by comparable transactions.

Hypothetical rent review provisions are unlikely to be repeated where the landlord has employed them to enhance the rent artificially. Where the provisions fairly assist the determination of rent, for example where comparable evidence is weak, they are likely to remain.

Upwards-only review clauses will generally remain, but upwards/downwards provisions may be imposed by the court where the current lease contains no review provisions. The provisions of the Landlord and Tenant (Covenants) Act 1995 can be reflected in the new lease and can influence the new rent.

If the tenant is not satisfied with the terms granted by the court, he can, within 14 days, decline to take a new lease and vacate the property, although the court may extend the current tenancy to allow the landlord to secure a reletting.

Tenants are not obliged to pay the costs incurred by the landlord in renewing the lease. However, where the tenant has requirements in addition to the entitlements of lease renewal, the landlord may take the opportunity to negotiate the recovery of costs.

Grounds for possession

Section 30(1) of the Act provides the landlord with grounds to oppose the tenant's application for a new lease. The grounds must be specified in the landlord's section 25 notice or in his counter-notice to the tenant's section 26 notice.

The grounds are:

(a) the tenant's failure to repair the property,
(b) persistent delay in paying rent,
(c) other substantial breaches,
(d) the landlord can provide suitable alternative accommodation,
(e) the landlord wishes to remove a subtenant in order to let the whole,

(f) the landlord intends to redevelop ('demolish or reconstruct') the property,
(g) the landlord intends to occupy the property himself (in which case he must have been landlord for five years before the date of termination).

The finer requirements of the provisions of the Act will need to be studied before seeking to remove a tenant. For the redevelopment ground, for example, at the date of the hearing, the landlord will have to establish an intention to redevelop. His case will be helped by having planning permission, building regulations approval, and finance in place or having negotiated a building lease with a developer.

Where the landlord is successful under grounds (e), (f) or (g), compensation may be due to the tenant for disturbance (section 37). This would be the rateable value of the holding where the tenant has been in occupation for less than 14 years up to the date of the section 25 notice, or twice the rateable value if 14 years or more (subject to any transitional provisions). The lease may provide that compensation is not payable where the tenant has been in occupation for less than five years.

Compensation may also be payable in respect of improvements undertaken by the tenant. The amount would be the lesser of the current cost of carrying out the works, and the increase in value due to the works, but would not be payable if the landlord intended to demolish the property.

The parties are often able to negotiate a settlement without requiring the court's assistance. The landlord may be prepared to offer increased compensation to secure the certainty he requires, and could still grant the tenant continued occupation by way of a 'contracted-out' tenancy. The contracted-out tenancy excludes the renewal provisions of sections 24–28 of the Act. The landlord is therefore guaranteed possession at lease expiry or break.

Tenant's ability to break

Tenants should ensure that the lease is broken on the correct day, and could seek to append the form of the break notice to the lease, to include the relevant dates.

The exercise of a break clause may be condition-precedent on total compliance with covenants. The repair covenant can be a particular trap, especially where the landlord is unco-operative and reluctant to provide a schedule of dilapidations.

At lease expiry, in accordance with section 18(1), Landlord and Tenant Act 1927, the landlord's claim for damages for disrepair is the lesser of the cost of undertaking the works to satisfy the terms of the lease, and the diminution in the value of the landlord's reversion that results from those wants of repair.

Tenants can be exposed to a greater liability as a result of disrepair if there is a condition-precedent break. The tenant's obligation to satisfy the repair covenant to preserve the right to break could give the landlord scope to secure a bullish cash settlement in exchange for dilapidations not being attended to (and, unlike lease expiry, even where the landlord intends to redevelop the property). Alternatively, a tenant may have to vacate the property in advance of lease expiry in order to deliver up the property in the required condition.

Such factors should be borne in mind when decisions are being made to enter into a relatively short lease or a longer lease with break provisions. Tenants should seek break facilities that are conditional only on the payment of outstanding amounts.

Some break clauses are personal to a particular tenant. A break would therefore not be available after assignment. Inter-company transfers may need careful consideration. Sublettings may also influence the ability to break.

Although break facilities are granted to tenants to enable them to quit the property, some tenants may seek to invoke the procedure to secure a new tenancy, particularly where the property is over-rented and a market rent could be secured. The courts have ruled that tenants are unable to do this – a further illustration of the need for the surveyor to be familiar with evolving case law.

Conclusion

Because of the procedural and legislative requirements of lease renewal, the consequences of notices not being served or being invalid and the depth and evolving nature of case law, it is essential that surveyors work closely with solicitors. The parties should begin formulating their options at least a year before lease expiry and be aware that the other party may be doing likewise.

Contributed by Austen Imber

CHAPTER 34

Scottish Landlord and Tenant

Published as 'A slightly different world up north', 15 June 2002

Surveyors responsible for national portfolios, or working on a cross-border basis, need to understand both English and Scottish landlord and tenant systems. Here we examine the basic differences

Scotland has few statutes governing leases of commercial property and is unaffected by any Landlord and Tenant Act legislation that applies in England and Wales. The relationship between the parties is therefore governed mainly by contract/lease terms. Leases are similar in the two countries, drawing on English case law in areas such as rent reviews, where the processes are virtually identical. (For an introduction to English landlord and tenant law and practice, see Chapter 32.)

Lease expiry/renewal

Under the English system, at the end of their lease, commercial property tenants have security of tenure under the Landlord and Tenant Act 1954. This means that they have the right to a new lease/tenancy, unless the landlord can establish a ground for possession, as prescribed by the 1954 Act, such as the intention to redevelop the property.

Leases in England may be 'contracted out' of the 1954 Act, denying the tenant the right to a new lease at lease expiry. This can place the tenant at some risk, owing to the landlord's negotiating strength when determining the terms of a new lease. This includes the ability to require the tenant to vacate.

In Scotland, commercial property tenants are in the same position, as there is no security of tenure. Here, the lease is brought to an end by either the landlord serving a 'notice to quit' or 'notice of removing', or a tenant serving a 'notice of removal'. This usually needs to be at least 40 days prior to lease expiry, as prescribed by statute (Sheriff Courts (Scotland) Act 1907), but the parties may have negotiated a longer period, as contained in the lease.

The Scottish system has two exceptions to its security of tenure rule:

- Tacit relocation – This provides that where neither of the parties serve notice to end the lease, it either continues for a further year from the expiry date if the lease was for a term of one year or more; or, if the term of the lease was less than one year, it continues for the same duration as the term of the expired lease.

  The 'continuation lease' carries the same terms as the expired lease and is extended similarly if neither of the parties serve notice. This is similar to 'statutory continuation' under section 24 of the 1954 Act in England, where the lease continues on the same terms until either the landlord or the tenant serves notice bringing the lease to an end by a section 25, 26 or 27 notice.
- Shops – A retail tenant, on receiving a landlord's notice of removing, can apply within 21 days to a Sheriff Court for a renewal. The Sheriff can grant an extension of up to one year on terms that they consider reasonable. But this procedure is rarely used.

The lack of security of tenure in Scotland means that tenants in particular need to plan ahead well in advance of lease expiry, seeking to negotiate new terms and/or identify options for relocation.

Compensation for both disturbance and improvements is not available in Scotland unless there is express provision in the lease, which is unusual.

The ease of removing a tenant also simplifies development strategies, whereas in England the landlord may have to establish to a court a ground for possession, as well as having to deal with tenants seeking to gain the maximum from their rights.

Alienation

In England, 'privity of contract' means that for leases granted before 1 January 1996, in the event of default of assignees the original tenant becomes liable for the payment of rent and performance of covenants for the duration of the lease, irrespective of the number of times, and to whom, the lease may be assigned.

For leases granted after 1 January 1996, in accordance with the

Landlord and Tenant (Covenants) Act 1995, the tenant ceases to be liable following assignment, but leases will typically impose an authorised guarantee agreement, which makes the tenant liable for the performance of covenants by his assignee.

On assignment in Scotland – which is known as 'assignation' – the outgoing tenant ceases to be liable. Landlords of Scottish property therefore ensure that suitably protective alienation provisions are drafted – typically on the lines of the assignee having to be respectable, responsible, of sound financial standing and demonstrably capable of performing the tenant's obligations under the lease.

Especially for larger properties and higher rents, and in the case of anchor tenants, there may be specific conditions relating to financial strength, such as credit rating, turnover and/or profitability. This is similar to pre-assignment conditions, which have existed in England since the 1995 Act.

If a landlord of a Scottish property does not consider an assignee to be of the requisite financial standing, he may seek a substantial deposit against rent and other default, or alternatively a guarantee from a parent company or other substantial covenant.

Some Scottish leases provide that the assignor will be jointly and severally liable with future assignees. This is worse than the English concept of privity of contract, as it binds every tenant in the chain, not just the original tenant. The effect on rental value of such onerous provisions, plus the strong resistance of tenants to it, means that in practice its use is limited.

Sub-leases in Scotland automatically end when the headlease expires, or is forfeited. The risks to a sub-tenant are therefore greater in Scotland, compared with England, where the sub-tenant may gain relief against forfeiture and become the direct tenant of the landlord.

Sub-tenants can seek a separate agreement from the landlord, providing that on the ending of the headlease in mid term, they can continue the sub-lease as a direct relationship with the landlord.

In the event of disagreement between landlord and tenant on the suitability of an assignee or sub-tenant, the matter is resolved by the court – or an arbiter, if this is provided in the lease. This is in accordance with such tests as specified in the lease, as there is no equivalent to England's Landlord and Tenant Act 1988.

A tenant of Scottish property wishing to claim damages for a deal lost has the task of proving that its landlord has unreasonably withheld or delayed consent. Some recent cases have seen

Scottish law move slightly closer to the English position by indicating that the landlord cannot refuse consent to acquire a commercial benefit to itself, and that consent should be given unless the tenant is unsuitable either in its ability to pay the rent or to carry out other lease obligations.

Dilapidations/repair

Scottish common law obliges a landlord to maintain the property so that it is windproof and watertight and to a standard reasonably fit for the purpose for which it is let. Landlords almost always ensure that leases provide alternative provisions to obtain the most appropriate balance between the landlord's and tenant's responsibilities, having regard to investment value and management issues, as in England. Service charge positions are the same in the two countries.

Scotland has no statutory equivalent law to sections 18 (1) and (2) of the Landlord and Tenant Act 1927, which limit damages for disrepair to the lower of the cost of undertaking the works, or the diminution in the value of the landlord's reversionary interest resulting from the disrepair. The position is instead covered by case law. Scottish courts are inclined to accept the ascertainable cost of carrying out the repair works as the appropriate measure of damages due to the landlord, unless the tenant can prove that the true loss is less.

Where, for example, the landlord intends to dispose of the property for redevelopment and it is to be demolished, damages may be minimal. This gives a similar result to section 18 of the Landlord and Tenant Act 1927.

Other differences

Scottish law is similar to English law with regard to rent reviews but differs in terms of titles and contracts.

Freehold in Scotland is known a 'feuhold' or 'heritable title'.

- The law governing title and contracts is very different in Scotland. Contracts could be created verbally – if this can be proved – and also by assembling a trail of correspondence – although a lease for more than one year must be in writing. Scotland is undergoing reform to its land tenure system.
- Leases of commercial property entered into after 9 June 2000 cannot be of a term greater than 175 years. Exceptions include

leases where contracts were concluded prior to the above date and sub-leases where the existing headlease has an unexpired term in excess of 175 years. Some long leasehold investment structures can be affected by this, but it is worth noting that long leasehold interests are much less common in Scotland than in England.
- Most Scottish residential properties are held as feuhold, with few being held on long leases of 99 years or more. New residential leases cannot be granted for a term of more than 20 years.
- As mentioned, for rent review, the English and Scottish systems are similar. But in the case of arbitration, different law applies.
- In Scotland, there is no implied provision that consent is not to be unreasonably withheld, as in the case of alienation in England, nor is there a prohibition of a fine or premium being secured in the case of a change of use. Leases in Scotland must include the term 'reasonable' and tend to go further than that to set the criteria for consent in the relevant circumstances.
- 'Keep-open' clauses – also called 'continuous trading' clauses in Scotland – are still enforceable in Scotland. In England, damages are more likely to be awarded to a landlord if a tenant ceases to trade, but in Scotland, 'specific implement', known in England as 'specific performance', is the primary remedy. Damages can be awarded as an alternative if the keep-open obligation is no longer capable of performance, or where it would be unjust to enforce it.
- Scotland uses only the terms 'landlord' and 'tenant', and not 'lessor' and 'lessee'.
- 'Covenants' or 'obligations' in England are simply known as obligations in Scotland.
- The modern Scottish quarter days for rent collection are 28 February, 28 May, 28 August, and 28 November. These were changed from the historic Scottish quarter days of 2 February, 15 May, 1 August and 11 November. In contrast, the traditional English quarter days are 25 March, 24 June, 29 September and 25 December – although modern quarter days of 1 January, 1 April, 1 July and 1 October are now more frequently used in England.
- Different rules apply to forfeiture, known in Scotland as 'irritancy', and to distraint, known as 'diligence'. Irritancy is one area affected by statute: the Law Reform (Miscellaneous Provisions) (Scotland) Act 1985.

- If a Scottish property is destroyed or sustains minor damage, the law of frustration terminates the lease automatically. However, in institutional leases this common law provision is always overridden by express provision to the contrary.
- Most of the environmental law applying to England also applies to Scotland. Planning law is also similar, although legislation is separate. The rating system is very different.

Contributed by Austen Imber

CHAPTER 35

Alienation

Published as 'Rights and rents', 26 January 2002

Alienation provisions, which govern lease assignments and sublettings, balance tenants' requirements with landlords' need to protect their returns. Here we cover the basics

Tenants of commercial property usually require the ability to assign their leasehold interest, and to be able to sublet the whole or part of their demise. This enables the leasehold interest and/or the business to be sold, and helps minimise the liability for accommodation which is surplus to requirements.

Landlords wish to optimise the investment value of their interest by preserving security of rental income, and by controlling the identity, use and behaviour of occupiers. Regard is also given to the effect of onerous alienation provisions on the ability to secure tenants, and on the level of rent that can be secured at rent review.

Landlords and tenants may need to give consideration to the principal issues considered below, but with such a general overview, there may be qualifications, exceptions, related legislation, case law and particular lease terms which warrant the need for detailed advice to be taken.

Preserving value

A tenant's ability to assign their lease, together with the provisions of security of tenure afforded by the Landlord and Tenant Act 1954, helps to uphold the value of their leasehold interest and their business. This is particularly so where the business operates from a single property.

A leasehold interest could have value, because the tenant paid a premium at the commencement of the lease, because the tenant erected buildings on the site and pays a ground rent, because the tenant has undertaken improvements to the property which cannot be reflected in the rental payable or because the current rent will remain below the open market rental value until a rent review or lease renewal can take place. The leasehold interest should therefore command a 'premium' if sold/assigned. In some situations, such as where market value is less than the passing rent, and the property is over-rented, the value of the tenant's leasehold interest could be negative. Here, the tenant would pay a 'reverse premium' to the new tenant to take on the lease.

Landlords have traditionally required tenants to make a commitment to a relatively long lease term, preferring to incorporate suitable alienation provisions, rather than provide tenants with the ability to break the lease. Break clauses are, however, increasingly common in modern leases, and there is also a trend towards shorter leases. Shorter, more flexible leases sometimes command higher rents.

The three types of alienation provisions included in leases are:

- an 'absolute' covenant which prohibits assignment. This can have a depressive effect on the rent and is most suitable for short leases not subject to rent review, and contracted out of sections 24–28 of the Landlord and Tenant Act 1954 (thus avoiding a depressive effect at lease renewal as well as rent review);
- a 'qualified' covenant, which permits assignment 'subject to consent'. This, however, is subject to the statutory provisions of section 19(1) Landlord and Tenant Act 1927 which implies that 'consent is not to be unreasonably withheld';
- A 'fully qualified' covenant, which permits assignment 'subject to consent – such consent not to be unreasonably withheld'. The qualified and fully qualified covenants are therefore of the same effect. In modern leases, assignment provisions will usually be fully qualified.

Alienation, user and rental value

As the range of potential assignees or subtenants for a property can be restricted by the user provisions contained in the lease, the effect of alienation and user provisions should be considered together.

An 'absolute' user covenant, which prohibits a change of use, enables the landlord to secure a consideration in exchange for allowing the tenant to operate a different use from the property.

A 'qualified' user covenant, which permits a change of use subject to consent, enables the landlord to refuse consent to a change of use, as there is no implied requirement that consent should not be unreasonably withheld. Section 19(3) of the Landlord and Tenant Act 1927 specifically prevents the landlord from demanding a lump sum or an increase in rent as a condition of giving his consent if the change of use will not entail any structural alterations – as is often the case – but does allow the landlord to insist on reasonable compensation for any diminution in the value of the premises or any neighbouring premises that he owns.

A 'fully qualified' user covenant expressly provides that consent cannot be unreasonably withheld for a change of use.

The landlord should aim to secure the optimum balance between controlling the use of the property and avoiding restrictive user provisions, which depress market value.

It is only the fully qualified user covenant that provides the certainty that market value will not be restricted. With a qualified user covenant, the valuer can attribute weight to the possibility that the landlord may grant consent, but rental value may still be significantly restricted. With an absolute prohibition against a change of use, the valuer cannot give regard to the possibility that the landlord may accommodate the tenant's requirements.

Preserving security of income: Landlord and Tenant (Covenants) Act 1995

The landlord's ability to preserve the security of their rental income has recently been influenced by the Landlord and Tenant (Covenants) Act 1995. The Act contains provisions for 'new leases', which are those granted on or after 1 January 1996 (unless in pursuance of an agreement, option, right of first refusal or court order before that date), and other provisions for all leases.

Old leases

'Privity of contract' provides that the liability of the original tenant continues during the term of the lease/contract, even though the lease may be assigned several times, and despite variations such as rent reviews taking place.

'Privity of estate' provides that the liability of an assignee continues while they are the tenant, and ends when the lease is next assigned. However, the liability of an assignee does not end where, as a condition of an assignment taking place, the landlord secures a direct covenant from the assignee, and/or where the assignee provides an indemnity to the assignor.

The liability of original tenants and assignees can therefore extend beyond their occupation of the property. Former tenants can be particularly exposed in weak market conditions – such as during the early 1990s recession, which prompted the 1995 Act – and especially where assignees are of poor financial standing.

New leases

The 1995 Act automatically ends the liability of the tenant (as original tenant or assignee) of a new lease, once the lease is assigned. However, within the lease the landlord can require the tenant who is seeking to assign his interest (T1) to guarantee the performance of the assignee (T2) by entering into an 'authorised guarantee agreement' (AGA). When the lease is further assigned, the original assignor (T1) is released from liability under the AGA, and the current assignor (T2) similarly enters into an AGA to guarantee the performance of the new tenant (T3). Note that the Act releases tenants from liability under their leases, or any authorised guarantee agreement only if the assignment is lawful – meaning that the landlord must approve assignees in accordance with the terms of the lease. Unlawful assignments are also a breach of the lease terms.

All leases

The 1995 Act also includes provisions which apply to all leases in respect of former tenants and guarantors – where there is either a liability through privity of contract for leases granted prior to 1 January 1996, or through an AGA for leases granted thereafter.

In order to preserve the right to take action, landlords are required to notify former tenants and guarantors of arrears of 'fixed charges' such as rent or service charges within six months of them becoming due. In certain circumstances, former tenants and guarantors who are pursued by the landlord can take an overriding lease, and become the immediate landlord of the current tenant.

If landlords agree to lease variations which they could have refused, and to which former tenants or guarantors were not a party, the liability of former tenants and guarantors may cease, or may be restricted.

Landlords need to operate an effective management system that maintains details such as the current addresses of former tenants and guarantors, and their current financial standing. A decision may have to be made as to which one of a number of parties should be pursued, and regard should be given to the consequences of an overriding lease being taken.

Note also that it is not possible to contract out of the 1995 Act, or generally seek to restrict its operation.

Pre-assignment conditions

The form that modern alienation provisions take depends on the size, nature and value of the property, the covenant strength of current and typical future tenants, the requirements of funding institutions, market conditions, the ability to attract new tenants, the possible diminution in rental value as a result of onerous alienation provisions and, overall, on the effect of the alienation provisions on the investment value and the saleability of the property.

Pre-assignment conditions, which specify conditions in new leases, could include:

- the requirement for the outgoing tenant to enter into an AGA;
- the provision of a guarantor;
- the provision of a rent deposit/bond;
- a requirement for an assignee or guarantor to be of a minimum financial standing, which could, for example, be assessed by reference to market capitalisation, a balance sheet structure, an assets test, a profits test (as a level of pretax profit or as a multiplier of the rent), strength of covenant or the financial standing of the current tenant. The requirement for an assignee to be of equivalent covenant strength to the current tenant could cause particular difficulties for strong and/or strengthening covenants, especially for properties that typically attract weaker covenants;
- compliance with covenants, especially the payment of rent and other sums, but possibly also other covenants;
- the prohibition of intra-group transfers or imposition of suitable conditions. Generally, landlords should be alert to the potential difficulties that can arise with associated companies. Weaker subsidiaries could be sold and some companies could even be established for the purpose of relinquishing lease commitments. The ability to make intra-group transfers may, however, provide certain companies with significant financing or taxation advantages, and landlords may need to be flexible;
- the requirement for the value of the landlord's reversionary interest not to be diminished;

- the requirement to obtain the consent of a superior landlord or mortgagee;
- the payment of the landlord's costs.

It can be difficult to set financial tests which take everything into account: FTSE 100 companies may fail a profits test, and a requirement for a tenant to have three times profit cover on the rent may not be stringent enough if the assignee occupies other properties. The trend of profitability is also an important consideration when selecting tenants/approving assignees. Where conditions are discretionary, the 1988 Act's test of reasonableness does of course apply (see p245).

Absolute prohibition on alienation

An absolute prohibition on alienation may be contained in short leases/tenancies, or in commercial periodic tenancy agreements (which can typically be determined by six months' notice at any time by either party). Such agreements are more common for lower-value properties, and where smaller businesses place less importance on the finer contractual requirements when negotiating their agreement, sometimes without professional representation. Also, landlords may wish to avoid the potential implications of allowing a tenant to assign or sublet the property, as well as generally wishing to avoid a management burden.

The inability to assign the agreement may prevent the value of a leasehold interest or a business being realised. A landlord may seek financial gain from such a situation, but should give regard to the consequences of the tenant relocating the business, especially for secondary properties where it may be difficult to secure a new tenant.

A landlord could allow the current tenant to introduce a new tenant who will take a new agreement at a market rent, leaving the current tenant and the new tenant to reach agreement on the sale of the business.

When a business is being sold, if the agreement is held in the name of a limited company, it may be feasible to sell the company, together with the tenancy, as the tenancy remains with the company. The lease may, however, impose restrictions on the change in the ownership of the company. With a company sale, guarantors may continue to be liable, and therefore need to be released. As an alternative to individuals or companies acting as guarantor, a bond could be provided to a landlord, which would effectively be returned by the purchaser of the business.

Rent review, lease renewal or the availability of break provisions may present an opportunity for tenants to renegotiate suitable terms, even though there may be no obligation for landlords to agree to variations to the terms of the current agreement.

In some cases an unauthorised assignee or subtenant may be of distinct identity, but in other cases the position may not be clear because of intra-company relationships, the use of trade names or informal arrangements. Where the tenant is in breach of covenant, the landlord could seek to forfeit the lease, sue for damages or seek an injunction. Or it may be possible to negotiate new terms with the tenant, including an increased rent.

Sub-letting: Securing rent and retaining control

Tenants may sublet, or 'underlet' their demise where, for example, they wish to retain occupation of part of the premises, wish to re-occupy or retain the lease for other reasons, or are unable to assign owing to factors such as a long unexpired lease term or other onerous lease terms.

The landlord's requirement to uphold the investment value of the property, and generally control the occupation of the building, can limit the tenant's ability to sublet the whole or part of their demise. Landlords and tenants may need to give regard to the following issues.

The need to recover possession

Tenants may require the ability to gain possession from the subtenant in order to run their business from the property again, or to preserve their right to secure a renewal of the lease in accordance with the provisions of the Landlord and Tenant Act 1954. To prevent subtenants gaining security of tenure, the sublease should be contracted out of sections 24–28 of the 1954 Act. The sublease should also expire in sufficient time for the tenant to recover possession before its own lease expires.

In modern leases, tenants are usually obliged to contract out sublettings anyway. The landlord may wish to avoid a subtenant gaining the right to the renewal of the sublease, which would be direct with the landlord, especially where the sublease is on terms that could restrict the level of rent payable.

Securing an open market rent
The lease may provide that the rental payable on a subletting has to be open market rental value, and may also provide that a premium cannot be secured from a subtenant.

Market value could be defined as a proportion of the open market value of the whole property, or could represent the market value of the actual facility which is being sublet. It may not therefore be possible to exact premiums from prospective tenants, although there may be more flexibility to do so where, for example, improvements, size, particular lease terms or the general attractiveness of the sublet part of the property enable a higher market rent to be commanded than the level of market rent that reflects the basis of valuation specified by the landlord.

Landlords may contend that the rental agreed on a subletting does not represent market value. Tenants may be able to help their case by being able to demonstrate that they have effectively marketed the property, have provided attractive terms, have sought competitive bids and can provide comparable evidence to support their assertion that full value has been secured.

Both parties should be aware that the level of rent established for a subletting may create evidence for rent reviews and lease renewals.

Other requirements
The lease may permit a certain number of sublettings to take place, permit a maximum percentage of the demise to be sublet or permit a maximum number of floors to be sublet. Subtenants may not be able to assign or sublet.

The sublease may have to contain identical terms to the headlease. The landlord's approval may be required to the full terms of the subletting. Rent reviews in the sublease may have to correspond with rent reviews in the head lease.

The tenant may wish to align rent reviews for cash flow purposes and, similarly, may impose rent payment dates on the subtenant which precede the dates in the head lease.

Landlords often also insist on direct covenants from the incoming tenant, creating a contractual relationship allowing action to be taken in respect of serious breaches of the terms of the sublease.

Lettings/agency
Generally, for certain properties, the opportunity to become a subtenant can be less attractive to prospective occupiers than

having a direct relationship with the landlord, where consent to the transaction, and to other requirements during the period of occupation, does not need to be determined by a superior landlord. The lack of security of tenure afforded by a contracted-out tenancy can also be unattractive.

Estate management matters
Arrangements may need to be made in respect of matters such as the separation and submetering of services, access and security, signage, alterations to the property, responsibility for insurance, responsibility for business rates, and the apportionment of service charges, insurance premiums or other amounts.

Whether consent should be granted: Landlord and Tenant Act 1988

In accordance with the provisions of the Landlord and Tenant Act 1988, when dealing with an application from a tenant to assign or sublet the lease, the landlord must be able to demonstrate that the refusal to grant consent, or the imposition of any conditions to the granting of consent, is reasonable.

The landlord must state any reasons for refusal and must respond within a reasonable time. The burden of proof is on the landlord and if consent is deemed to be unreasonably withheld, damages are available to the tenant. These can include a sum to cover the existing tenant's future liability under the lease.

The test of reasonableness is not governed by any specific rules, and primarily has regard to the circumstances of the current tenant, the proposed tenant and the landlord. The criteria will, for example, differ depending on whether the lease is being assigned, sublet in whole or sublet in part.

The landlord may, for example, be deemed to reasonably withhold consent to an assignment when an assignee is of poor financial standing or is in financial difficulty, when the demised property or the landlord's adjoining property could be injured because of the proposed use of the assignee, when the lease does not contain a requirement for an AGA, but it is still a reasonable condition for the landlord to impose, or when the assignment will damage the value of the landlord's reversion – although this may depend on whether the landlord intends to realise the value of his reversion or not: the landlord may be unable to withhold consent if he is only likely to suffer a 'paper loss'.

The landlord's withholding of consent may, for example, be deemed to be unreasonable when guarantors or a rent deposit are required unnecessarily, when consent is refused because the assignee is relocating from another property owned by the landlord that will be difficult to let, or when the landlord requires possession himself and wishes to negotiate a surrender.

When granting or refusing consent, the landlord is not under a duty to former tenants and guarantors who have a vested interest in successive tenants being able to meet their liabilities.

When in receipt of an application to assign or sublet, unless provision for the payment of costs is expressly provided for in the lease, it is generally considered to be reasonable for landlords to seek an undertaking that the tenant will meet the landlord's reasonable costs incurred in the matter before proceeding with the application. A landlord may be deemed to be acting unreasonably where a demand is made for an excessive level of costs.

Contributed by Austen Imber

CHAPTER 36

Dispute resolution – rent review

Published as 'How to decide what is fair', 20 April 2002

In the first of a two-part feature on dispute resolution, we concentrate on the processes available to landlords and tenants seeking to settle rent reviews

When negotiations cannot, for example, be easily concluded between a landlord and tenant, the parties have to consider the best means of reaching agreement.

For smaller-value cases, the surveyor's knowledge of dispute resolution processes, and the confidence to progress such a route if need be, can help secure an expedient and successful settlement. This is especially so where the other side may not be so familiar with dispute resolution, and are forced to re-assess their position quickly once faced with the possibility of court action or the appointment of a third party. For cases involving larger amounts, the parties will typically draw on a strong knowledge and experience of dispute resolution, including the appointment of experts if need be.

During negotiations, relationships between the parties will sometimes have deteriorated. Individuals may be entrenched in their personal unwillingness to concede, and eagerness to win, and may even be unable to agree on procedures. In other situations there may be an amicable difference of opinion between surveyors which they feel can only be resolved by a third party. In all cases, the parties need to know about dispute resolution methods.

This feature provides only a basic insight into dispute resolution at rent review, noting that statute, case law and lease terms can present many complexities in practice, often warranting detailed legal advice.

Arbitration

For most general practice surveyors, involvement in arbitration will be in respect of rent review work, but other valuation, landlord and tenant or construction disputes could also be settled this way. The provision for the appointment of an arbitrator will typically be set out in a lease or other contract.

Appointing an arbitrator

To appoint an arbitrator for a rent review, the parties can agree on a particular arbitrator themselves, or, as is often the case, one of the parties will apply to the president of the RICS to make the appointment. Although it is important to stress that the selection of an arbitrator is at the RICS's discretion, the parties may still suggest a number of names of arbitrators to the RICS who they agree would be able to satisfactorily conduct the arbitration, or may advise of particular arbitrators that should be avoided, such as where there is a conflict of interest.

This could, for example, be where an arbitrator is negotiating a rent review for or against one of the parties as part of their day-to-day case work in the same building as the rent review requiring determination, is acting in a separate but similar matter in the vicinity of the subject property, or is acting for or against one of the parties elsewhere – provided this is not too remote as may be the case with large companies/agents.

RICS criteria

The key criteria adopted by the RICS for the appointment of arbitrators is that they have the required knowledge and experience of arbitration generally and of the subject-matter, and also that they are free from conflict of interest. In the case of rent review, the arbitrator needs to be familiar with the technical areas of valuation and sometimes law which are in dispute. Experience of working in a particular locality is not essential, but it is helpful if the arbitrator already understands market norms, local valuation practice and so on, and does not need to be educated by the parties, as may more likely be the case, for example, with remotely located or particularly unusual property types. An arbitrator may, in fact, specialise only in West End offices, or out-of-town retail, for example. Also, arbitrators – and independent experts – must have recently completed the relevant RICS training course, followed by an assessment and interview.

Once in place, the arbitrator will make contact with the parties, advise them of the procedures and set out the basis of his fees.

Format and procedures

Arbitration procedures, the role of the arbitrator and the obligations placed on the parties are governed by the Arbitration Act 1996 and by general contract law.

A particular feature of the 1996 Act is the scope for the parties to agree on procedural matters, helping ensure that the arbitration is progressed as effectively as possible having regard to the nature of the dispute. Nevertheless, the arbitrator exercises complete discretion over all matters of procedure and evidence when the parties do not agree.

The arbitrator's initial directions, or orders, are typically outlined in writing to the parties, covering issues including:

- a request for an 'agreed statement of facts', such as a description of the property, measurements, comparable evidence and so on. This helps narrow down the areas of dispute, saving time and cost;
- the format of submissions, such as 'written representation', which will usually be the case with rent review – rather than an 'oral hearing', also known as a formal hearing, which tends to be more common with construction or contractual disputes – or, indeed, larger rent review cases;
- the procedures for submissions. For rent review, this will usually be a 'submission' being prepared by each of the parties, which are then exchanged via the arbitrator, and followed by a 'counter submission' from each party, all of which are then considered by the arbitrator. It is worth noting that counter submissions cannot introduce new primary evidence, only evidence by way of rebuttal;
- the timetable for submissions. During the process, there may, however, be requests to extend time scales, which will be decided at the arbitrator's discretion;
- reminders of matters such as 'without prejudice' correspondence not to be included within submissions;
- whether a 'reasoned award' is required, which is usually the case with rent review. The arbitrator is obliged to give reasons unless the parties agree that this is not necessary;
- the procedures for dealing with costs, which will mean either awarding costs at the same time as the arbitration award, or considering costs afterwards, possibly after inviting the parties to make submissions in respect of costs.

In some situations, a 'preliminary meeting' will take place to determine such issues.

Considering the evidence
The arbitrator's decision is based on the evidence submitted by the parties, including:

- evidence of fact, such as comparable evidence of an open market letting or rent review signed off by the surveyors acting for either side in that transaction;
- evidence from an expert witness, such as opinions on market conditions, trends and values, and comparable evidence;
- hearsay evidence, such as an unconfirmed claim that a tenant is thought to have agreed a certain rent on a nearby property. It was the Civil Evidence Act 1995 that allowed hearsay evidence to be considered.

The arbitrator apportions weight to the evidence submitted by the parties. He or she cannot introduce his own evidence, but can draw the parties' attention to factors which may warrant further investigation, including, for example, comparable evidence of which the arbitrator is aware.

It is important for the arbitrator to remain impartial and be seen to be impartial, and not, for example, be seen drawing the parties' attention to factors of benefit to one of the parties, or be seen putting one of the parties' cases for them. The arbitrator may however, provide greater guidance in respect of procedural aspects to a party with limited experience in conducting arbitrations.

Also, one change introduced by the Arbitration Act 1996 to the previous Acts of 1950 and 1979 was that arbitrators can now carry out their own investigations of the evidence, rather than rely only on the other side to challenge points. The arbitrator must, however, advise the parties of his findings so that they can comment. Note also that until the Civil Evidence Act 1995, arbitrators' and independent experts' decisions in other cases/comparables did not count as admissible evidence, but can now be included in submissions, with the arbitrator apportioning weight as appropriate.

Appealing against the award
The arbitrator's 'award' is enforceable in the same way as a court judgment.

An appeal is available on a point of law, and not on matters of valuation. A tenant could not, for example, contend for a rent review of a city centre shop that £2,500 per m^2 zone A should have really been determined in the order of £2,250 per m^2. But if the £2,500 per m^2 had derived from an incorrect interpretation of statute, case law and/or lease terms, for example, as to whether certain tenant's improvements fell to be rentalised or disregarded, this would count as a point of law. If a reasoned award has not been made, there will, of course, be no information available to the parties on which an appeal could be based.

The other ground for appeal is serious irregularity, which could include failure to comply with the duty to deal with the matter expeditiously and cheaply, conflict of interest, bias, departing from agreed procedures, or an award that has been obtained by fraud, such as misrepresentation of comparable evidence. An appeal is to the High Court, and must be made within 28 days of the arbitrator's award.

Award of costs

The arbitrator is obliged to make an award of costs, and has wide discretion over their apportionment between the parties (except where the parties have notified the arbitrator of an agreement they have reached between themselves).

The award of costs usually follows the event, which means the arbitrator gives regard to the extent to which one of the parties may be regarded as a clear winner.

Costs typically include the arbitrator's fees and the costs incurred by a landlord and tenant, for example, on appointed surveyors and lawyers and any expert witnesses. The administration fee paid by one of the parties to the RICS to appoint an arbitrator, currently £275, may also be recoverable.

In-house costs of the landlord or tenant in addition to that of appointed representatives may not typically be recoverable, especially where this effectively represents double/ liaison time. If, however, an in-house property team pursued arbitration themselves without appointing external agents, costs may typically be recoverable. Recoverable costs include the seeking of legal advice, but this may not, for example, be included in an arbitrator's award where the relevant party should reasonably have possessed the requisite knowledge.

Costs need to be proportionate to the matter being determined, and although the parties may be at liberty to bring in numerous expensive experts in order to support their case, all such costs may not be recoverable. Indeed, the arbitrator has the power to place a cap on recoverable costs.

It is worth noting that if a lease prescribes an apportionment of costs for arbitration proceedings, this is actually null and void, and discretion remains with the arbitrator. This would include leases in which some landlords, as a means to bring about undue negotiating pressure at rent review, provide that the tenant should bear the arbitrator's costs, and even also all of the landlord's costs.

Arbitrator or expert?

An alternative to arbitration is the appointment of an independent expert, whose detailed knowledge of a particular market enables him to determine rental value. The expert's remit is governed by the terms of the lease, including whether a reasoned determination is required, and the position in respect of costs – which will usually be shared equally. In a limited number of situations, the expert is required to award costs, and *Calderbank* letters (see p253) may be a feature. The parties cannot appeal against an expert's 'determination', but although rare, can sue for negligence, in which case damages will be received rather than a determination being revised.

Perceptions vary among surveyors as to whether an arbitrator or an independent expert is preferable in certain situations. Their respective merits depend on factors including property type, location, level of rent, market conditions, availability of comparable evidence and, of course, whether the choice is from the landlord or tenant's perspective.

In lower-value situations, the independent expert alone may be able to reach a determination expediently, without the need for the parties to make representation, with its attendant cost. But in larger-value cases, the parties' respective professional representation may be as extensive as with arbitration, thus making little difference to costs.

The differing remits of an arbitrator and an independent expert can influence the level of rent that is awarded, or indeed whether a landlord considers it worthwhile proceeding with a rent review and/or third-party determination. A remotely located property, for example, may offer little, if any, comparable evidence to a landlord to submit to an arbitrator in order to justify a rental increase at review, and the rent may have to remain at its current level. An independent expert, however, should be able to judge a suitable market rent from his own expertise, if not directly from comparable evidence, and will also have more scope to reflect factors such as a general rise in market values since the current rent was set.

In the case of prime city-centre commercial investment properties, for example, in a buoyant market, the comparable evidence available to an arbitrator may be somewhat historic, but an independent expert may be better positioned to consider the latest trends. Here an expert may determine a higher rental than an arbitrator, but if, for example, market conditions turned for the worse, and rental values were falling, a landlord may benefit from the more historical nature of evidence submitted to an arbitrator, noting also that in weakening market conditions, evidence of new lettings may become thin. With either third-party route, however, the determination may be some time after the valuation date and the historical nature of the evidence may therefore be less relevant.

Expert determination is less prone to settlements being influenced by the ease at which the parties are able to secure evidence, the quality of the submissions made and the extent of any imbalance between surveyors experienced in dispute resolution and novices. An expert may also be best placed to determine issues such as whether rent-free periods and works allowances reported as part of a new letting genuinely represent market conditions – rather than being designed so that, on paper, they can be analysed favourably by one of the parties.

In view of the above, at the initial letting of the property, the parties must consider the basis of third-party determination to be included in the lease.

Notwithstanding the merits of independent experts in small-value cases and other situations, the common view among landlord and tenant surveyors is that arbitrators are preferable, particularly in view of the greater control and flexibility afforded to the parties regarding issues of procedure and evidence as a result of the Arbitration Act 1996.

Calderbank letters

As mentioned below, the award of costs at arbitration follows the event, and gives regard to the extent to which one of the parties may be regarded as a clear winner. If, for example, a landlord's aspirations at rent review were £120,000 pa, the tenant's were £80,000, and the arbitrator awarded £100,000, the arbitrator's costs may be apportioned equally, with the parties bearing their own other costs. If the award was £118,000, an arbitrator may consider that such a near miss was sufficient for the landlord to be awarded costs, but may alternatively apportion costs equally. Awards would very rarely be made on a proportional basis, such as 75% landlord, 25% tenant.

One of the features of an arbitration process is the possible service of a '*Calderbank* letter', or '*Calderbank* offer' by one of the parties to the other. The letter would be headed 'Without prejudice save as to costs' – in other words, without prejudice in the usual way so as not to be admissible to a court or arbitration process, but presented pursuant to the determination of costs.

If, for example, the landlord had served a *Calderbank* letter prior to the tenant's application to appoint an arbitrator, offering to settle at £95,000, and an award was made at £100,000, this may see the tenant judged to have pursued the entire arbitration unnecessarily, and all costs may be awarded against him. However, if, for example, the £100,000 award hinged on a point of legal interpretation legitimately pursued by the tenant, costs may still be awarded equally. And if one of the parties had won, despite having lost on a major point which took a long time and expense to resolve, an award of costs may not be in their favour. The arbitrator would also consider the timing of any *Calderbank* letters, bearing in mind that that costs may have been incurred up to that point. Arbitrators may also give regard to any delay or other tactical mischief promoted by one of the parties.

Note also that a *Calderbank* letter must be a genuine offer to settle, and not simply be a mechanism to influence costs and/or pressurise the other party. It must also give the other side reasonable time to consider their position, including informing a client and obtaining instructions.

A *Calderbank* letter can indeed be an effective tactical weapon to concentrate the other side's mind, and facilitate settlement. Tactical opportunities at rent review will be considered in future *Mainly for Students* features. This includes 'disclosure' (previously 'discovery'), which, for example, could entitle a tenant to obtain details of all a landlord's lettings in an office block or industrial estate, when ideally they would prefer to confine submissions to the deals that are most favourable to their case.

Contributed by Austen Imber

CHAPTER 37

Dispute resolution – other Landlord and Tenant

Published as 'Many paths to a just settlement', 18 May 2002

The first part of this feature on dispute resolution concentrated on the settlement of rent review disputes through arbitration or independent expert – as governed by the terms of the lease/contract

For lease renewal cases, among other property disputes including damages for dilapidations, determination is by the court, having regard to the new Civil Procedure Rules 1998 (part of the Woolf reforms which emanated from Lord Woolf's report *Access to Justice*).

CPR aims to make dispute resolution more straightforward and less expensive than was often the case under the old County Court and High Court rules, and reduces the parties' scope to exploit the court system as part of case tactics, including for the purpose of delay. Most property cases will be heard in the County Court.

The new system

The new system includes the ability for courts/judges to:

- direct or encourage the parties to attempt to reach settlement outside the court by means of alternative dispute resolution (ADR). This could include mediation, arbitration or independent expert;
- impose on the parties a 'single joint expert' who reports to the court – instead of each of the parties appointing their own experts pursuant to conducting the full case in court. This is distinct from the ADR route above.

In some situations, statute provides that certain disputes shall be resolved by arbitration (and also 'adjudication' for construction disputes) despite this not being provided in the lease/contract.

Examples include the Agricultural Holdings Act 1986, the Housing, Grants, Construction and Regeneration Act 1996 and the Party Wall Act 1996.

Conduct, and costs

CPR introduces 'pre-action protocols' which set out certain procedures that the parties should follow before legal action commences. Protocols are not yet finally in place for lease renewal or dilapidations, but the draft versions represent good practice.

Another feature of CPR is the encouragement to the parties to exchange 'pre-action correspondence' in order to facilitate settlement between themselves, or to at least help narrow down the areas of contention to be dealt with by the court.

The court's judgment naturally reflects the facts of the case and the quality of the parties' respective representations, but in respect of the award of costs, the court's discretion under CPR operates on a much wider basis than apportionment on the traditional winner-and-loser approach – and could mean that a successful party still has to bear all costs. Factors considered by the court in respect of the award of costs could include:

- whether a claimant has acted reasonably in bringing an action or was aggressively litigious;
- whether a defendant acted reasonably in resisting an action;
- compliance with protocols, or consistency with draft protocols not yet formally in place;
- whether the parties have conducted themselves appropriately, or, for example, have taken an overtly tactical approach to gain from court procedures;
- whether the areas of contention are all genuine or have been included as wider perceived benefit (such as to trade certain points as may be typically the case during negotiations);
- the extent to which the parties have genuinely sought to negotiate (as opposed to sending letters suggesting mediation or the appointment of a single joint expert merely in hope of currying favour with the court);
- the attitude of the parties to mediation, independent expert or other non-binding means suggested by the court to help reach settlement by agreement;
- the level of the claim relative to the sum awarded or any settlement offers.

As well as a punitive award of costs, the court has the power to determine rates of interest on any sums awarded, at higher or lower rates than the standard rate of interest. Where a claimant has made a part 36 offer (see p261) which the defendant has not beaten at court, the court may award interest at a rate up to 10% above the base rate. No such provision is available where the defendant makes the part 36 offer.

Revising traditional strategies

The new system should end practices such as, in the case of dilapidations damages, inflating claims by submitting unduly high costings and/or not reflecting the precise lease terms or the statutory basis of section 18(1) damages.

Importantly, as is outlined above, certain dealings between the parties, which under the old system may not have had a bearing on any ultimate court decision, can now influence the court's determination of costs.

A landlord is, of course, at liberty to negotiate in the way he may have done before the new CPR, in the hope that a settlement can still be reached. But if taking such an approach, a landlord must balance whether this can actually achieve a bullish and expedient settlement, or whether non-compliance with protocols presents a negotiating edge to the other side, who would inevitably draw the court's attention to such a serious departure from the protocols – thus influencing the court's award of costs, as well as creating an overall unfavourable impression that may affect the court's judgment.

Although the protocols mean that the landlord would typically commence legal proceedings/court action once the tenant's response has been received to a claim, or at least after time for negotiation had taken place, he could still technically commence proceedings at any time. Although it is against the protocols, and risks an adverse award of costs, the expedient of securing damages may be paramount in some cases.

One of the early criticisms of CPR in the case of dilapidations, among other disputes, is the extent to which the landlord, for example, has to commence negotiations by preparing a full case upon which he has to rely. This allows tenants simply to refuse to negotiate until the landlord has incurred relatively considerable expense.

On the other hand, the overall procedures help reduce speculative claims, and encourage a generally more genuine, less tactical approach. It also ensures that both sides look hard at the evidence they will be relying on if the case does get to court. This is often a powerful persuader to settle.

The courts in control

Another feature of CPR is the greater control the courts have to manage the progression of a case, including its time scales for action. This reduces the scope for delaying tactics, and again may mean that landlords and tenants have to revise traditional strategies.

For an opposed lease renewal, for example, a landlord may have to establish an intention to redevelop at a sooner court hearing than planned, and may not be in a position to do so. Also, it may not be as wise, for example, for a landlord to claim spuriously a ground for possession such as redevelopment for the initial purpose of making a tenant anxious about their future as a means to secure a more expedient lease renewal on more favourable terms than if the tenant had the comfort of a landlord being prepared to grant a new tenancy. Here, the landlord may be hurried into court by a tenant.

Similarly, a tenant who unnecessarily fights a landlord's claim for possession may face an unfavourable costs award. Another of the early criticisms of CPR in the case of lease renewal is that the tenant has to serve all his evidence before he is aware of the details of the landlord's case.

The new system will inevitably experience teething problems, and its success will also be also dependent on the resourcing of the legal system. Case law, and an increased familiarity by surveyors and solicitors with the system, will help narrow any uncertainties. Litigation is, of course, an area of practice where it is imperative for surveyors to work closely with lawyers.

It is worth noting also that the recently launched Code of Practice for Commercial Leases in England and Wales, which outlines best practice for lease negotiations and conduct during a lease, recommends that where disputes cannot be settled by agreement, both sides should always consider speed and economy when selecting a method of dispute resolution. It also states that mediation may be appropriate before embarking on more formal procedures.

Mediation is not binding, but aims to help the parties consider disputes more dispassionately, and reach compromise.

Uncontested lease renewals – and PACT

At lease renewal, tenants' applications for a new tenancy will commonly be unopposed by the landlord, leaving the parties to agree the terms of the new lease and the rent themselves, or otherwise seek their determination by the court.

Professional Arbitration on Court Terms (PACT) is a scheme initiated in 1997 by the RICS and the Law Society to provide a voluntary alternative to the court process. The terms of the new lease and the rent payable are decided by a surveyor or a lawyer acting either as an arbitrator or an independent expert. This is in compliance with the Arbitration Act 1996 and Civil Procedure Rules 1998.

After initially protecting their positions through the usual service of section 25, section 26 and counter notices as appropriate, and making the necessary applications to the court, PACT procedures for the parties can broadly be summarised as follows.

- First, decide whether it would be advantageous to refer aspects of the lease renewal to a third-party solicitor or surveyor, rather than going to court.
- Second, identify which aspects of the lease renewal, if any, are agreed.
- Next, decide which aspects to refer to the third party: the interim rent, the new rent, other terms of the lease, the detailed drafting of terms or any combination of these.
- Choose those aspects that are to be resolved by a third-party solicitor, and those to be resolved by a third-party surveyor.
- Choose the third-party's capacity – arbitrator or expert.
- Draft the court application, making use of, or adapting, PACT model orders/forms (as set out in the RICS's main PACT brochure).
- Apply to the court for consent.
- Apply to the RICS or the Law Society for the appointment of a third party (if not already agreed between the parties).
- Proceed with the appointment.
- Receive the decision.

The procedures are a good illustration of how the parties are encouraged to confine their case to genuine areas of dispute, rather than tactically including other matters in order to secure beneficial trade-offs.

PACT is quicker, cheaper and more flexible than full court

processes and, arguably, more effective given that decisions are made by property specialists rather than judges – including surveyors in respect of valuation.

The arbitrator's or expert's decision is binding in the same way as in rent review cases, subject to the remedies outlined in the previous feature (and subject to any agreements the parties may have reached as to the ability to appeal). As with all lease renewals, the tenant can, of course, decline to accept the terms of the new lease, and vacate the property.

The PACT scheme has been slow to take off, particularly in view of its voluntary nature, although it is expected to become an increasingly used method of dispute resolution, with courts, for example, imposing a PACT appointment on the parties as part of CPR.

Regard also needs to be given to possible changes in landlord and tenant legislation. For an overview of the latest proposals, see the *Estates Gazette* feature by Suzanne Lloyd Holt and Allyson Colby of Wragge and Co, (30 March 2002, p94).

Other property disputes

Other property-related disputes which would ordinarily be the subject of court action include:

- possession/forfeiture by a landlord for breach of a tenant's covenant;
- a tenant's application for relief against forfeiture;
- pursuit of rent arrears and other amounts;
- matters of lease/contract interpretation and/or rectification;
- injunctions sought by a landlord against a tenant in respect of a keep-open user clause, or by the local planning authority in respect of enforcement action for unlawful use;
- tenant's compensation assessments for disturbance and/or improvements;
- removal, modification or enforcement of restrictive covenants;
- negligence claims against surveyors;
- boundary disputes;
- disputes arising from the dissolution of business partnerships.

Examples of where other procedures, such as tribunals for valuation and related matters apply include rating, compulsory purchase compensation, residential leasehold acquisition/valuation, capital gains tax and inheritance tax. Further rights of appeal may of course eventually bring such disputes to the courts. Planning appeals will be to the Secretary of State for Transport, Local Government and the Regions.

It is worth noting also that although some construction disputes will be governed by arbitration, adjudication may also be appropriate, particularly for smaller disputes. Here, the adjudicator reaches a decision on his or her own knowledge having regard also to the evidence presented by the parties.

Part 36 offers/payments

Part 36 of CPR is similar to the position in respect of Calderbank letters typically served at rent review, as outlined in the previous feature.

A tenant/defendant has always been able to make a payment into court of an amount designed to prompt a landlord's acceptance (and the ending of proceedings, with the parties bearing their own costs), but if not, otherwise influence the ultimate award of costs by the court.

A landlord or a tenant can make a 'part 36 offer' before or after proceedings commence. This must be in writing, making it clear that it is made pursuant to part 36, remain open for acceptance for at least 21 days, and in the case of a defendant's offer, include an offer to pay the other party's costs.

In the case of a money claim, the defendant must make a payment into court of the sum offered for the part 36 offer to be effective.

Expert witnesses

An 'expert witness' is appointed by one of the parties to a dispute in order to provide expert evidence, on an independent basis, as part of court proceedings or any other form of dispute resolution. This is clearly distinct from the role of independent expert as mentioned in the previous article.

Chartered surveyors who are appointed as expert witnesses should refer to the RICS practice statement and guidance note, Surveyors acting as expert witnesses, 2nd ed. Following the practice statements is mandatory, and although the accompanying guidance notes are for assistance, and do not strictly have to be followed, they represent best practice. Compliance may help provide partial defence against allegations of negligence.

The extent to which expert witnesses are truly independent, and do not effectively act as advocates, is a common area of debate, bearing in mind that they are appointed by one of the parties seeking the most favourable presentation of their case. There is a separate RICS guidance note, Chartered surveyors acting as advocate. (Note also the relevant RICS publication for arbitrators and independent experts: Guidance notes for surveyors acting as arbitrators and as expert witnesses in commercial property rent reviews, 7th ed)

An expert witness requires experience, expertise in the subject-matter, good courtroom skills if appearing in court, and, of course, familiarity with the relevant RICS publications and general procedures. As with arbitrators and independent experts, appointments will often be made through the RICS.

'Single joint expert witnesses' are often also appointed by the RICS pursuant to directions given by the courts under CPR. Here, the single joint expert would ordinarily obtain representations from the parties as part of the process of compiling his report for the court. Single joint experts have the same duties and responsibilities as the expert witness who is instructed by one party.

RICS Dispute Resolution Service

The RICS Dispute Resolution Service is the world's largest provider of property-related dispute resolution services, making around 10,000 formal third-party appointments each year. They additionally help parties make appointments themselves by providing names of arbitrators, independent experts, expert witnesses, mediators, adjudicators and so on.

The RICS maintains panels of dispute resolvers that satisfy demand for appointments, and ensures that each receives sufficient work in order to maintain the requisite knowledge and experience and to spread the time and cost incurred by both the RICS and the individual surveyors on training.

The RICS monitors the performance of dispute resolvers using surveys with the parties involved in the dispute. Performance determines the levels of work allocated, noting also that the good arbitrators receive work directly from the parties as well as from the RICS. Good decisions are seen as those that are conscientious and correct, and not those which may appear, for example, to be split down the middle without real merit.

Monitoring of performance includes matters such as conduct, identification of the issues and the application of the law and practice of arbitration. It is not concerned with the substantive merits of any third-party decision.

Owing to the courts' increasing encouragement of ADR, including the appointment of single joint experts, the RICS Dispute Resolution Service's business development initiatives include the promotion of the chartered surveyor as a key dispute resolver in a range of property-related matters.

The RICS Dispute Resolution Faculty serves the wider membership of the RICS, not just those on RICS panels of dispute resolvers. This includes the provision of bespoke education and training, weekly legal updates, the drafting and publication of guidance notes and practice statements, and the general promotion to members and the public of the use of dispute resolution procedures. The faculty is also about to introduce an expert witness registration scheme for the wider membership.

For more information on the role of the RICS Dispute Resolution Service, or further information on PACT, contact the RICS Dispute Resolution Service (020 7222 7000, e-mail drs@rics.org.uk; see also www.rics.org/resources/services/drs).

Contributed by Austen Imber

CHAPTER 38

Dilapidations (part 1)

Published as 'It's time to get it fixed', 28 July 2001

In the first of a series of features on dilapidations, we provide an overview of the main issues affecting landlords and tenants of commercial property, including liability for repairs

Tenants require their liability for repairs to be fair, reflecting factors such as the nature, size, value, age, character, condition, and use of the property, having regard also to the length of lease term.

Landlords wish to optimise the investment value of their interest, and will generally aim to secure a clear income by placing the responsibility for repairs on the tenant, but avoid causing rental value to be depressed as a result of the tenant's responsibilities being unduly onerous.

Landlords and tenants may need to give consideration to the issues covered below but, with such a general overview, there may be qualifications, exceptions, related legislation, case law and particular lease terms which warrant the need for more detailed advice to be taken. Future features will consider some of the points in more detail.

Issues at lease commencement

Tenants should ensure that they are not responsible for any disrepair which exists at the commencement of the lease, without such a liability being reflected elsewhere in the transaction. Where there is disrepair, tenants will require this to be recorded in a schedule of condition in order to avoid liability.

An obligation to keep a property in repair generally includes an obligation to put the property into repair. Therefore, if the tenant does not include a schedule of condition in the lease, the tenant can be held responsible for any disrepair which existed at the commencement of the lease.

Also, the level of rent which is determined at rent review and lease renewal can assume that the tenant is in compliance with repairing obligations, and if a schedule of condition is not included, the rent could reflect a superior condition of repair than that which existed at lease commencement.

At lease commencement, tenants may sometimes also wish to commission a full structural survey and may also check for contamination, asbestos, difficulties with air conditioning systems, high alumina cement, defective cladding and the like.

Requirement to undertake works

Rather than include a schedule of condition in the lease, the landlord or the new tenant may require works to be undertaken. Because new tenants will usually require the property to be in good condition, the landlord may undertake works as soon as the current tenant departs, thus making the property more attractive when marketed, and also sometimes helping works to be undertaken during a void period, rather than granting a new tenant a rent-free period or other allowance when a full rent could otherwise be immediately secured. However, where tenants are likely to have specific requirements in respect of facilities, condition and design, the landlord may rather wait, and grant an allowance to the new tenant to undertake the work themselves.

In order to help optimise the investment profile of a property, and therefore its capital value, the landlord needs to achieve a market rent which reflects a property in good condition and repair (rather than making allowance at rent review for initial disrepair), and obliges the tenant to keep the property in full repair. Means of achieving this include giving the tenant a capital contribution to undertake works, or granting a rent-free period or other allowance/incentive as part of the transaction.

The landlord may, alternatively, prefer to pay the tenant upon the satisfactory completion of the works and, particularly at the lower end of the market, could take a bond from the tenant on the grant of the lease, which is returned once the works are complete – thus helping ensure that the works are actually undertaken.

The repair covenant

Repair covenants within leases vary widely and could, for example, include 'to keep in wind and water tight condition', 'to keep in structural repair' and 'to keep in good and substantial repair and condition'. These are sufficiently distinct to create a different liability, but there are many finer variations in terminology within repair covenants which may or may not create differential liability depending on the nature, age and character of the property.

A tenant's liability for repair does not generally involve making improvements, or modernising the property.

In longer leases particularly, the repair provisions may incorporate potentially onerous obligations, such as the requirement to 're-build', 'renew' or 'replace'.

The repair covenant may also require specific actions to be undertaken, such as the periodic redecoration of the property.

At the expiry of the lease, tenants are usually required to 'leave', 'deliver' or 'yield up' the premises to a required standard. Alterations may also have to be reinstated, with consent usually having been granted initially by way of a 'licence to alter'.

The repair covenant generally applies to alterations and improvements undertaken at the tenant's expense, and to landlord's fixtures.

Inherent defects do not generally constitute disrepair, but defects could still be the cause of certain items of disrepair for which the tenant is liable.

Failure to repair could also be a breach of the Building Acts, resulting in the service, for example, of a dangerous structures notice by the local authority.

If the lease does not contain obligations for either party to repair the property, neither of the parties are generally obliged to carry out repairs, and cannot oblige the other party to do so. There is no implied condition of fitness that the landlord has to provide, and it is for the tenant to be satisfied that the property is fit for its intended use. Certain repairs may, therefore, have to be undertaken by the party with the greater need.

For properties in multiple occupation, a service charge may be administered which includes a contribution to the cost of repairs. The service charge helps avoid individual tenants having an onerous liability for the cost of major and unexpected works, typically by the administration of a sinking fund/reserve fund.

A form of lease may therefore be termed IRI (internal repairs and insurance) which may involve the tenant only painting and decorating, as against FRI (full repairs and insurance) which includes both internal and external repairs. The precise liability for insurance will also vary accordingly.

Schedules of condition and schedules of dilapidations

A 'schedule of condition' records the condition of repair of the property, typically at the commencement of the lease, and comprises descriptive comment and/or photographs, and, sometimes, also videos. The schedule should be appended to the lease, and/or the lease should make express reference to the existence and purpose of a schedule held separately. The separate availability of a schedule of condition does not necessarily limit a tenant's liability for repairs.

A 'schedule of dilapidations' details the items of disrepair for which the tenant is considered to be liable. The terms 'interim', 'terminal' or 'final' schedule are loosely used to mean mid-lease, towards the end, and at or beyond the end of the lease respectively.

During the lease, the schedule details works requiring remedy, but where the tenant has vacated following lease expiry, the claim is for the cost of the works. Statutory continuation/holding over and interim continuation counts as being during the lease.

A 'reverse' schedule involves a tenant serving a schedule on the landlord responsible for remedying disrepair.

A 'Scott' schedule takes different forms, but generally comprises both the landlord's and tenant's claims, costs and comments within the same schedule, prepared for the purpose of the court determining a settlement.

A 'repairs notice' is usually a contractual notice, that is served under the terms of the lease, which calls for specific repairs to be carried out within a given timescale.

The landlord's remedies for disrepair

The investment value of a property is influenced by its condition of repair. External disrepair can also affect the value of a landlord's neighbouring interests. Landlords may therefore give greater consideration to the state of repair when, for example:

- they wish to sell or raise finance on the property;
- the tenant is of poor covenant strength or is known to be in financial difficulty;
- the tenant is in breach of other covenants;
- the lease is due to expire; or
- the tenant has exercised a break facility.

Landlords also consider factors such as:

- the possibility and consequences of forcing the tenant into bankruptcy or liquidation;

- the need to preserve the right to sue former tenants and guarantors;
- the ability to relet the property – possibly on more favourable terms;
- the opportunity to re-negotiate terms with the current tenant as a result of the issue of disrepair; and
- the damage that could be caused to the landlord-and-tenant relationship.

The landlord's principal remedies for disrepair during the term of the lease are to sue for damages or, provided the lease contains a forfeiture clause, seek to forfeit the lease. Also, a 'self-help' remedy, outlined in the second part of this feature, may enable the landlord to undertake the necessary works themselves, and recover the cost from the tenant.

To seek to forfeit the lease or to sue the tenant for damages as a result of disrepair, a notice has to be served on the tenant in accordance with section 146 Law of Property Act 1925. This 'section 146' notice does not have to be in a prescribed form but must state why the tenant is in breach of the repair covenant and state what needs to be done to remedy the breach. The notice should give the tenant a reasonable period of time to undertake the works. If the works are not undertaken, the landlord can seek an order for possession from the court. Restrictions placed on the landlord's ability to forfeit the lease, owing to the Leasehold Property (Repairs) Act 1938 are outlined in the second part of this feature (see p272).

It is worth noting also that if rent is outstanding, it may be possible to gain possession by peaceable re-entry and subsequently sue the tenant for damages for disrepair – but noting that the tenant may obtain relief against forfeiture by paying outstanding rent arrears.

The tenant's failure to repair the property is also a ground of opposition at lease expiry for the tenant's application for a new tenancy, either as a single ground, or coupled with other grounds.

Another remedy for the landlord is to seek an order for specific performance from the court, but in practice this is very rare.

The second part of this feature, which will appear on 25 August, includes an examination of the valuation basis upon which damages for disrepair are assessed, together with other factors influencing the approach taken by the parties to remedy disrepair.

Repairs and the market rent: The effect of the repair covenant on rental value

Rent review provisions, and also the basis of valuation at lease renewal, usually assume that the tenant is in compliance with the terms of the lease, including the repairing covenants. The tenant cannot therefore benefit from non-compliance with repairing obligations, and pay a lower rent based on poor condition.

If the landlord is deemed to be in breach of their repair covenants, the rent can usually reflect the disrepair which results from the landlord's neglect.

If a tenant's repair covenants are onerous, having regard to factors such as the nature of the property and the term of the lease, the property should command a lower rent.

Disrepair at lease commencement can give landlords particular scope to construct beneficial investment profiles. This includes, for example, granting a rent-free period as a works allowance, which unlike a rent-free period granted as an incentive, would not warrant a downward adjustment to determine the true 'effective', or 'day-one' market rent. As well as artificially raising the apparent market rent for the property for the benefit of sale or financing, the transaction may be structured by the landlord having regard to its favourable impact on rental levels secured for rent reviews or lease renewals on their other interests nearby.

When evaluating comparable evidence, tenants must therefore be satisfied that reported works allowances are genuine, as evidenced, for example, by establishing the true extent of the works required, checking that the lease actually obliges all of the suggested works to be undertaken, quantifying the reasonable cost of the works, distinguishing between general remedial expenditure and works specifically relating to the particular tenant's business, ensuring that landlord's improvement works are not incorporated, contacting the previous tenant to establish the extent of disrepair and its cost/remedy (if any) that the landlord may have pursued, and being satisfied that the time allowed to undertake the works is reasonable and is not effectively a rent-free period/incentive.

Estate management systems: The value of effective administration

As well as ensuring that property inspections are made periodically, and consideration is given to tenants' compliance with repair covenants, administrative systems must ensure that details of original tenants and their guarantors are maintained, including changes of address and company names. Under the Landlord and Tenant (Covenants) Act 1995, any original tenants, former tenants and guarantors liable for the performance of a current tenant's covenants must be served with a 'section 17' notice by the landlord, notifying them within six months of liability arising. For repairs, this will be usually from the date that damages are claimed or other proceedings commence. However, while former tenant liability can help underpin income security and property value for institutional-grade investments particularly, for smaller landlords and in the case of lower-value properties, it will often be impractical and/or inappropriate to maintain systems and pursue former tenants, not least because many lettings will be on shorter leases granted initially to the current tenant.

It is worth noting that a seemingly straightforward consent which permits a tenant to undertake alterations could result in former tenants/guarantors escaping liability, because the consent effectively varies the lease. This is one illustration of the importance of seeking good-quality legal advice, and also of the need to maintain effective management systems, including checklists, for example, which make case surveyors and also administrative staff aware of the implications and financial consequences of certain, sometimes apparently innocuous, actions. The inadvertent acceptance of rent which can 'waive' the ability to take action against tenants for certain, 'once and for all', breaches of covenant (such as user or alienation provisions), is a common situation to be alert to, but in the case of repairs, the breach is ongoing, enabling rent to be accepted for the duration of forfeiture proceedings or damages claims.

Records also need to be maintained of deeds of variation, licences to undertake alterations, consent to undertake improvements, previous schedules of condition and dilapidations, and general correspondence – all of which may be required to help settle dilapidations claims, compensation for improvements and compensation for disturbance, and also to help determine, for example, the basis of rental valuation and therefore the market rent at rent review and lease renewal. Note, for example, that although compensation for improvements may appear to mitigate a tenant's liability for disrepair, tenants may still have to demonstrate that their improvements were undertaken with the landlord's consent, and will still have to serve the required notice (the time frame for which may have passed before the landlord instigates a dilapidations claim). It is also important that leases determine the extent of the demise, including responsibility for maintenance of access ways, roof space, party walls and so on. When repairs are being undertaken, regard may also be given to other legislation such as the Party Walls Act 1996 or the Access to Neighbouring Land Act 1992.

Contributed by Austen Imber

CHAPTER 39

Dilapidations (part 2)

Published as 'How to patch up repairs disputes', 25 August 2001

In the second part of our introduction to dilapidations, we look at how disrepair damages are worked out, together with other factors affecting landlords and tenants

Mainly for Students of 28 July 2001 gave an overview of the main issues affecting landlords and tenants of commercial property in respect of dilapidations. In this issue we examine the valuation basis upon which damages for disrepair are assessed, together with other factors influencing the approach taken by the parties to remedy disrepair.

Section 18 (1) of the Landlord and Tenant Act 1927 provides that both during the lease and at its expiry, damages for a breach of a repairing covenant by a tenant are limited to the diminution in the value of the landlord's reversion, if any, which results from the breach.

Landlords usually pursue dilapidations when leases expire. 'Reversion' therefore generally refers to the landlord's interest at the expiry of the lease when the tenant vacates, but can also apply mid-term.

Determining diminution in value

The cost of undertaking remedial works listed in a schedule of dilapidations may not equate to the diminution in the value of the landlord's reversion.

For example, when a lease expires on an old industrial or warehouse property, the cost of remedying items of disrepair may be greater than the impact of that disrepair on the demand from prospective tenants for functional, low-specification, cheap accommodation. Consequently, disrepair may have little affect on the rental value and investment value of the property.

Similarly, the degreasing of floors and painting of walls required by a landlord of a car mechanic's garage is unlikely to concern a new occupier whose activities will soon deposit oil and dirt around the property.

A costed schedule of dilapidations is more likely to equate to the diminution in the value of the landlord's reversion where, for example, at the expiry of a lease on prime office premises, prospective new tenants require the property to be in 'good and substantial repair' at the start of their lease.

Where the landlord pursues a claim for damages during the term of the lease, the diminution to the value of the reversion is likely to be lower where the lease has a relatively longer period still to run. However, diminution in value may be more evident where disrepair is serious, and/or where a landlord is wishing to sell, and can demonstrate the effect of disrepair on the price that could be achieved.

Assessing the landlord's intentions

At lease expiry, there could be a large difference in the tenant's liability depending on whether a re-letting, refurbishment or redevelopment takes place.

Section 18 (2) of the 1927 Act provides that if, for example, the property is to be demolished for redevelopment, the value of the landlord's interest is not diminished by the state of disrepair, and damages would not be payable. A refurbishment of the property may limit a damages claim to external repairs.

Tenants should establish the landlord's aspirations for the property, especially where they are vacating by choice and the landlord has not had to establish a ground for possession, such as the intention to redevelop the property. A landlord's plans to redevelop but also seek cash settlement from tenants may be revealed by a planning permission being in place.

Discussions between the landlord and planners will be confidential, but tenants could consider which option for the property may be the most commercially viable, having regard to market potential (although in some cases, options may be influenced by the landlord's financial position or other special factors).

Tenants may be able to enhance their case by showing, for example, that the landlord has not sought to market the property for re-letting. Note that a landlord's claim for damages relating to the cost of undertaking repair work generally has more weight where it is intended that such work actually be carried out.

Note also that if, to obtain maximum damages for disrepair, a landlord purports no intention to redevelop, but after receiving damages does redevelop, the tenant may be able to seek redress. This is based on misrepresentation and is a very difficult area, with such situations rarely arising in practice.

Negotiation and litigation

The Civil Procedure Rules 1998, also known as the Woolf Reforms, have changed the procedures by which landlords and tenants conduct litigation. In the case of damages for disrepair, the onus is on the landlord to demonstrate loss in accordance with section 18's basis of diminution in value.

However, as part of their negotiating strategy, some landlords may still adopt a traditional starting point of providing the tenant with a costed schedule of dilapidations. In situations such as where a new tenant would require all disrepair to be remedied on reletting, or require an allowance to undertake the work itself, a costed schedule may reasonably equate to diminution in value, and therefore may be a legitimate approach.

But where a cost-based approach is clearly inappropriate – such as with some older, secondary, properties – using such an approach merely to test a tenant's alertness to the correct basis of valuation is not good practice. Indeed, some landlords may deliberately overstate the extent of remedial works to influence negotiations and/or to assist possible litigation. Some schedules of dilapidations may give little regard to the repair covenants in a lease, or to statute or case law.

Landlords may also be seeking a cash settlement without intending to undertake any work. As shown above, it is important, therefore, for tenants to closely examine the lease terms and establish the landlord's true intentions for the property.

Note also that it is for the landlord to prove disrepair. Unless expressly provided for in the lease, a schedule of dilapidations should not, for example, require the tenant to test all electrical services or commission a contamination survey.

The position with relettings

In determining damages, consideration would also be given as to whether the need for repairs prevented the building being let, or whether, as a result of market conditions, there would likely to be a void period anyway. The fact that the departure of the tenant may enhance the value of the landlord's reversion is ignored. Damages are still available if the value of the reversion is negative, such as where a tenant of an over-rented property pursues a sub-tenant for dilapidations. Note that the valuation date is the date of termination of the lease.

Sometimes a landlord's claim for damages will be based on a capital contribution, rent-free period or other allowances granted to the new tenant in respect of work that needs to be done to the property. In this case, the departing tenant should be satisfied that any allowance represents the extent of its liability for disrepair, and does not, for example, include the cost of higher specification works required by the new tenant, or is not part of a wider package of incentives.

The deal with the new tenant could have been constructed having regard to the dilapidations claim, and to the overall objective of enhancing the investment profile of the property by granting incentives. Outgoing tenants could also check that the new tenant is actually obliged to undertake the works.

Other issues

Other issues arising include:

- The landlord's claim for damages could include the loss of rent and service charge contributions and the payment of empty rates charges or other liabilities. Fees incurred by the landlord in procuring repair work could also be recovered, but surveying fees or legal fees incurred in connection with notices and negotiations could only be recovered if the right to do so was provided in the lease. The costs of taking legal action may, of course, be recovered through the court's award of costs.
- Yielding up and reinstatement provisions are generally also subject to section 18 (1), so there may not be a liability, for example, to redecorate or reinstate alterations despite such obligations being stated in the lease.
- Complexities can arise where a property has been sublet. A tenant may have to take action against sub-tenants because it is being pursued for disrepair by its landlord. The liability of tenants and sub-tenants could differ because of the nature of their reversionary interests, the length of their respective unexpired terms and because repair covenants differ.
- At the expiry of a lease, departing tenants may wish to prepare a schedule of condition themselves where the landlord has not

prepared a schedule of dilapidations, or where the tenant wishes to contest the extent of the landlord's schedule of dilapidations. This will also help to protect against any liability for disrepair occurring after the lease expires.
- A tenant does not generally have a right to enter the property following lease expiry, and may not therefore be able to minimise their liability by undertaking the works itself – which can be cheaper than when the landlord procures the work. Tenants should consider their position in advance of lease expiry, possibly even with a view to offering the landlord a cash settlement.

The Leasehold Property (Repairs) Act 1938

Under this Act, if a lease was granted initially for a term of seven years or more and still has at least three years to run, a landlord must seek the court's permission before proceeding with an action for damages or before proceeding to forfeit the lease.

Action against a tenant still begins by serving a section 146 notice (requiring a forfeiture clause within the lease), but the notice must also advise the tenant of its right to claim the protection afforded by the 1938 Act by serving a counter notice within 28 days. If the tenant does not serve a counter notice, the landlord can continue with proceedings in the usual way.

If the tenant serves a counter notice, the court must be satisfied that the state of disrepair is serious, and that the work needs to be undertaken. To be granted permission, the landlord has to establish one of the following five grounds:

- The value of the reversion has been substantially diminished by the state of repair, or will be substantially diminished unless repairs are undertaken immediately.
- Repairs must be undertaken immediately in order to comply with any Act.
- Where the tenant is not in occupation of the whole of the property, repairs need to be undertaken immediately to protect the interests of another occupier.
- The cost of undertaking repairs immediately would be low compared to the cost of undertaking repairs in the future.
- It is just and equitable to grant leave because of special circumstances.

The provisions of section 18 (1) and the requirements of the 1938 Act often discourage landlords from seeking to remedy disrepair during the term of the lease. Indeed, the argument for mid-term damages may be particularly difficult to sustain, unless, for example, the landlord is selling the property and can demonstrate a capital loss.

Self-help approach
As an alternative to claiming damages or seeking to forfeit the lease, a landlord may be able to undertake the necessary repairs itself, and recover the costs from the tenant.

For landlords to be able to successfully employ this self-help remedy, the costs need to be recoverable as a debt, and not as damages. Unlike a claim for damages, a claim for debt falls outside the provisions of the 1938 Act and, also, is not covered by the provisions of section 18(1).

To provide an effective remedy of self-help, the lease should enable the landlord to enter the property for the purpose of inspection, provide the ability to serve a notice detailing the work required, specify a date by which the works should be completed, provide the necessary rights to enter the property to undertake repairs and recover the cost from the tenant, and state that the cost is recoverable as debt.

When pursuing the self-help remedy, it is particularly important that landlords prepare an accurate, rather than a negotiable schedule of dilapidations, and are aware that tenants will not be liable for the cost of work beyond their liability under the repair covenant.

Self-help provisions can place landlords in a strong negotiating position, although the tenant's financial standing will always have to be considered. Tenants should look to exclude such clauses, or impose suitable qualifications on the rights of the landlord. The landlord could, for example, be expressly made liable for any damage it causes and be obliged to cause minimal disruption to the tenant's occupation of the property.

The tenant's remedies for disrepair
The landlord is in breach of its repairing covenants once they have been given notice of the state of disrepair, or are aware of it, and is not in breach of covenant merely because the property is in disrepair.

Remedies for the tenant include:

- suing the landlord for damages;

- seeking an order from the court for specific performance (compelling the landlord to undertake remedial works);
- seeking the appointment of a receiver which will then manage the property and fulfil the obligations of the landlord; and
- undertaking the work itself then deducting the cost from the rent as it becomes due – known as 'setting-off'. Tenants cannot 'set off' in this way if the lease states that rent should be paid 'without any deduction whatsoever' or similar terminology. A landlord's inclusion of such a clause also prevents tenants from tactically concocting reasons for deductions when their true intention is to avoid rent payment.

Tenant's break, and repair

The ability of a tenant to exercise a break clause may depend on compliance with the terms of the lease, including repairing covenants. The tenant may be forced to remedy even relatively minor items of disrepair to preserve the right to break – and this would apply even where the landlord intends to take the tenant's break as an opportunity to redevelop/demolish the property.

Where landlords are uncooperative and possibly reluctant to provide a schedule of dilapidations, tenants should be in a position to undertake the works themselves if necessary – even if this means vacating the property well before lease expiry. Tenants may take the lead in negotiating a cash settlement, but should note that the break clause requirements may be very onerous.

At the start of a lease, tenants should resist the requirement for break clauses to be conditional on the performance of repair covenants. They should aim to be in the same position as they would be at lease expiry: facing only a damages claim for disrepair, rather than liability for rent and the performance of other covenants for the remainder of the lease, notwithstanding their ability to assign or sub-let, and noting also that their interest could be over-rented.

Contributed by Austen Imber

CHAPTER 40

Remedies for rent default

Published as 'Remedies for rent default', 9 January 1999

Landlords have various options when tenants won't pay up – but their surveyors must be careful not to advise steps that work against landlords' own interests

When tenants of commercial property default on rent or other payments due, surveyors may be asked to formulate an appropriate course of action on behalf of the landlord.

This article will outline how the problems of rent default can be minimised – but readers should be aware that there may be qualifications, exceptions, related legislation and particular lease terms which warrant the seeking of more detailed advice. Particular care must be taken when tenants become embroiled in an insolvency process, such as liquidation, bankruptcy or administration. In those circumstances, statute intervenes to restrict the landlord's remedies.

Initial considerations

The course of action formulated must have regard to the possibility that the pursuit of rent arrears could result in the termination of the lease or in the business failure of the tenant.

Issues which landlords need to consider include the following:

- The landlord may wish to preserve the right to receive rent from the current tenant or preserve any rights that may be available against previous tenants or guarantors (having regard to the Landlord and Tenant (Covenants) Act 1995). The preservation of the existing lease terms may uphold the investment value of the property. A landlord may wish to be particularly protective of over-rented interests.
- The landlord will wish to avoid responsibility for insuring the property, avoid liability for empty rates, avoid having to absorb service charges, and avoid incurring any other costs that result from the property being vacant.

- Regard should be given to the level of rent passing, to the state of the market, to the prospect of securing a reletting, and to the likely rent and other terms that could be achieved on reletting.
- Repossession could be attractive for a landlord where the rent passing is significantly below market value, where the tenant has paid a premium at lease commencement, or where the tenant pays a ground rent.
- Where the landlord has redevelopment aspirations, repossession may avoid the need to negotiate a surrender, avoid the need to establish an intention to develop in order to secure possession, and avoid having to pay the tenant compensation. Alternatively, the landlord may wish to occupy the property himself.
- The capital value of a property with vacant possession may be greater than the investment value of the property, therefore providing the landlord with a welcome opportunity to sell.
- The landlord may wish to preserve the right to enforce other terms such as the repair covenant. Disrepair may result in a rent-free period, or a contribution towards expenditure having to be granted to a new tenant, with little or no prospect of securing damages from the previous tenant. Other breaches of covenant such as unlawful subletting or a wider than permitted use of the property may provide the landlord with an opportunity to secure an enhanced rent, or more favourable other lease terms, instead of securing possession.

Wider considerations could include the disadvantage of having a vacant unit on an industrial estate. Rent reviews on other units may, for example, be influenced by the inability to relet the vacant unit.

It may not be wise to prejudice additional commercial relationships that may exist between the landlord and tenant, such as where the tenant rents property elsewhere from the landlord, or where one of the parties is a trade customer of the other.

The course of action taken by the landlord will be influenced by the level of rent arrears, by the rent payment history and by the financial position of the tenant. A different approach would be taken to a tenant of sustainable covenant strength than to a smaller company or sole trader in severe financial difficulty.

If amicable discussions have failed to secure payment or establish a satisfactory repayment pattern, consideration should be given to the options set out below – remembering that the terms of the lease should initially be examined, and that it may be necessary to work closely with solicitors to ensure that the correct procedures are followed. Some of the relevant legislation is archaic and complex.

Forfeiture

The landlord can seek to forfeit the lease for the non-payment of rent only where the lease contains a forfeiture clause (a right to forfeit/proviso for re-entry). The lease usually provides that payment must be 14 or 21 days overdue before the right to forfeit can be exercised. Unless the lease dispenses with the need to do so, the rent must have been formally demanded.

The landlord may also be able to forfeit the lease upon the tenant's insolvency, even if no rent or other amounts are outstanding, although to do this, a 'section 146 notice' (Law of Property Act 1925) must first be served.

The lease is forfeited by the landlord 're-entering' the property, either by physical re-entry or by commencing proceedings to recover possession, and obtaining a judgment for possession.

Forfeiture terminates the lease, and also terminates the continuing contractual liability of former tenants and guarantors. It also brings subtenancies to an end.

- *Relief*. Once the property has been repossessed, a tenant can nevertheless 'revive' the lease by applying to court for 'relief against forfeiture'. If the rent, interest on the rent and landlord's costs are paid, the tenant is likely to obtain relief. The tenant has up to six months from the date of the possession order or re-entry to do this. However, the right to relief is not automatic. The court may refuse it, for example, if the landlord wishes to relet the property and informs the disappointed tenant of his intention.

    Subtenants and mortgagees can also apply for relief against forfeiture. If successful, they obtain a new lease on similar terms to those of the forfeit headlease but, in the case of a subtenant, only for the length of the sublease.

    A landlord must serve forfeiture proceedings on subtenants and mortgagees. However, there is no obligation to inform them of an intention to physically re-enter. This does not prejudice a subtenant in occupation who will naturally be aware of the re-entry, but mortgagees may be unaware of events.
- *Waiver*. Any conduct by the landlord consistent with recognition of the continued existence of the lease will amount to 'waiver'

of the right to forfeit. Examples include negotiating a surrender, requiring disrepair to be remedied or accepting rent.
- *Practical issues*. The threat of repossession may prompt the payment of arrears, but could alert the tenant to the need to oppose physical re-entry, knowing that it is a criminal offence for the landlord or bailiffs to use violence to gain access. The tenant does not have to be warned in advance that the landlord intends to repossess the property and, unlike breaches of other covenants, a 'section 146 notice' need not be served.

The surveyor should be alert to the possibility that the tenant may seek to break back into the property to continue running the business or to facilitate relocation. Returning tenants sometimes cause substantial damage.

Distraint

The right to distrain need not be included in the lease and can be exercised as soon as arrears are due. However, distraint can only be undertaken where the arrears comprise rent or other sums expressly reserved in the lease as 'rent'.

To distrain, the lease must be in existence (so distraint could not take place following forfeiture). Also, distraining presupposes a landlord and tenant relationship, and therefore waives any existing right to forfeit. Accordingly, if a landlord wishes to repossess because rent is outstanding, but wishes also to effectively recover arrears by distraint, then distress must be completed before a fresh right to forfeit arises.

The bailiff gains entry to the property and produces an inventory of the tenant's goods that could eventually be sold to meet the debt. The goods must be physically present on the property.

The goods can either be impounded on the property (deemed seizure) where the tenant enters into a 'walking possession' agreement, or be impounded off the premises (actual seizure) by removal and storage. If payment is not made within five days following seizure (or 15 days if the tenant requests an extension), the goods can be sold. Arrears and amounts such as the bailiff's fees or an auctioneer's costs will be deducted, with any surplus being returned to the tenant. The landlord is obliged to achieve the best price for the goods, although is not compelled to arrange a public auction.

Distraint may not be able to be levied on items in actual use/ tools of the trade, on fixtures and fittings or on goods belonging to third parties. Third parties can make an appropriate declaration to recover impounded goods, but goods belonging to unlawful subtenants are not protected.

Managing surveyors should be aware of whether the tenant is likely to have goods of sufficient value on the property to make distraint effective. Forfeiture could be a fall-back option but, unlike distraint, would bring the lease to an end.

Serving a statutory demand

The service of a statutory demand for payment on the tenant can be an effective pressure tactic, as ultimately it could result in the insolvency of the tenant. The amount claimed must be certain, and must exceed £750. Landlords should avoid giving tenants the opportunity, tactically, to engineer contention, such as claiming that the rent has not been calculated correctly, or that service charge expenditure has not been evidenced in accordance with the terms of the lease.

Unlike forfeiture, the initial action need not prejudice the continued existence of the lease. If, however, within 21 days of the service of the demand, the tenant has not settled the debt, or has not applied to the court to have the demand set aside, the landlord must consider whether to begin bankruptcy proceedings against an individual, or winding-up proceedings against a company.

Issuing proceedings

Proceedings tend only to be issued against tenants where other courses of action are considered inappropriate, such as where the tenant is not in occupation of the property, or where the tenant is withholding rent because of a dispute about another matter.

Proceedings may be appropriate if the tenant has no seizable assets but owns property elsewhere; in which case, the landlord could obtain a judgment, and then secure payment of the debt by way of a charging order over other property. Proceedings could also be issued to recover arrears following repossession.

Lastly, there are the additional options for the landlord detailed below.

Additional options open to the landlord

- The landlord could serve notice on subtenants, detailing the amounts due, and requiring that future payments are made

direct until arrears are cleared. Distraint could be levied if the subtenant fails to pay.
- The landlord could utilise a rent deposit/bond already provided by the tenant, and then seek replacement funds to preserve the level of the bond (after initially ensuring that the lease obliges the tenant to pay additional funds).
- A lease surrender could be negotiated with the tenant.
- Rent arrears could be used as a ground for opposing the renewal of the lease. This would be feasible only where lease expiry or an appropriate break facility is imminent, or where the tenant has a periodic tenancy.
- The service of a notice opposing the renewal of the lease can help to concentrate the tenant's mind. The new lease may be concluded earlier and on more favourable terms.
- The use of the ground for possession of 'persistent failure to pay rent' could be added to other grounds upon which the landlord is seeking to recover possession of the property.

Good relations

A good landlord and tenant relationship often results in a good rent payment record, and also makes it easier for the surveyor to determine whether the tenant is in genuine need of assistance to clear arrears, or whether immediate and forceful action needs to be taken. Consideration of the consequences of losing the tenant, or the opportunities presented by vacant possession, is essential in order to preserve or enhance value for the landlord.

How landlords can pre-empt rent default

- Tenants should be credit vetted in the first instance. Company accounts should be used to assess the tenant's financial position and future prospects. Previous rent payment records or other credit histories will usually be more revealing than bank or trade references. However, landlords may sometimes just have to take a risk with start-up businesses or poor quality tenants.
- The landlord could require guarantors, who could be associated companies of the tenant, separate companies or individuals. Securing the directors of the company as personal guarantors can be particularly effective.
- A bond could be secured from the tenant. A strong reluctance by a prospective tenant to pay a bond, particularly to a landlord of reasonable repute, could be a sign that the tenant is seeking

cost-effective and possibly short-term occupation. The landlord is particularly exposed to the problems of disappearing tenants where rent for only one period is paid in advance, and at the end of the period, the landlord has no rent or other security.

The repayment of a bond could be conditional on rent being paid by the due date (or within, say, 10 days). Late payment could be subject to interest charges. A break facility could be conditional upon all payments being made on time.

- The most favourable terms that could be included in a new lease include a forfeiture clause, which can be effective whether rent is formally demanded or not, and the reservation of all amounts due as rent. Provisions should minimise the tenant's ability to claim set-off or to counter claim against any amounts demanded by the landlord. This also deters tactical claims by the tenant that seek to disrupt courses of action undertaken by the landlord to recover arrears. Covenants to pay rent 'without deduction' or 'without any deduction whatsoever' may not be conclusive. Tenants may be able to statutorily deduct certain items and regard should also be given to the Unfair Contract Terms Act 1977.
- Where there is a good landlord and tenant relationship, and where the surveyor has been able to build a rapport with the tenant, there is a greater tendency for the rent to be paid on time. Particularly in the case of industrial estates, there is also a greater chance of finding out about the financial fortunes of other tenants.
- Rent recovery should not be the sole responsibility of the bookkeeper or accountant. The surveyor's attention should be drawn to default within, say, a week of the amounts becoming due.
- Surveyors should be alert to the tactics that tenants may employ. Some tenants will telephone to apologise that the rent has not been paid and seek a restructured payment pattern. Other tenants will wait for the landlord to chase arrears. Where the tenant usually waits to be chased, but offers profuse apologies and repeated promises of imminent payment, it may be a sign that the tenant is planning to disappear. Tenants may also pay part of the rent, or pay the rent but not the VAT, or not the service charges or insurance payments.
- The fortunes or the intentions of a tenant could also be demonstrated by factors such as changes or reductions in

staff; the departure or unavailability of key personnel; the build-up, decline or absence of stock; an absence or increase in the amount of goods being stored or company vehicles being parked outside the property; unusual opening hours; changes of use and a deterioration in the condition of the property.
- Administration and management systems need to ensure that rent is not inadvertently demanded or accepted (as this could, for example, recognise the continuing existence of the lease following forfeiture, and amount to waiver). Tenants should not be able to tactically make payment direct into the landlord's or his agent's bank account.
- Cash payments should not be accepted without the managing surveyor's approval, and tenants should not, for example, be able to pay cash and secure receipts from receptionists. The problem is that even if such action by the tenant is eventually deemed to be insufficient to act as a waiver, it may cause temporary disturbance which is of great value to the tenant.

Legislative changes enabling easier remedies

For some time there has been a clamour for rationalisation and reform of the law relating to the remedies of forfeiture and distress. These have long been perceived as too complex and confused.

Forfeiture

In the context of non-payment of rent, the Law Commission proposed, among other things, the abolition or repeal and modification of (a) the present rules governing forfeiture by physical re-entry, (b) automatic waiver by acceptance of rent and (c) the regimes relating to the grant of relief to subtenants and mortgagees.

Broadly speaking, it is proposed that when a 'termination order event' (ie failure to pay rent) occurs, the landlord will have six months to apply for a 'termination order'. It is envisaged that this order will either be 'absolute' (stating a date when the tenancy will end) or 'remedial' (providing that the tenancy will end on a specific date unless certain specified action is taken).

The termination order will end subtenancies, but the courts will not make an order unless satisfied that subtenants and mortgagees have had the chance to apply for relief. The landlord can preserve subtenancies; and subtenants and mortgagees can apply for their interests to be preserved.

Physical re-entry will become illegal unless the landlord first serves a 'preliminary notice' requiring the tenant to pay the rent. The landlord will also be obliged to inform subtenants and mortgagees that he has served a preliminary notice on the tenant. The landlord will then have six months to re-enter, and the tenancy will end either three months after the re-entry or earlier, if the landlord can prove that the tenant has 'abandoned' the property.

It is proposed that landlords will not be able to physically re-enter if the rent payable under the lease is less than the market rent. This proposal is aimed at leases granted in consideration of a premium or at a ground rent.

Subtenants and mortgagees will be able to apply for relief at any time from the date of service of the preliminary notice until the tenancy ends.

Any demand or acceptance of rent will no longer automatically amount to 'waiver'. Whether or not waiver has occurred will be a question of fact to be determined by the court.

Distress

Distress is a relic of feudalism. The Law Commission has noted that it is an archaic and anomalous remedy which is inappropriate for modern society. While recognising the case for abolition altogether, the Law Commission has not gone that far. In the absence of any more efficient debt recovery mechanism suited for society's needs, the Law Commission has recommended that distress be retained as a remedy.

However, if it is to be retained, the Law Commission recommended that there is a strong case for codification, in modern terms, of the statutes and principles laid down in case law.

Contributed by Austen Imber

CHAPTER 41

Peaceful re-entry

Published as 'They come in peace', 27 July 2000

The legal principle of peaceful re-entry is well established, but what does it mean and how effective is this procedure as a means of forfeiting a lease?

A landlord may exercise his right to forfeit a lease either through a 'breach of condition' or for a 'breach of covenant' in a lease. Whether a term is a condition depends on the interpretation of the words used.

In *Doe d Henniker* v *Watt* (1828) 8 B&C 308 the words 'stipulated and conditioned' were used in relation to a clause concerning assignment and subletting. It was held that this obligation constituted a condition.

Where a covenant (not amounting to a condition) has been breached, there must be a forfeiture clause in the lease reserving a right of re-entry and covering the activity that the tenant is said to have breached. The most usual procedure is for forfeiture to be pursued through the courts through an action for possession. However, it is also possible (in the right circumstances) to gain possession without the court's assistance by the self-help procedure known as 'peaceable re-entry'.

Peaceable re-entry may also be used by the landlord where the lease has come to an end by some other process, for example by surrender or by effluxion of time, where the lease does not come within the ambit of any statutory protection. If, for instance, the court has given its approval, a business lease may be excluded from the statutory protection given by the Landlord and Tenant Act 1954 Part II: see section 38(4).

Residential tenancies

The Protection from Eviction Act 1977, as amended by the Housing Act 1988, precludes eviction of residential occupiers without court proceedings. Although there are some exceptions to this rule (including lettings under section 3A – see p292), these exceptions apply only to post-Housing Act 1988 tenancies.

In all cases, section 6 of the Criminal Law Act 1977 must be borne in mind. This makes it a criminal offence to use or threaten to use violence to secure the entry to any premises where there is someone on the premises at the time who is opposed to entry, and the person threatening or using violence knows this to be the case. This section curtails the circumstances in which the process of peaceable re-entry can be used.

Forfeiture process

Whether the lease is to be forfeited through the courts or by peaceable re-entry, the provisions of section 146(1) of the Law of Property Act 1925 must be adhered to. Except where the breach of covenant related to non-payment of rent or to some further exceptions (such as agricultural or pastoral land, mines and minerals), the landlord must serve a notice on the tenant. A section 146 notice must:

(a) specify the particular breach complained of; and
(b) if the breach is capable of remedy, require the tenant to remedy the breach (a reasonable time must be allowed for the tenant to do this); and
(c) in any case, it must require the tenant to make compensation in money for the breach.

The particulars of breach must always be included in the notice to the tenant. The landlord must then decide whether the breach is capable of remedy. If he decides that it is not – and if the court decides otherwise – the landlord's failure to specify the remedy will invalidate the notice: see *Expert Clothing Service & Sales Ltd* v *Hillgate House Ltd* [1985] 2 EGLR 85. If the landlord decides that the breach is capable of remedy then a reasonable amount of time must be specified in the notice, otherwise the action will fail.

As to the question of damages, it was established in *Rugby School* v *Tannahill* [1935] 1 KB 87 that a notice is not invalid merely because it fails to ask for compensation.

Where the breach in question relates to a failure to repair with more than three years remaining on the lease, the provisions of the Leasehold Property (Repairs) Act 1938 will apply. (There are some exceptions to this provision, contained in section 1(1), section 3 and section 7(1) – such as where the original lease was for less than seven years.)

If the 1938 Act is applicable then the section 146 notice must contain a statement, in characters equally readable or equally sufficient to the body of the notice, informing the tenant of his right to serve a counternotice within 28 days. If this is subsequently served by the tenant, leave of the court will be needed before the landlord can proceed with the re-entry. The court will only give leave if circumstances fall within section 1(5) of the said 1938 Act.

Waiver

Landlords and their managing agents must take great care, once they have made a decision to forfeit the lease, not to carry out any action that would 'waive' the breach.

Waiver of the breach will arise if, with knowledge of the breach, the landlord or his agent acts in such a way as to give the tenant the impression that the landlord has elected to treat the lease as continuing.

The courts consider this objectively. For example, waiver can arise if, with knowledge of the breach, a rent review clause is operated or a demand for rent is sent out. This applies even if done mistakenly. This occurred in the case of *Central Estates (Belgravia) Ltd* v *Woolgar (No 2)* [1972] 223 EG1273, where an instruction from the landlord not to send out a rent demand did not reach one of the clerks and it was issued in error.

Relief from forfeiture

Section 146(2) of the Law of Property Act 1925 provides that a tenant can apply for relief from forfeiture by the courts.

Lord Templeman in *Billson* v *Residential Apartments Ltd* [1992] 1 EGLR 43 stated:

The need for such intervention was and is manifest because otherwise a tenant who had paid a large premium for a 999-year lease at a low rent could lose his asset by a breach of covenant which was remediable or which caused the Landlord no damage. The forfeiture of any lease, however short, may unjustly enrich the Landlord at the expense of the tenant ... In practice this discretion is exercised with the object of ensuring that the landlord is not substantially prejudiced or damaged by the revival of the lease.

In *Billson* the landlord argued that, under section 146(2), a tenant could not apply for relief against forfeiture after the landlord had peacefully re-entered business premises. The landlord's argument was that, after peaceful re-entry, he was no longer 'proceeding' against the tenant (with a view to obtaining forfeiture of the lease) but, by self-help, had already succeeded in exercising his right of re-entry. The House of Lords rejected this proposition and held that a tenant could apply for relief against forfeiture under section 146(2) of the 1925 Act even after the landlord had forfeited by re-entry without first obtaining a court order for that purpose.

Landlords should be aware that there is always the risk that an aggrieved tenant may be successful in thwarting an apparently successful peaceable re-entry by applying to the courts afterwards for relief from forfeiture.

Peaceable re-entry – when and how?

Peaceable re-entry may be a sensible alternative to court proceedings where, for example, the tenant of business premises appears to have abandoned those premises or where there appears to be little chance of relief against forfeiture ever being given.

If business premises are still being used by the tenant or by his employees, section 6 of the Criminal Law Act 1977 means that re-entry should take place in the early hours of the morning before the property is occupied (provided that there are no security guards employed by the tenant, thereby preventing entry).

Peaceable re-entry is usually effected by smashing or picking locks, and by fitting new ones, but it can also occur through reletting the property.

The recent case of *Re Lomax Leisure Ltd* [1999] 2 EGLR 37 the High Court decided that:

a Landlord was ... entitled to exercise a right of peaceable re-entry even though the tenant was the subject of an administration order or petition.

From another recent case it appears that, once the lease has been forfeited by peaceable re-entry, a tenant cannot remove his fixtures and claim damages. In *Re Palmiero: debtor 3666 of 1999* [1999] 3 EGLR 27 the value of the tenant's fixtures amounted to over £19,000. His counsel argued that the law gives a tenant a reasonable time after re-entry to remove his fixtures. However, although this appears to be a fair assertion, Mr Registrar Jacques felt compelled to follow the authority of *Pugh* v *Arton* (1869) LR 8 Eq 626, in which Sir Richard Malins V-C declared:

unless the tenant protects himself by a contract, giving him a right to take away fixtures after the expiration of the term, either by lapse of time or of his own act, he cannot do so.

Conclusion

Peaceable re-rentry obviously is a quicker and cheaper alternative to re-entry through the courts. However, because of the dangers inherent in the process, it should only be used with legal advice.

The Law Commission has advocated the retention of peaceable re-entry in recognition of the frequency of this process in practice and has said that it will be included in a bill on Termination of Tenancies by Physical Re-entry if and when it is published.

Residential tenancies where eviction is permitted without a court order

Protection from Eviction Act 1977

Section 3A(2)
(a) Under its terms the occupier shares any accommodation with the landlord or the licensor; and
(b) immediately before the tenancy or licence was granted and also at the time it comes to an end, the landlord or licensor occupies as his only or principal home premises of which the whole or part of the shared accommodation formed part.

Section 3A(3)
Accommodation is shared with a member of the landlord' s or licensor' s family and the landlord or licensor were occupying shared accommodation as their only or principal premises at the end of the tenancy and immediately before the commencement.

(This also includes accommodation in the same building as the landlord or licensor that is not a purpose-built block of flats.)

Section 3A(6)
A tenancy or licence granted as a temporary expedient to a person who entered as a trespasser.

Section 3A(7)(a)
A tenancy or licence granted for a holiday only.

Section 3A(8)
A tenancy or licence granted free of rent.

Section 3A(8)
Hostel accommodation within the meaning of the Housing Act 1985 provided by public sector landlords.

Contributed by Monica Dawson

CHAPTER 42

Forfeiture and surrender of leases

Published as 'Two ways to leave your tenant', 16 December 2000

When landlords are faced with an unsatisfactory tenant, they have the choice of forfeiture or surrender. But what do these each entail?

A landlord may be faced with the following (not unusual) problem: rent has not been paid on time, and, as a result, arrears are mounting. The building itself is becoming increasingly dilapidated and ever more underused.

Landlords' choice
In these circumstances, it might be a good idea for the landlord to take advantage of an offer from the existing tenant to vacate the premises and to return the keys, even if the lease has many years still to run. After all, someone could be waiting in the wings with an offer to take a lease of the premises at a higher rent; this someone could even be willing to refurbish the premises. This may seem a simple solution to a complex problem. However, it is a solution that, if not handled correctly, could trap the landlord in a mesh of conveyancing problems, and could render the premises unlettable.

Faced with an unsatisfactory tenant, there are two ways in which a lease can be brought to a premature end: by surrender or forfeiture. As its name implies, forfeiture is a unilateral act, whereby the landlord snatches back a property following a tenant's default. Surrender, however, is a bilateral act that is subject to negotiation between the parties. Both procedures have advantages and disadvantages, as explained below.

Forfeiture
Every conventionally drawn lease contains a forfeiture clause. Upon a strict interpretation of such clauses, a landlord's right to forfeiture will usually arise if rent is more than a few weeks in arrear or if the

tenant has breached any of its other leasehold obligations. Some forfeiture clauses go further, by giving landlords an instant right to forfeiture in the event of a tenant's insolvency, although a provision of this type will usually make a lease unmortgageable.

Does this mean, therefore, that if a rent is scarcely a month in arrear, or if any other technical breach of the lease exists, the landlord can simply walk in, repossess the property and relet to someone else? Unsurprisingly, the answer is 'no'.

Over the centuries, both parliament and the courts have laid down procedures to which landlords must adhere if they wish to forfeit a lease. This is to ensure that tenants are treated fairly and that landlords are prevented from enjoying windfalls at a tenant's expense following a technical breach of covenant. Such procedures also treat rent arrears differently from other breaches of the lease.

In the case of simple rent arrears, a landlord can, in theory, walk in and repossess a property from a non-residential tenant as soon as that tenant falls into arrears. However, matters do not end there. Provided that the tenant subsequently pays off those arrears within a reasonable time, and reimburses any associated out-of-pocket expenses incurred by the landlord as a result of that default, the law will require the landlord to reinstate the tenant. The law's willingness to grant relief against forfeiture has always existed in relation to rent arrears, but it was not until the Conveyancing and Law of Property Act 1881 that relief was extended to other forms of breach.

Procedure

A landlord can never forfeit a lease immediately, other than for rent arrears (or insolvency). It must first follow the procedure laid down in section 146 of the Law of Property Act 1925.

Section 146 requires the landlord to serve formal notice upon the defaulting lessee, specifying the particular breach of covenant complained of, requiring the lessee to remedy the breach (if it is capable of remedy) and, in all cases, requiring the lessee to make fair compensation for the breach.

As with rent arrears, a tenant facing forfeiture can now seek relief under section 146(2) of the 1925 Act. The court may, of course, grant or refuse relief, having regard to the conduct of the parties and other relevant circumstances.

Where a section 146 notice relates to breach of covenant relating to internal decorative repairs, section 147(1) allows the court, in appropriate cases, to relieve the lessee, wholly or partially, from liability for such repairs. A landlord seeking to repossess premises for an alleged breach of any repairing covenant must also comply with the Leasehold Property (Repairs) Act 1938 if the lease has at least three years to run.

To comply with the 1938 Act, a section 146 notice must give the tenant the right to serve a counternotice upon the landlord claiming the benefit of the 1938 Act. If a counternotice is served within 28 days, the landlord cannot then proceed with the forfeiture without first obtaining leave from the court. This will normally be given only if the landlord's reversionary interest is under immediate threat.

Forfeiture can take two forms:

peaceful re-entry into possession; or
an application to the court for a possession order.

It should be noted that peaceful re-entry is usually an option only if no one is in residential occupation of the property. For most residential leases or tenancies, section 3 of the Protection from Eviction Act 1977 states that eviction can take place only under a court order.

A landlord that is considering forfeiture of a lease for breach of any covenant (other than rent arrears) must refuse to accept any future rent until such time as the situation is resolved. If a landlord continues to receive rent, a court may infer that the landlord has 'waived' the breach, which effectively means that it has elected to continue the lease, notwithstanding the breach.

The leading case on forfeiture is currently *Billson* v *Residential Apartments Ltd* [1992] 1 EGLR 43, in which the House of Lords affirmed the general rule that a tenant's right to apply for relief remains preserved, even after peaceful re-entry has taken place.

Surrender

A surrender of a lease can take place only by agreement between the landlord and the tenant. Under such an arrangement, the landlord takes back the premises and releases the tenant from future liability under the lease. If the lease has either a capital value or a negative value, money may then change hands.

Unlike forfeiture, a surrender of a lease is final, and the landlord is therefore free to relet the premises immediately to someone else. However, whereas forfeiture can be regarded as a hostile act on the part of the landlord, a surrender constitutes a conveyancing transaction in which the landlord essentially buys out the tenant's leasehold interest. The appropriate conveyancing searches and inquiries must be made to ensure that the leaseholder has the necessary 'capacity' to effect a surrender. Such capacity may not exist if the lease has been mortgaged or if subtenancies have been created out of it. In such circumstances, the landlord must ensure that these third-party interests have been cleared before the surrender is completed. Alternatively, it must ensure that any respective third parties concur in the surrender.

A physical inspection of the property should also be undertaken before completion of the surrender in order to identify any existing breaches of covenant on the part of the tenant that may affect the value of the landlord's interest, and to ensure that there are no other persons in occupation of whom the landlord was previously unaware. Any such matters can then be taken up with the tenant before the surrender is made final. Otherwise, once the tenant has been released from the lease, it may be too late for the landlord to do anything about it.

The surrender itself can be carried out in one of two ways:

by operation of law; or
by a deed of surrender.

Surrender by operation of law means nothing more than the tenant handing back possession of the property to the landlord, together with the original lease and any associated documentation. Provided the landlord, by its actions, 'accepts' the surrender, the law will treat the lease as being at an end and the tenant will be released from further liability under it. While no formal documentation is required, the fact of the surrender will normally be recorded in correspondence, and a receipt may be issued for any payment handed over by either party to the other.

Stamp duty

Until section 128 of the Finance Act 2000 came into force, the advantage of a surrender by operation of law was that it was always free of stamp duty, even if a large premium had been paid by either party to the other. However, this exemption has been closed, and stamp duty is now payable upon any written document evidencing a surrender. For leases of more than 21 years, an undocumented surrender may no longer be possible, because the Land Registry is insisting upon a statutory declaration setting out the circumstances of any surrender by operation of law.

A deed of surrender is a stand-alone document that records both the surrender of the lease and the former tenant's release from future liability. The deed will also record details of any payment made for the surrender and other associated terms. With the abolition of the stamp duty exemption on surrenders by operation of law, deeds of surrender may now become the norm.

Closing the leasehold title

Any modern lease of more than 21 years requires registration at the Land Registry. A new leasehold title will be created, and a land or charge certificate issued in respect of it. Thus, when a registered lease is surrendered, the landlord must ensure that the registered leasehold title is closed before entering into any dealings with its reversionary interest or granting any new leases out of it. To achieve closure, the landlord must provide the Land Registry with appropriate documentary evidence to prove that the lease has indeed been terminated.

Conclusion

It will be seen from this article that terminating a lease is more complex than simply taking back the keys. In the case of a tenant defaulting, a landlord must choose between forfeiture and a negotiated surrender, and it must weigh up the advantages and disadvantages of each.

Forfeiture versus surrender: Main differences between the two options

Forfeiture	Surrender
Unilateral act	Bilateral act
May not be final, as tenant can seek relief from forfeiture	Always final
No stamp duty implications	May be stamp duty implications
Statutory procedure must be followed	Conveyancing transaction
Overrides third-party interests	Takes subject to third-party interests unless released

Choice between two options: peaceful re-entry and a court application for possession	Choice between surrender by operation of law and a deed of surrender
Registered leasehold title must be closed	Registered leasehold title must be closed

Contributed by VC Ward

CHAPTER 43

Service charge disputes

Published as 'Service record', 16 June 2000

Service charges are notorious for causing problems between landlords and tenants, and if matters turn litigious, several jurisdictions may be involved

Service charges are a common source of dispute between landlords and tenants. They are levied, in addition to rent, to compensate a landlord for services carried out by him for the benefit of all his tenants. Such services will include, among others things, buildings insurance, the maintenance of the block, common areas, lifts, car parks, gardens and other communal external areas, and the provision of caretaking services.

Uncertainty of service charges

Unlike rent, which is fixed in advance and for which a tenant can budget, service charges are variable, and the final amount may not be calculated until after the end of the financial year to which the services relate. They may cover costs for unforeseen emergency work; costs that might not be covered by insurance. Under most leases, landlords enjoy reasonable flexibility in deciding which services they wish to provide and how those services are procured and paid for. It is then left to the tenant to pick up the bill.

A liability to pay service charges will normally be built into a lease when a building is split into separate lettable parts, either as flats or offices. Where a building is let to a single tenant on a long-term basis, it will usually be the tenant's direct responsibility to effect its own essential insurance and to carry out maintenance and redecoration*.

---

* Leases of a 'dwelling-house' (a term that includes flats) are subject to section 11 of the Landlord and Tenant Act 1985 if they are for a term of less than seven years. This includes periodic tenancies (weekly, fortnightly, monthly, yearly etc) even if they might last, or have lasted, for seven years or more. In the case of such leases, the landlord cannot impose significant repairing obligations on the tenant or charge him for the cost of carrying them out.

However, it would be impractical, in the case of residential flats or offices, to expect each individual leaseholder or office tenant to put in place buildings insurance or to undertake structural responsibility for their own section of the building. It could also lead to inconsistencies between different parts of the building regarding the adequacy of insurance and the quality of repairs. It therefore makes sense for the landlord to undertake these responsibilities to a common standard and to share the cost between individual tenants.

Most leases containing service charge provisions also require leaseholders to pay interim payments on account of future services, with a final adjustment being made after the end of the financial year, when the exact amount becomes known.

Common sources of disputes between landlords and their tenants include:

the item for which the charge was made was not something that the landlord could lawfully charge for under the lease;
the service charges were excessive for the work carried out, or the work could have been carried out more economically;
the works were unnecessary.

Starting point

At this stage, it is necessary to distinguish between commercial service charges, which are regulated by the terms of the lease alone, and service charges charged to residential leaseholders, which are now governed by a statutory regime to ensure that leaseholders are properly consulted on major service charge issues and that the charges themselves are fair and reasonable. Either way, one must first look at the lease to ascertain whether the particular item is chargeable, and, if so, whether the landlord has followed the appropriate contractual procedures. For instance, a lease that allows a landlord to charge leaseholders for 'repairs', cannot also charge for items that go beyond simple repair: the law may regard these as 'improvements'.

The issue of commercial service charges was recently considered by Blackburn J in *Fluor Daniel Properties Ltd* v *Shortlands Investments Ltd* [2001] 2 EGLR 103. This concerned a landlord's demand for an estimated £2m to cover air-conditioning and structural repairs to a modern office building. This sum was largely to be recovered by an additional reserve fund contribution of £750,000, coupled with an increased service charge demand of a similar amount. However, although the lease allowed the landlord to 'renew' as well as 'repair' the existing air-conditioning, Blackburn J held that the lease did not entitle the landlord to incur expenditure on plant that was in proper working order and operating to the standard required under the lease.

In reaching his decision, Blackburn J also reviewed several earlier cases, including the judgment of Nichols LJ in *Holding & Management Ltd* v *Property Holding & Investment Trust plc* [1990] 1 All ER 938, in which he (Nichols J) listed the factors a court would take into account when considering a tenant's obligation to reimburse a landlord for 'repair':

The circumstances to be taken into account in a particular case may include some or all of the following: the nature of the building, the terms of the lease, the state of the building at the start of the lease, the nature and extent of the defects sought to be remedied, the nature, extent and cost of the proposed remedial works, at whose expense the proposed remedial works are to be done, the value of the building and its expected lifespan, the effect of the works on such value of lifespan, current building practice, the likelihood of any recurrence if one remedy rather than another is adopted, the comparative cost of alternative remedial works and their impact on the use and enjoyment of the building by the occupants.

Residential leases

The Landlord and Tenant Act 1985 now sets out a statutory code to which landlords must adhere in order to recover service charges against residential leaseholders. The governing rules are:

Service charges can be levied only to the extent that they are reasonably incurred and relate to the provision of services or the carrying out of works to a reasonable standard: section 19(1). Likewise, payments on account of future service charges must be reasonable and contain provision for adjustments: section 19(2).

Service charges relating to capital works exceeding the greater of £1,000 or £50 multiplied by the number of flats cannot be charged unless the landlord has: (i) obtained at least two estimates for the proposed works; and (ii) copied these to each of the leaseholders or displayed them in a conspicuous place, with a formal notice describing the proposed works and inviting observations within one month. Unless the works are urgent, they cannot begin until the end of the time limit for consultation.

Landlords have only 18 months from the date the expenditure was incurred to levy a demand for service charges in respect of that expenditure: section 20B.

A right for leaseholders to request a summary of expenditure incurred in respect of service-charged items and a right to inspect the landlord's accounts, receipts and other documents supporting the summary and to obtain copies or extracts from them: sections 21 and 22.

Role of leasehold valuation tribunals

The 1985 Act (as amended by the Landlord and Tenant Act 1987 and section 83 of the Housing Act 1996) enables residential service charge disputes to be referred to a leasehold valuation tribunal (LVT), on the application of either the landlord or the tenant, for a determination of the reasonableness of the charge. Unless the amount of unpaid service charge has been agreed, or a suitable alternative arbitration provision is contained within the lease, it is compulsory for a landlord who is intending to commence forfeiture proceedings for non-payment to refer to an LVT. Where works have been carried out, or services are currently being provided (or are proposed for the future), the LVT can determine whether:

the costs were (or would be) reasonably incurred;
the works or services are (or would be) of a reasonable standard;
the size of the advance payment is (or would be) reasonable.

Anyone applying to an LVT must pay a one-off fee. The LVT has no power to award professional costs, but it may order the application fee to be reimbursed by the other party. Where a lease includes provision for a landlord's legal costs to be included in service charges, leaseholders may ask the LVT for an order, under section 20C of the 1985 Act, that the landlord's costs arising from the proceedings are not charged to the tenants. The procedure adopted by most LVTs is informal. The panel members are experts in their own fields, and each panel must include someone with a legal qualification and someone else who has a surveying or valuation qualification. Either party can appeal to the Lands Tribunal against the LVT decision.

However, the LVT's function is to deal only with valuation and issues of reasonableness. It has no automatic jurisdiction to provide a legal interpretation on the wording of a lease. Such matters must continue to go to the civil courts. How this works in practice is illustrated by Judge Michael Rich's decision in *Gilje* v *Charlegrove Securities Ltd* [2000] 3 EGLR 89.

Legal interpretation

Here, the question was whether a landlord could require leaseholders to reimburse the notional rental value of a caretaker's flat situated within the block, or whether the landlord was entitled only to reimbursement of its out-of-pocket expenses in housing the caretaker. The issue involved both a legal interpretation of the lease and an adjudication upon whether the charge was 'reasonable'. On a previous hearing, the LVT had ruled that it could not deal with questions relating to the interpretation of the lease. Legal interpretation had to be the subject of separate proceedings in Central London County Court.

Following an appeal from certain aspects of the LVT decision, the case also went to the Lands Tribunal. In the event, both the county court and the Lands Tribunal proceedings were heard by the same judge, who rejected the landlord's claim on a legal interpretation of the lease and also on the ground that the charge would be unreasonable. However, in his judgment in the Lands Tribunal on 15 August 2000, Judge Rich gave helpful advice on how parties could avoid duplication of expense when the case involved both a legal interpretation of the lease and issues of reasonableness. He suggested that:

the parties could jointly invite the LVT to adjudicate on legal matters relating to the interpretation of a lease in the same way as the county court was empowered to do; or

the LVT could adjourn its proceedings while the parties sought an appropriate declaration from the county court; or

legal problems could be anticipated by seeking county court declarations on the issues and then leaving it to the county court to transfer to the LVT issues relating to the reasonableness of the amounts charged.

Contributed by VC Ward

Planning, Development and Environment

44. Water pollution and the law. 307
45. Human rights and the law of sewers 312
46. The law relating to waste disposal. 317
47. Public and private nuisance 322
48. Statutory nuisance 327
49. Noise nuisance and the doctrine of implied repeal. 332
50. Conservation areas and the law 337
51. Listed buildings. 343
52. Planning contravention notices 348
53. ISVA assignment submission/development scheme 352
54. Urban regeneration/RDAs 360

CHAPTER 44

Water pollution and the law

Published as 'Clear waters', 10 January 1998

EC legislation covering water supplies is constantly evolving, with huge implications for the property sector

One of the mechanisms for achieving and maintaining a single European market is the harmonisation of laws across member states. Environmental law is one of the areas where the EC now has competence to legislate.

The European controls in respect of water fall into two categories: (1) water used for specific purposes; and (2) dangerous substances in water.

Drinking water

There are three EC directives which control the quality of drinking water. The first, *Council Directive Concerning the Quality Required of Surface Water Intended for the Abstraction of Drinking Water in Member States* (75/440) was passed in 1975.

It divides surface water into three categories of quality, each requiring different purification treatments.

Surface water, which falls within category A1, requires simple treatment and disinfection. Category A2 requires normal physical and chemical treatment and also disinfection. Category A3 requires intensive treatment.

In 1979 the European Community passed a directive on the sampling and analysis of surface water for drinking (79/869). This prescribes the sampling procedures to be carried out to ensure that drinking water complies with the requirements of the 1975 directive.

In 1980 the EC passed a more extensive directive (80/778). Whereas the 1975 directive was limited to surface water, the 1980 one relates to all water intended for human consumption, including water used in food-processing operations.

It contains three annexes of scientific information relating to the testing of water. Values are set which may be 'Guide Levels' (set at the discretion of member states) or 'Maximum Admissible Concentrations' (values which must be set and met). These levels are called parameters.

Technical advisers have set the parameters to determine the amount of particular substances which are permissible in drinking water. They relate to a number of factors affecting quality, such as taste, smell, transparency, and the presence of a number of substances such as copper, aluminium, lead and bacteria.

In all, 62 different standards are specified. In addition, the directive provides that regular monitoring of drinking water must take place.

It was the 1980 directive which resulted in the UK government enacting regulations to tighten up the quality of drinking water. These introduced more stringent controls on chemicals used in the leather-processing and dry-cleaning industries.

As a result, the Cambridge Water Co closed down its bore-hole at Sawston and unsuccessfully sought compensation from Eastern Counties Leather plc. *Cambridge Water Co Ltd* v *Eastern Counties Leather plc* [1994] 1 ALL ER 53 is now always included in tort lectures at every English university.

Bathing water

The Council Directive on the *Quality of Bathing Water* (76/160) provides for the reduction of pollution of bathing water. The use of limit values within certain parameters (which are flexible and subject to determination) are deployed in the same manner as in the drinking water directive. The directives make use of 'I' values and 'G' values. 'I' values are imperative and must be followed, while 'G' values are guidelines.

Member states must use their best endeavours to follow these values when they test bathing water.

The directive requires that bathing water is sampled, and that this sampling should take place on those days when the daily average density of bathers is at its highest. The sampling should begin two weeks before the beginning of the season.

If the analysis of the samples shows that the value limits have been exceeded there is no sanction provided in the directive itself. It is an interesting question whether an individual bather could bring proceedings against a defaulting member state if he or she was poisoned by swimming in waters which had been allowed to remain contaminated in breach of the directive.

Fish and shellfish

There are two EC directives which prescribe quality standards for freshwater supporting fish life and for shellfish waters (78/659 and 79/923). These directives also make use of 'I' values and 'G' values.

The values relate to the physical and chemical parameters to be observed. The freshwater fish directive applies to waters designated by member states as needing protection or improvement in order to support fish life. It excludes natural or artificial fish ponds used for intensive fish farming.

Dangerous substances in water

The directive which relates to the dangerous substances in water is 76/464 – *Council Directive on Pollution Caused by Dangerous Substances Discharged into the Aquatic Environment*. This 'framework directive' sets out a programme of action and has been followed by later directives. These deal with individual substances, such as mercury, cadmium, carbon tetrachloride, DDT and chloroform.

The framework directive (known as the Dangerous Substances Directive) classifies substances into two lists. The first contains these which are particularly unpleasant and which should be eliminated. The second contains a substances which should be reduced.

List one – known as the black list – contains substances selected because of their toxicity, persistence and bioaccumulation. List two – the grey list – contains families and groups of substances, including a number of metals such as copper, nickel, lead and uranium, which affect the smell or taste of drinking water. It also list substances which affect the balance of oxygen in water, such as ammonia and nitrates.

The Dangerous Substances Directive does not fix the limit values for these substances. This is done through the directives – known as the daughter directives – which deal with individual substances. It is a basic requirement of the framework directive that any discharge into the aquatic environment must be authorised and that emission standards must be prescribed.

The aquatic environment, for these purposes, includes most types of surface waters within the territory of each member state, inland surface waters, territorial waters and internal coastal waters. Groundwater was originally included but it is now covered by a separate directive (80/68).

Groundwater

The groundwater directive deals with the quality of groundwater, much of which now constitutes the drinking water of the EU. The directive is similar in style to the Dangerous Substances Directive and has two lists annexed to it which require either the elimination or reduction of substances in water. There are some differences in the content of the lists. The Groundwater Directive includes all mineral oils, hydrocarbons and cyanides.

Nitrate controls

The Drinking Water Directive sets as a maximum admissible concentrate 50mg of nitrate per litre of water. Specific controls for nitrates in water are provided by a directive on the protection of waters against pollution caused by nitrates from agricultural sources, which was passed in 1991 (91/676).

This directive recognises the need for good agricultural practices and recommends the creation of areas designated for particular protection. Waters must be designated which are, or which may be, affected by pollution by nitrogen compounds.

The member state must then designate as 'vulnerable zones' all the known areas of land which drain into such waters. Prohibitory measures must then be taken, such as the banning of certain types of fertilizer.

Sewerage controls

There is a directive on urban waste water treatment (91/271). This is concerned with the treatment of sewage and industrial effluent. The directive's objective is to safeguard the environment from the effects of the discharge of industrial effluent over a specified period of time. It is mainly concerned with the collection, treatment and discharge of waste water from urban areas and covers both domestic and industrial waste water.

The obligations imposed by the directive are dependent upon the size of the population served by the particular sewerage system. Population size is determined by reference to the organic biodegradable load requiring to be treated. One 'pe' (population equivalent) means an organic biodegradable load having a five-day biochemical oxygen demand (BOD 5) of 60g of oxygen per day*.

---

* In effect, this provision has imposed a duty on member states to maintain sewage treatment works wherever a certain density of population exists.

The directive also requires the identification of more sensitive areas where more stringent treatment will be required.

There is also a directive which deals with the protection of the environment from sewage sludge (86/278). This provides for the treatment of sludge and the soil where sludge is being used.

The future

In December 1993, a European Council decision endorsed a commission report which set out proposals for future changes in the European regime on water. With the insertion of the principle of 'subsidiarity' in the Treaty of European Union there has been much pressure from member states for reform in this area.

Further proposals, issued in February 1997, are for a wide-ranging Water Framework Directive which will replace directives covering groundwater, surface water, fish water and shellfish water.* A new *Integrated Pollution Prevention and Control Directive* (96/61/EC) has also been introduced which will supplement the existing UK system on integrated pollution control. It is expected that this directive will eventually replace the Dangerous Substances Directive.

The Water Framework Directive is intended to cover surface and groundwater, as well as estuaries and coastal waters. It will prevent further deterioration in aquatic ecosystems, promote sustainable water consumption and contribute to the supply of water in terms of both quality and quantity.

It is expected to create a framework directive for a community water policy. An overriding requirement of the Water Framework Directive will be to ensure that member states will achieve a 'good' status for all waters by the end of 2010. But much debate is envisaged before these far-reaching proposals are adopted.

Contributed by Rosalind Malcolm

---

* The Water Framework Directive 2000/60/EC(1) is now in the process of implementation.

CHAPTER 45

Human rights and the law of sewers

Published as 'How to fall foul of the law of sewers, 9 March 2002

There was a time, well within the memory of many law lecturers who are still teaching, when the syllabuses for 'Administrative Law' consisted of such subjects as sewers and drains, education committees, police committees, public highways, markets and fairs, refuse disposal services, and many other subjects that were redolent of Victorian and Edwardian England. In short, they were syllabuses on local government law.

The growth of judicial review in the past 30 years has, of course, put paid to syllabuses of this parochial nature. Nevertheless, two recently reported cases have shown that there is indeed some academic interest to be found in the law relating to sewers and drains.

Because landowners undoubtedly suffer physical damage if their premises are flooded, and suffer financial damage if their property cannot be connected to a public sewer, this aspect of the law can occasionally be of particular interest to property developers, planners, surveyors, and real property lawyers.

Flood damage

In *Marcic* v *Thames Water Utilities Ltd* [2002] EWCA Civ 64; [2002] 07 EG (CS) 122, the claimant's home was flooded because of Thames Water Utilities' failure to carry out suitable repairs to surface and foul water sewers. His claims at common law (for negligence, nuisance and breach of statutory duty) were dismissed by the judge. In doing so, the judge was following precedents dating back to the 19th century: see *Glossop* v *Heston and Isleworth Local Board* (1879) 12 ChD 102. He also rejected a claim under the rule in *Rylands* v *Fletcher* (1868) LR 3 HL 330. However, there is now some doubt as to whether this is a separate head of liability from the tort of nuisance: see *Cambridge Water Co* v *Eastern Counties Leather plc* [1994] AC 264.

The claimant also relied upon his rights under Article 8 and

Protocol 1 (Article 1) of the European Convention on Human Rights. It has been permissible for litigants to rely upon such rights in the courts and tribunals of England and Wales since 2 October 2000, the date upon which the Human Rights Act 1998 came into force in those jurisdictions. (The Convention had come into force approximately one year earlier in Scotland because of the limitations imposed upon the Scottish parliament by the devolution provisions of the Scotland Act 1998.)

Convention rights

The judge awarded damages to the claimant for breach of those Convention rights cited on p316, commencing 2 October 2000. These were awarded to take account of the effect on the value of the claimant's home, particularly having regard to the fact that Thames Water Utilities would not be taking any steps in the foreseeable future to prevent further flooding. (Thames Water Utilities had argued that it would cost more than £30,000 per house, and more than £1,000m in total, to alleviate all the flooding problems of each householder within its area.)

Appeal and cross-appeal

Thames Water Utilities appealed to the Court of Appeal against the award of damages. The claimant cross-appealed against dismissal of his common law claims.

The Court of Appeal held that the inadequacy of the sewers constituted a nuisance at common law. The conduct of Thames Water Utilities in continuing to use the sewers (albeit passively) to perform its statutory duties amounted to a continuation and adoption of that nuisance.

Moreover, the conduct of that public utility also amounted to negligence, given that it had actual knowledge of the problem and had failed to take reasonable steps to abate it: see *Goldman* v *Hargrave* [1967] 1 AC 645 and *Leakey* v *National Trust for Places of Historical Interest or Natural Beauty* [1980] 2 WLR 65. (Both these cases related to nuisances that had arisen naturally – lightning in one case, and movement of an ancient burial mound in the other. Even so, the landowners in question were held to be under a duty to take reasonable steps to protect their neighbours from the effects of such catastrophes.)

Given that the Court of Appeal had interpreted the common law in favour of Mr Marcic's claim, it was not necessary to confine his right to damages to the period following 2 October 2000. Instead, he was entitled to damages at common law for the entire period of his claim. There was, in fact, very little need for the Court of Appeal to refer to the Human Rights Act 1998, since it did not add anything to the validity of Mr Marcic's claims at common law.

It is important to realise that this case turns upon proven defects in a public sewer. These defects had, over many years, been brought to the knowledge of the water and sewerage undertaker. A flood is not, in itself, sufficient evidence of negligence: see *Pritchard* v *Clwyd County Council* The Times 16 July 1992 (a case where a pedestrian was injured because a street had been under 3in to 9in of flood water).

Failure to connect to public sewers

In *R (on the application of Anglian Water Services Ltd)* v *Environment Agency* [2002] 06 EG 155 (CS), the Court of Appeal considered the extent of the Environment Agency's statutory powers under section 101A(7) of the Water Industry Act 1991. The agency had made decisions under that section, stating that the water and sewerage undertaker (Anglian Water Services Ltd) was under a duty to provide a public sewer to serve four villages.

Anglian Water Services had successfully challenged these decisions in the High Court, and in respect of two of these villages (Wretton and Bent Hill) the Environment Agency appealed to the Court of Appeal.

The Appeal Court upheld the judge's ruling that section 101A(7) of the Water Industry Act did not give the agency the power to require sewers to be laid throughout a locality merely because some of the premises required first-time sewerage. Instead, the Environment Agency was under a duty to consider alternative solutions: for example, a private treatment plant.

Private law and public law

Unlike *Marcic*, *Anglian Water Services* did not involve any private rights, even though private property owners would (no doubt) have benefited had the Environment Agency's decisions been upheld by the courts. The question the courts had to consider was one of public law: had the agency acted within its statutory powers, or 'beyond its powers' (*ultra vires*)?

To make a decision in respect of a matter that is not within the statutory terms of reference of the decision-maker is known as 'substantive *ultra vires*'. Failing to take into account a material consideration, such as the alternative methods of providing sanitation, is known as acting 'irrationally'. It is a form of unlawful decision making, which is every bit as serious (in the eyes of an administrative lawyer) as a penchant for taking into account irrelevancies.

Expectations

There is also another type of *ultra vires*, known as 'procedural *ultra vires*'. This refers to the failure of a decision maker to comply with correct procedures, either statutory procedures, or, where applicable, procedures arising from the rules of natural justice or from any legitimate expectation that the decision maker has somehow created.

In *Anglian Water Services*, the water and sewerage undertaker (Anglian Water) had argued that the Environment Agency had transgressed this legal principle. Anglian argued that earlier correspondence had taken place with the Environment Agency, in which the agency had led Anglian to believe that a sympathetic approach would be taken to its proposition that only partial first-time sewerage would be required in Wretton.

As it happened, the Court of Appeal found in favour of Anglian regardless of this argument. Nevertheless, if this procedural point had been the only argument that Anglian had been able to put forward, it would have lost the case. The Court of Appeal held that the only legitimate expectation that Anglian could have formed about this matter was that the Environment Agency would bring an open mind to the facts.

Public purse

Anglian Water Services was an exercise in statutory interpretation, carried out in order to decide which of two public, or quasi-public, bodies had the final say in how and where public money should be spent. In so far as the result favoured the water and sewerage authority (and, no doubt, disadvantaged certain private property owners), it was an example of judicial self-restraint.

By contrast, *Marcic* favoured private property rights over the alleged discretion of the water and sewerage authority to refuse to spend public money on better services. Taken together, the two cases support the well-known principle that the common law more readily sympathises with those who have suffered physical damage (either to themselves or to their property) than it does to those who have suffered economic loss only.

Indeed, the type of loss (if such it be) that is suffered by a landowner whose property has never been connected to a public sewer is far more like the 'loss of a hope' than any sort of economic loss. By contrast, the loss suffered by a homeowner whose home collapses because of defects in its construction is (pace the House of Lords in *Murphy* v *Brentwood District Council* [1991] 1 AC 398) tragically physical and emotionally devastating.

Convention rights breached in Marcic – What the rights specify

Article 8(1) of the European Convention on Human Rights states:

Everyone has the right to respect for his private and family life, his home, and his correspondence.

Protocol 1 (Article 1) commences with the words:

Every natural or legal person is entitled to the peaceful enjoyment of his possessions...

Postscript: After publication of the above article in the *Estates Gazette*, Thames Water plc successfully appealed to the House of Lords against the decision of the Court of Appeal in *Marcic*, see [2004] 1 All ER 135.

Contributed by Leslie Blake

CHAPTER 46

The law relating to waste disposal

Published as 'Don't rubbish the rules', 25 July 1998

Controls on the disposal of waste are tightening and, for those who step out of line, imprisonment is a real prospect

There is now a much greater awareness about the toxicity of waste than there used to be. And it is at the planning stage that fears about its possible effects on the health of the community are first raised.

All developments, including those for the disposal of waste, require planning permission at the outset. Once this has been obtained, it will be for the Environment Agency to determine whether a 'waste management licence' (or an 'integrated pollution control authorisation') should be granted. Planning Policy Guidance Note 23 deals with the division of duties between the local planning authorities and the Environment Agency. (This guidance note is currently being revised – see *Waste Disposal and Management, Department of the Environment and Transport*, PPG 10, February 1998.)

Planning Policy Guidance Note 23 adopts something of the approach taken by the High Court in *Gateshead Metropolitan Borough Council v Secretary of State for the Environment* [1994] 1 PLR 85.

Here, there was a planning application for the construction of a clinical waste incinerator in Gateshead. The pollution which the public feared would be caused by this incinerator led the local authority to refuse planning permission. On appeal, however, the Secretary of State granted planning permission.

It was this decision which was challenged by the local planning authority in the High Court. (This, of course, could be a challenge only on grounds of law, not on grounds of fact or planning policy.) The High Court upheld the Secretary of State's decision.

The court took the view that there was no reason to believe that Her Majesty's Inspectorate of Pollution (now the Environment Agency) would not be able to take an independent and objective view of the application for a waste management licence. It was not for the local planning authority to presume to take that role upon itself.

Europe and waste

At European level the management of waste has been identified as a key task for the 1990s. The emphasis has been placed upon the need to reverse the upward trend in the amount of waste being generated and the increase in the environmental hazards which waste poses. A European Community strategy for waste management up to 2000 has now set out a hierarchy of options. This is underpinned by the so-called 'preventative principle'.

Recycling and reuse of materials are the primary objectives of the strategy, together with improved 'final disposal techniques' for the treatment of waste which cannot be reused. The preventative principle requires the use of clean technologies, ecolabelling, product criteria and behavioural changes by producers and consumers.

In the UK the Secretary of State is obliged, by statute, to produce a national strategy for waste. This will replace local waste management plans which were formerly required of waste regulation authorities.

On June 9 1998 the UK government launched its consultation process for a national waste strategy for England and Wales. It has been made clear that the recycling of household waste and the use of incineration (with energy recovery) would be its cornerstones. These consultations build on the White Paper, Making Waste Work: A Strategy for Suitable Waste Management in England and Wales, which was published in 1995.

A draft national strategy for Scotland was produced in March 1997 by the Scottish Environmental Protection Agency, A Blueprint for Progress 1997–2001. It can now be seen that the order of priority, both in Europe and in the UK, is prevention, reuse or recycling of materials and final disposal of waste.

UK legislation

The European definition of 'waste' has been implemented in the UK by the Waste Management Licensing Regulations 1994. These are accompanied by a lengthy and detailed Circular, *Environmental Protection Act 1990: Part II; Waste Management Licensing: The Framework Directive on Waste*, which provides guidance on the statutory meaning of waste:

'Waste' means any substances or object [set out in Part II of Schedule 4 to the Waste Management Licensing Regulations] which the holder discards or intends or is required to discard.

Waste is considered to be something which poses a significantly different threat to human health or the environment than other human activities, partly because of the manner of disposal and partly because the holder of it no longer has any sense of obligation. Waste, therefore, falls out with the normal cycles of commerce and chains of utility. This is the general test.

A European case, *Vessoso and Zanetti* [1990] 1 ECR 146; 2 LMELR 133, has held that the concept of waste was not to be understood as excluding substances and objects which are capable of economic reutilisation. This has been confirmed in another recent decision of the European Court of Justice, *Tombesi* [1997] 3 CMLR 673. The implication of these decisions is that, even though a byproduct might constitute a secondary raw material, it may nevertheless fall within the definition of waste and therefore be subject to the licensing and regulatory framework.

Waste offences

The current legal regime on waste in the UK is contained in Part II of the Environmental Protection Act 1990. There is an offence, under section 33(1)(c) of that Act, of 'treating, keeping, or disposing of' controlled waste in a manner likely to cause pollution of the environment or harm to human health. This offence can be committed even if a waste management licence is in force and the conditions imposed on the licensee are being complied with.

Section 33 of the 1990 Act also contains offences of 'knowingly causing or knowingly permitting' the deposit etc. of waste without a waste management licence. Similar offences existed under earlier legislation.

Changes were made to the law in 1990. Parliament enacted a duty of care: see section 34, Environmental Protection Act 1990 imposed significant controls on producers of waste and on all others involved in the management of it. Liability now extends beyond the moment when the waste leaves their control. Valuations (eg for insurance purposes) will have to reflect this liability.

Due diligence

The defence of 'due diligence' is a common theme in offences relating to environmental health, food safety, trading standards and similar regulatory areas of the criminal law. This defence is similarly available in the law relating to the management of waste.

One case concerning the defence of 'due diligence' in the context of the management of waste is *Durham County Council* v *Peter Connors Industrial Services Ltd* [1992] Crim LR 743, decided under similar legislation, prior to the implementation of the Environmental Protection Act 1990.

In this case a waste producer left waste in a skip, ready for collection at regular intervals. On one occasion a quantity of special waste was left in the skip, contrary to the terms of the licence. It was held that the 'due diligence' defence had not been proved because the producer should have informed himself, on each occasion, of the contents of the skip. It was not enough that he merely trusted that the system would work.

The defence of 'emergency' has also been the subject of judicial interpretation. In *Waste Incineration Services and Jacob* v *Dudley Metropolitan Borough Council* [1992] 4 LMELR 200 the court held that the defendant must clearly prove that an emergency existed. Clinical waste had been incinerated over a Bank Holiday period when, because of a delay in maintenance work on a hospital incinerator, bags of waste were piling up in an area to which the public has access. The emergency had not been proved because the court declared that temporary storage could have been found and, in any event, the defendant had not sought prior approval from the authority.

Special waste

The 1991 Directive on Hazardous Waste prescribes more stringent rules for dealing with dangerous waste: waste has to be recorded and identified when it is tipped, while rules are laid down for the mixing of such waste.

This directive has been implemented in the UK by the Special Waste Regulations 1996. These regulations prescribe a system of consignment notes identifiable by codes allocated by the Environment Agency (and other agencies). Prenotification procedures are also prescribed so that information regarding the destination of special waste is made available to the agencies. Documentation must be kept by all involved in the handling of special waste for three years.

It is an offence not to comply with these regulations, except where that failure is caused by an emergency or grave danger with all reasonable steps taken to minimise the threat to the public or the environment and the rules complied with as soon as was reasonably practicable.

The main defences – Section 33, Environmental Protection Act 1990

- 'all reasonable precautions and all due diligence', or
- 'acted on instructions from his employer and neither knew nor had reason to know that his acts constituted a contravention', or
- 'acts done in emergency to avoid danger to human health and ... taken to minimise pollution to the environment and harm to human health and the authority was informed as soon as reasonably practicable'.

Contributed by Rosalind Malcolm

CHAPTER 47

Public and private nuisances

Published as 'Nuisance values', 16 September 2000

They share a common name and sometimes overlap, but the differences between public and private nuisances are significant

What is the difference between public and private nuisances? Given the fact that they share a common name, it should come as no surprise that there are probably as many similarities between these two areas of the law as there are distinctions.

Areas of overlap

For example, the same activity can be both a public and a private nuisance: noise, smell and air pollution being just a few of the more obvious areas of overlap. The potential defendants are also similar: not only the creators of a nuisance but also owners liable for the acts of third parties on their land.

In *Sedleigh-Denfield* v *O'Callaghan* [1940] 3 All ER 340 (HL), an owner was found liable in private nuisance for the actions of a trespasser on his property. In *R* v *Shorrock* [1993] 3 All ER 917 (CA), an owner was convicted of public nuisance for allowing a licensee to hold an extremely noisy 'acid house' party on his land.

In both areas of law, there may be circumstances that could give rise to an actionable tort when a foreseeable injury is suffered. In *Sedleigh-Denfield*, the defendant's blocked drains created a state of affairs where flooding of the claimant's land was a foreseeable result.

In *Castle* v *St Augustine's Links* (1922) 38 TLR 615, the frequent occurrence of golf balls being hit onto the highway created a state of affairs that was hazardous to the public. This was particularly so for the claimant, as he lost an eye when one of the golf balls smashed through the windscreen of his car.

Defendant's conduct

In both public and private nuisance the reasonableness of the defendant's conduct is a factor in determining liability.

In *Dymond* v *Pearce* [1972] 1 All ER 1142 (CA), the parking of a lorry, although an obstruction of the highway, was not deemed to be an actionable nuisance as it was parked in a highly visible way. On the facts, the defendant had not acted unreasonably in leaving the lorry where he did. As a result, the claimant could not succeed in a tort action for public nuisance when the motorcycle upon which he was a passenger ran into the back of the lorry.

Give and take

When talking about the liability of the defendant in private nuisance, Lord Goff, in *Cambridge Water Co Ltd* v *Eastern Counties Leather plc* [1994] 1 All ER 53 (HL) referred at p71 to the 'principle of reasonable user'. This concerns the principle of 'give and take' between neighbouring occupiers of land. He explained it in this way:

> if the user is reasonable, the defendant will not be liable for consequent harm to his neighbour's enjoyment of his land; but if the user is not reasonable, the defendant will be liable, even though he may have exercised reasonable care and skill to avoid it.

In both public and private nuisance, unreasonable interference results in an actionable nuisance. Again, in appropriate circumstances, it is possible to obtain an injunction to restrain the unreasonable interference in both spheres of law. However, in spite of these common areas, the distinctions, as always, are probably of more significance than the similarities.

Distinctions

Perhaps the most fundamental distinction is that private nuisance is a tort: a civil area of law where actions are commenced in a county court or in the High Court. Public nuisance, on the other hand, is primarily a crime, for which a defendant will normally be proceeded against in the Crown Court.

Public nuisance is defined as an unreasonable interference that materially affects the reasonable comfort and convenience of the public in general or a section of the public. However, a claimant who suffers particular damage, over and above that suffered by the public in general, may bring a tort action to recover compensation in public nuisance.

Does the claimant have to be a landowner?

Another significant difference is that a person wishing to bring an action in private nuisance must hold an interest in the land. This was decided categorically in the case of *Hunter* v *Canary Wharf* [1997] 2 All ER 426 after a period of some uncertainty.

The interest can take various forms. Lord Goff in *Hunter* v *Canary Wharf Ltd* stated at p435 that an action could be brought by a person in actual possession, either as the freeholder or the tenant or the licensee, and with exclusive possession of the land. In addition, a reversioner could sue if permanent damage was caused to his reversion. It was decided that the spouses, children and other relatives, with no interest in the land, who shared the house with the interest-holders in *Hunter*, had no right to sue in private nuisance.

This was applied in a commercial context in *Butcher Robinson & Staples Ltd* v *London Regional Transport* [1999] 3 EGLR 63, where subsidiary companies occupying business premises without exclusive possession were unable to maintain an action in private nuisance.

Private nuisance is an unreasonable interference with the claimant's use or enjoyment of his rights over land. Lord Lloyd in *Hunter* v *Canary Wharf Ltd* stated at p441:

Private nuisances are of three kinds. They are (1) nuisance by encroachment on a neighbour's land; (2) nuisance by direct physical injury to a neighbour's land; and (3) nuisance by interference with a neighbour's quiet enjoyment of his land.

There is no need to have an interest in land to maintain a tort action in public nuisance. The claimant merely needs to establish that, as a result of the actions of the defendant, he or she has suffered particular damage over and above the damage caused to the public in general.

Thus, in the case of *Tarry* v *Ashton* [1876] LR 1 QBD 314, a pedestrian who was injured by a falling lamp was able to recover for particular damage, ie personal injury, suffered as a result of the public nuisance that had been created by the hazard.

However, having an interest in land is no bar to an action in public nuisance if the claimant suffers particular damage. In *Tate & Lyle Food and Distribution Ltd* v *Greater London Council* [1983] 1 All ER 1159 (HL) the claimant was able to recover the cost of dredging the riverbed when the defendant caused it to silt up, thus obstructing the public's right to navigate along a navigable river. The claimant suffered particular damage, as its vessels were unable to reach its jetty as a result of this public nuisance.

A claimant in private nuisance, on the other hand, does not have to show particular damage once it has been established that his interest has suffered unreasonable interference.

While it is possible to plead the defence of prescription (20 years' continuous user amounting to nuisance) in private nuisance, it is not possible to plead prescription as a defence in public nuisance, as one can never acquire the right to commit a crime.

Personal injuries

When considering damage and what can be compensated for in the two areas of nuisance, there are, once more, some significant distinctions. While it is clear from cases already referred to (*Castle v St Augustine's Links* (1922) 38 TLR 615 and *Tarry v Ashton* (1876)) that it is possible to recover for personal injury in public nuisance, this issue remains contentious among judges and legal authors in relation to private nuisance. Lord Lloyd in *Hunter v Canary Wharf Ltd* stated at p442:

> If the occupier of land suffers personal injury as a result of inhaling the smoke, he may have a cause of action in negligence. But he does not have a cause of action in nuisance for his personal injury, nor for interference with his personal enjoyment.

Thus, unlike public nuisance, compensation in private nuisance is very closely related to the use and occupation of the land by the interest-holder. The compensation will either be for damage to the property or for loss of amenity resulting from the defendant's interference with the claimant's enjoyment of the land. Lord Hoffmann in *Hunter v Canary Wharf Ltd* stated at pp451–452:

> in addition to damages for injury to his land, the owner or occupier is able to recover damages for consequential loss. He will, for example, be entitled to loss of profits which are the result of inability to use the land for the purposes of his business. Or if the land is flooded, he may also be able to recover damages for chattels or livestock lost as a result. But inconvenience, annoyance or even illness suffered by persons on land as a result of smells or dust are not damage consequent upon the injury to the land.

Conclusion

It would seem fair to suggest that we have probably not heard the last on this issue. Lord Goff in *Hunter v Canary Wharf* referred, at pp438–439, to the views of various eminent legal authors. He made reference to a school of thought that suggests that not only should personal injury claims be excluded from the domain of nuisance, but that claims in respect of physical damage to the land should also be excluded from private nuisance. Such extreme views have not, as yet, been applied in the courts.

Therefore, for the present, it would seem more than likely that the main distinctions between the two forms of nuisance will remain as set out in this article.

Contributed by Gail Price

Postscript:

In *Pemberston* v *Southwark London Borough Council* [2000] 2 EGLR 33, the Court of appeal held that a 'tolerated trespasser' (i.e. a Council tenant against whom a possession order had been made but not enforced) was entitled to maintain an action for nuisance against her landlord. The decisive point was that she was still in exclusive occupation of the land at the time of the nuisance (an infestation by cockroaches from premises still occupied by the council).

CHAPTER 48

Health and nuisance

Published as 'Something of a nuisance', 11 November 2000

The concept of statutory nuisance continues to be defined according to the sanitation statutes of the 19th century

The power of local authorities to issue abatement notices – to curtail overflowing drains, dust pollution, pest infestation, unsanitary housing conditions, etc – depends upon whether the inconvenience can be termed a statutory nuisance.

Statutory nuisances

Statutory nuisance includes those activities or circumstances listed in section 79(1) of the Environmental Protection Act 1990 (see p000). For surveyors, the most important nuisance is found in section 79(1)(a): 'premises in such a state as to be prejudicial to health or a nuisance'. This expression has its legislative origin in early Victorian statutes: the Nuisances Removal and Diseases Prevention Acts 1848 and 1849, in which the precise phrase was 'a nuisance or *injurious to health*' (author's italics). The modern phrase, defined in section 79(7) of the 1990 Act, includes injury to health. Thus, no difference exists between the words used in the original legislation and the current expression.

The origin of this phrase is not simply a matter of historical comment. In recent decisions, judges have harked back to the original meaning of statutory words and the original purpose of the law.

At common law, a recent noteworthy example in private nuisance is *Hunter* v *Canary Wharf Ltd* [1997] 2 All ER 426, where the House of Lords returned to the original purpose of the tort of private nuisance – the protection of property rights, not of the environment. (Their lordships saw no reason why the law of nuisance should be developed so as to give protection to those who are not property owners or tenants, but merely occupiers of a house or flat.)

In statutory nuisance, this tendency to interpret the law according to its original purpose (even if that purpose dates back 150 years) can be seen in two recent cases: *R v Bristol City Council, ex parte Everett* [1999] 2 All ER 193 and *R v Falmouth and Truro Port Health Authority, ex parte South West Water Ltd* [2000] 3 All ER 306. One issue in *Bristol* was whether the words 'prejudicial to health' included the risk of injury from falling down a narrow staircase. In *Falmouth and Truro* (which concerned one of the few statutory nuisances still to be found outside the 1990 Act), the meaning of 'watercourses' (in the Public Health Act 1936) was in dispute. The Court of Appeal determined its meaning by a close analysis of the original legislative intent of parliament, which intent was held to exclude the estuary of a river.

Thus, in defining the terms used in the Environmental Protection Act 1990 or the Public Health Act 1936, close regard must be had to the history of that legislation and to the presumed legislative intent of parliament in the reign of Queen Victoria.

The first point to note about the phrase 'prejudicial to health or a nuisance' is that it contains two limbs, separated by the word 'or'. These two limbs are to be kept separate: 'or' does not (in this context) mean 'and'.

In *Malton Board of Health* v *Malton Manure Co* (1879) 4 Exch D 302, the judge held that the statute was not to be read as though it said a 'nuisance injurious to health', since this would run against the literal meaning of the words. This point was repeated in *Bishop Auckland Local Board* v *Bishop Auckland Iron Co* (1882) 10 QBD 138. In 1975, in *Salford City Council* v *McNally* [1975] 2 EGLR 28, the House of Lords concurred with this view, emphasising that different requirements existed for each limb of a statutory nuisance.

Nuisance limb

No further definition of 'nuisance' is found in the Environmental Protection Act 1990. The common law meaning of nuisance is to be imported into the statute, but it encompasses two different concepts: private and public nuisance. The definitions of each are well known, and were discussed in *Estates Gazette* 16 September 2000 at p152.

However, the common law definitions cannot be read literally into the legislation relating to statutory nuisances. In that context, parliament intended to deal with the problems of disease control and public health, which were becoming manifest in the mid-19th century. To subsume all aspects of common law nuisance under this legislative regime would have been absurd. Judges have made this clear over the centuries. But where is the borderline to be drawn?

In *Great Western Railway Co v Bishop* (1872) 7 LR QB 550, the court held that the purpose of the statute was to deal with public and private health issues and was aimed primarily at urban and suburban dwellers. It was not to be used to provide a method of abatement of private and public nuisances in general. A link with matters of health was a prerequisite. Water dripping from an overhead bridge (for example) was not the sort of mischief at which the law of statutory nuisances was aimed.

Health and the nuisance limb

If a case is being brought under the nuisance limb, the nuisance does not also have to be 'prejudicial to health'. The two limbs are, of course, alternatives. So, how tenuous a link with health can there be if the case is being argued under the nuisance limb?

In *Malton*, it was said that a statutory nuisance could arise even if it was not injurious to health. What was essential was to show that it 'affected' public health, and this could include the 'diminution of comfort'. Thus, the effluvia from a bone-crushing factory that caused the local populace to feel nauseous and 'made sick people worse' was sufficient to found a statutory nuisance, even though the medical evidence was divided as to the permanent health effects of the problem.

In *Bishop Auckland*, where strong fumes and effluvia rose from burning heaps of cinders and ashes, it was held that a nuisance 'either interfering with personal comfort or injurious to health' was a necessary condition.

This was confirmed by the House of Lords in *Salford City Council v McNally*, where it was held that personal comfort was appropriate when defining the nuisance limb, but would not be sufficient for the health limb.

Internal nuisances

A characteristic shared by the nuisance limb and private nuisance is that the offending activity must be transmitted from a neighbouring property. This could be from one flat to another, as in classic noise cases, or from a factory blowing fumes or smoke over neighbouring houses. If that is the case, then the transmission of the offending activity, plus interference with personal comfort, will do. This will often be appropriate in noise cases, and cases involving bad smells, where it is notoriously difficult to establish adverse health effects.

However, there is one crucial type of case where the nuisance limb can never be satisfied. This involves those cases in which the problem arises on or within the premises, the most obvious example of which is where residential property suffers from the effects of condensation. These cases will fall under section 79(1)(a) of the 1990 Act: 'premises in such a state as to be prejudicial to health or a nuisance'. The problem is not transmitted from one property onto a neighbouring property. Thus, the circumstances must always be considered under the health limb. It would be necessary to show the adverse effects of condensation on the health of the occupants. This is a more complex standard than that required by the nuisance limb.

Salford City Council v *McNally*, a case falling under this heading, concerned a house that was to be demolished in a slum clearance programme. In the meantime, the occupier alleged that the house was prejudicial to health. The court agreed, holding that a statutory nuisance could arise in such a case because, and only because, the health of an occupier had been affected.

Cases such as *National Coal Board* v *Neath Borough Council* [1976] 2 All ER 478 appear to confirm this. In that case, guttering and skirting boards were defective, but there was no injury to health, either actual or threatened. This could not be brought under the health limb. The only way forward was if the defects satisfied the common law requirements of the nuisance limb. The claim failed, the court finding that the occupiers of the defective building alone were inconvenienced.

R v *Carrick District Council, ex parte Shelley* [1996] Env LR 273 involved the deposit of sewage and sanitary products from a sewage outfall onto a beach. The judge considered the extent of the nuisance limb. He examined the definition of a 'public nuisance' at common law, namely: 'an act or omission which materially affects the material comfort and quality of life of a class of Her Majesty's subjects'. He held that this was the appropriate test when considering the nuisance limb of statutory nuisances, and that it did not have to be limited to health in any direct sense. Similarly, in *Wivenhoe Port* v *Colchester Borough Council* [1985] JPL 175, the judge concluded that to be a statutory nuisance, a nuisance had to interfere materially with the personal comfort of residents, 'in the sense that it materially affected their well-being, although it might not be prejudicial to health'.

Health limb

The health limb, on the other hand, (although it can embrace the health of anyone) demands more than mere discomfort or annoyance, and requires proof of harmful health effects.

Ex parte Everett was a 'premises' case, falling under the health limb of section 79(1)(a). The occupier alleged that the threat of injury from the risk of falling down a narrow staircase was a statutory nuisance. The Court of Appeal did not agree. The judges drew their interpretation from 19th century cases and the context of the law of public health in those days. They considered that the health effect being struck at was the risk of disease. Accidental injury, such as a broken ankle, was not the type of health effect intended to be covered by the legislation. This followed the viewpoint expressed in the earlier case of *Coventry City Council* v *Cartwright* [1975] 2 EGLR 112, where inert matter was dumped on wasteland. The fact that trespassers on the site might suffer injury was not enough to bring the case within the type of health problems anticipated by the legislation. As Lord Widgery CJ stated in *Cartwright*: 'that which is struck at is an accumulation of something which produces a threat to health in the sense of a threat of disease, vermin or the like'.

Modern environmental statutes

The modern interpretation of statutory nuisances is still determined in accordance with 19th century sanitation statutes. Evidence of rat infestation in *Cartwright* would have been sufficient to make the nuisance a statutory nuisance. Design, maintenance and estate-management problems, eg defective electrical wiring or gas installations, inadequate stair handrails and bannisters, etc will not fall within the statutory nuisance regime. However, if personal injuries are caused by such defects, the injured party could sue the landlord and/or the designer for damages for negligence: see *Rimmer* v *Liverpool City Council* [1984] 1 EGLR 23 and *Targett* v *Torfaen Borough Council* [1992] 1 EGLR 275.

Contributed by Rosalind Malcolm

CHAPTER 49

Noise nuisance and the doctrine of implied repeal

Published as 'Words writ on water', 19 June 1999

Parliament has the right to repeal or rewrite its own legislation at any time, and it can do so in a variety of ways, not all of them straightforward

Parliament is the writer of our statutes. But unlike the moving finger in the Rubaiyat of Omar Khayyam, which

...writes; and having writ,
Moves on: nor all thy Piety or Wit
Shall lure it back to cancel half a line,
Nor all thy Tears wash out a word of it...

parliament constantly repeals or amends provisions in the 'British statute book' – the name given to all the statutes in force at any given time. There is no theoretical limit to this process.

As long ago as 1686 an English judge, Herbert CJ, remarked that:

if an Act of Parliament had a clause in it that it should never be repealed, yet without question, the same power that made it could repeal it.
Godden v *Hales* (1686) 11 St Tr 1165

The verb 'to repeal' relates to the legislative undoing of an Act of Parliament. An Act of Parliament is a form of primary legislation, otherwise known as a 'statute'. If secondary legislation (such as a 'statutory instrument') is being dealt with in this way, the provision in question is said to be 'revoked'. If a rule of common law is to be abolished or replaced by a statutory rule, the common law rule is said to be 'abrogated'.

Express repeal

It is common for modern Acts of Parliament to contain schedules that list the statutory provisions that have been repealed, amended, or otherwise superseded. This is known as the 'doctrine of express repeal'. The prevalence of this practice is one of the reasons why it is not safe to rely on the original text of a statute, once a few years – or, sometimes, even a few months – have gone by.

Not only may the statute have been repealed in its entirety (an event which is unlikely to have happened without a certain amount of publicity) – more insidiously, it may have been amended by the deletion of certain words or sections, and by the insertion of new words or new sections (a process which is known as 'posting'). Like the 'Ministry of Truth', therefore, in George Orwell's *1984*, parliament can rewrite its own publications on a day-to-day basis.

An example of how the doctrine of express repeal can be used to rewrite the text of an earlier Act of Parliament is provided by section 604 of the Housing Act 1985, which defines 'fitness for human habitation'. This section was substantially rewritten by the Local Government and Housing Act 1989, thereby rendering earlier copies of the Housing Act 1985 dangerously out of date.

Implied repeal

Problems arise if two Acts of Parliament appear to be in conflict, but the later one does not expressly repeal or amend the earlier one. In such circumstances, it is the duty of the courts to reconcile the two statutes, if this is possible, but, if not, the courts must prefer the later statute over the earlier one.

The two cases usually cited in textbooks on this point relate to the law of compulsory purchase: *Vauxhall Estates Ltd* v *Liverpool Corporation* [1932] 1 KB 733, and *Ellen Street Estates Ltd* v *Minister of Health* [1934] 1 KB 590. In both cases it was held that certain rules of compensation law laid down in the Acquisition of Land (Assessment of Compensation) Act 1919 had been impliedly repealed by less generous rules contained in the Housing Acts of 1925 and 1930 – even though the 1919 Act was still 'on the statute book'. This is known as the 'doctrine of implied repeal'. In the *Ellen Street Estates* case, Scrutton LJ put the matter like this:

[The claimant's] contention is that, if in a later Act provisions are found as to the compensation to be paid for land which are inconsistent with those contained in the Act of 1919, the later provisions are to have no effect. Such a contention involves this proposition, that no subsequent Parliament by enacting a provision inconsistent with the Act of 1919 can give effect to the words it uses... That is absolutely contrary to the constitutional position that Parliament can alter an Act previously passed, and it can do so by repealing in terms the previous Act... and it can do it also in another way – namely, by enacting a provision which is clearly inconsistent with the previous Act.

The *Haringey* case

A recent example of the 'doctrine of implied repeal' is provided by *Haringey London Borough Council* v *Jowett* [1999] EGCS 64. In that case a tenant complained to the magistrates' court that a 'statutory nuisance' existed at her council flat in London N8. She relied on section 79(1) of the Environmental Protection Act 1990, which contains a list of statutory nuisances.

She claimed that her council flat was in 'such a state as to be prejudicial to health or a nuisance' (section 79(1)(a)) because of the lack of sufficient sound insulation and acoustic ventilation to protect the premises from the noise of traffic. In submitting this argument the tenant relied on *Southwark London Borough Council* v *Ince* (1989) 21 HLR 504, where it was accepted that insufficient protection from traffic noise could be a 'statutory nuisance'.

The *Southwark* decision had been based on the wording in section 92(1)(a) of the Public Health Act 1936, but this was the same as the wording in section 79(1)(a) of the Environmental Protection Act 1990. The significant change was not the express repeal of (the relevant parts of) the 1936 Act by the 1990 Act – the wording, after all, was the same – but rather the implied repeal of the original scope of section 79(1)(a) by an Act passed in 1993.

This was the Noise and Statutory Nuisance Act 1993, which was passed to enlarge the list of statutory nuisances by 'posting' a new paragraph into section 79(1) of the 1990 Act, namely para (ga):

noise that is prejudicial to health or a nuisance and is emitted from a vehicle, machinery, or equipment in the street.

This new paragraph now sits between section 79(1)(g) and (h) in revised editions of the 1990 Act. Car alarms, stereo equipment, and generators are the obvious examples of the nuisances intended to be dealt with by this new amendment. Parliament has made it clear that it was not intended to deal with the ordinary street noise by adding a new subsection, namely section 79(6A) – which, of course, has been 'posted' into the 1990 Act after section 79(6).

This new subsection states that para (ga) does not apply to noise made by 'traffic', or by the armed forces, or by political or other public demonstrations.

The divisional court in *Haringey* interpreted the amendments made by the 1993 Act to be an implied cutting down of the scope of section 79(1)(a). It therefore took the view that parliament had impliedly lifted a load from the shoulders of landlords and property developers: they were no longer to be held liable for inadequate insulation from traffic noise under section 79(1)(a) of the 1990 Act.

Strange interpretation

This is, indeed, a strange interpretation of amendment which was intended to enlarge the list of statutory nuisances, not to reduce them or to limit their scope. Moreover, the decision seems to be confusing traffic noise (for which there is no liability) with the shoddy nature of adjacent premises (for which the *Southwark* case says there can be liability). But if the case is correctly decided it provides an up-to-date example of the doctrine of implied repeal at work.

It is a timely reminder that parliament's words to its public often have something in common with the promises described by the poet Catullus:

A woman's words to her lover
Be on wind and running water writ.

Statutory amendment – How section 604(1) of the Housing Act 1985 has changed

Section 604(1), Housing Act 1985 (Original version)

In determining for any of the purposes of this Act whether premises are unfit for human habitation, regard shall be had to their condition in respect of the following matters:
repair,
stability,
freedom from damp,
internal arrangement,
natural lighting,
ventilation,
water supply,
drainage and sanitary conveniences,
facilities for the preparation and cooking of
food and for the disposal of waste water;
– and the premises shall be deemed unfit if, and only if, they are so far defective in one or more of those matters that they are not reasonably suitable for occupation in that condition

Section 604(1) Housing Act 1985 (as substituted by Local Government and Housing Act 1989)

Subject to subsection (2) below, a dwelling-house is fit for human habitation for the purposes of this Act unless, in the opinion of the local housing authority, it fails to meet one or more of the requirements in paragraphs (a) to (i) below and, by reason of that failure, is not reasonably suitable for occupation –
(a) it is structurally stable;
(b) it is free from serious disrepair;
(c) it is free from dampness prejudicial to the health of the occupants (if any);
(d) it has adequate provision for lighting, heating, and ventilation;
(e) it has an adequate piped supply of wholesome water;
(f) there are satisfactory facilities for the preparation and cooking of food, including a sink with a satisfactory supply of hot and cold water;
(g) it has a suitably located water-closet for the exclusive use of the occupants (if any);
(h) it has, for the exclusive use of the occupants (if any), a suitably located fixed bath or shower and wash-hand basin each of which is provided with a satisfactory supply of hot and cold water; and
(i) it has an effective system for the drainage of foul, waste, and surface water;
– and any reference to a dwelling-house being unfit for human habitation shall be construed accordingly.

Contributed by Leslie Blake

CHAPTER 50

Conservation areas and the law

Published as 'Green is for caution', 27 July 2002

With more of the country coming under conservation area control, developers must be aware of the rules governing development in conservation areas

There are over 8,000 conservation areas in England. All of them are designated by local authorities under section 69(1) of the Planning (Listed Buildings & Conservation Areas) Act 1990. The criteria for inclusion is whether the character or appearance of the area is worth protecting or enhancing. On their website, English Heritage state that:

> conservation areas vary greatly in their nature and character. They range from the centre of our historic towns and cities, through fishing and mining villages, 18th- and 19th-century suburbs, model housing estates, and country houses set in their historic parks, to historic transport links and their environs, such as stretches of canal. [www.english-heritage.org.uk].

It is vital that property developers know that a potential development site falls within a conservation area. This information can be obtained from the relevant local authority, as the designation of an area as a conservation area will be registered as a local land charge.

New development

What are the practical implications for developers of such designation? Any new proposed development will come under more careful scrutiny and the public will be made aware that an application will take place. PPG 15 acknowledges that new development in conservation areas cannot be prohibited:

> Conservation ... cannot realistically take the form of preventing all new development; the emphasis will generally need to be on controlled and positive management of change.

It goes on to state that within a conservation area there will be:

> buildings that make no positive contribution to or indeed detract from the area ... New designs don't have to mirror existing styles but they should be designed with respect for their context, as part of a larger whole, which has a well-established character and appearance of its own.

Planning applications in conservation areas may require more detailed plans than those in non-conservation areas:

> including elevations which show the new development in its setting or ... general planning standards should be applied sensitively in the interests of harmonising the new development with its neighbours in the conservation area. [PPG 15]

Therefore, even if planning permission is granted, there will be less freedom over the design and layout.

Duty of the authority

A local planning authority have a duty, under section 72 of the 1990 Act, to preserve or enhance the character or appearance of a conservation area. In *South Lakeland District Council* v *Secretary of State for the Environment* [1992] 1 PLR 143, Lord Bridge interpreted this in the following way:

> It is entirely right that, in any such area, a much stricter control over development than elsewhere should be exercised ... but where a particular development will not have any adverse effect on the character or appearance of the area and is otherwise unobjectionable on planning grounds, one may ask rhetorically what possible planning reason there can be for refusing to allow it.

However, PPG 15 states that section 72 must also be considered in the planning authority's handling of development proposals that are outside the conservation area but would affect its setting, or views into or out of the area. Local planning authorities are required by section 73 to publish a notice of planning applications for development that would, in their opinion, affect the character or appearance of a conservation area. Therefore, a proposed development may be affected by being on the fringe of a conservation area, rather than within the area itself.

In the case of *Trafford Metropolitan Borough Council* v *Secretary of State for the Environment Transport and the Regions* [2000] PLSCS 118, planning permission was obtained to demolish a house in a conservation area and to build a new one. The new house was larger than permitted, and a terrace at the back of the house was substantially bigger. An enforcement notice was served and an appeal was lodged against it.

The inspector, whose decision was upheld on appeal, made the following interesting remark:

> In this particular part of the conservation area, I consider the character or appearance which it is in the public interest to preserve or enhance, to be the character or appearance of those parts which are visible from the highway; and it is with this approach in mind that I intend to determine these appeals.

So, in granting permission, it would seem that those parts of a building that are publicly visible, for example from highways, are scrutinised more carefully than new buildings or parts of buildings that are completely private.

Demolition of buildings

Where the development involves demolition (either total or substantial), an application must be made to the local planning authority, and there will be a presumption in favour of retaining buildings that make a positive contribution to the area. Demolition was defined in *Shimizu (UK) Ltd* v *Westminster City Council* [1996] 3 PLR 89 as:

> pulling down a building so that it was destroyed completely and broken up. It followed that works which involved the demolition of a part only of a listed building, falling short of the destruction of the whole listed building... did not constitute demolition... unless the works... were so substantial as to amount to a clearing of the whole site for redevelopment.

Lord Hope made it clear that this case, although particularly concerned with a listed building, also applied to conservation areas. However, developers should err on the side of caution and seek advice if there is ambiguity over the issue of demolition. The government is inviting consultation about proposals to strengthen controls over works of partial demolition in conservation areas, although there are some exceptions to this, in section 75 (2) of the 1990 Act (see p341).

A planning authority may not be keen to grant consent for a demolition if the issue of redevelopment has not been made clear at the same time. It may be:

appropriate to impose on the grant of consent for demolition a condition... to provide that demolition shall not take place until a contract for the carrying out of works of redevelopment has been made and planning permission for those works has been granted. In the past, ugly gaps have sometimes appeared in conservation areas as a result of demolition far in advance of redevelopment. [PPG 15]

Benefits to the community
It is sometimes argued that a building should be demolished because of the positive public benefits that will ensue from the proposed new development, for example a new use of gain to the community.

Alterations
Where a developer is considering altering an existing building, as opposed to demolishing it or constructing a new one, it may need permission where it is not usually required. For example, the size of permitted extensions is reduced, and various types of cladding and the insertion of dormer windows into roof slopes are not permitted without permission. Any alterations, therefore, may need to be referred to the local planning authority to confirm whether planning permission is needed. Under Article 4(2), local planning authorities can, without the consent of the Secretary of State, restrict certain permitted development rights relating to houses in conservation areas where the development is fronting a highway, waterway or open space. However, this is rarely applied in practice.

Trees
The final restriction that arises, in the case of a developer who is clearing a site for development, relates to the cutting, lopping or outing of a tree. Section 211 of the 1990 Act gives trees in a conservation area, with some exceptions, the same protection as a tree preservation order. The implication is that a tree cannot be cut down, uprooted, topped, lopped, or wilfully destroyed, without the written consent of the local planning authority.

If the development site includes any individually listed buildings, then the controls are much more stringent. Section 9 of the Listed Buildings Act 1990 states that:

no demolition or alteration or extension of a listed building in any manner which will affect its character as a building of special architectural or historic interest may be carried out.

Any such work must have listed building consent: see Chapter 51 (pp343–347).

Overall, although conservation area control is not as stringent as listed building law, it can still prevent, or impede, a proposed development from taking place, or severely curtail its extent and nature.

Permitted demolitions – Statutory control over demolition

The following demolitions are permitted under section 75(2) of the Planning (Listed Buildings and Conservation Areas) 1990.

- Buildings or part of buildings with a total cubic content not exceeding 115m^3.
- Buildings erected after January 1914 and used for agriculture.
- Gates, walls, fences, or railings less than 1m high if abutting onto a highway or public open space (2m in any other case).

Any building required to be demolished because of a condition of a planning permission.

Permitted demolitions – Statutory control over demolition

The following demolitions are permitted under section 75(2) of the Planning (Listed Buildings and Conservation Areas) 1990.

- Buildings or part of buildings with a total cubic content not exceeding 115m^3.
- Buildings erected after January 1914 and used for agriculture.
- Gates, walls, fences, or railings less than 1m high if abutting onto a highway or public open space (2m in any other case).

Any building required to be demolished because of a condition of a planning permission

Positive public benefit – Recent examples
- In inspector's decision Harrow LB 15/5/89, six conservation area houses were demolished, and a new 21-house development financed a new theatre for Harrow school. The inspector held that the overall development would enhance the site.

- In inspector's decision Melton BC 7/8/86, a building was to be demolished for a link-road scheme, and the environmental gain from this was felt to justify the demolition.

Gallard Homes recently won the right to demolish two buildings in St John's Wood conservation area, London, on the basis that the development is of outstanding quality and will improve the existing buildings

Contributed by Monica Dawson

CHAPTER 51

Listed buildings

Published as 'Respect for the aged', 14 July 2001

Developers face criminal liability if they do not comply with the strict rules governing the listing of buildings

A property developer can ascertain from the relevant local authority whether the building he is considering developing is one of the 360,000 listed buildings in England. The powers of listing are contained in section 1(1) of the Planning (Listed Buildings and Conservation Areas) Act 1990:

In relation to buildings of special architectural or historic interest, the Secretary of State should compile lists of such buildings, or approve, with or without modification, such lists compiled by the English Heritage or by other persons or body of persons and may amend any lists so compiled or approved.

Unfortunately, from the developer's point of view, property owners are not informed of the Secretary of State's intention to list a building, as this could lead to its hasty demolition. A building can be listed shortly after its acquisition or even possibly between exchange of contracts and completion. Furthermore, the frustrated developer has no remedy, as there is no appeal available against a listing. However, an appeal can be made against a refusal of an application for listed building consent. Listed building consent is required before carrying out any alteration or demolition works.

The developer can obtain a certificate of immunity from listing, under section 6(1) of the Act, if he is seeking or has obtained planning permission. The developer can apply for this with an application for planning permission. Then he is safe against listing for a period of five years. Even when such a certificate has been granted, if the building is in a conservation area the developer will require consent for demolition. However, few developers apply for a certificate of immunity as the application could result in the building becoming listed!

Non-statutory guidance

PPG 15 paragraphs 6.10 and 6.11 set out the main criteria that the Secretary of State applies in deciding which buildings should be listed (see p346).

Once a listed building has been acquired, no demolition, alteration or extension in any manner that would affect its character as a building of special architectural or historic interest, is permitted. Any such work must have listed building consent. Even if the developer intends to do minor work before resale, consent may be needed. Paragraph 3.2 of PPG15 states:

> consent is not normally required for repairs, but, where repairs involve alterations which would affect the character of a listed building, consent is required. Whether repairs actually constitute alterations which require consent is a matter of fact and degree which must be determined in each case. Where painting or repainting the exterior or interior of a listed building would affect the building's character, consent is required.

Extent of the listing

One big problem is identifying the extent of the listing. Objects and structures fixed to the principal building at the time of the listing are included, provided they are fixtures and ancillary to the building – for example, a garage. Therefore, removing wall panels and chimney pieces would not be permitted without permission.

Any object or structure within the curtilage of the building that, although not fixed to the building, forms part of the land, and has done so since before 1 July 1948, is included under section 1(5) of the Act. However, where the building in question is clearly independent of the listed building, it will not be included in the listing.

In *Debenhams plc* v *Westminster City Council* [1987] 1 EGLR 248 it was argued that Hamleys toy shop, which was not listed, was subordinate to another Regent Street store that was listed (the two stores were linked by a subway). In this case it was held that the buildings were historically independent.

The exact extent of the curtilage of a listing can be difficult to ascertain. In some listings the description can be brief and when part of the land, for example a barn, is sold out of common ownership, the extent of the original listing can be overlooked.

The recent case of *Skerritts of Nottingham Ltd* v *Secretary of State for the Environment, Transport and Regions* [1999] 2 PLR 109 provides a good example of the problems that can arise, and the issues that have to be considered, when identifying curtilage. The case involved a stable block that was located 200m from a listed building, Grimsdyke Hall. The block had had double-glazing installed without consent, and an enforcement notice had been served. The stable block itself was not listed.

The issue therefore was whether the block was within the curtilage of the hall. Mr George Bartlett QC identified a number of useful factors, contained in PPG15, that should be considered. The building at issue:

must be ancillary to the principal building, that it must have served the purposes of the principal building at the date of the listing, or at a recent time before the date of the listing, in a necessary or reasonably useful way and must not be historically an independent building. Where a self-contained building was fenced or walled-off from the remainder of the site at the date of listing ... it is unlikely to be regarded as having a separate curtilage. The structure must form part of the land, and this probably means that there must be some degree of physical annexation of the land.

Another issue that the developer should bear in mind is the impact on other buildings. In *R* v *Bolsover District Council, ex parte Paterson* [2000] EGCS 83, the owner of Brookhill Hall was given permission to demolish a garage. The owner of a coach house, situated about 50 yards from the garage, which was separately listed, appealed on the ground that the planning services manager failed to consider the impact of the proposal on the coach house as a separate listed building. Collins J held:

The impact on each individual listed building has to be taken into account. Equally, consideration of the impact on the setting of a group of buildings might, in the given circumstances, inevitably cover the impact on a particular individual member of the group.

Developers should be aware, when acquiring land for development, that the definition of building under the Act covers any structure. Bridges, fountains, summerhouse and telephone boxes have been included within the definition. It can never be assumed therefore that the listed buildings laws have no relevance.

Penalties

A developer who is in breach of the listed buildings consent, or in breach of a condition attached to a consent, will find himself criminally liable, under section 9 of the Act. If he is found guilty in the Crown Court, the developer faces the prospect of an unlimited fine and/or a two-year term of imprisonment.

The relevant local authority also have the power to issue a listed building enforcement notice, under section 38, requiring the building to be restored to its former state or further works to alleviate the effects of the work. The offence is one of strict liability, which means the offender will be held liable even if he is not at fault or has not been negligent.

Furthermore, the wording of section 9 covers anyone who 'executes or causes to be executed' the works. A property developer who has not legally acquired ownership of the land within the listed building may still be liable. If the listed building is demolished without consent, an offence will have been committed – but it must be a total demolition. Partial demolition will count as an alteration.

A listed building that has been demolished can be required to be rebuilt, as in *R* v *Leominster District Council, ex parte Antique Country Buildings Ltd* [1988] 2 PLR 23 where a 16th century barn was dismantled prior to being sent to the US. As 70% of the timbers were traceable, the court ordered that it be re-erected.

Although there are no proposals to alter the current law on listed buildings, human rights arguments may well have an impact on this particular area of the law. Time will tell.

Listed building criteria – Extracts from PPG15 notes, paras 6.10 and 6.11

Architectural interest

The lists are meant to include all buildings which are of importance to the nation for the interest of their architectural design, decoration and craftsmanship, also important examples of particular building types and techniques (eg buildings displaying technological innovation or virtuosity) and significant plan forms.

Historical interest

This includes buildings that illustrate important aspects of the nation's social, economic, cultural or military history.

Close historical association

With nationally important people or events

Group value
Especially where buildings comprise an important architectural or historic unity or a fine example of planning (eg squares, terraces or model villages).

Not all these criteria will be relevant, but a particular building may qualify for listing under more than one.

Age and rarity are relevant considerations ... Thus all buildings built before 1700 which survive in anything like their original condition are listed and most buildings of about 1700 to 1840 are listed, though some selection is necessary. After about 1840, because of the greatly increased number of buildings erected and the much larger numbers that have survived, greater selection is necessary and only buildings of definite quality and character are listed. Buildings less than 30 years old are normally listed only if they are of outstanding quality and under threat.

Contributed by Monica Dawson

CHAPTER 52

Planning contravention notices

Published as 'Once more into the breach', 14 November 1998

Taking action against breaches of planning controls used to be a slow and difficult process for local planning authorities. However, the introduction of planning contravention notices has made the process somewhat simpler. We explain how they work in practice

The discovery by a spotter plane of a village built by environmentalists, without planning permission, in a national park in Pembrokeshire, has again raised the issue of the enforcement of planning control. This was an area of environment law seen as slow, complicated and uncertain to succeed. The main reasons for this (at least, prior to 1991) were as follows.

First, a local planning authority might encounter difficulties in deciding who was responsible for the breach of planning control and who, therefore, should be served with an enforcement notice. Gypsies occupying caravans were one example of such a doubt: see *Beech* v *Secretary of State for the Environment* [1993] EGCS 214. Another example was the case of an agent or manager of an estate, or a contractor on a site, who did not necessarily enjoy possession of the land and who did not have any proprietary interest in it.

Second, the very definition of 'development' gave rise to areas of doubt. For example, it was not always easy to know whether a change of use was a 'material change', eg an increase in work done by a professional man or a skilled worker at his home address. It was also sometimes difficult to know the precise date on which a material change of use took place or the date on which operational development was completed, thereby leading to doubts about whether an enforcement notice would be time-barred. Other problem areas for local planning authorities were whether or not land formed part of the curtilage of a dwelling-house (*Hill* v *Secretary of State for the Environment* [1993] JPL 158) or whether or not a building was being used for agricultural purposes (*Sykes* v *Secretary of State for the Environment* [1981] 1 EGLR 137). In many cases the facts known to the local planning authority were insufficient to formulate the wording of an enforcement notice. The result was that a very high percentage of enforcement notices were appealed, and many of these appeals were successful.

Carnwarth Report

At the request of the Secretary of State for the Environment, Robert Carnwarth QC prepared and submitted a report in 1989. This suggested a number of amendments to the enforcement procedures contained in the Town and Country Planning Act 1971 (soon to become the Town and Country Planning Act 1990). Almost all the suggestions were accepted by the government and they found their way into the Planning and Compensation Act 1991, which amended the Town and Country Planning Act 1990 by 'posting' new sections into it.

One of the most important amendments to the 1990 Act was the posting of two new sections, 171C and 171D. These created a new type of notice called a 'planning contravention notice'.

Planning contravention notices

Section 171C(1) states that when it appears to the local planning authority that there may have been a breach of planning control in respect of any land, they are empowered to serve a notice to that effect on any person who is 'the owner or occupier of the land' or who 'has any other interest in the land or is carrying out operations on the land or is using it for any purpose'. (This clearly includes contractors, managers or employees working on the land.)

It should be noted that the local planning authority must have a suspicion that a breach of planning control has occurred. It is not enough that they may have received complaints about an activity that is clearly permitted by the general development order: see *R* v *Teignbridge District Council, ex parte Teignmouth Quay Co Ltd* [1995] 2 PLR 1; [1994] EGCS 203. If a planning contravention notice is served in such flimsy circumstances, it may be quashed by the High Court in proceedings for judicial review.

Section 171C(2) provides that the planning contravention notice may require specified information about:

- any operations being carried out on the land;

- any use of the land;
- any other activities being carried out on the land; and
- any matter relating to the conditions or limitations subject to which any planning permission in respect of the land has been granted.

This clearly shows that the notice can be served to investigate an alleged breach of a planning condition or limitation on the grant of a previous planning permission; it is not limited to investigations relating to land with no relevant planning history.

A planning contravention notice may ask for the following additional information from the recipient:

- whether the land is being used for a purpose specified in the notice;
- whether any operations or activities specified in the notice are being carried out, or have been carried out, on the land;
- the date on which the specified activities began;
- the names and addresses of persons involved in the use of the land or who are (or were) carrying out activities on it;
- details of any existing planning permissions relating to the land; and
- the interests in the land of the recipient and of any other persons.

Responding to the notice

Section 171C(4) states that a planning contravention notice may give notice of a time and place at which the recipient may make representations to the local planning authority; or at which he may make an offer to apply for planning permission; or to refrain from carrying out certain operations or activities; or to undertake remedial works. Whether or not the local planning authority give the recipient notification of this opportunity, they must make it available to him if he asks. Needless to say, the authority are free to reject the recipient's proposals, but the whole purpose of this consultation process is to avoid formal enforcement action – and the expense and delay of appeals – if possible.

A planning contravention notice must inform the recipient of the consequences of failing to respond to the notice. Not only is this failure a criminal offence (and the recipient may be prosecuted more than once if his failure is repetitious), but the ordinary enforcement notice procedure, and stop notice procedure, can be used against him. If, for example, he is served with an enforcement notice and a stop notice, he may find that his failure to respond to the planning contravention notice adversely affects his claim to compensation – assuming he launches an appeal against the enforcement notice and wins that appeal.

The maximum fine for failing to reply to a planning contravention notice is £1,000 for each offence. If the recipient gives a reply that he knows to be false or misleading in a material particular, or recklessly makes such a statement, the maximum fine will be £5,000 for each offence. Recklessness in this context means that the statement was made by a person who did not care whether it was true or false: see *Large* v *Mainprize* [1989] Crim LR 213. Gross carelessness is not enough. The test is substantially the same as the test for fraudulent misrepresentation, as explained by Lord Herschell in the famous case of *Derry* v *Peek* (1889) 14 App Cas 337: 'fraud is proved where it is shewn that a false representation has been made (1) knowingly, or (2) without belief in its truth, or (3) recklessly, careless of whether it be true or false'.

The time-limit for complying with a planning contravention notice is 21 days (section 171D). All replies must be given in writing. These replies will, of course, be admissible as evidence in any future planning appeal (or enforcement notice appeal) relating to the land. It is doubtful, however, whether these new provisions override the common-law right to refuse to answer questions if the answers might incriminate the recipient of the notice (eg if he is using the land in breach of an abatement notice served by an environmental health officer or illegally using the land for an activity that requires a licence, or using the land for processing stolen goods). Section 171D(3) provides that it is a defence for the recipient to prove that he had a reasonable excuse for failing to comply with the notice. Presumably, the privilege against self-incrimination is a 'reasonable excuse'. If it is not, a very interesting conflict with the European Convention on Human Rights is likely to emerge.

Contributed by Adam Lominiki

CHAPTER 53

ISVA assignment submission/development scheme

Published as 'This is your assignment', 11 December 1999

Development work can involve a range of complexities, as illustrated by the pre-qualification assignment for ISVA students presented below

The assignment instruction from April 1998, set out below, was given in a letter from Bitehornes Properties entitled Open-air market relocation, Bull Ring Centre.

Bitehornes Properties' letter gave details of the instruction as follows:

As part of the overall proposals for the redevelopment of the Bull Ring area of central Birmingham, we are looking at one particular aspect which requires your assistance.

Historically, this part of Birmingham has always held a variety of markets, both open-air and indoor. They are an integral part of this area and it is a planning requirement that they are retained within any future redevelopment. However, one of these open-air markets, established over 20 years ago, is situated well within the proposed retail scheme and needs to be relocated. The planners will accept a degree of relocation, provided it is within a quarter of a mile of the existing site.

A suitable site has been identified (plans excluded here) but there are problems in securing the freehold. The owners already have an outline planning consent for office development extending to 8,000m^2 (86,112 sq ft), granted in 1990 and renewed in 1995. The owners are willing sellers but are taking the stance that the site is worth more to us than the residual office site value because, arguably, it is required if the scheme is not to be held up.

There are over 100 traders involved who are, generally speaking, hostile to any move (having been moved once already in the past 20 years). Indeed, several already claim statutory tenancies (or squatters' rights, as one put it). They occupy the site on a daily stall charge basis, although many have been doing this for years. Any relocation will have to be treated with care, not only in securing the site but also in making it sufficiently attractive for the traders to move.

We therefore require the following information to make a case for relocation:

(1) An estimate of the existing use value of the 'office site' with the benefit of the outline planning consent.
(2) Your suggestions as to how we can obtain vacant possession and some guide as to the costs involved.
(3) Your view as to whether all the alternative site will be required and, if not, your suggestions for the remainder.
(4) As we would like to avoid managing the market once relocated, we would like your advice as to how this might best be accomplished, preferably with us retaining some ongoing financial interest.

Please DO NOT make contact with the planners or any of the traders on this matter as negotiations are already at a critical stage. Please accept the planning information provided in this letter for the purposes of your report.

The task

Following a format that would be required if you were undertaking such an instruction in practice, the student must provide a report to the client, Bitehornes Properties.

Titled photographs and plans should be included. Plans will need a north point, scale, title, 'crown copyright reserved' statement and so on. The report should be written in a formal style.

Appendices can include information not usually included in a report to a client, but which is necessary in order to demonstrate, in particular, the research undertaken. This would, for example, include valuations, annotations to valuations, schedules and analysis of comparable evidence, or a more detailed commentary on market conditions or factors affecting value.

In addition, terms of instruction should be confirmed in writing. Guidance on the points to be covered may be found in the Red Book – the RICS Appraisal and Valuation Manual, produced in association with the ISVA and the IRRV. Also, a covering letter to the client is likely to accompany the report.

An 'office file' is required to record additional information. Some of this will have been derived from actual work undertaken, such as notes from discussions with a solicitor to establish a legal point. Other entries will be more hypothetical. On confirmation of planning matters, for example, it could be that a particular road is an adopted highway, or that previous uses on the site do not give rise to concern about the presence of contamination and its effect on value (note that the planners must not be approached as part of the project).

Students are free to make sensible assumptions. These can help define the task, enabling the report to concentrate on the main issues while demonstrating an awareness of related matters. The initial instruction advises that queries can be made in writing only to the ISVA, which is thus putting itself in the position of the client. It should not usually be necessary to refer back, particularly as all students will have attended a full briefing. Here, members of the assessment panel will be on hand.

Key detail
The instruction should be examined to establish the key details, some of which are:

- The client, Bitehornes Properties, is looking at only one aspect of the Bull Ring redevelopment. Its obvious familiarity with the redevelopment means that a detailed commentary on the scheme is unnecessary for the report. Descriptive detail should concentrate on advice specifically required, namely the office site and the relocation of the traders. Generally, students are best able to demonstrate their abilities by setting out options, evaluating possibilities and then making recommendations. Although providing descriptive detail is relatively easy, information deriving from good-quality research will gain particular credit.
- Students will need to understand the aims and overall requirements of the client in order to give the best advice. The initial site visit, and any subsequent visits, will help students to appreciate the area, and what the Bull Ring redevelopment is likely to involve. An A–Z may be helpful. A note should be made of surrounding uses. Is there any development activity or evidence of forthcoming developments in the area? Plenty of photographs should be taken. Site inspection notes should be included in the office file. *Estates Gazette*'s Birmingham/West Midlands 'Focus' (and previous 'Centrefolio') may be of value. Birmingham libraries should have local newspapers. Students will have their individual approach and will obtain different information.
- The statement that one of the open-air markets needs to be relocated would suggest that it may not be appropriate for the report to contemplate the incorporation of the market into the retail development, or even mention it as an option.

1 Office site – existing use value

For a city-centre office development, a residual valuation is required. The value of the completed development has to be worked out, with the construction cost deducted, in order to establish the residual site value, or acquisition price. The valuation exercise therefore involves consideration of occupational, investment, development and construction issues.

The gross area of 8,000m^2 (86,112 sq ft) can be adjusted to produce a suitable net internal area of office space, to which can be applied the appropriate rental per m^2 and a suitable yield/multiplier.

Research should be undertaken on such factors as national and local office market trends, influences on occupier demand, the amount of unoccupied space on the market, rental levels, typical void periods, rent-free periods or other incentives, typical lease lengths, the type of tenants likely to be attracted, their typical covenant strength and the requirements of funding institutions.

Would the property be let as a whole or in parts? Would smaller suites command a disproportionately higher rate per m^2, a greater total income and/or a more favourable yield than a letting to a single tenant (account also being taken of management costs)?

The comparable evidence presented to support the market rent for the offices could include details of actual lettings, rent reviews or lease renewals of similar properties. Notes could be made of discussions with agents and other bodies. Asking rents on vacant properties may be helpful (although they may not always be a reliable guide). Research briefings and other published statistics may provide assistance. Are there any rating issues? Do service charge arrangements need to be considered? Are markets subject to any special rules?

Students familiar with Birmingham, and/or those who have made thorough enquiries, may discover that offices situated outside the inner ring road command a relatively lower rent than similar space located within the ring road.

It may be considered useful to analyse a key comparable in particular detail, making an appropriate allowance, for example, for a rent-free period in order to determine the effective market rent/day-one rent.

Specific consideration could be given to car parking. The instruction brief does not mention it, or the density/number of floors within the development, but as city-centre parking is generally of premium value, and so enhances both rental and investment value, students have the opportunity to gain credit by perhaps commenting on the potential for the design of the offices to maximise parking within the scheme.

Evidence will be required of yields, with valuations again being suitably annotated, and of costings for the elements of construction within the residual valuation.

Although land values for city-centre office developments may not provide reliable comparable evidence in view of varying densities, design requirement, development constraints, infrastructure requirements and so on, notes could be included in the office file of discussions with agents to the effect that they generally concur with the residual land value determined.

Students taking on this brief may actually have found agents declaring that office development would not, in practice, be viable on the subject site. After all, the planning consent obtained in 1990 may have been in very different market conditions. Do you then value the site at a negative figure? If so, where does your report go from there? Would it be better to produce a valuation at a positive figure, and comment on the finding that the viability of office development may, in fact, be marginal?

Although the instruction does not expressly ask for comment on the issues beyond the provision of a valuation, the valuer would, in practice, draw attention to all relevant factors, such as:

- The sensitivity of the residual method of valuation – demonstrated by making adjustments to rents, yields and costs to establish how changing these variables affects residual land value.
- The finding that the viability of office development may, in fact, be marginal.
- The possibility that the owners could seek consent for uses more valuable than offices. It may be useful to raise such an issue but, equally, it may be preferable not to distract from the main issues by pursuing it.
- The effect of the owner's contention that the site can command more than office values in view of the special value to the clients. Does the acquisition have to be negotiated, or are CPO powers available to the developer? Would the owners of the office site gain additional value under compulsory purchase valuation rules, or would the additional value be attributable to the scheme underlying the acquisition, and thus confine compensation to office values ignoring the effects of the redevelopment?
- The possibility that the acquisition of the office site so

substantially adds to the value of the overall scheme that it may be preferable to accept the commercial reality and negotiate a deal expediently with the owners. An appreciation of the concept of worth, and its relationship with market value, could be demonstrated.
- The raising of issues that could influence negotiations, and therefore the price paid. There may be benefit in knowing that the owners are willing sellers (as described in the instruction), and may be unlikely to be adopting an obstinate and tactical stance of being content to await the Bull Ring's redevelopment, and secure complementary uses of a higher value than offices. The owners' options may actually be blighted by the uncertainty surrounding the Bull Ring scheme, and the opportunity to sell may be welcome. The owners may be known to have a pressing requirement for capital receipts. The planing permission for office development appears due for further renewal in 2000 (around a year from the submission date of the assignment), and may not be renewed. Alternative uses may be less valuable.

Standard caveats to valuation reports could include deeds and other documents not having been inspected, contamination surveys not having been undertaken, or ground conditions being considered satisfactory for development.

Site specific caveats (which are ideally stated separately to standard caveats) could include an assumption in respect of vacant possession. On inspection, students would actually have seen National Car Parks (NCP) occupying the site. It may be unnecessary to establish the nature of the company's occupation, but at least gain credit by identifying their presence as an issue. It could be stated in the report that 'it is understood that vacant possession can be secured at sufficiently short notice and that compensation would not be payable'.

Alternatively, the office file could include a note that an inspection revealed that there was an occupier on the site, that clarification was sought from the client and that the occupation was to be disregarded.

Considering other issues – Landlord and tenant, CPO and other land use options
2 Vacant possession
It is not entirely clear whether the request to advise on how to obtain vacant possession relates to the office site mentioned in

point 1 (and whose occupiers may have been identified from a site visit), or relates to the open-air market. However, comment in the question about statutory tenancies and squatters' rights suggests that it is more likely to be the market. Issues could include:

- What is the legal nature of the occupiers' rights? What is meant by 'statutory tenancies'? Does reference to 'squatters' rights' have any legal basis?
- Are the occupiers actually tenants enjoying Landlord and Tenant Act protection/security of tenure? What grounds for possession could be established in order to remove them? Would it be possible to establish the requisite intention to develop the property under ground (f) of section 30(1) of the Act in view of the relocation of the traders being a planning requirement, and therefore a prerequisite for development taking place?
- Would compulsory purchase powers be needed? Whereas the traders may be entitled to compensation for disturbance under ground (f) under the Landlord and Tenant Act, their legal interest may not be sufficiently substantial to warrant compensation for their property interest under a CPO scenario. Landlord and Tenant Act compensation would not be due under ground (d) where suitable alternative accommodation can be provided – but would the relocation to the office site be considered reasonable? Appropriate assumptions will help in reaching conclusions, while also enabling other issues to be raised.
- Legal fees, surveyors' costs and other expenditure might be incurred.
- A comment could be made on how the rights of the tenants, who could delay the scheme and therefore create uncertainty, could affect the overall project and its value.

Students should also note that special common law provisions may apply to the markets – traders may not fall within landlord and tenant legislation, especially when they have access during limited (trading) hours only.

3 Alternative use of surplus land

The inspection of the site and the surrounding area would help to clarify this issue. Students may wish to pick up the point made above in respect of car parking.

Could additional parking increase custom for the relocated market, and could this be a key to securing the willingness of traders to relocate? Would extra parking so close to the city centre present any planning gain benefits to the overall scheme? Would any leisure or retail uses be appropriate? What alternative uses might complement the overall redevelopment? And is there current and potential income from the advertising hoardings alongside the site?

4 Retained interest
Opportunities for Bitehornes Properties to avoid managing the market, but retaining a financial interest, could involve granting a leasehold interest to the local authority or to a private concern which would then manage the market. A full rent could be payable, or a turnover-based arrangement may be suitable.

A premium plus ground rent structure may not be the most effective arrangement. There may still be some residual development potential, and it may be necessary to preserve the ability to gain possession. A joint venture/partnership arrangement could be contemplated.

Other issues, such as requiring the owner to restrict retail/market trader activities to those compatible with the overall Bull Ring scheme, could also be considered.

Conclusion
There has only been scope here to cover some of the issues. Many areas are open to the imagination of the student. Effective use should be made of assumptions and notes in the office file in order to cover the full range of relevant issues. Some issues will be covered in depth whereas others will merely require acknowledging.

The criteria adopted by the assessment panel includes factual content (adequacy and accuracy); layout and presentation (use of plans, headings and appendices); validity, clarity and logical development of advice; market analysis and valuations; balance and professionalism and overall assessment.

Contributed by Austen Imber

CHAPTER 54

Urban regeneration/RDAs

Published as 'Pump priming for prosperity', 7 September 2002

Strengthening weak economies within cities and towns requires specialised regeneration bodies. Here we offer a guide to their functions and remits

The aim of urban regeneration is to stimulate growth in weaker local economies, achieved through a combination of property- and business-related initiatives. Chartered surveyors involved in the sector increasingly have to apply a range of business skills, with a multi-disciplinary approach often being the key to the successful delivery of projects.

Regeneration initiatives

Since the Urban Programme was launched in 1968, the UK's regeneration initiatives have included enterprise zones; urban development corporations (UDCs); City Challenge; English Partnerships; Single Regeneration Budget Challenge Fund; and Regional Development Agencies (RDAs).

Weaknesses such as an overreliance on inward/foreign investment, and new homes not being accurately located in relation to areas of employment mean that current initiatives look to create new sustainable mixed-use communities which draw housing and employment together. Rural communities are also supported.

Regional development agencies

The RDAs were established in England in 1999 (except London the following year), and are:

- Advantage West Midlands
- East Midlands Development Agency
- East of England Development Agency
- London Development Agency

- North West Development Agency
- One North East
- South East England Development Agency
- South West England Regional Development Agency
- Yorkshire Forward.

There are similar bodies in Scotland, Wales and Ireland, but with a different scope and structure from their English counterparts.

Role of the RDAs

Regional development agencies focus on economic regeneration, although they have considerable portfolios of physical regeneration activity.

Their roles include:

- acquiring and assembling sites;
- preparing sites for development by the private sector, such as through the remediation of brownfield sites and the provision of infrastructure;
- entering into partnerships/joint ventures with the private sector, local authorities etc;
- attracting relocating companies to their regions;
- securing inward investment;
- providing finance, loans, guarantees;
- working with the local planning authority on master planning for an area;
- assisting with the formulation of long-term strategic planning:
- undertaking direct development;
- carrying out the usual property management functions.

Regional development agencies are able to compulsorily acquire land but, unlike their predecessor urban development corporations, do not have any statutory planning powers. Instead, they operate within the usual planning system.

Whereas previous regeneration initiatives were predominantly property specific, the RDAs' roles extend to bringing about the long-term overall economic growth of an area. This is achieved by the provision of support to new and existing businesses and the promotion of training and development initiatives for local communities and businesses.

RDAs also seek to build a strong brand to assist in dealings with businesses and the general public.

Other players in the sector
There are in fact many overlapping roles among the UK's various bodies involved in regeneration.

Local authorities often look to take co-ordinating roles in regeneration schemes and may also provide land and buildings, with other major landowners contributing through the sale/development of their property holdings. Housing associations lead in the development of new social housing and the government recognises the need for key worker housing in expensive urban areas.

The private sector frequently leads in regeneration, with institutions, investors and developers recognising its potential. English Partnerships leads many regeneration initiatives at a national level, bringing forward a number of strategic sites, including within new towns. Urban regeneration companies (URCs) are tripartite joint ventures between a local authority, RDA and EP.

The Office of the Deputy Prime Minister oversees the majority of urban regeneration initiatives, with the Department of Trade and Industry (DTI) playing a wider key role, including securing funding from the European Union (EU), and acting as the ministry responsible for the RDAs.

Funding regeneration
Public funding of UK regeneration is through three principal sources: the RDA Single Pot, the Single Regeneration Budget, (which is administered by RDAs but falls outside their Single Pot), and the European Union's European Regional Development Fund (ERDF), which covers development costs. The SRB is being wound down, and the ERDF is guaranteed only until 2006. Through the Single Pot, RDAs will therefore have increasing influence over the shaping of physical regeneration priorities and investment. Additionally, Regional Selective Assistance (RSA) focuses on supporting businesses rather than providing direct regeneration funding.

The many other sources of funding include local authorities, English Heritage and the National Lottery. Enterprise zones continue to provide financial incentives such as exemption from business rates and favourable capital allowances, but few remain as their life is limited to 10 years. Through its European Social Fund (ESF), the EU also contributes to training and education and also to community initiatives.

The ways in which public sector monies can be invested in regeneration have been heavily affected by the EC's state aid rules. In December 1999, the EC declared gap funding (which filled the gap between end-value and development costs in order to make development commercially viable) under the Partnership Investment Programme (PIP) constituted illegal state aid, and breached its Competition Directorate's rules on fair competition within the single market.

In summer 2001, the EC approved a suite of replacement schemes, providing new mechanisms for gap funding. The RDAs are generally reluctant to use the new gap funding regime within their Single Pot allocations, favouring greater use of direct development and joint venturing. This requires greater initial funding, and involves longer delivery times – one factor being the need for additional skilled personnel, and hence a greater emphasis on training.

Uplifting an area and strategic acquisition

Once sufficient development activity has been undertaken by an RDA in an area, the viability of further development opportunities is usually much improved.

This then draws the private sector to the commercially viable opportunities available. Such a process is known as pump-priming.

RICS Regeneration Forum

The RICS Regeneration Forum comprises a multi-disciplinary group of professionals, including surveyors, town planners, economists, engineers, architects, commercial developers, housebuilders, local authorities and other government bodies.

Lead initiatives include researching the success of regeneration schemes and helping steer government regeneration strategy. The Forum also investigates a range of issues through CPD seminars, study tours, conferences, newsletters, research papers and articles.

2003 sees the full implementation of the Forum's education strategy, focusing on the many macro-inputs which all players in the sector must understand in order to deliver successful regeneration. This includes surveyors leading a multi-disciplinary team, and demonstrates more widely how RICS's new lifelong-learning and business skills initiatives directly affect surveyors' performance as well as the contribution that property makes to the economy and local communities.

The Forum's expansion will enable the hitherto London-based conferences to be rolled out to locations including Birmingham and Manchester (in addition to events connected with imminent research projects at Plymouth and Sheffield). The Forum is planning to expand internationally and enhance RICS's position as a global leader in regeneration strategy. It is anticipated that a separate RICS regeneration faculty will be established in due course, with regeneration in the meantime falling under the Planning and Development Faculty.

RICS Policy Unit

The RICS Policy Unit's work in the sector draws on its links with UK government and the European Union. Current initiatives include:

- working with the Office of the Deputy Prime Minister (ODPM) on fiscal incentives for urban regeneration;
- launch of a new ODPM/RICS website in October, which will act as a one-stop shop for those seeking information about funding for regeneration;
- input into the Urban Summit, 31 October to 1 November in Birmingham;
- responding to the London Draft Plan;
- working on a new RICS campaign on sustainable communities; and
- input into the EU seminar on 'Strategies for Financing Urban Regeneration' in Brussels on 27 November.

From offices in London and Brussels, the Policy Unit also lobbies government on behalf of RICS members and the public. Market commentaries and legal updates are regularly prepared, and the evolvement of government regeneration policy is also monitored.

Advantage West Midlands: RDA business development built on training

Advantage West Midlands (AWM) sees training and development as a key element of its 10-year plan for delivering major development projects in the city of Birmingham and wider West Midlands areas. This approach aligns with government and RICS lifelong-learning initiatives.

Business skills
It is essential that RDA surveyors understand the operational objectives of the businesses and developers with whom they work and are familiar with the more strategic, and indeed sometimes political, elements of the regeneration process. With two-thirds further growth in staff numbers planned over the current financial year, AWM's management training accounts for ever-changing organisational structures, as well as the usual people management issues.

APC support to the sector
For all general practice and planning and development APC candidates taking the RICS Assessment of Professional Competence (APC), open training events for final assessment submissions and for the interview/presentation are run on a free-of-charge basis in London and Birmingham.

CPD Centre
The AWM CPD Centre is being launched shortly to provide CPD seminars free of charge to local surveyors for mainstream subject areas, and to regeneration professionals on a national basis. Speakers include AWM's current and prospective consultants, and RICS and government personnel.

Note also that AWM is one of an increasing number of organisations incorporating consultants' commitment to lifelong learning as part of selection criteria.

Recruitment benefits
AWM's internal commitment to training and development has helped in the recruitment of surveyors and other staff. A comprehensive in-house structured APC training programme attracts graduates, and the rapid promotion prospects often available in RDAs attract qualified surveyors. Administrative staff too have been attracted by the opportunity to secure qualifications such as NVQs and the Assessment of Technical Competence (ATC).

Various consultee input

Procedure and Evidence

55. The rule against bias 369
56. Expert witnesses (part 1) 375
57. Expert witnesses (part 2) 380
58. Similar fact evidence 385

CHAPTER 55

The rule against bias

Published as 'The rule against bias', 20 March 1999

Last year's House of Lords' decision to extradite General Pinochet was overturned because of an ancient principle that applies to anyone sitting in judgment

The rule that 'no man should be a judge in his own cause' applies not only to judges but also to arbitrators, members of tribunals, and anyone else exercising judicial or quasi-judicial functions. This rule is so universal that it does not depend upon an Act of Parliament, or even upon the legal system of any particular nation state. It is a rule of natural justice, the origin of which predates the English language, and is often quoted in its Latin formulation: *nemo judex in causa sua*.

Rent assessment hearings

A case on fair rents provides one of the most important authorities on this rule in recent times. It also illustrates why this rule is sometimes called 'the rule against bias'.

In *Metropolitan Properties Ltd* v *Lannon* [1968] 1 QB 577 an application for the registration of a fair rent of a flat in Kensington, London, was heard by a Rent Assessment Committee. The landlord was a company in the Freshwater Group. The father of the chairman of the committee was the tenant of a similar flat nearby, owned by another company in the Freshwater Group. The chairman lived with his father and was advising him about his rent for that flat.

The Court of Appeal held that the chairman ought to have disqualified himself from hearing the case because he could not be a judge in one case and an advocate in another case when those cases involved inter-related issues.

In the month that has seen the death of Lord Denning at the age of 100, it is fitting to recall the clarity of thought that he brought to this case:

if [the chairman] were to have asked any of his friends: 'Do you think that I can properly sit ?', the answer of any of his good friends would surely have been: 'No, you should not sit. You are already acting, or as good as acting, against them. You should not, at the same time, sit in judgment on them.'

Absence of actual bias

It is important to note that where the 'rule against bias' applies, it is not necessary to argue or to prove that the judge or arbitrator was actually biased. The 'rule against bias' is wide enough to be a 'rule against interest' also.

The two most famous cases in this regard were relied upon recently by Senator Pinochet (former president of Chile). In December 1998, he applied to the House of Lords to set aside a previous decision of five law lords. On 25 November 1998, their Lordships had decided (by a majority of 3 to 2) that Pinochet did not have 'state immunity' for such alleged crimes as torture and hostage-taking: see *R* v *Bow Street Metropolitan Magistrates and others, ex parte Pinochet* [1998] 4 All ER 897.

The two cases in question were *Dimes* v *Grand Junction Canal* (1852) 3 HL Cas 759 and *R* v *Sussex Justices, ex parte McCarthy* [1924] KB 256 (see p373). In the first case, the Lord Chancellor, Lord Cottenham, had been the trial judge in a case involving a canal company in which he himself had had a substantial shareholding. Lord Cottenham's judgment was set aside by the House of Lords. Lord Campbell observed:

Since I have had the honour to be Chief Justice of the Court of Queen's Bench, we have again and again set aside proceedings in inferior tribunals because an individual, who had an interest in a cause, took part in the decision. And it will have a most salutary influence on these tribunals when it is known that this high court of last resort, in a case where the Lord Chancellor of England had an interest, considered his decree not according to law, and was set aside.

Non-financial interests

In the *Sussex Justices* case, Lord Hewart emphasised that the conflict of interest that arose was more important than any financial interest that might or might not exist. This was very much to the point in Pinochet's application to set aside the decision of the House of Lords given in November 1998. None of the law lords had any financial or proprietary interest in the outcome of the case.

The dispute about the validity of the judgment arose because the House of Lords had allowed Amnesty International Ltd to become an 'intervening party'. Amnesty has a reputation for opposing the human rights infringements committed by those who 'wade through slaughter to a throne and shut the gates of mercy on mankind'. It is an organisation with wide knowledge of the history and context of international treaties, including those that outlaw torture and hostage taking (on the one hand), or give certain immunities to former heads of state (on the other hand).

In a procedure that seems to have been copied from the US Supreme Court, the House of Lords sought to hear the arguments that such an organisation could place before it.

After the November judgment had been given, it transpired that one of the appeal judges, Lord Hoffmann, was an (unpaid) director and also chairman of Amnesty International Charity Ltd. This company was, technically speaking, a separate legal entity from Amnesty International Ltd. This is because English law does not allow political campaigns to be treated as charities. Accordingly, the non-political work of Amnesty has to be treated as a separate legal entity in order to secure the tax advantages that charities enjoy.

Lord Hoffmann, was one of three judges who voted against Pinochet's claim to 'state immunity', and fate so decreed that his vote was vital.

A differently constituted House of Lords decided, on 17 December 1998, that the previous decision could not be allowed to stand: see *R* v *Bow Street Metropolitan Stipendiary Magistrate, ex parte Pinochet (No 2)* [1999] 2 WLR 272. Their Lordships noted that, whatever the niceties of tax law and company law might be, Amnesty International Ltd and Amnesty International Charity Ltd were labourers in the same vineyard. Lord Hoffmann had therefore been an interested party.

Dangers for arbitrators?

More depends upon this decision than the question of how the House of Lords is to constitute its appellate committees in the future. For example, should an arbitrator disqualify himself if asked to assess the rent for premises occupied by a charity to which he has made out a covenant, or to which he pays a subscription, without actively participating in its work? Is a magistrate to 'recuse himself' (to use the legal term) if he is a member of the RSPCA and the case before him involves cruelty to a dog?

In fact, there is authority on the last point. In *R* v *Deal Corporation and Justices, ex parte Curling* (1881) 46 JP 71, a magistrate who was a member of the London Society for the Prevention of Cruelty to Animals was held not to be disqualified from hearing a prosecution brought by the parent society. This precedent is still included in the standard reference book used by magistrates' courts – Stone's *Justices' Manual*. It seems likely that this way of thinking (with its refusal to equate charitable work with financial interests) must have been in Lord Hoffmann's mind when he allowed himself to become a member of the committee hearing the *Pinochet* case.

Interest sufficient

In 'vacating' (ie setting aside) the judgment of November 1998, the House of Lords placed great emphasis on *Dimes* v *Grand Junction Canal* – particularly on the point that there needs to be no investigation as to whether a judge was actually biased, or even whether there was an appearance of bias. Once the 'interest' is shown to exist, the judge is disqualified.

On the particular point of involvement in a charitable organisation, Lord Browne-Wilkinson said that Lord Hoffmann would have been disqualified had he been a member of Amnesty International Ltd (apparently, even if he had been an inactive member). It made no difference that he was a member of the sister organisation, Amnesty International Charity Ltd.

Implications

The effect of all this is to make it very unwise for an arbitrator or any other person presiding over judicial or 'quasi-judicial' proceedings to conceal his membership of a charity, pressure group, etc. if that organisation (or a closely related one) is a party to the case. Although *R* v *Deal Corporation and Justices, ex parte Curling* is not mentioned by the House of Lords in their December judgment, it is dangerous to assume that this decision is still good law.

Yet the December judgment of the law lords is very unhelpful to lesser judicial figures, trying now to decide whether they can adjudicate in a case where they are inactive members of a litigating (or arbitrating) organisation. The House of Lords has also left open the wider question of what happens when it is the wife or husband of a judge or arbitrator (etc) who is the 'interested party', not the judge or arbitrator himself.

It would certainly be a sad state of affairs if professional men and women had to recuse themselves from charitable work and public-spirited endeavours because of the need to flaunt, like Robespierre, the fact that they are 'sea-green incorruptibles'.

'Justice seen to be done' Why Sussex Justices *case made history*

In *Sussex Justices*, Mr McCarthy, a motorcyclist, was prosecuted for dangerous driving after a collision with another motorcycle. McCarthy pleaded not guilty. The clerk to the magistrates was a partner in a firm of solicitors acting for the other motorcyclist. (Civil proceedings had been threatened against McCarthy by this firm.)

The conviction was set aside because the magistrates had retired with the clerk when they had left the courtroom to consider their verdict.

Lord Hewart CJ gave a judgment which contained one of the most memorable phrases in English law – indeed, it has passed into ordinary English parlance:

'It is not merely of some importance but it is of fundamental importance that justice should not only be done, but should manifestly and undoubtedly be seen to be done.'

Contributed by Leslie Blake

CHAPTER 56

Expert witnesses (part 1)

Published as 'Tricks of the trade', 27 January 2001

The lot of an expert witness under cross-examination is not a happy one. This article discusses the most famous instance of a such a witness being discredited by a trick question

Surveyors, engineers and other professional persons are often called upon to be expert witnesses in legal proceedings. The idea that such a person can be called, by one party or the other, to assist the court with the benefit of his or her opinions – even if those opinions are to be given in answer to hypothetical questions – dates from the 18th century.

Genesis of expert witnesses

One of the earliest reports of an expert being allowed to give opinion evidence in an English court relates to the famous engineer John Smeaton (1724–1792). He was the pioneer of modern lighthouse construction, having built the third Eddystone lighthouse in 1757. In addition to being an expert on lighthouses, he had also studied the canal and harbour systems of the Netherlands. In *Folkes* v *Chadd* (1782) 3 Doug KB 157, he was called to give his opinion on whether the building of an embankment (allegedly being an act of trespass) had caused the silting up of a harbour. Lord Mansfield, the judge, noted that the courts were regularly receiving the evidence of handwriting experts in civil and criminal cases. He therefore welcomed the evidence of John Smeaton as an expert engineer:

> Mr Smeaton understands the construction of harbours, the causes of their destruction, and how remedied. In matters of science, no other witnesses can be called.

Smeaton's expert opinion was that the embankment had not caused the silting-up of the harbour, an opinion that was confirmed by evidence that other harbours on the same coastline had been silted up, even though they were not in close proximity to any embankments.

Estates Gazette has always been in the forefront of those authorities who have emphasised the duties of expert witnesses. The evidence of valuers, surveyors, engineers, and similar experts is often vital in proceedings before arbitrators, tribunals and public inquiries, as well as courts of law.

National Justice Campania Naviera SA v *Prudential Assurance Co Ltd (The 'Ikarian Reefer')* [1993] 2 EGLR 183 set out the duties of an expert witness, as summarised by Cresswell J (see p379).

London & Leeds Estates Ltd v *Paribas Ltd (No 2)* (see p378) indicates the risk that expert witnesses face when they are called to give evidence, and paid their professional fees and expenses, by one party or the other to litigation. It may seem (and, in some instances, it may be true) that they are acting as advocates, not as experts who are required to assist the court, tribunal or arbitrator before whom they are appearing. (The story of an over-enthusiastic valuer, in a 19th century land compensation case, has already been covered in this series on 26 June 1993, reprinted in *The Best of Mainly for Students* vol 2, pp141–149.)

Among lawyers, the most often-quoted example of an expert witness being cross-examined so as to destroy his credibility occurred when an 'engineer' was called as a witness in *R* v *Rouse* (1931) Notable British Trials Series, usually known as the 'blazing car case'.

Blazing car case

Alfred Arthur Rouse was born in Herne Hill, South London, in 1894. He had worked briefly as an office boy for a firm of estate agents. By 1930 he had long worked as a commercial traveller, or 'bag man', as he would have been known in those days. This job, and his possession of a car, gave him a degree of mobility around England and Wales that was unusual in the days before motorways were built and car ownership became commonplace. Taking advantage of this mobility, he had fathered illegitimate children in various places, had contracted a bigamous marriage and had financial obligations to the mothers of his children. A desire to escape his obligations by faking his death seems to be the only logical motive for the dreadful crime he embarked upon in November 1930.

We now know, from a confession that Rouse made prior to his execution, that he offered a lift to a man whom he had met in the

Swan and Pyramid public house in Whetstone High Road. He then strangled him into unconsciousness near the village of Hardingstone in Northamptonshire. He soaked his victim in petrol and set fire to the car. To ensure that the fire would be fed by a constant flow of petrol, he loosened the union joint at the carburettor end of the petrol tank, thereby destroying the body to such an extent that it could not afterwards be identified. Luckily for the interests of justice, however, Rouse was seen leaving the scene of the crime. He was subsequently charged with the murder of 'a certain man, whose name is unknown'.

Rouse's defence, at his trial, was that the car had caught fire accidentally while the unknown man was smoking a cigar (given to him by Rouse) after filling the tank with petrol from a petrol can. Rouse's failure to call help, and his subsequent jocular and talkative disposition, was seen as strong circumstantial evidence against him. Today, this conduct might well be explained as the bizarre after-effects of shock, or the result of changes to his personality brought about by injuries received in World War I.

Expert evidence

It was vital to the prosecution case to prove that the union joint had been deliberately loosened in order to feed the fire. Obviously, Rouse was not disposed to admit this at his trial. The Crown called Colonel Cuthbert Buckle, a man who had had 26 years' experience as a fire loss assessor. In the four years prior to the trial, he had inspected 56 burnt-out cars, and his firm (Ellis & Buckle Ltd) had inspected 83. In his evidence, he excluded every accidental cause for the fire, and stated that the union joint could not have become loosened accidentally or by the effects of the fire itself. If the joint had been loosened prior to the fire, while Rouse and his passenger were travelling in it, the fumes of the petrol would have become overpowering and would not have gone unnoticed.

Giving evidence in his own defence, Rouse was, by all accounts, a hopeless witness. In an attempt to rebut the evidence of Colonel Buckle, the defence called two expert witnesses. The first of these was Herbert Bamber, a mechanical engineer and automobile engineer. He stated that it was possible for the union joint to become loosened by vibrations if it had not been firmly and properly tightened to begin with. He believed that a 'weeping' leak of petrol could go on for some time without being noticed, and could then be ignited by a spark from the electrics of the car.

In cross-examination, however, he admitted that he had never seen a car so thoroughly burnt, and that his experience related principally to motor car collisions and to crane accidents. He also admitted that he had not told Sir William Morris (the manufacturer of the car) of this risk. His cross-examination ended with this interchange:

Q: I think we can leave it like this: you do not profess to be an expert on fire?
A: No.

Cross-examination as to credit

Mr Bamber had principally been cross-examined on the issues raised by his evidence, although the cross-examiner's common ploy, of alleging that he was straying beyond his field of expertise, had also been used. The second expert called by the defence was treated very differently. He was 'cross-examined as to credit'.

This expert was Mr Arthur Isaacs, the managing director of a firm specialising in the heat treatment of metals. He described himself as an 'engineer and fire assessor', although (unlike Mr Bamber) he was not a member of any engineering institution. Whereas Mr Bamber had submitted that the union joint could have been accidentally loosened prior to the fire, Mr Isaacs' opinion was that the fire itself (even if accidentally started) could have caused the expansion and loosening of the joint. 'I go so far,' he said, 'that in the last 25 cases that I have done, where the fire has been intense, these nuts have always been loose.'

Mr Isaacs was cross-examined by Mr Norman Birkett, who was making a rare appearance as a prosecutor, for his reputation survives to this day as a great defence lawyer in murder trials. In mounting his cross-examination, Birkett had been guided by Colonel Buckle's intuition that Mr Isaacs was not an expert. Having in front of him a table in an engineer's diary, Birkett's first question was:

Q: What is the co-efficient of the expansion of brass?
A: I am afraid that I cannot answer that question off-hand.
Q: If you do not know, say so. What do I mean by the term?
A: You want to know what is the expansion of the metal under heat?
Q: I asked you what is the co-efficient of the expansion of brass. Do you know what it means?
A: Put that way, I probably do not.
Q: You are an engineer?
A: I dare say I am...

Further questions about Mr Isaacs' experience followed, and then:

Q: I am suggesting to you that the roadside fire is a less common case than a fire in the garage. How many of the 15 to 20 [fires you saw] last year were roadside fires?
A: I could not be sure.
Q: Did you not look up your notes before you came?
A: I do not think that I had much time

The cross-examination was effective not because of the use of a trick question (no engineer could have answered this without referring to his diary – the co-efficient of the expansion of brass is 0.0000189). Rather, it was the witness's inability to recognise the question as a trick, or to give the jury any reassurance that he was the expert engineer that he claimed to be. If he had known the answer, Birkett afterwards said that he would have asked about the co-efficient of the expansion of other metals, and if the correct answers had been given, he would have gone on to deal with other issues, as if the questions were of no importance at all.

What of those expert witnesses who really are highly qualified academics, not merely practical do-it-yourself men? Even they cannot escape the cross-examiner's scorn. At least one professor, giving evidence, has been met with the jibe: 'It may be very difficult for a man who gives lectures to answer questions, but you must answer mine!'

A case study – The risk faced by expert witnesses

In *London & Leeds Estates Ltd* v *Paribas Ltd (No 2)* [1995] 1 EGLR 102, a valuer was called to give expert evidence for a landlord in a rent review arbitration. It was alleged that, in an earlier rent review arbitration (relating to property in the same locality), he had given contradictory evidence on the state of the market. On the previous occasion, he had been called to give evidence for the tenant of the property. The court ordered him to produce a copy of his proof of evidence in the previous proceedings so that he could be cross-examined on its contents in the present proceedings. In short, the valuer's previous (allegedly inconsistent) statements could be used to attack his credibility when appearing as an expert witness for the landlord in the present arbitration proceedings. This procedure is permitted by the Criminal Procedure Act 1865 (a statue that, despite its title, applies to civil and arbitration proceedings as well as to criminal trials).

Duties of an expert witness – *National Justice Naviera SA* v *Prudential Assurance Co Ltd (The 'Ikarian Reefer')* per Cresswell J

1. Expert evidence should be, and should be seen to be, the independent product of the expert, uninfluenced as to form or content by the exigencies of litigation.
2. An expert should provide independent assistance to the court by way of objective and unbiased opinions.
3. An expert should never assume the role of an advocate.
4. An expert should always state the facts or assumptions upon which his or her opinion is based.
5. An expert should not omit to mention, or consider, material facts that could detract from his or her opinion.
6. An expert should make it clear when a particular question or issue falls outside his or her expertise.
7. If an expert's opinion is not properly researched, because not enough data is available, this must be stated, together with an indication that the opinion is no more than provisional.
8. In cases where an expert witness has prepared a report, but cannot assert that it contains the truth, the whole truth and nothing but the truth, without some qualification, that qualification should be stated in the report.
9. If, after an exchange of experts' reports between the parties, an expert changes his or her view on a material matter, this should be communicated to the other side without delay, and, if appropriate, to the court.
10. Where the expert's evidence refers to photographs, plans, calculations, analyses, measurements, surveys etc, these must be provided to the opposite party at the same time as the exchange of reports.

Contributed by Leslie Blake

CHAPTER 57

Expert witnesses (part 2)

Published as 'Stick to one's honest guns', 19 May 2001

An expert witness is called upon to give the court the benefit of his honest and unbiased opinion, not to act as a partisan hired gun and sacrifice truth in the pursuit of a particular outcome

The article appearing in *Mainly for Students* (27 January 2001, see Chapter 56 in this book) has excited a certain amount of interest among practitioners, as well as students. It dealt with the problem that faces expert witnesses when they are called by one party or the other in English legal proceedings – a problem that (in civil proceedings) the concept of a single joint expert is now supposed to overcome.

The article reprinted the list of 10 rules (something of a lecture, intended for expert witnesses) that Cresswell J set out in his judgment in *National Justice Compania Naviera SA* v *Prudential Assurance Co Ltd 'Ikarian Reefer'* [1993] 37 EG 158. All of these rules could be looked upon as particular applications of the first and third rules:

1. 'Expert evidence should be, and should be seen to be, the independent product of the expert, uninfluenced as to form or content by the exigencies of litigation'; and
3. 'An expert should never assume the role of an advocate.'

Keith Gaston, a partner in the commercial litigation department of Ipswich-based Merricks solicitors, has been kind enough to draw attention to a further display of judicial impatience with expert witnesses. This was reported in *Fleet Street Law Reports* (FSR), a specialist series of reports that deals with copyright infringements, patent rights and other intellectual property disputes. On occasion, these disputes involve the construction industry: for example, where an architect seeks to claim copyright to his drawings and plans. One such case was *Cala Homes (South) Ltd* v *Alfred McAlpine Homes East Ltd (No 1)* [1995] FSR 818.

Cala Homes

In *Cala Homes*, the design director of the Cala group of companies, and all the companies individually, sued McAlpine for allegedly infringing their copyright in drawings of elevations and floor plans for a commercially successful range of houses. It was also alleged that McAlpine had induced a breach of contract on the part of a firm of technical draughtsmen that Cala Homes had previously used for the purpose of producing various drawings and plans.

At the end of a long judgment reviewing the law and examining the complex facts of the case (and finding that there had indeed been a breach of copyright and an inducement to commit a breach of contract), Laddie J turned to the evidence of the defendants' expert witness. The witness was a Mr Goodall, an eminent architect, who had previously written an article entitled *The Expert Witness: Partisan with a Conscience* in the *Journal of the Chartered Institute of Arbitrators* (August 1990). This article had presumably been the subject of the cross-examination of Mr Goodall in *Cala Homes*, and, for this reason, Laddie J was able to refer to it (see pp383–384).

Hired gun?

Mr Goodall's article had postulated that there are three phases in an expert's work: first, the client's 'candid friend' (telling him all the faults in his case); second, 'a hired gun'; and, third, the witness in court (where 'shades of moral and other constraints begin to close upon him').

In his judgment, Laddie J recognised, as a fact of life, that some witnesses are driven by a desire to achieve a particular outcome to the litigation, and feel it necessary to sacrifice truth in the pursuit of victory. However, his lordship continued: 'in the case of expert witnesses the court is likely to lower its guard'. The court will usually assume that the expert is more interested in being honest and correct than in ensuring that one side or another wins.

Laddie J made it clear that it is not the job of an expert to 'stand shoulder to shoulder, through thick and thin, with the side which is paying his bill'. He criticised Mr Goodall's threefold analysis of the expert's role by stating that the 'pragmatic flexibility' commended by Mr Goodall was merely a euphemism for 'misleading selectivity', which would only give place to 'something closer to a true and balanced view' when the expert was being cross-examined, and was faced with the possibility of being found out.

In fairness to Mr Goodall, Laddie J also pointed out that an expert witness would not usually be prepared to admit (as Mr Goodall had done) that he was approaching the drafting of his report as a 'partisan hired gun'. But this reluctance would only increase the risk that the court would receive evidence that was 'contaminated by [an] attempted sleight of mind'.

Role of the advocate

It follows from this analysis of the role of the expert witness that it is entirely different from the role of an advocate appearing for a party in civil or criminal proceedings. The expert witness gives evidence to assist the court with the benefit of his opinion, honestly given. It should be a matter of mere coincidence that his honest opinion tends to favour, to a greater or lesser extent, the party who is calling him to give that evidence.

By contrast, an advocate has no business to give the court, or arbitrator, his opinion about the truth or justice of his client's case. In a famous murder trial in 1856 (*R v Palmer*), the defence lawyer made the mistake of beginning his speech by assuring the jury that he believed the defendant to be innocent. (This, it might be noted, was an almost impossible belief to hold on any impartial view of the evidence.) The trial judge, Lord Campbell CJ afterwards directed the jury as follows:

> I most strongly recommend to you that you should attend to everything [defence counsel] said to you with the exception of his own private opinion. It is my duty to tell you that opinion ought not to be any ingredient in your verdict. It would be disastrous if a jury was led to believe that a prisoner is not guilty because his advocate expresses his perfect conviction of his innocence. And, on the other hand, if an advocate withholds his opinion, the jury may suppose that he is conscious of his client's guilt; whereas it is the duty of the advocate to press his argument upon the jury, but not his opinion.

The reason for Lord Campbell's warning to the jury had been eloquently stated by Dr Johnson in the previous century (see p384).

The starkly contrasting duties of the advocate and the expert witness make it unwise for a surveyor, engineer, architect, planning consultant or other professional expert to act as the person presenting (or defending) a case if he is also expected to give his expert opinion as a witness in those proceedings.

However, it has recently been held that it is not a bar to being an expert witness in a case if the party calling that witness is a friend, colleague or employer: see *Liverpool Roman Catholic Archdiocesan Trustees Inc* v *Goldberg (No 2)* The Times 9 March 2001. But, of course, the duties that the expert witness owes to the court take precedence over loyalties of friendship, business or employment. This is why, for example, planning officers giving evidence at a inquiry often have to admit that they had advised their planning committee against the action or decision it subsequently decided upon.

No expert witness is entitled to make a court, or arbitrator, believe that the worse case (as he believes it to be) is, in fact, the better case. Advocates are often duty-bound to do so, for the reasons that Dr Johnson gave. Nevertheless, even advocates are seldom likely to be confronted with the moral dilemma that faced Charles Phillips, a barrister, in 1840.

Sailing close to the wind

While conducting a brilliant defence on behalf of a man charged with murder, the prisoner privately confessed to Phillips that he had committed that crime. He then said to him: 'And now I rely on you to do the best you can to prove that I have not'. This admission certainly prevented Phillips from accusing any other person of the crime. To that extent, he could not be a 'hired gun'. The defendant, however, had not instructed him to make any such accusation. Phillips was advised that it was his duty to continue to defend the accused man. He solved the problem by using the following words in his closing speech:

But you will say to me, if the prisoner did not do it, who did do it ? Ask not me, a poor finite creature like yourselves. Ask the prosecutor who did it. It is for him to tell you who did it; and until he shall have proved by the clearest evidence that it was the prisoner at the bar, beware how you imbrue your hands in the blood of that young man.*

Expert witnesses never have any right to sail this close to the wind.

Laddie J's opinions on Mr Goodall's article: The Expert Witness – Partisan with a conscience

Mr Goodall said the following:

---

* The case was *R* v *Courvoisier* (1840) 9 C&P 362. Despite Phillips' efforts, the verdict was guilty.

How should the expert avoid becoming partisan in a process that makes no pretence of determining the truth, but seeks only to weigh the persuasive effect of arguments deployed by one adversary or the other? the man who works the three card trick is not cheating, nor does he incur any moral opprobrium, when he uses his sleight of hand to deceive the eye of the innocent rustic and to deny him the information he needs for a correct appraisal of what has gone on. The rustic does not have to join in: but if he chooses to, he is 'fair game'. If by an analogous 'sleight of mind' an expert witness is able to present the data so that they seem to suggest an interpretation favourable to the side instructing him... it is no more than a suggestion, just as the Three Card Trick was only a suggestion about the data, not an outright misrepresentation of them...

Laddie J commented as follows:

No doubt it is currently fashionable to say that our legal system makes no pretence to determining the truth. I accept that some people not only say it but also believe it. If it were true, then Mr Goodall would be right in thinking that anything short of outright misrepresentation is permissible in an expert's report and that, not only the other party but also the person trying to decide the issue – the 'rustics' – are fair game. On reflection, if Mr Goodall were right, I am not sure that even outright misrepresentation should be avoided. If litigation is to be conducted as if it were a game of three card trick, what is wrong with having a couple of aces up your sleeve? The whole basis of Mr Goodall's approach to the drafting of an expert's report is wrong. The function of a court of law is to discover the truth relating to the issues before it. In doing that it has to assess the evidence adduced by the parties. The judge is not a rustic who has chosen to play a game of three card trick. He is not fair game. Nor is the truth...

from [1995] FSR 818 pp841–843

Dr Johnson explains the duty of a lawyer

Sir William Forbes said he thought an honest lawyer should never undertake a case that he was satisfied was not a just one.

'Sir,' said Dr Johnson, 'a lawyer has no business with the justice or injustice of the cause which he undertakes, unless his client asks his opinion, and then he is bound to give it honestly. The justice or injustice of the cause is to be decided by the judge. Consider, Sir, what is the purpose of courts of justice? It is that every man shall have his case fairly tried by men appointed to try causes... A lawyer is not to usurp the province of the jury or the judge and determine what shall be the effect if the evidence or the result of legal argument... If lawyers were to undertake no such causes until they were sure that they were just, a man might be precluded altogether from a trial of his claim, though if it were judicially examined it might be found a very just claim.'

From *Boswell's Life of Johnson*

Contributed by Leslie Blake

CHAPTER 58

Similar fact evidence

First published 4 April 1998

Press coverage of a murder trial alerted a court to coincidences in a defendant's past and helped set a precedent for civil and criminal cases today

In 1912 a magistrate, Frederick Wilbee, owned several houses in Herne Bay, Kent, which he rented out. He employed Miss Carrie Rapley to assist him in the business. She had worked for him for 34 years when, in May 1912, a man calling himself 'Mr Williams' called to say that he wanted to rent 80 High Street, Herne Bay.

Rapley asked for references, but Williams could not give any. She asked whether he had a bank account and he produced a Post Office savings book, but refused to show her the contents. 'You need not be afraid,' he said, 'there is between £50 and £60 there.'

Rapley observed that, if he was going to furnish the house, £50 or £60 would not leave him much to live on. 'Oh,' he replied, 'my wife has a private income paid monthly. I have not got anything except that. I dabble in antiques.' He then added another remark about his wife: 'I might just as well tell you, she is a notch above me. She is the daughter of a bank manager, and I met her in a boarding house. Her friends did not at all approve of the marriage.'

Chances are Miss Rapley did not think very much of Williams. But, as fate would have it, Wilbee entered the office and he and Williams agreed a rent of £18 pa for the house, payable monthly in advance. The first month's rent was paid on May 20.

During the succeeding weeks, Rapley saw Williams many times. He came frequently to the office to complain about the house. His wife came on two occasions, but she never came alone.

On July 16, Williams arrived at Rapley's office in an extremely agitated state. He put his head down on Rapley's desk and sobbed. When Rapley asked him what the matter was, he replied: 'Have you not heard? She is dead.'

'Who is dead?' said Miss Rapley.

'My wife...She had a fit during the week. I went out. She went to have a bath, and she must have had another fit, for when I came back I found her dead in the bath.'

Rapley was shocked. Williams then looked up. 'Was it not a jolly good job I got her to make a will?' he observed.

Death by misadventure?

The coroner's inquest returned a verdict of death by misadventure. Williams rapidly left Herne Bay with Wilbee's consent. Rapley never forgot her suspicions, but it was not until two-and-a-half years later that she was called to give evidence in a criminal court about her encounters with Williams.

When it was put to her by the defence counsel that she could not possibly remember details of conversations so long ago, she replied: 'I have a very excellent memory.' The prosecuting counsel then re-examined Rapley and, in doing so, demonstrated how this opportunity can be used to neutralise an opponent's otherwise skilful cross-examination:

Q: 'During the 36 and a half years you have been in Mr Wilbee's service, has anyone come and put his head down on his hands and wept in your office?'
A: 'No. I am in a magistrate's office, and we have all sorts and conditions of people come, but they do not do that sort of thing.'

When Rapley commented about furnishing the house, she knew of one thing which was lacking at 80 High Street, Herne Bay – a bathroom. The bath in which the drowning occurred was first seen by the so-called Williams (as it turned out, this was a false name) in July 1912. It was for sale in a shop in Herne Bay for £2. Williams sent his wife to bargain down the price, to 37s 6d.

The bath was delivered on July 9, but was never paid for. Four days later, the woman who had transacted the bargain was dead in that bath. A few days later, Williams asked the ironmonger to take the bath back, without giving any reason. The bath was returned and Williams never had to pay for it.

Knowing what we now know about 'Williams', it is clear that he had used the victim of his intended crime to bring the means of death into their home.

Death by counsel's opinion?

If the means of death had been delivered to the house on July 9, the death warrant had arrived one week earlier. And of all the unlikely documents to serve this purpose, it was an opinion from a Chancery barrister, Mr G F Spear, of 2 Paper Buildings, Temple.

'Williams' had been anxious to know whether his wife could alter a trust fund, set up after the death of her father, so that she could get all the capital – about £2,500 in gilt-edged securities – instead of receiving the modest income of £8 per month. If this was not possible, he wanted to know whether she could leave the capital to him by will. In return, he was prepared to make a will in her favour – although he did not have any property of his own to leave to his wife.

Williams had cheated and stolen money from women before 1912, but he had left them alive. But in the case of 'Mrs Williams' (whose name was Beatrice, or Bessie, Mundy), counsel's opinion persuaded him to kill her.

Spear advised that the trust or 'settlement' could not be broken in Bessie Mundy's lifetime, but that she had a 'power of appointment' under the terms of the settlement, which she was entitled to exercise by will.

This would be effective to pass all the capital of her trust fund to her intended beneficiary upon her death. The perceptive barrister added these words of caution:

> Generally I am bound to add that I do not consider the proposed arrangement (of mutual wills) very satisfactory. The courts regard married women jealously, and discourage dealings with their property in favour of husbands ... I do not see how it can possibly be for her benefit to make such a covenant (promising not to revoke her will), and I think that it is the duty of her advisers to point this out.

Spear's opinion arrived on July 2. On July 3, the solicitor acting for 'Mr and Mrs Williams' saw 'Mrs Williams' and advised her of the content of counsel's opinion. On July 8 'Mr and Mrs Williams' executed mutual wills, each making the other their sole beneficiary. And, as we have seen, 'Mrs Williams' (Bessie Mundy) died in her bath on July 13.

The trust fund had been intended to protect her capital from a predatory husband. Instead, it had made her the victim of a murderous one. And the ease with which he had got away with the crime then gave him the idea that the exercise could be repeated ...

Death at Blackpool

Of course, to repeat such a crime would require a change of name. But that was no disincentive to Williams. The name Williams was not the first false one he had used.

Even his marriage to Bessie Mundy was not valid. He had been married twice before, and so all his marriages after the first one were bigamous and void.

The man's real name was George Joseph Smith. He had been born in Bethnal Green, London, in 1872.

It is interesting to note, in passing, what Smith did with his ill-gotten gains. Bessie Mundy's estate had a net value of £2,571 13s 6d. Williams/Smith became a property dealer, specialising in Bristol: during the autumn and winter of 1912–13 he bought 167 North Road for £420; 34 Beach Road for £180; 80 Ashley Down Road for £215; 49 Cranbrook Road for just less than £400; 81 Brynland Avenue for £210; 31 Wolsely Road for £187.10s; and 10 Zetland Road for £575. Shortly afterwards, Smith sold these houses for a total of £1,455, thereby making a substantial loss.

By November 1913, Smith, using his real name this time, married Alice Burnham at Portsmouth. As with Bessie Mundy, the woman's family had vehemently objected to Smith, but he an hypnotic influence over his intended victim. Alice had far less money than Bessie, but he got it from her none the less and then insured her life, using her own money to pay the premium.

On December 10 1913, Mr and Mrs Smith viewed a flat at 25 Adelaide Street, Blackpool, but declined to rent it because it did not have a bath. Instead, they rented a room with use of a bathroom at 16 Regent Road, Blackpool. On the evening of the next day, Alice was found dead in the bath.

Smith received £506 under the insurance policy and whatever property remained in Alice's estate. Once again, the coroner's jury brought in a verdict of death by misadventure. It was, of course, ignorant of the incident involving 'Williams' in Herne Bay. And like Rapley, however, Smith's landlady in Blackpool had her own views.

When he wrote down a forwarding address on a postcard, she wrote on the back: 'Wife died in bath. I shall see him again some day.' Later, at Smith's murder trial, the jury was allowed to see what Smith had written on the front of the card, but not what the landlady had written on the back.

Death in London

In December 1914, after an intervening non-murderous but still bigamistic marriage, Smith married Margaret Lofty at Bath. (There was no humour in the man whatsoever, but he no doubt felt very clever to use a town with this name.) Smith gave his name as John Lloyd and his occupation as land agent.

On the same day as the marriage, Mr and Mrs Lloyd travelled to London and eventually found lodgings at 14 Bismarck Road, Upper Holloway (now Despard Road). The next day, Mrs Lloyd went to see a solicitor in Islington High Street and made a short will leaving her entire estate to her husband. In fact she had very little money, but she had a life insurance policy in favour of her estate.

By 8.15pm on the same day (it was December 18 1914) Margaret Lofty (Mrs Lloyd) was found dead in the bath. On this occasion, however, the first day of the inquest was reported in The News of the World under the headlines: 'Found Dead in Bath: Bride's Tragic Fate on Day after Wedding'.

Two readers immediately recognised Smith's handiwork and contacted the police. One was Charles Burnham, father of Alice, the Blackpool victim. The other was the son-in-law of the landlady in Blackpool, the lady who had written 'I shall see him again some day'.

After various police forces had co-ordinated investigations, three charges of murder were laid against Smith. Those relating to the deaths at Blackpool and Herne Bay were transferred for trial to London under Palmer's Act – an Act which was passed to allow William Palmer, the poisoner, to be tried in London in 1856 because of the local prejudice against him in Staffordshire.

An evidential problem

In the days when murder was punishable with the death penalty, there was rule of practice that murder was always charged alone and that different charges of murder, relating to separate incidents, could only be tried in separate trials. In other words, Smith could be charged with only one murder at a time.

And yet, if this was to be the case, how could any single death be shown to be murder in the case of Smith? There were no marks of violence nor evidence of drugs. Each one had died consistently with a fainting fit, causing their accidental death by drowning.

In short, the conundrum was this: if the prosecution was not allowed to refer to all three deaths, Smith could not be convicted of murdering any one of his three brides. On the other hand, if the defence was not allowed to exclude this evidence, Smith could not hope to be acquitted of murdering whichever bride the prosecution chose to name in their indictment. In fact, the prosecution chose to begin with the first death – Bessie Mundy – who died at Herne Bay.

The defence, led by 'the Great Defender', Sir Edward Marshall Hall, relied on the rule of common law that a defendant in a criminal case does not come to court to answer for his entire past life. He comes only to answer a specific charge, and his other criminal convictions or examples of bad character are not usually admissible evidence against him.

Indeed, this rule is valid in civil cases also. Even equity, when demanding that 'he who comes to equity must come with clean hands', does not expect its litigants to have led entirely blameless lives.

The essential decision in *R* v *Smith* (1915) was one for the judge, not for the jury. It was for the judge to decide whether the jury could be allowed to learn of the deaths of Alice Burnham and Margaret Lofty, as well as the death of Bessie Mundy. The question is usually discussed in textbooks on the law of evidence under the title 'similar fact evidence'.

The judge was Scrutton J (afterwards Scrutton LJ). He is mainly remembered today as a sound judge on matters of property and commercial law. He ruled in favour of the prosecution. When the time came afterwards to explain this decision to the jury he did so using an example:

You are playing cards for money with three men; suddenly in the pocket of one of them is found a card of the pack you are playing with... Cards do sometimes tumble into odd places. If it happened to be the ace of trumps in the game you are playing at that time you might regard the matter with more suspicion... [but] you might say that, in that one case, only, you could not form any opinion about it. But supposing on your mentioning it to someone else it turned out that on five separate occasions of playing for money the gentleman had had the same fortunate accident of finding the ace of trumps in his coat pocket, what would you think then? What the law says you may think is that that series of fortunate accidents does not usually happen... [and] that it was not an accident at all, but that it was designed.

The jury convicted Smith of Miss Mundy's murder and this decision (and the judge's ruling on the law of 'similar fact evidence') was upheld by the Court of Appeal: see (1915) 11 Cr App Rep 229.

After the dismissal of his appeal, Smith was hanged for the murder of Bessie Mundy. (There was no need to try him on the other two charges.) Scrutton J had observed, when passing the death penalty, that 'exhortation to repentance would be wasted on you'.

Similar fact evidence

The exceptional situations where similar fact evidence can be used to establish the truth of a disputed matter are sometimes to be found in civil cases.

A tenant's argument that he has only accidentally infringed the covenants in his lease (eg by causing a nuisance to neighbours) might be rebutted by evidence of his misconduct towards other neighbours in other properties.

An argument that an apparent breach of copyright was a mere coincidence might be rebutted by evidence of other 'coincidences' with regard to other copyright owners: see *Mood Music Publishing Co v De Wolfe* [1976] Ch 119.

An argument by a defendant that he would not cheat or defraud his mother might be rebutted by evidence that, on a previous occasion, he admittedly cheated and defrauded his sister: *Berger v Raymond Sun Ltd* [1984] 1 WLR 625.

But whether in civil cases or criminal prosecutions, the degree of relevance which 'similar fact evidence' must achieve has never been better illustrated than in the criminal career of George Joseph Smith – one of the most undesirable and certainly one of the most systematically evil tenants that there has ever been.

Contributed by Leslie Blake

Property Law and Trusts

59. Proprietary estoppel 395
60. Restrictive covenants on land 400
61. Secret trusts 406

CHAPTER 59

Proprietary estoppel

Published as 'A rural family at war', 24 February 2001

In a case that shatters the dream of the rural idyll and illustrates the vagaries of friendship, the Court of Appeal has reviewed the scope of the equitable doctrine of proprietary estoppel

One of the circumstances in which a court will take notice of an agreement about land, even if that agreement is not in writing and not signed by the parties to it, is if that agreement gives rise to a 'proprietary estoppel'. The scope of this doctrine has recently been reviewed by the Court of Appeal in *Gillett* v *Holt* [2000] 2 All ER 289.

An everyday story of country folk

In 1952 a 12-year-old boy, Geoffrey Gillett, and a 38-year-old gentleman farmer (and bachelor), Ken Holt, formed a friendship that lasted for more than 40 years. The boy left school at 15 despite the doubts of his teachers and his parents, who wanted him to gain formal qualifications. He accepted an invitation to work for Ken Holt on his farm, gradually learning the business. He finally became the manager. When he married, his wife and sons became a surrogate family for Mr Holt. They became closely involved in the farm's complex financial arrangements and in Mr Holt's landed estate. Indeed, they sold their own home to live on the estate.

Mr Gillett was an efficient farm manager and the business prospered. He was treated like a son by Mr Holt, who, at one point, proposed to adopt him so that he could inherit the agricultural tenancy. He involved him fully, throughout this lengthy period, in his social life and various sporting activities.

Mr Holt's promise

On many occasions, Mr Holt assured Mr Gillett that he, and his family, would benefit from the estate. He even drafted various wills under which Mr Gillett and his family stood to gain. Mr Gillett became anxious about the degree to which he had enmeshed his life and prospects, and those of his family, in the affairs of Mr Holt. As wills (even if properly signed and witnessed) can always be revoked during the lifetime of the testator, he sought formal assurances from Mr Holt that he would, indeed, receive the benefits he had been promised.

Mr Holt never put the arrangement on a more formal footing, and Mr Gillett, believing him to be a man whose word could be trusted, tolerated this situation.

End of the friendship

Mr Gillett's fears were not without foundation. In 1992 the relationship between Mr Holt and the Gilletts deteriorated suddenly and rapidly. The cause of this breakdown was the fact that Mr Holt had transferred his loyalty to a trainee solicitor, a Mr Wood. The position changed so dramatically that, by 1994, Mr Wood had replaced Mr Gillett as the principal beneficiary in Mr Holt's will and, in 1995, Mr Gillett was summarily dismissed from his job as farm manager. A police investigation was instigated against him. This came to nothing.

The effect of this breakdown in family relations was to jeopardise the Gillett family home, livelihood and good name. They were left with none of the benefits that they had believed they would be receiving under Mr Holt's will, and felt that, in committing themselves, without reservation, to the interests of Mr Holt, they had relied upon such prospects to their detriment.

With little left to lose, they started a legal action against both Mr Holt and Mr Wood, who, by this time, had become the legal and beneficial owner of a large portion of the estate. (Unlike many previous cases involving promises to make a will, the litigation did not arise upon the death of the promisor, but was commenced during his lifetime.)

The basis of the original action was twofold. The first cause of action was in contract, but this was abandoned at the trial. The lack of a written agreement was, no doubt, a considerable barrier to the success of such a claim, given that land was involved. The second cause of action was the doctrine of proprietary estoppel.

Proprietary estoppel: the five basic requirements

Proprietary estoppel is an equitable doctrine and, as such, is subject to the discretion of the court. Nevertheless, certain elements must be established before a claim can succeed. These elements have changed over the years. In early cases, five requirements needed to be satisfied. Failure to prove any one of these requirements would prove fatal to the claim:

1. the claimant must have made a mistake as to his legal rights;
2. the claimant must have spent money, or done some act, based upon his mistaken belief;
3. the defendant, as holder of the legal right, must be aware of the existence of his own right and that it is inconsistent with the right claimed by the claimant;
4. the defendant must know of the claimant's mistaken belief; and
5. the defendant must have encouraged the claimant in his expenditure of money or in the other acts that the claimant performed – either directly or by abstaining from asserting his own legal rights.

These strict tests (which imply a unilateral mistake on the part of the claimant) come from *Willmott* v *Barber* (1880) 15 ChD 96. This case followed the reference to the equitable doctrine of 'encouragement and acquiescence' in the dissenting opinion of Lord Kingsdown in *Ramsden* v *Dyson* (1866) LR 1 HL 129. The object of establishing these criteria was to show that it would be tantamount to fraud for the defendant to assert his own legal rights.

Relaxing the requirements

The extent to which the five basic criteria of proprietary estoppel have been followed has varied. In some cases, all the requirements have been insisted upon (*Matharu* v *Matharu* (1994) 68 P&CR 93); in other cases, some of the requirements have been ignored (*Inwards* v *Baker* [1965] 2 QB 29). In *Inwards*, the defendant had built a bungalow on his father's land on the understanding that he would be allowed to live there. This was no unilateral mistake; both knew the state of the title. The court allowed the claim to succeed on the basis that expenditure had been incurred based upon an expectation. It was felt that equity must intervene to prevent an injustice.

A similar result ensued in *ER Ives Investment Ltd* v *High* [1967] 2 QB 379, where, again, both parties were aware of the state of the title. One of the parties acquiesced in the encroachment under his land of foundations from the neighbouring building in return for the right to an easement over his neighbour's land. As a result of the agreement, he built a garage for his car, which could only be reached by making use of the easement. The court held that the acquiescence, reliance and expenditure involved in the construction of the garage were enough for the court to allow an equity to arise as a result of a proprietary estoppel.

Modern approach

Oliver J gave a key judgment in *Taylors Fashion Ltd* v *Liverpool Victoria Trustees Co Ltd* [1982] QB 133. He held that: the strict fivefold test was not absolute; the doctrine of estoppel required a broader approach; and each case should be examined on its facts:

> The more recent cases indicate that the application of the *Ramsden* v *Dyson* principle – whether you call it proprietary estoppel, estoppel by acquiescence, or estoppel by encouragement is really immaterial – requires a very much broader approach which is directed rather at ascertaining whether, in particular circumstances, it would be unconscionable for a party to be permitted to deny that which, knowingly or unknowingly, he has allowed or encouraged another to assume to his detriment, than to enquiring whether the circumstances can be fitted within the confines of some preconceived formula serving as a universal yardstick for every form of unconscionable behaviour.

Notwithstanding this *dicta*, key elements must still be established, albeit ones that are not formulated in the restrictive way of the earlier case law. First, there must be unconscionability. In other words, the defendant's action (in denying the claimant his expectation) must shock the conscience of the court. Second, this unconscionable conduct must rest on the actions of the claimant, who must show encouragement given to him and detrimental reliance suffered by him.

Future wills: difficulties of relying upon a promise

Clearly, one of the difficulties in cases such as that of Geoffrey Gillett and Ken Holt is that the promise – to leave property by will – related to an action that might not be carried out or (if carried out) might be revoked. A will is effective only on the death of the testator. A testator can write as many wills as he chooses and revoke them all, one by one. However, the fact that a will has been revoked, or that a promised will has never been made, will not affect the equity of the situation if the promisee has acted, to his detriment, upon a promise, to the knowledge of the promisor. At that point, the promise (as opposed to the will itself) becomes irrevocable.

Promises in cases of this sort, whether they are to leave property by will (as is often the case) or to transfer property during the promisor's lifetime, are revocable. If they are embedded in a contractual agreement or executed as a deed, they become enforceable. They can result in damages for breach of contract (or breach of covenant) or to specific performance of the promise. If, therefore, there is no equity to address, the matter can be safely left to the common law. It is precisely where the promise is revocable and has not been fulfilled that the problem arises, as in the case of Geoffrey Gillett and Ken Holt. Equity, a creation of the middle ages, remains as relevant in the 21st century as it ever was.

Gillett v Holt

In *Gillett*, the relevant circumstances were considered by the Court of Appeal. The court took the view that the circumstances were sufficiently compelling for Mr Gillett to benefit from equity's intervention. Mr Holt was estopped from reneging on his various promises to Mr Gillett 'to see that he was all right' and 'all this will be yours'. Mr Gillett's actions in forgoing a formal further education, in giving up his own home, in devoting himself for 40 years to his friend and employer constituted sufficient detrimental reliance upon these promises.

In *Gillett*, the complex financial arrangements surrounding ownership of the farms was such that the court made a broad order transferring part of the estate to Mr Gillett, together with £100,000 compensation. The precise disposition of the property, which was necessary to accomplish this, was left to the parties themselves (with a right to return to the court if they could not agree). The equity is satisfied either by transferring the freehold of the estate to the claimant; by granting a life interest; or by monetary compensation.

Thus, this unhappy, modern tale of a family at war was resolved in Solomon fashion by the Court of Appeal, using that very ancient weapon – equity.

Contributed by Rosalind Malcolm

CHAPTER 60

Restrictive covenants on land

Published as 'Restrained behaviour', 19 September 1998

Restrictive covenants can stop new owners from building on land. But some restrictions are vulnerable to change

Students nowadays come across the phrase 'restrictive covenant' in two different contexts. In recent times, it has come to mean the covenants that are often included in contracts of employment which seek to restrain the employee from working for a competitor – or setting up a competing business – within a specified time after leaving the employer's business.

These covenants are more properly known as 'restraint clauses' because, in the eyes of the common law, they constitute a 'restraint of trade'. They are therefore valid only if they are reasonable in space and time and do not seek to overprotect the legitimate interests of the employer. It is for this reason that contracts of employment often impose obligations on the employee not to resign without reasonable notice, and give to the employer the right to send a defecting employee on 'gardening leave' while this period of notice expires (see *Mainly for Students*, March 16 1996).*

The more traditional use of 'restrictive covenant' is to be found in English land law. It is the name given to the equitable interest in land first recognised in *Tulk* v *Moxhay* (1848) 2 Ph 774.

Tulk v *Moxhay*

In 1808 Mr Tulk sold the open land in the centre of Leicester Square, London, to a Mr Elms. This sale was subject to a covenant that the land would be kept 'in an open state, uncovered by any buildings, in neat and ornamental order'. Elms and his immediate

---

* See *The Best of Mainly for Students*, Volume 2, Chapter 54.

successors-in-title did not build on the land, but by the 1840s it was overgrown and unsightly.

The then owner, Mr Moxhay, decided to build houses on the land. Thinking only of the common law, with its strict rules about privity of contract, Moxhay reasoned that the covenant of 1808 was not binding on him because he had not been a party to that agreement. Who, after all, was Mr Tulk to him; or he to Mr Tulk, that he should weep for him?

As it happened, Mr Tulk was still alive and still owning land nearby. He sued Moxhay and claimed an injunction to prevent the redevelopment. The Lord Chancellor, Lord Cottenham, granted the injunction because it seemed to him to be an act of fraud for a purchaser of land to buy it cheap, knowing that there was a restriction on its use, and then have the right to disregard that restriction and sell at a higher price. It was not disputed that Mr Moxhay had known all about the old covenant when he had bought the land from his predecessor in title.

The decision of Lord Cottenham LC to grant an injunction against Moxhay was based upon the maxim: 'Equity acts upon the conscience.' The essential point in the case was the fact that Moxhay had had notice of the covenant in the 1808 agreement. The result of the litigation would have been different had he not known about the restriction and, from the current available documents, could not reasonably have been expected to know about it. 'Notice', it should be emphasised, is a wider concept than 'knowledge', and equity does not give any advantages to lazy purchasers or to their lawyers, or to persons exhibiting 'Nelsonian blindness'.*

After the decision in *Tulk* v *Moxhay* it became the earnest purpose of property developers, and other persons imposing restrictive covenants on land, to ensure that no purchaser could ever emerge who did not have notice of the restriction in question. This was an important objective to achieve, given the indefinite lifespan of restrictive covenants.

Restrictive covenants exist for the benefit of neighbouring land – not for the benefit of a named individual, wherever he or she might

---

* 'Nelsonian blindness' is an expression which has entered English law from Nelson's conduct at the Battle of Copenhagen, when he put his telescope to his blind eye in order to disregard the signal of his commanding admiral ordering him to cease fire.

happen to be. In other words, if Mr Tulk had been dead by the time Mr Moxhay hatched his plan to build houses on the gardens in Leicester Square – or if he had sold his own house and had moved to some other locality – it would have been possible for his successor-in-title to have brought the proceedings for an injunction against Moxhay. Indeed, the very covenant which gave rise to the dispute in *Tulk* v *Moxhay* was the subject of litigation as recently as 1989: *R* v *Westminster City Council, ex p Leicester Square Coventry Street Association Ltd* [1989] EGCS 38.

As every law student knows, English land law underwent a radical reform in 1925. One of the changes was that all new restrictive covenants had to be registered at the Land Registry or, if the land itself was not registered, at the Land Charges Registry. This new provision came into force on January 1 1926. If a restrictive covenant (created on or after that date) was not duly registered, it would not be binding on subsequent purchasers of the land – even if they bought that land with actual knowledge of the existence of the covenant.

Conversely, if the covenant was duly registered it would be good against the whole world. No purchaser of land would ever be able to come forward claiming that he did not know of the covenant's existence.

Lands Tribunal

The Lands Tribunal was given jurisdiction to hear applications for the modification or discharge of restrictive covenants by the Lands Tribunal Act 1949. The power to award compensation to the persons harmed by the discharge or modification was inherent in the Law of Property Act 1925 but that power was enlarged by the 1969 Act.

In *In re University of Westminster* [1998] EGCS 118, the Court of Appeal held that the Lands Tribunal has the power to refuse an application for the discharge of a restrictive covenant, even if no one opposes the application.

In exercising its jurisdiction to discharge or modify a restrictive covenant, the Lands Tribunal is sometimes asked to act like a planning authority. Developers often put in a planning application to change the use of property and they argue that one isolated project cannot harm the amenities of an area or cause disadvantage to anyone. Often, the objectors have no argument other than that the development will be 'the thin end of the wedge'. As Portia said in *The Merchant of Venice*:

It will be recorded for a precedent,
And many an error by the same example
Will rush into the state.

Such arguments by developers are not always very attractive to local authorities or to central government. Nevertheless, if a planning application is rejected because it is perceived to be 'the thin end of the wedge', no error of law is committed.

In *Collis Radio Ltd* v *Secretary of State for the Environment* [1975] 1 EGLR 146, Lord Widgery CJ said that it was of the greatest importance when considering a single planning application to take into account what the consequences, or 'side-effects', of granting it would be. An application for planning permission for site A had to be judged according to the consequences to sites B, C and D; this was the most elementary planning procedure.

Thin end of the wedge

In *McMorris* v *Brown* (1998) The Times August 29, an application for modification of a restrictive covenant was made in Jamaica. As already mentioned, Jamaica uses grounds for such an application that are modelled on section 84(1), Law of Property Act 1925 (before it was amended in 1969).

The application related to a covenant that stipulated that there should be no subdivision of six plots of land in a residential suburb of Kingston, Jamaica. (Each plot was about three-quarters of an acre and there was one house on each of the plots.) The Court of Appeal of Jamaica granted an application to modify this covenant so that it now read: 'There shall be no subdivision of the said land ... save and except into two lots for residential purposes.'

The reason for this decision was the court's opinion that this change would not injure the persons entitled to the benefit of the restriction.

As discussed in *Mainly for Students* on May 2 1998, Jamaica is one of those independent nations that still retain the right of appeal to the Judicial Committee of the Privy Council in London. The Privy Council has now upheld an appeal by the neighbours of the applicant, stating, in so doing, that such arguments as 'the thin end of the wedge' and 'the first is the worst' were legitimate concerns in such cases as this.

Lord Cooke (giving the judgment of the board) cited a decision of Judge Bernard Marder in the Lands Tribunal: *Re Snaith and Dolding's Application* (1995) 71 P&CR 104. In that decision, Judge

Bernard Marder observed that it was legitimate to have regard to the scheme of covenants as a whole and to assess the importance to the beneficiaries of 'maintaining the integrity of the scheme'.

Lord Cooke applied the same principle in the Jamaican appeal and restored the decision of the trial judge – the onus was on the applicant to show that the first relaxation of the covenant would not constitute a real risk as a precedent. The applicant had failed to discharge that onus and the judge had not been wrong to seek to protect 'an unusually spacious enclave from any fragmentation of titles'.

One of the dissenting judges in *Donoghue* v *Stevenson* [1932] AC 562 (Lord Buckmaster) said: 'If we take this one step, why not 50?' However wrong the judge may have been to take such an attitude, he would have been entirely right to voice such fears in the context of relaxing restrictive covenants on land.

The Amended Grounds for Modifying or Discharging a Restrictive Covenant (in England and Wales) – after the Law of Property Act 1969

(a) that by reason of changes in the character of the property or the neighbourhood or other [material] circumstances... the restriction ought to be deemed obsolete; or

(aa) that ... the continued existence thereof would impede some reasonable user of the land for public or private purposes ...

[if] the Lands Tribunal is satisfied that the restriction, in impeding that user, either does not secure to persons entitled to the benefit of it any practical benefits of substantial value or advantage to them, or is contrary to the public interest; and that money will be an adequate compensation for the loss or disadvantage (if any) which any such person will suffer from the discharge or modification; or

(b) that the persons ... entitled to the benefit of the restriction...have agreed, either expressly or by implication, by their acts or omissions, to the same being discharged or modified; or

(c) that the proposed discharge or modification will not injure the persons entitled to the benefit of the restriction.

Note: The Lands Tribunal is expressly required to take into account the development plan in the relevant areas, and also 'any declared or ascertainable pattern for the grant or refusal of planning permission': see section 84(1B), LPA 1925 – 'posted' into the 1925 Act by section 28, LPA 1969.

Changes in the neighbourhood

Because of the indefinite life of restrictive covenants (particularly those created on or after January 1 1926 and duly protected by proper registration), it has been necessary for Parliament to create some mechanism for modifying or discharging any covenants which are manifestly out of date. That mechanism was created by section 84(1) of the Law of Property Act 1925. As originally drafted, that subsection listed three grounds for modifying a restrictive covenant affecting land. This subsection was amended in 1969 by section 28 of the Law of Property Act 1969 (see below).

The changes made to the law in 1969 were not necessarily duplicated in jurisdictions that modelled their legislation on the 1925 law. Jamaica still uses legislation that is modelled on section 84(1) in its original form.

Contributed by Leslie Blake

CHAPTER 61

Secret trusts

Published as 'Keeping a secret', 17 October 1998

Family disputes and court cases can result when, contrary to the Wills Act 1837, the true beneficiary of gifts specified in a will is concealed. But the courts are at pains to enforce the maxim that 'equity will not allow a statute to be used as an instrument of fraud'

A secret trust is a trust that does not name the true beneficiary, but makes it look as if some other person (the secret trustee) is the donee of the gift. Typically, but not exclusively, such a trust arises where a testator makes a will leaving property – usually money – to a friend, who has undertaken with the testator to hold that property for the benefit of the testator's mistress or illegitimate child. The heyday of these trusts was in the Victorian era, when outward respectability was important; there was far less candour about second families.

Wills Act 1837

A secret trust contained in a will is a disposition of property fails to comply with the formalities laid down in section 9 of the Wills Act 1837 because the true beneficiary is not named in the will, and the testator is seeking to bestow the benefit of the gift by means of a secret, non-testamentary, agreement.

The approach of equity to this problem was explained by Lord Buckmaster in *Blackwell* v *Blackwell* [1929] AC 318:

> The trustee is not at liberty to suppress the evidence of the trust and thus destroy the whole object of its creation in [an act of] fraud . . . [against] the beneficiaries.

This *dicta* suggests that the rationale for the enforcement of a secret trust is the prevention of fraud. This would mean that a secret trust is a species of 'constructive trust'. A constructive trust was defined by Lord Denning MR in *Hussey* v *Palmer* [1972] 1 WLR 1286 as a 'trust imposed by law whenever justice and good conscience demand it'.

In *Blackwell*, however, Lord Sumner did not agree with Lord Buckmaster. He took the view that a secret trust arose out of the testator's agreement with the secret trustee, not because a constructive trust was imposed on the secret trustee whether he liked it or not. This reasoning was approved more recently by Megarry J in *In re Snowden dec'd* [1979] 2 WLR 654.

Law of Property Act 1925

If, as Lord Sumner believed, a secret trust arises out of an agreement between the testator and the secret trustee, the trust in question would be an express trust. This would create a problem if the property in question was land, because section 53(1)(b) of the Law of Property Act 1925 lays down certain formalities in the case of an express trust of land (see p384).

The recent case of *Gold* v *Hill* [1999] 1 FLR 54, raised issues similar to those that arise when a secret trust is created. The deceased, Mr Gilbert, had had dinner with a friend, Mr Gold (the plaintiff). This was shortly before Mr Gilbert was about to leave for Nigeria. During the course of the dinner, Mr Gilbert told Mr Gold that he intended to nominate him as the beneficiary under a life insurance policy so that he (Mr Gold) could look after the financial needs of Mr Gilbert's common-law wife and their child if anything should happen to him. Mr Gilbert's forebodings about his trip to Nigeria were well founded: he died there.

In the insurance policy Mr Gilbert had described Mr Gold as his 'executor'. This was not true. The executor of his will was a solicitor, who, representing the estate of Mr Gilbert, claimed that the life insurance money should be paid to the estate and not to Mr Gold. This dispute between the two claimants, both of them claiming in a representative capacity and not for their own financial benefit, went to the High Court. The nomination of Mr Gold to receive the life insurance money (instead of the true executor) was challenged on two grounds.

First, it was alleged that a person who had no right to receive the insurance money as a beneficiary could not be nominated to receive that money for the purpose of holding it on trust for someone else unless, of course, he was the executor of the deceased's estate.

Second, it was argued that such a nomination needed to comply with section 53(1)(c) of the Law of Property Act 1925 because it was a 'disposition' of an equitable interest away from the true executor to Mr Gold. (It should be noted that section 53(1)(c), unlike sections 53(1)(a) and 53(1)(b), is not confined to trusts of land, but relates to equitable interests in any property.)

The answer to both these points was to be found in *Re Danish Bacon Co Ltd Staff Pension Fund Trusts, Christensen v Arnett* [1971] 1 WLR 248.

Bringing home the bacon

In dealing with the question of Mr Gold's right to receive the money for the benefit of Mr Gilbert's common-law wife and her child, Carnworth J drew an analogy with the law of secret trusts. The nomination, like a disposition under a will, could not take effect until the death of the policyholder. Nevertheless, the nomination at any time before the death was effective to dispose of the interest arising upon death – even if the nominee had no insurable interest in his own right.

It is important to remember that it is not permissible to be a beneficiary under a life insurance policy unless such an insurable interest exists. It is this concept of an 'insurable interest' that distinguishes insurance contracts from gambling transactions.

In the *Danish Bacon* case the court had found that the nomination of a beneficiary to receive benefits upon the death of a member of the pension fund was valid, even though this nomination was ineffective during the member's lifetime and could also be revoked by him at any time. The court also decided that section 53(1)(c) of the Law of Property Act 1925 did not apply to the nomination because the equitable interest in the death benefits provided by the pension fund did not arise until the person making the nomination died. It was not a subsisting interest at the time the nomination was made.

The nomination in *Gold v Hill* was similar to the nomination in *Danish Bacon*. It was a nomination of a beneficiary to take a future interest in property; it did not transfer any existing interest under a trust fund. Section 53(1)(c), therefore, had no application to the case.

The conversation between Mr Gilbert and Mr Gold over dinner created a secret trust. This made no difference to the validity of that nomination; the grafting of a secret trust on to it did not invalidate it. Consistent with the principle in *Blackwell*, Carnworth

J held that the secret communication to Mr Gold was binding and effective. If Mr Gold had declined to accept the trusteeship, Mr Gilbert would, no doubt, have notified the insurance company that someone else was to be his nominee.

This part of the decision is at variance to some extent with obiter *dicta* in *Kasperbauer* v *Griffith* (unreported) November 21 1997. In that case, the Court of Appeal held that an alleged secret trust did not exist because the testator, who had changed his mind several times, had never intended to impose any obligation on his wife as to how she should deal with certain property. The essence of any kind of trust is that it imposes a legal obligation on the trustee to deal with the property in a particular way. In *Kasperbauer* the discussions within the family were consistent with 'a mere moral or family obligation': *per* Megarry J in *Re Snowden*.

The *Kasperbauer* case concerned an alleged secret trust of a death benefit under a pension scheme. In the absence of a specific direction this was due to pass to the widow of the deceased. Nourse LJ said:

> I have never met a case where A can declare trusts of property of which A is not the owner ... I find it extremely improbable that equity would hold that a secret or any other trust could be imposed by such a declaration.

Mutual wills

Although secret trusts are comparatively rare nowadays, the courts have had to deal with a number of recent cases concerning 'mutual wills'. These arise when two people both agree to make a will disposing of property in a particular way. Once the first of the two testators dies and the agreed legacy is received by the survivor, or by a third person, the survivor is under an obligation not to revoke the relevant provisions in his or her own will: see *In re Cleaver dec'd* [1981] 1 WLR 939 and *In re Dale dec'd* [1993] 4 All ER 129. It may be that all these circumstances are examples of the principle that a person who accepts property as a trustee will not be allowed to deny the trust, even if the requisite formalities for creating that trust are absent: see *Rochefoucauld* v *Bousted* [1897] 1 Ch 196.

Half-secret trusts

Half-secret trusts arise where the will, or other document creating the trust, uses such words as 'To A for purposes which I have communicated to him'. The existence of the trust is publicised, and it therefore becomes impossible for A to keep the secret entirely to himself. However, the ultimate beneficiary is concealed. This type of disposition no doubt causes many family disputes. It certainly causes legal problems if, in fact, A has not been told about the 'purposes' or gets to hear of them only after he has received the property.

How gifts of land can fall foul of express trusts

Section 53 of the Law of Property Act 1925*
(1) Subject to the provisions hereinafter contained ...
   (a) no interest in land can be created or disposed of except by writing signed by the person creating or conveying the same, or by his agent thereunto lawfully authorised in writing, or by will, or by operation of law;
   (b) a declaration of trust respecting any land or any interest therein must be manifested and proved by some writing signed by some person who is able to declare such trust or by his will;
   (c) a disposition of an equitable interest or trust subsisting at the time of the disposition, must be in writing signed by the person disposing of the same, or by his agent thereunto lawfully authorised in writing or by will.
(2) This section does not affect the creation or operation of resulting, implied or constructive trusts.

Contributed by Margaret Wilkie

---

* The difficulties caused to executors, trustees and the Inland Revenue by this section were discussed in *Mainly for Students* on December 12 1987: (1987) 284 EG 1503.

Residential

62. Housing market. 413
63. Residential lettings 418
64. Anti-social behaviour orders 427

CHAPTER 62

Housing market

Published as 'Housing ups and downs', 24 July 1999

The 'feel-good' factor governs the housing market, fuelling the interaction between buyers and sellers, builders and lenders

Confidence has a great influence on the housing market. The market can rise substantially during periods of economic growth when the labour market is buoyant, wages are increasing and there is a general 'feel-good factor' about job security and financial comfort.

Yet overconfident borrowers sometimes give little consideration to the possibility of a downturn in the economy and the housing market or the prospect of unemployment. Such behaviour helps to account for the way prices can spiral, and for the extent of peaks and troughs in the market. Higher-value properties often tend to see the largest percentage gains, but may also experience the greatest falls.

Factors producing the downward spiral
Optimism can be hit by reports of slowing activity, prices levelling off or falling, deals taking longer to complete or falling through, and suggestions of a return to the misery of negative equity.

Falling prices can depress supply, leaving few buyers and sellers in the market. The reality of economic downturn is established and, although falling interest rates are beneficial, there is no measure of their favourable effect on the market.

The market can be hindered by vendors not accepting agents' opinion of a disappointingly low value of their home and, maintaining unrealistically high asking prices. In some areas, high repossession rates and forced sales will hit market values.

In a falling market, some owners will not sell once prices fall below the original purchase price. Similarly, in a market rising from a slump, owners may wait for prices to increase to the original purchase price before selling. Negative equity and other financial difficulties are not always the reason. Some owners delay moving and enjoy the rise in value of their current home, while the value of their next, typically larger, property rises similarly, thus producing a net deficit.

Emotional effects of loss

Loss is an emotionally negative experience. There tends to be a greater emphasis on price and profit performance with an existing home than with a new one. Vendors are usually more flexible over the price they are prepared to accept when profits are being locked in than when losses are being taken. Such factors can restrict market activity and can account for the slowness of recovery.

Poor market conditions can increase the preference to rent, with the desirability of homeownership being affected by job insecurity, the possible need to relocate to find work, the difficulty in selling, having to rent out the home and rent elsewhere, and the prospect of having to sell at a loss.

This situation is most typical of the younger, first-time buyer who, once eventually in the housing market, may bypass the traditional starter property. The demand for smaller properties may therefore lag behind a general recovery in the market but return to favour as first-time buyers become priced out of the market for larger properties.

Prices, particularly in a rising market, can be influenced by the lending policies of the banks and building societies. A rising house market can be of as much comfort to them as it is to their valuers, who may often be led by the agreed price.

Some buyers will seek to borrow the maximum amount available, whether through ignorance, greed or social factors. Borrowing habits can also be influenced by previous bouts of high inflation which historically helped to erode mortgage debt.

Financial shock of repayment

Incentives such as a discounted variable rate may be attractive, but can cause financial shock when the full rate is payable, as well as when interest rates rise generally. The same lending criteria, such as three times salary up to 95% of market value, can apply whether lending rates are at 7% or 9%, the difference often having a substantial effect on monthly repayments.

Relatively rigid lending policies do, however, help to prevent individual branches and decision-makers from having the collective capacity to cause excessive credit expansion, boom, bust and so on (a feature more common with the rise and collapse of commercial property markets).

The market is also influenced by the degree of competition between lenders. However, the profitability of lenders can appear disproportionately high given their vast representation in the market, and their apparent hunger for new business. Profitability is upheld by factors such as existing borrowers paying full rates while new customers receive incentives, the tendency of many borrowers to deal with their current bank or building society rather than shopping around, and apathy concerning remortgaging.

As interest rates fall, there tends to be less scope for lenders to exploit the margin between rates paid to savers and rates paid by borrowers.

Interest rates

Higher interest rates increase mortgage repayments, reduce demand and exert downward pressure on values. Interest rates will be set having regard to factors, such as the following:

- the current rate of inflation
- the rate of inflation expected around 18–24 months ahead, as there is a lag between interest rate changes and their reflection in the rate of inflation
- fiscal policy (taxation and spending), owing to its interrelation with monetary policy in controlling the economy and inflationary pressures
- the exchange rate or 'strength of the pound' against other currencies, because this affects the competitiveness of UK exports, the level of UK output, the cost of imports and inflationary pressures; and
- international factors, noting the increasing influence of foreign economies and financial markets

European economic and monetary union (EMU) and the single currency also affects the UK economy.

Issues for house builders

Land can account for between 20% and 50% of the price of a new house – the proportion mainly reflects the location and any abnormal development costs.

A healthy land bank tends to be beneficial when the outlook for the housing market is good, but can cause difficulties when the outlook is bad. Housebuilders used to benefit from continually rising house prices and inflation generally, but nowadays they are more exposed to market changes and price fluctuations in a less inflationary economic climate.

Market weakness may provide favourable opportunities to replenish land banks. The acquisition of another company can be an effective means of securing land.

Astute companies may anticipate a downturn and dispose of parts of their land bank. Regard also has to be given to the cost of financing land banks – another way that interest rates influence the sector.

The planning system is a major obstacle encountered by housebuilders. Developers prefer greenfield sites, but may, for example, experience difficulties in securing consents in view of the government's desire to see the redevelopment of brownfield sites, such as an inner-city land previously used for heavy industry.

Brownfield development involves different skills from greenfield development. Sites may need to be assembled, grant aid sought and contamination cleaned up. There may be a number of owners and occupiers with whom negotiations have to take place. Compulsory purchase powers may be required.

Complementary developments and other improvements may need to be completed or at least in progress before sales are feasible. Some urban sites may be suitable only for flats, starter homes and sheltered housing, whereas certain housebuilders will specialise in larger family homes.

Small firms can suffer cash-flow difficulties because of the time between site acquisition, the incurring of construction costs, and the development being completed and sold.

In a weak market, sales can take time, possibly also necessitating price reductions or the granting of incentives. It may be preferable to secure purchasers contractually prior to the completion of a development – although prices can sometimes rise significantly during the development process.

Private rented sector

Although most new lettings will be on the straightforward basis of an assured shorthold tenancy, the legislation governing the rights of landlords and tenants of residential property is more complex than that which applies to commercial property.

The reversionary potential of some residential interests can be realised only on the death of an ageing occupant, but even then, occupiers such as children or grandchildren may inherit certain rights.

Surveyors are well placed to include residential property in their personal financial portfolio. A well-located, readily lettable property incurring little management time can provide a substantially better income return than deposit accounts, as well as providing capital growth.

The need to instruct agents and incur agency and/or management fees can be avoided.

Surveyors should be able to draft tenancy documentation without employing a solicitor. Buy-to-let mortgages provide competitive rates of interest, and can help in constructing a suitably geared portfolio.

More recently, however, there has been a decline in the fortunes of the rental sector. Increased demand for property from private investors, supported by low interest rates and competitive buy-to-let financing, has increased the supply of properties available to let. At the same time, low interest/mortgage costs are increasing the attractiveness of home ownership against renting, thereby reducing tenant demand.

Contributed by Austen Imber

CHAPTER 63

Residential lettings

Published as 'Manage risks to ensure income', 10 March 2001

Surveyors dealing with residential lettings find that flexibility, experience and due diligence can reap rewards. But certain situations often demand a firm hand

The residential lettings sector covers most residential property types, with tenants ranging from foreign governments and company executives, to students and housing benefit claimants.

Landlords include property companies, local authorities, other public bodies, private investors – including surveyors – institutions such as universities, estates and trusts, local businesses and homeowners living away. They require their properties to be let expediently, and on favourable terms, to suitable tenants. The risk of rent default and other management difficulties should be minimised, and tenancy agreements must protect landlords' interests.

Landlords may undertake lettings themselves or appoint agents, such as the residential department of national surveying practices, local estate agents or specialist lettings agencies. Although some landlords may have the expertise, including in-house surveyors, traps await those who seek tenants without professional assistance.

Attracting tenants

Agents' advertising outlets include local newspapers, their office windows, site boards, their own availability lists and the internet.

For landlords seeking tenants themselves through classified/private lets, some areas enjoy a strongly established newspaper outlet to which tenants always turn. Private ads may not, however, be appropriate for certain property types and values, and agents will need to be appointed in order to provide the requisite profile.

Local property companies may attract regular enquiries without advertising and may see existing tenants introduce other tenants. Some landlords may also advertise directly through universities' housing departments, at places of work or in newsagents' windows.

Basic marketing particulars can be made available, including details of the property, local amenities, the availability of public transport and other attractions, and, ideally, a photograph. It can also be useful to state details such as the rent, deposit, council tax and water rates charges, average electricity and gas charges, furniture and appliances available and confirmation that the landlord bears any service charges/ground rent.

When making a comparison between several properties, tenants often cannot recall all they have been told verbally, and tend to focus on written information. Some tenants may never have rented property before, and be attracted to the landlord/agent making a special effort to assist.

Residential rents are usually expressed on a calendar monthly (pcm) basis, and are payable likewise. A rent of £325 pcm equates to £300 per four weeks or £75 per week. The quoting of rents on the four-weekly basis can sometimes make the accommodation appear more competitively priced. Reference to weekly rents can make any rental differences seem less significant when stressing the attractions of a property against others.

Flexibility

Rather than having to initially pay, say, one month's rent in addition to a deposit, the flexibility could be provided to pay a lesser amount of rent in advance, and allow rent payment dates to match a tenant's salary payment dates. This helps a tenant's cash flow, and reduces the possibility of delayed payment. Rents can be paid four-weekly rather than calendar-monthly if need be. The ability to depart at short notice and/or introduce a new tenant during a fixed term can be also attractive. Flexible terms can generally help make rentals appear more competitive.

Advantage can also be gained by landlords/agents who can receive calls and arrange viewings instantly – including evenings and weekends – judge tenants and their credit worthiness expediently, execute documentation quickly, and demonstrate an amenable landlord and tenant relationship. Agents may have numerous properties on their books, and a varying speed at which an individual property may secure a tenant, particularly in weak market conditions and/or for the less attractive properties.

Landlords can be frustrated if agents initially recommend over-optimistic rents to help secure an instruction, but have to lower their aspirations after a void period. Competitive rentals can often be the key to income security, minimal voids, ease of management, lower costs and reduced risk. Landlords sometimes enjoy more flexibility in respect of marketing and negotiations if letting the property themselves, possibly gaining an edge on agents, whose approach may be relatively standardised.

The approach taken to marketing will, of course, vary between property types and market conditions. An eye should always be kept on other rentals in an area, and on market trends. The development of 'buy-to-let schemes', for example, with their cheap rates of finance, and attraction to amateur landlords, helped to substantially raise the supply of rented accommodation in some areas at a time when low interest rates and a favourable economic outlook were encouraging occupiers to buy rather than rent. A weak rental sector sees falling rents, falling yields, longer void periods, more flexible terms, the need to improve properties to attract tenants and the quality of location being increasingly important.

Securing suitable tenants

Experience in residential lettings can help enable the suitability of tenants to be determined before formal checks are undertaken. When, for example, a prospective tenant's first question is the level of deposit required, their financial position may well be problematic. Particular interest in the flexibility of determination provisions may suggest that requirements may only be short term, even if not admitted as such.

Tenants may request that a property is held specially for them, pending viewing or subsequent issues. Loss of rent and further advertising costs can be minimised by advising tenants that it is 'first-come, first-served', by taking a deposit early (in whole or part, and as cash), by providing a tight deadline for tenants to return with funds and sign an agreement, and by continuing to deal with new applicants while others delay decision making. Tenants that seem enthusiastic on viewing can be too shy to express disinterest, and those having agreed to take a property often change their mind.

References provided by tenants may not always be reliable, but credit checks against previous addresses, or calls to former landlords, may highlight problem payers. Good tenants tend to be happy to provide details, including workplace and next-of-kin addresses, whereas suspicions should be aroused with those who are defensive or evasive. Some problem tenants may respond to private advertisements rather than use agents because they expect fewer, if any, checks to be made.

Outgoing tenants should be prevented from withholding a final amount of rent, typically of one month, because they consider that it covers a deposit due to be returned. The deposit may have to cover cleaning costs, disrepair or the replacement of items not attended to by the tenant prior to departure. Inspections of the property should take place during the tenancy, and will be particularly important prior to vacation, when tenants can be advised of any items requiring remedy. Rent may also be lost during the period that remedial works take place. Higher deposits could be taken at the initial letting, but this may deter applicants. A poor condition is unattractive to prospective new tenants at viewings.

It should be ensured that new tenants enter into direct relationships with the relevant bodies in respect of council tax and utilities for which they are responsible, and do not use the name of previous tenants, the landlord or others. It is preferable for landlords to advise the utility providers of new tenant details and meter readings at the start of the tenancy.

Recovery of rent from problem tenants

Effective letting processes should minimise the potential for subsequent rent default and management problems. Some tenants will still need chasing constantly for payment. Excuses such as cheques going astray in the post, and bank accounts being changed, are usually untrue. Direct debit difficulties, personal problems and forgetfulness may be given the benefit of any doubt initially, but not on further occasions.

Legal action for recovery can take time, incurs costs and can jeopardise the relationship with tenants in occupation, thus causing further problems. Although the assured shorthold tenancy will usually state that landlords can recover possession at 14 days' notice in the event the failure to pay rent or the breach of other covenants, a court order will still be needed.

Even if legal action against either current or former tenants, or guarantors, is not considered to be worthwhile for smaller amounts, these parties could at least be contacted by formal letter, outlining the threat of legal action, such as 'if payment is not received by 1 April 2001 a county court judgment will be sought against you. If this is necessary, you will additionally be liable for the court fee and any other legal costs which the court awards. You will be aware that a court judgment will affect your credit rating and hence your ability to take out loans, secure other credit or obtain a mortgage.' A copy could be enclosed of a completed claim form that would be submitted to the court if action proceeded.

For amounts above £750, a statutory demand could be served which could ultimately result in the bankruptcy of an individual, or the winding up of a company. A debtor could be advised that 'if payment is not received in full by 1 April 2001, solicitors will issue a statutory demand for payment. As you are aware, non-payment proceedings will commence which can lead ultimately to your bankruptcy. It will also involve immediate notification in local news media of your potential bankruptcy'. For a statutory demand, the amount will need to be certain – such as outstanding rent, as opposed to damages for disrepair or other losses which may be disputed by a tenant.

The landlord's position can appear stronger to a tenant by letters being sent recorded delivery, and/or by a solicitor. If a repayment pattern is agreed, post-dated cheques are preferable to the possibility of having to chase payment for each amount, and again contemplate legal action if payment is not forthcoming. This will be particulary useful in the case of debts falling below £750 removing the option of a statutory demand. It should be noted that it is easier to sue on a cheque not met than it is for a debt, as by issuing a cheque, the debt is acknowledged. Tenants should be made aware that, if payment is not received by the due date, or if cheques bounce, legal action will commence without prior notification to them.

The habitual debtor may be well-versed in creditor management, and be prepared to pay only once legal action is under way – a step a landlord may not be prepared to take. Although many occupants do not present problems, substantial losses can result from those who do.

Other requirements

Landlords must comply with certain health and safety requirements, including annual gas safety checks, the safe supply of electricity and satisfactory working of electrical appliances, the provision of fire-retardant furniture and, depending on the nature and size of the property, the availability of fire escapes, smoke alarms, extinguishers to meet fire regulations. The condition of the property must meet minimum standards in accordance with the

Landlord and Tenant Act 1985, notwithstanding the tenant's responsibility for repair provided in the tenancy agreement.

Mortgage providers may need to be informed of lettings, and with domestic mortgages, higher rates of interest may be payable. Insurance companies may also need advising, with the extent of cover sometimes requiring amendment. In the case of leasehold interests, consent to sublet may be required from landlords. Agents will notify the Inland Revenue of clients' details, and in the case of owners living abroad, will deduct income tax at the basic rate. Property income is generally classed as investment income, providing less favourable taxation arrangements to trading situations.

The instruction provided to an agent may be to simply find a tenant, or could be a request for a full letting and management service, including the completion of tenancy documentation, arranging stamping of the agreement – if appropriate – collection of rent, holding of deposits, periodic inspection of the property, arranging repairs and insurance, paying bills, obtaining any exemptions from utility/council tax payments during void periods, and dealing with relettings. Agents may also provide investment advice and undertake appraisals of individual opportunities.

Professional indemnity insurance should be obtained by agents, and client bank accounts held separately from company monies. Agents should exchange terms of instructions with clients, and may also vet landlords.

As with estate agency and residential sales, no professional qualifications are required to operate as a letting agent. In a market where unethical practices are often reported in the press, 'chartered surveyor' status should imply higher standards, and help to create fee-earning opportunities.

Legislation, tenants' rights and pitfalls for the landlord

For tenancies commencing prior to 15 January 1989, the Rent Act 1977 affords substantial security of tenure to tenants, and regulates the level of rent payable. The Housing Act 1988 introduced the modern type of 'assured' tenancies, which still provide significant security and 'assured shorthold' tenancies, which can be determined relatively easily.

To secure assured shorthold status, landlords previously had to serve a prescribed 'section 20' notice on the tenant. The Housing Act 1996 ended this requirement, and provided that all new private-sector tenancies commencing after 28 February 1997 would be assured shorthold tenancies unless notice was served to make them assured tenancies. If a new assured shorthold tenancy is granted to an existing tenant already enjoying rent act or assured tenancy protection, assured shorthold status will not apply. Purchasers of tenanted properties should therefore establish whether tenants were in occupation before the commencement date of the current agreement, and if so, should determine the nature of previous agreements and the extent of the tenant's rights. If a section 20 notice was not served originally, or if service cannot be proved, the protection afforded by assured status, rather than assured shorthold status, can depress property values. At the commencement of the tenancy, tenants should ideally have been requested to sign and date a copy of the section 20 notice for the landlord's own records.

Owners should obtain all documentation from agents at the time of letting. Agents should maintain suitable records, protecting them also against any claims of negligence. Tenant protection could also be influenced by rights of occupants – including family – not detailed on the agreement, and by rights of succession following death. Residential tenancy law is complex, and legal advice may have to be sought – especially if the landlord is seeking possession. Rent Act protection can warrant a substantial discount to vacant possession value.

Tenancy agreements
The maximum term of a tenancy by ordinary written agreement is three years, with a formal lease, by deed, being required for longer periods. Anyone can draw up tenancy agreements, but leases by deed, if being prepared for a fee or other reward, must be prepared by a solicitor or licensed conveyancer. Landlords and agents may have personalised tenancy agreements, or could use standard versions, such as those published by Oyez legal stationers or Estates Gazette.

Landlords can reassure tenants by advising that 'the agreement is a standard published document, which aims to strike a fair balance between landlord and tenant'. Tenants can be invited to seek independent legal advice if they wish.

Reassuring prospective tenants
Handwritten amendments to standard documents are ideally confined to matters such as the responsibility for utilities, or the inclusion of an inventory of the landlord's furniture and appliances and effects. Substantial amendments to standard terms can unnerve prospective tenants. Particularly at the lower end of the market, however, tenants may often sign agreements unconcerned about their contents, and without professional assistance.

A six-month term of occupation will commonly be granted by an 'assured shorthold tenancy'. This provides reasonable security to the landlord, while giving the tenant some flexibility against changes in domestic or work circumstances. On expiry, a new tenancy can be executed for a further fixed period. The tenancy of a fixed term does not, however, merely end when an expiry date is reached. To end the tenancy formally, two months' notice has to be served, in most situations, by the landlord, and one month's notice by a tenant, ending on the expiry date or thereafter on a rent day. The automatic continuation also means it is not necessary to incur fees for a renewal, unless greater security is required by either party. Even then, a new agreement could be created by an exchange of correspondence relating to the existing agreement, also providing for a revised length of term and any other changes, which could include a rent increase. This does not endanger assured shorthold status.

An assured shorthold tenancy could be granted for, say, three years to include the ability for sooner notice to be served by one or both of the parties to end the tenancy. Since the Housing Act 1996, there is no requirement for the term to be a minimum of six months, although even before the Act, any sooner right to depart earlier was easily provided by side letter.

The use of the property should be restricted to a private dwelling house, with business activities being prevented. Assignment and subletting is best prohibited in order to avoid management difficulties, and to more easily control the choice of tenant.

The extensiveness of the terms included in standard published agreements vary. Reasonable additional provisions could include restrictions on smoking, changing locks or duplicating keys, changing the telephone number or arranging other services, and requirements to respond immediately to requests for information from utility providers or other bodies, to forward the landlord's mail or otherwise notify the landlord, not to keep any pets at the property, to ensure that any furniture or appliances brought on to the property comply with the relevant gas/electric/fire regulations and confirmation that furniture and appliances are in a satisfactory condition and safe working order. It should also be ensured that viewings can be easily undertaken for reletting, or indeed sale.

Tenants may wish to include a schedule of condition of the property in the agreement. In the case of leasehold interests, such as flats, tenants should be expressly obliged to comply with the terms of the head-lease, avoiding the problem of a lessee being unable to take action against their tenant for breaches pursued by the head-landlord.

The tenant could be obliged to pay the reasonable costs incurred by the landlord – whether relating to in-house personnel or external agents – in connection with the breach of terms of the agreement, including the covenant to pay rent by a due date. Interest provisions on outstanding amounts, additional penalty rents/charges and the automatic loss of a deposit are provisions sometimes included.

Such arrangements may not find favour with a court, and the landlord of residential property generally has less scope to protect their position in this way than landlords of commercial property. Such terms may, at least, place a landlord in a more favourable negotiating position with a tenant in the event of problems. The securing of guarantors can also be useful.

Contributed by Austen Imber

CHAPTER 64

Anti-social behaviour orders

Published as 'Ain't misbehaving', 23 November 2002

Criminal proceedings have always followed a very different route to civil proceedings. The House of Lords has recently heard two cases in which it has had to decide whether applications for 'antisocial behaviour orders' should be treated as criminal or civil matters

Criminal proceedings can be differentiated from civil proceedings in a number of ways:

- Criminal proceedings involve conduct that is 'against the peace of our sovereign lady the Queen, her crown and dignity'.
- Civil proceedings are primarily intended to give individuals (and corporations) a remedy for injury to their private rights.
- Criminal charges have to be proved 'beyond reasonable doubt'.
- Civil proceedings permit allegations to be proved 'on the balance of probabilities'.
- Criminal prosecutions (whether brought by a public or private prosecutor) seek to impose penal sanctions.
- Civil proceedings do not seek to impose penal sanctions on any of the parties.
- Criminal proceedings place significant restrictions on the use of hearsay evidence.
- Civil proceedings do not now have any restrictions on the use of hearsay evidence.

Antisocial behaviour orders

Antisocial behaviour is often an estate-management problem on housing estates and in shopping centres. The Crime and Disorder Act 1998 gave magistrates the power to make antisocial behaviour orders against anyone aged 10 years or over. The social problem that this was designed to deal with was described by Lord Hope of Craighead in *Clingham* v *Kensington and Chelsea Royal London Borough Council*; *R (on the application of McCann)* v *Manchester Crown Court* [2002] UKHL 39, at [42]:

it is a sad fact that there are some individuals for whom respect for the law and for the rights of others has no meaning. Taken one by one, their criminal or sub-criminal acts may seem to be, and indeed often are, relatively trivial. But, taken together, the frequency and scale of their destructive and offensive conduct presents quite a different picture. So does the aggression and intimidation with which their acts are perpetrated. The social disruption which their behaviour creates is unacceptable. So too is the apparent inability of the criminal law to restrain their activities.

The police or the local authority for the area in question may apply for such an order to be made in the circumstances set out in section 1 of the 1998 Act (see p431).

Appeals

In *Clingham* and *McCann*, which were both judgments of the House of Lords, but which were otherwise unrelated, the question arose as to whether an application for an antisocial behaviour order (ASBO) was to be treated as a criminal or as a civil procedure.

Clingham had been subject to an appeal by way of case stated from a magistrates' court to the Divisional Court of the Queen's Bench Division. *McCann* had undergone a longer procedure, as if the case had been a civil case. An appeal had been made from a magistrates' court to Manchester Crown Court, a process that can be used for both criminal and civil cases (licensing appeals, for example). The three McCann brothers had then appealed to the Divisional Court and from there to the Court of Appeal (Civil Division). There is no jurisdictional problem in the cases of appeals from the Court of Appeal (Civil Division or Criminal Division) to the House of Lords, provided that the case involves a point of law of general public importance. But there can be no direct appeal from the Divisional Court to the House of Lords, unless the case is a 'criminal case or matter': see section 1 of the Administration of Justice Act 1960. Accordingly, in *Clingham*, the House of Lords had to examine its own jurisdiction: if the case were a civil case, the lords would not have had any jurisdiction to hear the appeal, although this was largely an academic point.

Standard of proof

The classification of an application for an ASBO as either 'civil' or 'criminal' was not primarily important in *Clingham* and *McCann*. The defendants in both cases wanted the procedures to be categorised as 'criminal' proceedings, in order for them to obtain the benefit (so they hoped) of the criminal standard of proof and the stricter rules of evidence that criminal courts use.

The general rule is that even if a criminal offence is alleged by one party to a civil case against the other, that allegation has only to be proved on the balance of probabilities: see *Hornal* v *Neuberger Products* [1957] 1 QB 247. This is one of the reasons why a defendant may sometimes be acquitted of a charge in a criminal court, only to be successfully sued in a civil court. The protection that the law gives to the person accused of a crime in a civil case is the law of probabilities itself. Some things are less probable than others. Fraud, for example, is less common than negligence, and negligence, if it be criminal at all, is rarer than innocent error. Thus, even in civil cases, there is a presumption of innocence.

Yet the American jurist Oliver Wendell Holmes observed that 'the life of the law is not logic, but experience'. In practice, some allegations in civil proceedings are so serious that the courts have insisted upon a 'heightened civil standard' of proof (in practice, 'proof beyond reasonable doubt'): see *Re H (Minors) (Sexual Abuse: Standard of Proof)* [1996] AC 563. If a party is alleged to have breached an injunction granted by, or an undertaking given to, a civil court, that allegation must be proved beyond reasonable doubt: see *Dean* v *Dean* [1987] 1 FLR 517.

So, it was argued by the defendants that even if an application for an ASBO were a civil and not a criminal proceeding, it was still possible for the House of Lords to hold that the factual allegations against the defendants would have to be proved 'beyond reasonable doubt'.

Civil or criminal?

The lords held that an application for an ASBO was a civil proceeding, even though a prosecution for breaking such an order would, of course, be a criminal proceeding. The application itself did not require proof that the defendant had committed any criminal offence – the emphasis was upon the result of the defendant's conduct to others, not upon the state of mind with which it was committed. The making of the order was not, in itself, a criminal punishment; if the defendant complied with the order, no criminal record would attach to him. Their lordships also reviewed the case law of the European Court of Human Rights, and came to the conclusion that the proceedings were civil proceedings under Article 6 of the European Convention for the Protection of Human Rights and Fundamental Freedoms.

Having decided this, their lordships went on to hold that the standard of proof, in all applications for an ASBO, was the criminal standard of 'proof beyond reasonable doubt'. Lord Steyn took the view that this would make the task of magistrates more straightforward, because they would not then be chasing a varying standard of proof, dependent upon the severity of the allegations made in each particular case.

Hearsay evidence

As hearsay evidence is now admissible in all civil proceedings, the lords' decision to designate ASBO applications as 'civil proceedings' led to the ruling that hearsay evidence was admissible in such proceedings.

Evidence of this nature is very likely to be relied upon in ASBO cases. It was almost certainly within the contemplation of parliament when it passed the 1998 Act. Residents of housing estates rarely come forward to give evidence against antisocial neighbours. As Schiemann LJ said in *Clingham* (in the Divisional Court):

If the policeman could only say that he had been told by such persons [who had seen the behaviour in question] that Mr Clingham had behaved in an antisocial manner, that would be hearsay evidence of the behaviour.

Of course, magistrates may still conclude that hearsay evidence, in a particular case, fails to satisfy the strict standard of proof now required in ASBO proceedings. In any event, a problem arises out of the wording of the Magistrates' Courts (Hearsay Evidence in Civil Proceedings) Rules 1999.

Rule 3 of this statutory instrument (SI1999 No 681) requires a notice of such evidence to be served not less than 21 days before the date fixed for the hearing. This notice must identify (among other facts) 'the person who made the statement': see r 3(4)(e). If, as is so often the case, the informant wishes to remain anonymous, it appears that local authorities and the police will face problems when using such evidence. This point was certainly raised in *Clingham*, but once their lordships decided that this case was not criminal, they had no jurisdiction to hear the appeal. The practical problem therefore remains unanswered.

Certainty or doubt?

It appears that the House of Lords wished to bring certainty to this new area of the law.

But, unintentionally, their lordships may have created a situation of doubt for local authorities and estate managers. Every landowner or proprietor of a business will demand proof 'beyond reasonable doubt' when he is served with an abatement notice (under the Environmental Protection Act 1990), or any other notice that threatens him with criminal prosecution if he does not comply: for example, under the Housing Act 1985, the Food Safety Act 1990, or the Health and Safety at Work Act 1974. It has already been held that proceedings under section 82 of the Environmental Protection Act 1990 (often brought by council tenants) are criminal: see *Botross* v *Hammersmith and Fulham London Borough Council* [1995] Env LR 217. See also Chapter 16 of *Statutory Nuisance: Law and Practice* (2002) by R. Malcolm and J. Pointing.

Antisocial behaviour orders – What the orders entail

The person against whom the order is sought must have acted in a manner that has caused, or that was likely to cause, 'harassment, alarm, or distress' to one or more persons 'not of the same household as himself';

The person against whom the order is sought must be 10 years old or more;

The order must be 'necessary' to protect persons in the local government area (where the harassment, alarm or distress was caused) from further such conduct;

The police and the local authority must have consulted with each other before one of those 'relevant authorities' makes an application to a magistrates' court.

Contributed by Leslie Blake

Valuation

65. Introduction to investment valuation 435
66. Surrender and renewal valuations 444
67. Valuation of trading properties. 450
68. Rating. 456
69. Quarterly in advance 465
70. Rent-free periods 473
71. Telecoms valuation 480

CHAPTER 65

Introduction to investment valuation

Published as 'Valuable lessons in the art of calculation', 18 September 1999

Grasping the general principles and procedures for investment property valuation is essential for those beginning their studies in estate management

Investors acquire property to secure a return through the rent paid by tenants, and seek rental and capital growth.

A 'market rent' is the full rental value of the property; also termed 'open market rental value', 'market rental value' or the 'rack rent'. The rent paid under the lease may sometimes be at a level below the market rent, in which case it is termed the 'rent reserved' or the 'rent passing'.

The rent passing is paid during the 'term', until the 'reversion' to a market rent. The reversion represents the remaining life of the investment and is referred to as 'in perpetuity'; during this time, there is likely to be a progressive growth in the market rental value of the property.

The reversion could be at the next rent review or at the expiry of the lease (when either a new lease could be taken by the tenant or the property relet). Rent reviews are usually three- or five-yearly, although students may encounter older leases where rent reviews take place every seven years, 14 years, a longer interval or not at all.

Rent, capital value and yields

The capital value of investment property is a function of the rental return produced by the property. The return is measured by the 'yield'. If, for example, a property is purchased for £250,000, and it produces a market rent of £20,000 pa, the yield is 8%, calculated by income (£20,000) ÷ capital value (£250,000).

When valuing investment property, the valuer has to apply an appropriate yield in order to 'capitalise' the rent. The yield will reflect the yields that have been secured on disposals of similar properties in the area (known as 'comparable evidence').

Comparable evidence may also be examined to establish the market rental value of the property which is to be valued.

Students at this level will normally be presented with comparable evidence in order to establish a market rent, but will usually either be told what yield to adopt, or be advised, for example, that 'similar property investments are securing 8%'. Sometimes, adjustments may have to be made to yields, as will be demonstrated later. Generally, students should explain why a particular yield has been adopted.

In practice, yields reflect a range of factors, such as the location, age, use, condition of the property, lease terms and the financial standing or 'covenant strength' of the tenant. Regard would be given to a range of international, national and local, economic and property market factors.

In addition, regard would be given to the yields obtainable from alternative types of investment (such as shares/equities, bonds/gilts and cash), and the respective qualities of those investments compared with property.

The balance of an investment portfolio has regard to the respective returns, which are available from such investments, and to the ability of each investment to help diversify risk. Property, for example, may be seen as offering diversification benefits within a portfolio because, if the value of shares fall, property may still continue to generate a steady income.

Gilts are government (gilt edged) securities that yield a fixed income. Gilts bought originally at £100 each may yield 9%, but if later traded in the market at £90, would yield 10% (9 ÷ 90).

Therefore 10% would be the yield to which investors would compare the yield on property.

In order to reflect the greater risks of property investment compared with government-backed securities, 2%, for example, could be added to gilt yields to establish an appropriate yield to value the property. Students are usually just advised, for example, that 'gilt-edged securities are yielding 10%'.

The majority of valuations considered at degree level have an inherent assumption that the properties are good quality, which will provide an income secure enough to allow students to concentrate on the mechanics of the valuation.

The time value of money

Because interest could be earned, a lump sum is more valuable if it is received now than if it were received in the future.

If, for example, £10,000 is received now, 'simple interest', at an interest rate of 8%, would be £800 pa, or £2,400 over three years. However, as well as earning interest on the original capital of £10,000, interest would be earned on the accumulated interest (provided of course that the interest is reinvested and not withdrawn). This is known as 'compound interest'.

From now on readers will need to refer to a set of valuation tables, such as *Parry's Valuation and Investment Tables*.

The amount of £1

The 'amount of £1' tables calculate the amount to which £1 invested now will accumulate at compound interest over a given number of years.

Ignoring the payment of income tax on the interest, £1 invested now for three years at 8% would accumulate at compound interest to £1.2597 (as per tables); £10,000 invested now would therefore accumulate to £12,597 after three years (£2,597 compound interest compared with £2,400 simple interest).

Present value

The 'present value' ('PV') of the amount of £12,597 is £10,000. If invested today, £10,000 would accumulate to £12,597 after three years at 8%. The present value of £1 is listed in the valuation tables for three years at 8% (no income tax) at 0.793822. £12,597 × 0.794 = £10,000 (or near enough, noting that it is necessary to work only to three decimal places and round off the last figure).

It may be necessary to 'discount' an element of a valuation to 'present value'. For a term and reversion investment valuation, for example, the term commences today, and is therefore a present value, whereas the reversion commences in the future, and requires discounting to present value. Examples are provided later.

Years' purchase

Until now, consideration has been given only to reflecting the time value of money in respect of a lump sum. Valuations also need to reflect the point in time at which rent is payable. Because compound interest can be earned, £40,000, for example, is worth more if received now than if it were received as a rent of £10,000 payable each year for four years.

'Years' purchase' ('YP') accounts for the timing of the receipt of the rent. The traditional YP tables assume that the rent is receivable at the end of each year, termed 'annually in arrears'.

Years' purchase is listed in the valuation tables for four years at 10% (no income tax, single rate) at 3.1699 (which can be rounded to 3.167). The figure 3.167 is known as the 'multiplier'.

The value of the four-year 'term' of income is £10,000 × 3.167 = £31,670 (less than the present value of the total income of £40,000 because the rent is received annually in arrears rather than received today).

Tables are also available which assume that the rent is received quarterly in advance, as is usually the case with most property investments.

Students at this level will work to the traditional basis of annually in arrears. This does not mean that an inadequate valuation is being produced. This is because yields are assumed to derive from evidence which will be consistent with the property being valued.

Years' purchase in perpetuity

Where a market rent is capitalised into perpetuity, the 'years' purchase in perpetuity' tables are used. 'YP perp' for a yield of 8% would be 12.5, so a rent of £20,000 would be capitalised by a YP/multiplier of 12.5 to produce a capital value of £250,000. YP perp can easily be calculated by 100 ÷ 8 = 12.5 without the use of tables.

Where the rent is capitalised into perpetuity at a reversion, following a term of income, 'years' purchase of a reversion in perpetuity' tables could be used.

For example, for two years at 8%, the tables list 10.717. £20,000 × 10.717 = £214,340, say, £215,000 (the value of the reversion). Alternatively, the rent could be capitalised in perpetuity, and then separately discounted, such as £20,000 × 12.5 = £250,000, × PV two years 8% (0.857) = £214,340, say £215,000.

The term 'say' is the valuer's terminology for rounding off the valuation.

Although the term 'interest' has been used above, in the context of property investment valuation, the rates of return/yields used in a valuation represent the initial return required on property.

Basic investment valuation

The purpose of investment valuation is to assess the present value of the income flow (rent) from the property.

The most straightforward valuation is to capitalise a market rent at an appropriate yield, such as:

Market rent	£20,000
YP perpetuity 8%	12.5
Capital value	£250,000

Term and reversion valuations involve a wider range of considerations. The following question introduces the basic methodology which students apply to preparing investment valuations, and also introduces further issues.

Question: You are required to value the freehold interest in an office property which is let on a 25-year FRI lease at a rent of £40,000 pa. Rent reviews are five-yearly and the next rent review is due in three years' time. The office has a net internal area of 500m^2 (5,382 sq ft). A similar office property, having an area of 600m^2 (6,459 sq ft), has recently been let on similar terms at a rack rent of £60,000 pa, and sold at a yield of 7%.

Students should note:

- The term of 25 years is the traditional length of term that is required by institutional investors (although the property market conditions of the early 1990s in particular have resulted in shorter terms being more common).
- An 'FRI' lease is where tenants are responsible for full repairs (internal and external repairs) and insurance. Tenants will also be responsible for business rates, water, electric and so on, enabling the rent paid by the tenant to represent the net income that the landlord secures from the property. If the property was held on an 'IRI' lease, where the tenant is responsible for internal repairs and insurance, it would be necessary to deduct, say, 5% from the rent to reflect the landlord's responsibility for external repairs.
- Letting fees incurred by the landlord do not form part of the valuation. In some circumstances, management fees may be reflected in the valuation.

A term and reversion valuation is clearly required. The rent passing for the three-year term to the next rent review is £40,000 pa. The market rent for the reversion is not known, but can be calculated from the comparable evidence provided of the similar office property.

£60,000 ÷ 600m^2 = £100 per m^2. The rate of £100 per m^2 is applied to the area of 500m² of the property being valued to produce a market rent of £50,000 pa.

A yield of 7% can be adopted to capitalise the market rent at the reversion because a similar rack-rented investment has been sold for 7%. An explanation for the yield of 6% adopted for the term is provided later.

Term

Rent passing		£40,000
YP 3 years at 6%		2.673
Value of term		£106,920

Reversion

Market rent		£50,000
YP perp at 7%	14.286	
PV 3 years at 7%	0.816	11.657
Value of reversion		£582,850
Capital value		**£689,770**
say		**£700,000**

Students can often be mystified at the apparent inconsistencies between the choice of yields that are found in valuation examples. The yield that investors require, among other factors, depends on whether the rental income is fixed, or whether there is scope for rental growth. The rent for the three-year term is fixed at £40,000, but the market rent of £50,000 is expected to grow into perpetuity as rental values increase.

The yield of 7% adopted to capitalise the market rent of £50,000 into perpetuity is known as the 'market yield', or the 'all-risks yield'. The all-risks yield implicitly reflects the potential for rental growth. Generally, the greater the prospect of rental growth, the lower the yield that investors are prepared to accept.

It may seem, therefore, that because the rent passing is fixed, it should be capitalised at a higher yield than the 7% which is applied to a market rent that can grow. However, investors would also give consideration to how long the income is fixed for, and to how secure the income is. A rent passing which is fixed for three years on a property with a five-yearly rent review pattern is not necessarily unattractive to investors, noting that, even if a market rent was paid, the investor may still have to wait five years to the next rent review before an increase can be secured. Until then, the income is fixed.

Six per cent is adopted for the three-year term of income because a rent less than market value is considered more secure than a market rent. This is because a tenant is less likely to default; and, even in the event of default, the property could be let for a higher rent.

In the case of a reversion being the expiry of a lease, the income for the term could, for example, be more secure because of the possibility that the tenant might vacate and, consequently, because a new tenant may not be found immediately.

Where there is a relatively longer term than the three years in the above example, greater regard will be given to the fixed nature of the income. With an older lease, for example, there may be, say, ten years before market value can be secured at rent review or lease expiry.

The return available on other fixed return investments could also be considered, namely gilts. A yield of 12% could, for example, be adopted to value the fixed income because gilts are yielding 10% (adding 2% to reflect the greater risks of property investment compared with government-backed securities). It should be noted that market yields/all-risks yields (which reflect the potential for growth in the current level of returns) should not be compared with gilts yields (which are fixed returns).

Leasehold interests

Investment valuations are also undertaken to establish the value of a tenant's 'leasehold interest'. A tenant's leasehold interest could have value where the tenant occupies the property and the rent passing is less than the market rent or, alternatively, where the tenant sublets the property at a higher level of rent than the rent passing which is paid to the landlord. The difference is known as the 'profit rent'.

From the example above, the value of the tenant's interest could be calculated as follows, using a 'dual rate' YP which is explained later.

	Market rent	£60,000
less	Rent passing	£40,000
	Profit rent	£20,000
	YP 3 years at 8%, 4%, 30%	1.86
	Capital value	**£37,200**
	say	**£37,000**

The rent is capitalised up to the point that an open market rent is payable and, consequently, the tenant ceases to enjoy a profit rent.

A yield of 8% is greater than the yields adopted for the valuation of the freehold interest because leasehold investments are generally considered to be less attractive than freehold investments. Investment and occupational disadvantages of leasehold tenure include the need to gain consents from a superior landlord, whereas a freeholder has greater flexibility and control over their interest.

When describing years' purchase earlier in the text, the YP of 3.167 for four years was stated as 'no income tax, single rate'. When undertaking valuations of leasehold interests at this level, 'dual rate' tables are usually used. YP three years at 8%, 4%, 30% was used in the above calculation.

The use of a single rate YP for freehold interests and a dual rate for leasehold interests occurs because the income (or profit rent) is received by a leaseholder for a fixed period of time (three years to the first rent review in the above example), whereas a freeholder receives income in perpetuity.

At the rent review of the leaseholder's interest, profit rent would cease and the leasehold interest would no longer be of value. The amount that was originally paid for the leasehold interest would be lost, whereas a freehold interest would always maintain a value because of the right to receive income in perpetuity.

The dual rate YP assumes that part of the income/profit rent would be retained in a 'sinking fund' in order to recoup the amount that was originally paid for the leasehold interest.

The sinking fund is effectively an investment which earns a return (4% in the above example). The return would be taxed, hence the rate of 30%.

The use of dual rate tables for the valuation of leasehold interests has its criticisms, but is an illustration of valuation issues which students may have to comment on in coursework and examinations.

Premiums

Sometimes it will be necessary to establish a market rent from a 'premium'. A premium is a capital sum which is paid, usually by a tenant at the commencement of a lease, in exchange for a nil rent (although sometimes it is for a lower rent or other benefit).

If a premium of £150,000 has been paid for a 15-year lease at a nil rent (known as a 'peppercorn rent'), the equivalent market rent, at a yield of 8%, would be calculated by £150,000 (YP 15 years at

8% ÷ 8.556) = £17,532, say £17,500 pa. The capital sum of £150,000 therefore represents the present value of £17,500, payable each year, annually in arrears for 15 years.

Study, coursework and exams

There are a range of textbooks available that cover the issues discussed here in more detail.

At first-year level, students will be presented with most of the information required for the valuation, but may be required to establish a market rent, or make adjustments to yields which have been provided. Beyond first-year level, less information will be supplied and students will increasingly be required to make their own assumptions.

Often in valuation, there is no one correct approach to take. Valuers have to examine comparable evidence and give regard to a range of factors that affect value. Students, in the same way as valuers, have to make their own judgments. The essence of the valuation is to be able to apply a reasoned and consistent methodology.

Contributed by Austen Imber

CHAPTER 66

Surrender and renewal valuations

Published as 'The price of surrender', 9 February 1999

When a landlord or tenant wants to renegotiate a lease, the surveyor must take into account and balance both quantifiable and less tangible factors

A landlord may wish to enhance the investment profile of a property in order to sell or to raise funds. He may require an open market rent, a longer lease term, a regular rent review pattern, generally more modern lease terms or he may wish to ensure that the income is 'clear' by placing responsibility for repairs, insurance and any other costs onto the tenant. Lease structures may need to be similar to those of the landlord's other tenants, or the landlord may wish to renegotiate the lease to facilitate redevelopment at a later date.

The tenant may require a longer lease to improve his security of tenure in order to develop the business, to assist the sale of the business, to enable funds to be raised or to make improvement expenditure viable. The tenant may wish to renegotiate other terms, such as the ability to undertake a wider use of the property, or being able to sublet.

The valuation principle behind surrender and renewal is that the market value of each party's present position should equate to the market value of their proposed position. The settlement would typically fall between the respective positions of the parties, and be influenced by their particular requirements and bargaining strengths. The consideration for the settlement could be a variation on the rent, a variation on other terms, a premium paid by the tenant or by the landlord.

Varying the rent
A tenant, for example, having six years to lease expiry without review, may wish to take a new, long lease. The landlord may be willing to grant a new lease provided that the rent passing of

£20,000 pa can be reviewed to market value after three years. The current market rental value is £27,000 pa.

The parties need to establish the revised rent to be paid over the three-year term to the rent review. For simplicity, the valuation adopts the same yields for the present and proposed interests of each party although, in practice, a new situation could command different yields. The leasehold interest is valued on a dual rate basis, and adopts a yield 1% higher than the freehold interest, to reflect the relative investment advantages of freehold tenure (see valuation below).

Landlord's present interest
Rent passing	£ 20,000
YP 6 years 10%	4.355
Value of term	**£ 87,100**
Rack rent	£ 27,000
YP perp. 10%	10
	£270,000
PV 6 years 10%	0.564
Value of reversion	**£152,280**
Capital value	**£239,380**

Landlord's proposed interest
Rent passing	£ x
YP 3 years 10%	2.487
Value of term	**£ 2.487x**
Rack rent	£ 27,000
YP perp. 10%	10
	£270,000
PV 3 years 10%	0.751
Value of reversion	**£202,770**

Capital value = £2.487x + £202,770
Proposed interest = present interest
£2.487x + £202,770 = £239,380
£2.487x = £36,610
Rent passing (x) = £14,720

Tenant's present interest
Rack rent	£27,000
Rent passing	£20,000
Profit rent	**£ 7,000**
YP 6 yrs 11, 3%, 40%	2.72
Capital value	**£19,040**

Tenant's proposed interest

Rack rent	£27,000
Rent passing	£ x
Profit rent	**£27,000 – x**
YP 3 yrs 11%, 3%, 40%	1.54

Capital value = £41,580 – 1.54x
Proposed interest = present interest
£41,580 – 1.54x = £19,040
1.54x = £22,540
Rent passing (x) = £14,636

The transaction is of equal benefit to the parties, and the agreed rent could be the average of £14,720 (landlord) and £14,636 (tenant) at, say, £14,675. Had the valuation of the tenant's interests adopted the same 10%, single rate, yields as the landlord's interest, the parties would have determined the same rent passing of £14,720. The more divergent the yields, the greater the difference between the valuations of the parties' interests. In other situations it may be considered appropriate to adopt a single-rate YP for the leasehold interest.

Paying a premium

Where the landlord wishes to maximise the investment value of the property, he may pay the tenant a premium to secure a market rent and other more favourable lease terms. In again adopting a rent passing of £20,000 pa and a market value of £27,000 pa, the parties' present interests are the same. The parties' proposed interests are formulated to establish the premium payable. The example demonstrates the marriage value that can be created by a surrender and renewal, where the improved investment profile of the property enables the landlord to sell at a lower yield (of 8% rather than 10%). The landlord's proposed interest is calculated as:

Landlord's proposed interest

Rack rent	£ 27,000
YP perp. 8%	12.5
Capital value	**£337,500**
less present interest	£239,380
Value of premium	**£ 98,120**

The tenant's proposed interest has no value because there is no profit rent where a rack rent is paid. The premium would thus be the value of the tenant's present interest of £19,040. The premium paid by the landlord would fall between £98,120 and £19,040.

Improvements

The landlord could also enhance the investment profile of the property by securing a rack rent that reflects the value of improvements undertaken by the tenant. In accordance with the '21-year rule', the landlord may not otherwise have been able to reflect the value of improvements in the rent until the end of the lease, or until 21 years after the improvements were completed, whichever is the latter.

For some investments, particularly secondary investments (and especially those towards the lower end of the market), investors may emphasise the rent passing, and give little regard to the reversionary potential offered by improvements or other factors. Substantial marriage value can therefore be created by establishing a full market rent together with a lower yield.

It is difficult to encapsulate accurately such market practice or sentiment into the valuation. This emphasises the importance of negotiating effectively.

Where the landlord wishes to redevelop or sell to a developer, the existing lease could be surrendered and compensation paid to the tenant. A 'contracted-out' tenancy could be granted to the tenant where the landlord requires the certainty of being guaranteed possession later. The valuation adopted to establish the premium would be the same as in the above examples, although the landlord's reversion would be to development value. In assessing the premium, account may be taken of the tenant's possible entitlement to statutory compensation for disturbance, or for improvements, which may be available where the landlord could otherwise secure possession at lease expiry, or at lease break.

A settlement could be influenced by the possibility that the tenant may not be able to relocate easily, and may even have to cease trading. The goodwill of the tenant's business may be extinguished, and previous investment expenditure may not be recovered. The landlord may have to make an attractive offer to buy out the lease.

There may still be a level of premium at which it would be preferable for the landlord to wait until lease expiry to realise development potential, thus having to pay the tenant only statutory compensation. In other situations, compensation at the statutory rate may be attractive to a tenant who can cost-effectively relocate. This could enable the landlord to secure possession relatively cheaply.

The premium payable by a landlord where development is an option would generally be higher where the development value is proportionately greater than the existing use value, where the tenant has greater security by way of a longer unexpired lease and where the tenant enjoys a higher profit rent.

The position becomes complex where the landlord has to conclude negotiations with two or more parties. Practical as well as valuation difficulties arise where tenants are indifferent about negotiating and/or each think that they can promote a ransom position. Where there is uncertainty about the landlord's ability to secure planning consent, a settlement could be conditional on consent being secured.

The settlement: factors to consider

- The parties are unlikely to prepare identical valuations and will have different perceptions of their positions.
- At a certain level of premium, it may be preferable for the landlord to wait until lease expiry to realise full value, and not have to pay the tenant a premium, despite the level of marriage gain that could be generated by a surrender and renewal. Where a tenant enjoys a significant profit rent, as lease expiry becomes nearer, the value of the tenant's interest generally diminishes, and the value of the landlord's interest appreciates.
- The finer consequences of other changes to the lease may not be incorporated into valuations (eg, by minor yield adjustment), but may influence the course of negotiations. The settlement could, for example, reflect the implications of the Landlord and Tenant (Covenants) Act 1995, which result from having to grant a new lease. The transaction could reflect the addition or the release of guarantors, or the payment or the return of a rent deposit/bond.
- There may be situations where the landlord has promoted surrender and renewal because the tenant is in breach of covenants; the tenant's alternative to taking a new lease is possibly forfeiture of the old one.
- The parties may have distinct liabilities for taxation or differing abilities to secure other accounting benefits from the transaction.
- The valuation is confined to the parties' property interests.

Additional benefits resulting from a longer term being granted to the tenant may include the enhancement of the value of the tenant's business as a going concern, or the benefits that would accrue from investing in the current property that could not be achieved elsewhere owing to the immobility of goodwill. The enhanced investment profile of the individual interest may be reflected by adopting a lower yield for the valuation of the landlord's proposed interest, but the enhancement to the landlord's overall property holding may not be reflected. A more detailed valuation may be required, or a 'calculation of worth' could be undertaken to establish the specific worth to the landlord or to the tenant of the transaction. Each party may still not be able to secure sufficient information to establish the full extent of the other party's position.

- There may be uncertainty as to the landlord's ability to secure an expected disposal price. The landlord may be exposed to, or may be able to benefit from, changes in values. The tenant could, however, be committed to executing a new lease when the landlord completes a sale, perhaps in exchange for the premium being proportionate in whole or in part to the eventual disposal price.

Valuations could be undertaken of an optimistic position and a pessimistic position of the parties' interests, with an average being taken. This would achieve a different result only where the valuation range of one of the parties' interests is wider than that of the other. Such a valuation can therefore enable differing levels of risk to be reflected

Conclusion

Where there is equal benefit to the parties from a surrender and renewal, the settlement should be nearer to the average of the parties' respective positions, and would more likely be based on a considered valuation approach.

Where the requirement for a new lease is predominantly from one of the parties, the settlement will be particularly influenced by the parties' special circumstances, by their respective bargaining strengths and by their knowledge of the other party's true position.

Contributed by Austen Imber

CHAPTER 67

Valuation of trading properties

Published as 'A price on the potential', 26 June 1999

Licensed and leisure properties are operational businesses. Unlike traditional commercial property, they are valued to reflect trading potential

Licensed and leisure property includes hotels, public houses, restaurants, cinemas, bingo halls, tenpin bowling alleys and casinos. At the outset of a valuation of such a property, the valuer must agree with the client the purpose of the valuation, its basis, and any assumptions which are to be made.

For bank loan purposes, for example, the basis of valuation could include one or more of the following, all of which are defined in the *RICS Appraisal and Valuation Manual* (the new Red Book):

- Open market value (OMV)
- Estimated realisation price (ERP)
- Estimated restricted realisation price (ERRP)
- Alternative use value

The Red Book defines trading related properties as 'the valuation of property fully equipped as an operational trading entity and valued having regard to trading potential'.

The Red Book also provides for clients to require additional valuations, subject to 'special assumptions'. These could be where accounts or records of trade would not be available to, or could not be relied upon, by a purchaser, that the business is closed, that the inventory has been removed or that the licences, consents, certificates and/or permits have been lost or are in jeopardy.

The valuer should consider how such assumptions might affect the value of the property, while a lender, for example, will wish to consider the degree of risk associated with the specified scenarios.

The valuation

The valuation of property fully equipped as an operational entity and valued having regard to trading potential comprises three elements, each of which are examined below.

- The value of the land and buildings.
- The value of the trade fixtures, fittings, furnishings and equipment.
- The market's perception of the trading potential of the property, excluding 'personal goodwill', together with an assumed ability to renew all relevant trading licences. This was formerly known as 'inherent goodwill'.

This is clearly different to the valuation of traditional commercial property types, such as retail, offices and industrial, where, usually, the capital value is established by capitalising the rental value of the property.

Land and buildings

The freehold interests in land and buildings should be relatively straightforward to value. However, planning consents, restrictive covenants, trading licences, and other relevant statutory consents and permits can limit the property's use. This will affect turnover and profit levels and must therefore be reflected in the valuation.

In valuing leasehold interests, regard must additionally be given to the length of the unexpired lease term, the rent paid, the actual open market rental value, the frequency and basis of rent reviews (and whether they tend to favour the landlord or tenant), the user and alienation clauses, repairing obligations, service charge provisions, the treatment of tenant's improvements, the inclusion of break clauses, whether the leasehold interest affords security of tenure and the potential for a new lease to be granted upon expiry of the current lease.

In 'frothy' market conditions, however, certain unfavourable lease provisions may be sometimes overlooked by acquiring tenants/assignees. This can have the effect of increasing leasehold values generally.

However, under more depressed market conditions, acquiring tenants/assignees are likely to pay far greater regard to the terms of the lease. They may seek to limit their offers, or even withdraw from negotiations, if the terms are considered onerous.

Trade fixtures, fittings, furnishings and equipment

Because trading properties are valued on the basis of being fully equipped as an operational entity, owned trade fixtures, fittings and equipment are included in the value of the property.

Items not in the ownership of the business and/or which are not available for sale with the property must be identified. These could include items held on hire purchase or leasing arrangements, or items personal to an operator. Consumable stocks are excluded from the valuation, but may separately form part of the transaction.

The market's perception of trading potential

The valuation definition for property fully equipped as an operational entity assumes that the exiting licences, consents, certificates and permits will be transferred to a purchaser and renewed (unless a declaration is made to the contrary).

These could include the Justices On-Licence, a restaurant licence, a public entertainment licence, a special hours certificate, gaming permits, fire certificates and food safety consents.

The licences will control the activities carried out at the property and may, for example, restrict the number of persons permitted within it, the hours of operation, or the areas of the property which can be used for specific purposes (such as drinking, gaming, eating).

Licences have an important effect on potential turnover and should therefore be inspected by the valuer.

Additional value may exist if extra or improved consents could be secured – for developing additional trading areas within a licensed property or obtaining planning consent for an extension, for example.

Goodwill relating to a trading property can represent a particularly difficult aspect of the valuation. The thrust of the valuation is to identify the type of purchaser for the property, and the levels of the fair maintainable turnover and profit which a 'reasonably competent operator' in the sector could generate.

In so doing, the valuer should ignore any personal trade or goodwill which is derived from the skills or personality of the actual operator, and which would depart with the operator if the property were sold.

For example, some operators may be able to generate relatively higher returns than a current operator of a licensed property, owing to their expertise in a particular market, brand names, a certain corporate identity or as a result of a particular theme that can be adopted.

An individual hotel may benefit from inclusion in the purchasing hotel chain's national promotional material.

In accordance with the definition of market value, account should not be taken of any additional bid which is made by a prospective purchaser with a special interest. But there may still be a number of operators in the market who can add value as a result of their particular identity or reputation – and, overall, still represent the reasonably competent operator.

Valuation methodology

The valuation method usually adopted for trading properties is the 'profits method', also known as the 'accounts method'.

The essential material needed to undertake a profits valuation will be the past three years' certified or management accounts, together with trading projections.

The valuer has to then assess the fair maintainable turnover and adjusted net profit levels that could be generated at the property by a reasonably competent operator (and from which a capital or rental value can be calculated). This may involve making adjustments to the accounts provided, such as the deduction of any turnover or expenditure which is personal to the current owner/operator. Consideration may also have to be given to changed trends in turnover and profitability levels which may, for example, reflect general economic changes, new or extinguished competition, changes in the layout of trading areas, different lines of activity or periodic fashions and trends.

It is necessary to arrive at an adjusted net profit level before bank interest, tax, depreciation, directors' remuneration, any extraordinary items of expenditure or charges which may relate to the owner's other property operations. Such outgoings should not be reflected in the valuation unless they represent costs which would reasonably be incurred by a purchaser.

For businesses currently operated by individuals but which would be sold to a company, an allowance may be required for a manager's salary or for head office costs, such as marketing, training or administration.

With some businesses, adjustments will need to be made to reflect seasonal variations in trade, in tourist locations for example, or for any leisure properties having large external areas that can be used for seating or other fine weather activities.

Capital valuations involve calculating the fair maintainable adjusted net profit level by the appropriate 'years' purchase' (YP), or 'multiplier'. The YP will reflect factors including the likely future profitability, local and national economic conditions, trends in the industry, existing and proposed competition, the property's attractiveness and adaptability, unexploited potential, and multipliers being paid for similar businesses.

The valuer will also need to consider any competing or complementary developments in the area, the location, the condition and life expectancy of the building, impending legislative changes, the calibre of staff and management, and the reliability with which the accounts represent the trading potential of the property.

Because the nature of trading properties varies, particularly their profitability, adjustments may have to be made to the multiples being obtained for comparable open-market transactions.

Freehold interests tend to command a higher multiple than leasehold interests because they represent a proportionately greater share of the value of the trading entity and therefore provide more security. Leasehold interests may restrict the operator's ability to raise funds, may make investment opportunities less viable or may allow less operational flexibility when compared with freehold interests.

Rental valuations of some trading properties, such as hotels, are carried out by allocating the adjusted net profit level before rent paid – the 'divisible balance' – between the landlord (which represents the tenant's rental bid) and the tenant (which represents the tenant's remuneration for operating the business). The allocation of the divisible balance will reflect the type of property being valued, operating risks such as obtaining (or losing) licences, likely demand for the property and the profitability associated with it, and the lease terms under which it is held. Tenant's rental bids can range between 25% and 50% of the divisible balance, depending on the nature of the property, and the above factors.

Although the profits/accounts method is generally accepted as the most appropriate for valuing most types of licensed and leisure properties, in certain sectors, including hotel development sites and larger-sized hotels, the discounted cash flow (DCF) method is becoming more popular. One advantage is that DCF can reflect future income and outgoings, and can help to smooth out volatility in a market sector. It is particularly useful when a property is about to be constructed or extended. A disadvantage is that DCF does not reflect extreme market fluctuations, and therefore may produce too high a value in a recessionary market, and too low a value in a boom. Also, it may calculate 'worth' to an operator, rather than 'value' in the open market. The merits of the DCF method, however, are the subject of much debate.

Specialist expertise

While general practice surveyors should appreciate the factors affecting the valuation of trading properties, the valuation exercise is highly specialist. Valuations should be undertaken only by surveyors who have sufficient expertise in the relevant sector.

Specialist valuers should be familiar with the nature of the property, the fair maintainable turnover and profit levels, trading risks, market conditions, type of likely purchasers, and the multipliers to adopt.

Various consultee input

CHAPTER 68

Rating

Published as 'Low value: High priority', 15 April 2000

The 2000 Rating Revaluation kicks in this month, prompting an analysis of ways to reduce rates liabilities on commercial property

In affecting occupational demand, rental levels, investment values and the like, rates liabilities influence the work of agents, landlord and tenant surveyors, valuers and developers, as well as rating surveyors. Here we provide an insight into the rating system for commercial property in England and Wales, including opportunities to minimise the liability for rates.

The rating system

The Local Government and Finance Act 1988 repealed the General Rate Act 1967. Domestic properties were excluded from the rating system, and the powers of each rating authority to set their own rate poundages were replaced by a nationally set 'National Non-Domestic Rating Multiplier' (NNDRM) – also known as the 'Uniform Business Rate' (UBR).

To calculate rates liability, the UBR is applied to the 'rateable value' (RV) of the 'hereditament' (the rateable unit) – such as RV £10,000 × UBR £0.416 = £4,160 rates pa for 2000–01 in England. RVs are based on the hereditament's annual rental value.

The Valuation Office Agency (VOA) of the Inland Revenue assesses the RV and compiles the 'rating lists': those for 2000 are posted on the VOA website (www.voa.gov.uk) and also on EGi.

Once collected by the local billing authority, rate payments are pooled, and then redistributed to the local authorities by central government.

Periodic revaluations redistribute rate liabilities depending on changes in market rental values. The 1990 Revaluation established rateable values with effect from 1 April 1990, based on an 'Antecedent Valuation Date' (AVD) of 1 April 1988. The 1995 Revaluation adopted dates of 1 April 1995 and 1 April 1993 respectively. The 2000 Rating Revaluation, which introduced new rateable values with effect from 1 April 2000, is based on an AVD of 1 April 1998.

The UBR is calculated once the revaluation exercise is complete, and has regard to factors such as the grand total of rateable values, changes in values since the last revaluation and inflation. In broadly preserving the real value of rating revenue, the new UBR multiplier for 2000–01 has been fixed at £0.416 or 41.6p in England and 41.2p in Wales. The 1999–00 UBR was 48.9p and 44.3p respectively. Until the next revaluation, the UBR is adjusted annually with a maximum increase based on the RPI – so that inflation does not erode the real value of rating revenue.

In 1997–98, the government introduced a category of 'small properties', with a lower UBR than large ones (48p compared with 48.9p in 1999–00). The qualifying RV for small properties has been increased for the 2000 Revaluation from £10,000 to £12,000 (and £15,000 to £18,000 in Greater London) but, in England, they will pay the same as large properties, 41.6p. Transitional arrangements, however, are more favourable for small properties (see later).

The basis of valuation for rating

Schedule 6 of the Local Government and Finance Act 1988 previously provided:

The rateable value of a non-domestic hereditament shall be taken to be an amount equal to the rent which is expected the hereditament might reasonably be expected to be let from year to year if the tenant undertook to pay all the usual tenant's rates and taxes and bear the cost of other expenses necessary to maintain the hereditament in a state to command that rent.

The hypothetical basis of occupation assumes that the property is vacant, and to let, on the basis that the tenant/occupier is responsible for repairs and insurance – similar to most commercial leases.

Hereditaments should be valued rebus sic stantibus (in their existing state). The potential for alternative use, conversion, improvement, refurbishment, development etc. is generally disregarded. The rebus principle does not, however, extend to valuing the actual condition of the property or its state of repair, or disrepair.

Assumptions in respect of repair were the subject of recent case law and legislation. In *Benjamin (VO)* v *Anston Properties Ltd*

[1998] 2 EGLR 147, the Lands Tribunal held that if a hereditament was in a state of disrepair that would depress its rental value, then the rating assessment should also reflect this.

This was contrary to the intended Schedule 6 valuation basis outlined above. The decision would have led to problems including rateable values being lowered by a deliberate action not to undertake necessary repairs, difficulties in establishing the actual state of repair at the date of valuation, RV listings reflecting divergent standards of condition, rental adjustments and analysis becoming problematic and the possible need to revalue following repairs being carried out. Anston could have led to a large number of appeals against buildings in varying states of repair, and to losses in rating revenue.

The Rating (Valuation) Act 1999 amended Schedule 6, to provide:

The rateable value of a non domestic hereditament none of which consists of domestic property and none of which is exempt from local non-domestic rating shall be taken to be an amount equal to the rent at which it is estimated the hereditament might reasonably be expected to let from year to year on these three assumptions;
(a) the first assumption is that the tenancy begins on the day by reference to which the determination is to be made;
(b) the second assumption is that immediately before the tenancy begins the hereditament is in a reasonable state of repair, but excluding from this assumption any repairs which a reasonable landlord would consider uneconomic;
(c) the third assumption is that the tenant undertakes to pay all usual tenant's rates and taxes and to bear the cost of the repairs and insurance and other expenses (if any) necessary to maintain the hereditament in a state to command the rent mentioned above.

At the date of the rateable value assessment, the actual state of repair may be ignored. The property is deemed to be in a reasonable condition consistent with the market rent achievable, with the property being maintained thereafter by the tenant to the same standard. Contention could still exist as to what constitutes a 'reasonable state of repair' and 'uneconomic repair', with variances depending on property types, their location, age and condition and market considerations.

Valuation methods

The four established valuation methods available to undertake rating valuations are:

- **Rental method** This has regard to rents established in the open market, and will be used for most retail, office and industrial properties.

  The actual occupier can be assumed to be in the market for the property, so the actual rent paid, and other terms, represent *prima facie* evidence of rental/rateable value, provided that it is on terms similar to the definition of rateable value and was agreed near the AVD.

  To gather valuation evidence, the Valuation Officer serves a notice on occupiers, legally obliging them to complete a form that includes details such as tenure, rent passing, rent review frequency, premiums, improvements, sublettings, service charges and, where necessary, trading figures.

  The initial rental form does not, however, inform the VO of all restrictive or onerous lease provisions that may affect the rent (although more detailed information can be requested). The VO may only in fact consider the finer lease terms if the rent is critical to the revaluation, or it is to be used as evidence in connection with an appeal.

  Note that the hereditament would be assessed, for example, as a shop, rather than butcher's shop or clothes retailer, as may be provided in the user clause of a lease. Whereas such a tenant may command a discount at rent review for a restricted user provision, that rental evidence may have to be uplifted in order to assess the RV.

  The decapitalisation of premiums should be undertaken by a market yield, although a consensus discount rate such as 8% may often be applied.

  Valuers will have to be satisfied also that rents are representative of open market value. Factors such as goodwill, the individual tenant's occupation and tenant desperation should be disregarded, but they may not be readily apparent.

  Where a rental market does not exist for some properties or locations, values can be interpolated from the tone of rents elsewhere, or profits or cost-based methods can be applied. It is unusual to decapitalise freehold values.
- **Receipts and expenditure/profits method** This is used for properties such as hotels and public houses, where value is dependant on trading potential and profitability, and warrants the examination of accounts.
- **Contractor's basis** This is used for properties which are rarely, if at all, available for letting on the open market, such as some

public buildings or specialist industrial installations. The valuation comprises land value (for existing not alternative use), the cost of constructing a similar facility, and a deduction for any obsolescence to the current hereditament. The resulting capital sum is decapitalised in order to produce an equivalent rental/rateable value. A standard decapitalisation rate of 5.5% is prescribed for most properties, yet schools, for example, would attract the lower rate of 3.67%.
- **Statutory formulae** This is used to value facilities such as gas, water and electricity undertakings and railway premises. Non-statutory formulae may be agreed between the VO and ratepayers for certain classes of property.

Plant and machinery may also be rateable.

Movements in values

Movements in rental values between 1993 and 1998 will result in some occupiers suffering a substantial increase in rateable values. Rate liabilities can also impact on market rents, as well as generally affecting the location decisions of occupiers.

Chesterton Research estimates, for example, that prime City of London office rentals increased around 100% over the period, contrasting with only a slight rise in prime Birmingham city centre office rentals. Rental growth for retail parks has been strong, exceeding 100% in some locations. In many areas, growth in prime industrial rents has been confined to 10% or less.

Government statistics state the national average increase in rateable value of all properties in England is approximately 25%.

Transitional relief

'Transitional relief' or 'phasing' will cushion increases, but also limit decreases in rates liability. Transition rates depend on changes in value being upward or downward, and vary between large properties and small properties, with adjustments also allowing for inflation.

Transitional arrangements pass with the property to new occupiers. A new hereditament coming into the list for the first time would not be subject to transitional arrangements, so new buildings completed after 1 April 2000 could place substantially different rates liabilities on occupiers compared with properties already in the list. Rental levels could consequently be affected. Note that Wales has a separate scheme of transitional relief to England.

Reducing the rates liability

All ratepayers should consider whether to appeal against their 2000 rateable value, but noting that the RV could actually be increased on appeal.

The new procedures for dealing with appeals termed 'programming' involves the VO timetabling appeals into groups determined by location and property type. The VO sets a 'start date' for negotiations with the rate payer to begin, and a 'target date' by which if agreement cannot be reached, the appeal would go forward to be listed for hearing by the Valuation Tribunal. There is a further right of appeal to the Lands Tribunal, and then to the Court of Appeal (and the House of Lords) on a point of law.

In assessing the rateable value, regard is given to the 'tone of the list' – the general level of value established over time by the settlement of appeals against entries in the rating list. When negotiating later appeals, the VO will have regard to previous appeal settlements. The new grouping arrangements under programming should, however, see the majority of appeals for a property type considered together.

An appeal against the RV in the 2000 list can be made at any time during the duration of the list. Unlike the provisions in respect of the 1995 lists, the effective date of the revised RV and rates liability may not, however, be backdated to the commencement date of the new lists. Appeals against the 2000 rateable value must be lodged before 1 October 2000 to ensure any revised RV commences at 1 April 2000. Appeals against compiled list entries lodged between 1 October 2000 and 31 March 2001 will have an effective date of 1 October 2000. Once into the new 2001-02 rating year, appeals against compiled list entries will have an effective date no earlier than 1 April 2001. This principle will apply to subsequent years. Appeals relating to material changes are not subject to the same limitations but should be served as soon as possible after the change.

After 31 March 2001, appeals cannot be made against assessments in either the 1990 or 1995 rating lists.

Other opportunities to minimise rate liability include:

- Where properties/uses are exempt, such as agricultural land and buildings, churches and fishing rights.
- Where relief can be obtained, such as charities' entitlement to 80% relief, which can be increased to 100% at the local billing authority's discretion. Hardship can gain 100% relief at the authority's discretion.

- Deletion of listing – such as when a building is demolished, or when there is no liability for business rates because the property is now used for residential purposes.
- Material change in circumstances – such as change to the locality or the property which reduces its value, including the proximity and effect of major infrastructure works or new property developments, or the refurbishment or alteration of a building.
- Merger – where, for example, the same ratepayer has several adjoining units on an industrial estate, a number of office suites within the same building or neighbouring retail units, which are 'contiguous', the merger may enable the total area to be valued for rating purposes, possibly at a significantly lower rate per m^2 than if the units were valued separately.
- Change of commencement dates of rateable occupation.
- Change of description, such as classification of the property as a different (less valuable) use. This may also affect the liability for empty rates.
- Change in the criteria which gives rise to rateable occupation.

The valuation date adopted for appeals/proposals is still the Antecedent Valuation Date adopted for the rating list, but with the valuation being based on any new circumstances pertaining at the material day, that is, compilation date or date of change.

Empty rates

'Empty rates' or 'void rates' are payable on empty retail and office properties at 50% of the occupied liability, following a three-month period of full exemption. This can represent a significant cost to landlords of empty or partially let buildings.

Note that a tenant who has vacated prior to lease expiry may benefit from the three-month period, leaving the landlord to pay empty rates as soon as he is in possession of the property. Suitable provisions could be included in the lease to protect the landlord from this happening.

Empty rates are not payable in respect of industrial/warehouse/distribution premises, nor for hereditaments having a rateable value of less than £1,900, listed buildings, or properties that are uninhabitable by statute.

It has been possible to undertake works, sometimes called 'constructive vandalism' or 'soft stripping', to make buildings unusable and avoid empty rates, such as removing a roof, bricking up fire exits and removing services.

Unused parts of a building may be suitable for void rates. It may be possible to create independently accessible and separately operable areas by reorganisation and/or by undertaking certain works. Billing authorities also have discretion to treat part of a property as vacant for limited periods.

Rent and rates

The distinction between the basis upon which market rents are typically established and the basis of rateable value means that rateable values are not reliable evidence for determining current open market rental values. The antecedent valuation date may be historic, there may be scope for an adjustment following appeal, and the value of improvements may not be reflected in the rent, but should be in the RV.

The assumption for RV assessment that the hypothetical tenancy is on an annual year-to-year basis means that there is a reasonable expectation that the tenancy will continue. It does not infer that security of tenure is unduly restricted and that rental/rateable values can consequently be discounted (as may be the case where redevelopment is pending, for example).

In theory, the year-to-year assumption infers an annual review which would warrant an adjustment between rental and rateable value because tenants will usually be prepared to pay a higher rent for a three- or five-year period between rent reviews – with the uplift being greater where values are rising more strongly. In practice, a downward adjustment does not tend to be made if the review frequencies within rental evidence represent the market norm. Valuation ranges, divergent evidence and many other differences mean that an overall view often has to be taken.

Consideration may have to be given to situations such as rateable values of offices being based on market rents that are inclusive of car parking, but car parking also being assessed as a separate hereditament, and therefore creating the need to avoid double counting. Also, the value of offices that have no car parking may not necessarily be the same as the value of those with parking, less market car parking rates. Similarly, shop rents in out-of-town retail parks reflect the centre's car parking provision, which could be double counted if valued separately.

Specialist advice

Many general practice surveyors undertake basic rating work, but for larger properties and/or for special situations, occupiers are advised to seek specialist rating advice.

Occupiers should instruct reputable practices, and be aware of the 'rating cowboys', who in their worst form, comprise teams of (non-property) salesmen who knock on the doors of businesses, take advance payment for the promise of being able to reduce rates liability, only to then disappear.

Various consultee input

CHAPTER 69

Quarterly in advance

Published as 'Time to move forward', 10 June 2000

Valuation should reflect the true timing of rental income receipt – quarterly in advance – even though the approach used may not affect property values

Investment valuation involves capitalising rental income in order to produce a capital valuation.

A 'rack-rented' investment producing a 'market rent' or 'open market rental value' (OMRV) of £30,000 pa could be valued at, say, £30,000 × YP in perpetuity 8% (12.5) = £375,000. The 12.5 multiplier is usually determined by dividing 100 by 8.

A 'reversionary' investment having, say, a three-year term of rent passing at £40,000, before the reversion to today's market rent or 'estimated rental value' ('ERV') of £50,000, could be valued at, say, £40,000 × YP 3 years 7% (2.624) = £104,960 (value of term) + £50,000 × YP perp 8% (12.5) × PV 3 years 8% (0.794) = £496,250 (value of reversion) = £601,210 total capital value – say £600,000.

YP 3 years 7% and PV 3 years 8% would be established from tables, although could be calculated manually.

YP accounts for rent being paid periodically during the three years rather than in advance at the start.

PV determines the present value of a reversion which is paid for now, but does not yield rent for three years.

The sooner income is received, the more valuable it is, as it can be invested to earn further returns (known as compounding).

However, the YP rates in traditional valuation tables, such as the 2.625 and 12.5 multipliers, assume that income is received annually in arrears. Valuers continue to adopt this basis, despite rental income from most property investments being received quarterly in advance. The Investment Property Forum has sought to change this practice, beginning primarily with institutional grade properties.

Valuation and comparable evidence

In capitalising a rent of £10,000 on the annually in arrears basis, £10,000 × YP perp 10% (10) = £100,000.

Yet on the quarterly in advance basis, the YP multiplier for 10% perp is 10.62, producing a capital value of £106,200. This is 6.2% higher than the in arrears basis because income is worth more if received in advance. The higher the yield, the greater the difference between the approaches.

The value of property does not, however, differ because of the in advance or in arrears basis of income timing adopted by valuers. Nor does any approach necessarily produce an incorrect valuation. This is because the yield/multiplier is taken from market transactions – what investors are prepared to pay for similar investments. The analysis of a comparable, and the valuation of the subject property, should be undertaken on the same basis of income receipt.

For example, a sale at £750,000 of a rack-rented investment producing £60,000 pa devalues to a yield of 8% by the calculation £60,000 ÷ £750,000. This simple analysis is the annually in arrears basis. Analysis on the quarterly in advance basis would produce a yield of 8.42%.

In applying these yields to a similar rack-rented investment producing £80,000, the annually in arrears basis is £80,000 × YP perp 8% (12.5) = £1m. The quarterly in advance basis is £80,000 × YP perp 8.42% (12.5) = £1m. The valuation is therefore the same.

Use of the 12.5 multiplier for both in advance and in arrears valuations reflects the combination of income received in advance, first, yielding a relatively higher yield/return (8.42% rather than 8% in arrears) and, second, having a relatively higher YP/multiple (12.5 rather than 11.87 if 8.42% was the in arrears basis).

Even if investors work to the annually in arrears basis to establish yields and their purchase prices, they are still pricing in the reality that income will be received quarterly in advance. And if the rent was actually received annually in arrears, investors would require a yield higher than that acceptable for income received quarterly in advance (notwithstanding the enhanced effect of income security/covenant strength; and also the possibility that rents would be higher if tenants could pay annually in arrears). The effect of income timing on valuation shows the need for clarity in reporting yields, property statistics and the like.

Departing from theoretical principles

It is rare that the perfect comparable is available which facilitates the type of valuation undertaken above. Furthermore, the valuer may adopt a figure as precise as 8.4% for institutional-type property, but in other situations may round off the yield to 8.5%. The difference in valuation may be small in this case, and the final figure rounded off anyway, but this shows how the in advance and in arrears approaches can produce valuation differences in practice.

With secondary properties particularly, the in advance and in arrears methodology may be seen as a disproportionately precise consideration compared with the reasonable range within which a single valuation figure could fall (notwithstanding the difference between in advance and in arrears approaches having a greater effect with higher yields).

Adjustments may be required for the many factors affecting value: location, age/character/condition of the property, tenant covenant strength, the unexpired term of the lease, other lease terms, voids, the potential for rental growth, overrenting, the effect of incentives and the like. Valuers will also rely on intuition, use information from property publications and assess opinion from other valuers. At the lower end of the market, yields could vary by several per cent for lesser quality industrial, or retail space, for example.

It remains important, however, that a credible and consistent approach is applied to valuation by the profession. While stressing the importance of meeting institutional client requirements particularly, the IPF accepts the place of straightforward traditional approaches to valuation, appraisal and analysis in certain situations.

This is reflected in the way valuers should now be embracing quarterly in advance methodology – or, more specifically, reflecting the true timing of income, as there may sometimes be a different payment basis to quarterly in advance.

Institutional investment

With prime institutional property investments, property characteristics, tenant profiles and lease terms are relatively consistent, and yield selection more precise.

Investors require valuations and appraisals to reflect the precise quarterly in advance timing of income receipt. It is only then that there can be accurate comparison with alternative investments such as gilts/bonds, equities and cash deposits. The annually in arrears basis does not provide that accuracy.

Mathematic modelling has become a more sophisticated means of comparing the relative performance of investment media. There has been an increased application of Discounted Cash Flow (DCF) techniques in order to develop a greater understanding of property valuation and its performance, and also to deal with the more dynamic nature of property markets (such as the mid-1970s and early 1990s crashes and their consequences).

With DCF, inputs such as an estimated growth rate are explicitly accounted for, and the timing of income accurately reflected. Computer packages such as Kel and Circle automate the valuation process, with quarterly in advance options typically being provided. It is increasingly common for clients to be provided with valuation calculations. Against these factors, the annually in arrears basis becomes increasingly invalid.

Equivalent yields

With a traditional valuation of a reversionary investment, the yield for the term of rent passing may be, say, 7% against an all risks yield of 8% used to capitalise the market rent at reversion. The 1% deduction for the term reflects the greater security afforded by the tenant enjoying a rent below market value or 'profit rent'.

With prime investment properties, the excellent covenant strength of tenants will often mean that a differential in yields is not warranted. The same, 'equivalent', yield could be applied to both the term and reversionary income.

The equivalent yield is also used to analyse other transactions, and often the way deals of institutional grade investments are reported in the property press.

With reversionary investments, the equivalent yield derives from a weighting analysis of initial income, the length of the term and the reversionary income.

With rack-rented investments, the initial yield/all risks yield and the equivalent yield would be the same (market rent ÷ capital value), but it is equivalent yield parlance with which institutional type property is associated.

Equivalent yields should now reflect the timing of quarterly in advance rental payments, and be referred to as 'True Equivalent Yield' or 'TEY'. This applies for both rack-rented and reversionary investments. 'Nominal' (annually in arrears) equivalent yields should no longer be used. A true equivalent yield of 6.5% would be expressed TEY 6.5% (Qly in Adv) in valuations, statistics, reported deals, marketing particulars and the like. In due course, Qly in Adv would be dropped.

Property owners/clients should ensure that valuations and marketing material adopt equivalent yields on the TEY basis. As well as quoting the true basis, agents may add the nominal basis, which is expressed 'NEY'. Although initial and reversionary yields will remain on the annually in arrears basis, they may also be expressed on the true basis.

For the time being, the all risks yields (such as initial and reversionary yields – see p470) will continue to be used on their 'nominal' annually in arrears basis (although can be expressed as true yields if surveyors wish). It is indeed the preserve of the equivalent yield among mainly institutional grade property that neatly divides the new quarterly in advance approach from some of the traditional methodology that retains its place. For some property types, typically good-quality/mid-market investments, there will, however, be an overlap of in advance and in arrears valuation practice, owing to institutional investors applying different appraisal methodology compared with less sophisticated investors.

The longer-term aim is that all property yields will be quoted quarterly in advance. For some purposes, yields may be quoted on a quarterly basis (such as 1.25% per quarter).

Student learning

Students initially gain an understanding of investment valuation with the traditional annually in arrears format. Concentration is on yield selection, and on the approach taken to different rack-rented and reversionary situations, as well as on the historical background to valuation work. Moving on to modern valuation methods and finer valuation analysis, students will study the quarterly in advance approach. This approach will then be used for valuations, but with an awareness of whether and when this takes place in practice.

Conclusion

Valuation practice must mirror the process by which typical investors formulate their bids, and therefore determine 'market value'. For mainly institutional type property, the quarterly in advance basis will be adopted for valuation, appraisal and analysis, involving especially the true equivalent yield (TEY).

Elsewhere, straightforward traditional methods retain their place for the time being. The profession as a whole must embrace new approaches, and present credibility to its markets.

Pricing and analysis of investments, comparing like with like

The price and yield performance of property and alternative investments is measured as follows.

Property

The 'initial yield' is the initial income divided by the capital value. If there was a term of £40,000 rent passing until a reversion at today's market value of £50,000, and the capital value was £600,000, the initial yield would be 6.66% (£40,000 ÷ £600,000). The initial yield also applies where the initial income is the market rent, such as 8% in the case of a £375,000 property producing £30,000 (£30,000 ÷ £375,000).

The 'reversionary yield', for reversionary investments only, represents the return provided at a reversion, such as 8.33% (£50,000 ÷ £600,000).

These yields are 'all risks yields', although ARY terminology commonly refers to the market yield – that deriving from a rack-rented investment. Valuations and yields would also reflect an allowance for purchasers' costs, such as the 'net initial yield' referred to often in marketing particulars.

The basis of the above yields are annually in arrears and are referred to as 'nominal yields' (as opposed to 'true' yields calculated quarterly in advance). They (as well as the equivalent yield described in the main text, and which is also an all risks yield) implicitly reflect the potential for the investment to secure rental/income growth. Income yields from other investments will do the same. For all investments, a measure is also required of total returns – the combination of income returns and changes in capital value (see later).

Gilt and bond yields

The income from gilts/bonds is fixed, but the price is adjusted to produce the appropriate yield. The Treasury 8% 2021 stock for example, when issued at £100, yields 8%. When gilt yields fall to 6%, the stock is worth £133 – calculated by £8 coupon interest ÷ £133 current price. The 6% is known as the 'running yield' or 'initial yield' and is a measure of income return on current gilt prices.

Because gilts will usually be redeemed at £100, as opposed to their current price, their value is influenced by any capital gain or loss that would be realised from now to redemption, or to any sooner sale in the market. The 'redemption yield' combines the current income earned with the effect of redemption on changes in capital value, such as the 6% income return, and the fall from £133 to £100 by 2021. It is the principal measure for investors, calculated by using a precise discount rate formula provided by the Institute of Actuaries. Account is made for the payment of gilt interest being half-yearly in arrears.

Equity yields

Yields from equities/shares are calculated by adding together the last two dividend payments, and dividing this by the current share price. The yield does not expressly reflect the timing of income. Although the share price will adjust to reflect the entitlement to dividends, with 'ex-dividend' prices being adjusted downwards for example, the dividend will be received some time later. The timing of income is effectively being lost in day-to-day price fluctuations but, in theory, is reflected in the share price.

Cash deposits

Bank and building society rates of interest will be quoted on the basis that income is earned. 4.7% for the annual receipt of interest is the same as 4.65% for monthly receipt. This is due to the effect of compounding – interest earned monthly being reinvested to earn further interest throughout the year.

Making comparisons

It is the redemption yield on long-dated gilts to which property returns are typically compared. The 'equated yield' for property, may be derived by adding a risk premium of, say, 2–5% to gilt yields, reflecting both property market risks and property specific risks.

The equated yield represents total annualised returns over the life of the investment, which are therefore fixed returns that account for rental and capital growth. They also represent the 'internal rate of return' of the investment. Investors will also consider total returns over an individual year or shorter period, combining income and capital performance. The equated yield can be adopted on the quarterly in advance basis in order to account for the in advance receipt of the income element.

Investors will seek the best-performing asset classes, subject to an optimum balance of investments being secured within a portfolio. The attraction of equities will often be the scope for capital gains, in both the shorter term and longer term, hence the acceptance of lower-income yields. Gilts provide secure income, and possibly also capital growth. Property is sometimes seen as a defensive hedge against equities and gilts.

For equities, gilts and property, total annual returns will sometimes be negative, owing to the disproportionately greater influence of variations in capital value against income returns. In poor and/or volatile market conditions, cash deposits may be an attractive option, and there may also be a 'flight to quality' – typically gilts, which carry less risk. It is risk in relation to return on which investors, fund managers and the financial markets focus. Investors will also look at taxation, trading costs, liquidity, portfolio issues, risk, and pre-defined strategy/objectives. Note that exposure to property could also be secured through holding equities in the sector's property investment or development companies or agents, through unit or investment trusts, through derivatives/index-based investment vehicles or through any new forms of securitised vehicles which may emerge.

On the quarterly in advance basis, the true equivalent yield could be, say, TEY 6.5%. On the former annually in arrears basis, this equates to a nominal equivalent yield of NEY 6.25% (assuming the investment is rack-rented). Therefore, although not expressly changing property values, the quarterly in advance basis helps to make property appear a more favourable investment. This increases its attraction to the good of the profession and, indirectly, can raise values. As any securitised property investment vehicles develop, they will bring the liquidity, divisibility and trading costs of property closer to that of other investments types, making the 0.25% differential increasingly significant. Accurate comparison between investments can be made only if analysis reflects the true timing of income receipt.

Quarterly in advance – the new calculations

Quarterly in advance YP multipliers are included in *Parry's Valuation and Investment Tables*, 11th ed. YP in perpetuity tables on p42 show both the in arrears and in advance YP multipliers, which for a 10% yield are 10 and 10.618 respectively. Quarterly in advance YP tables for a given number of years on pQ:22 show 2.705 for YP 3 years at 8%. The in-arrears multiplier on p34 is 2.577.

Valuers may also wish to convert between the nominal/in arrears basis and the true/in advance basis. The 8% nominal and 8.4166% true figures share the same multiplier of 12.5, as illustrated in the main text, and produced the same £1m value from a rent of £80,000.

Such straightforward conversions apply only to rack-rented properties. Equivalent yields for reversionary investments cannot be determined easily, unless of course they are an original input into the valuation.

There are many more detailed complexities related to quarterly in advance methodology. Some difficulties relate to converting between the two bases; difficulties that would disappear if all valuation practice was on the in advance basis.

Contributed by Austen Imber

CHAPTER 70

Rent-free periods

Published as 'The truth beyond the horizon', 30 November 2002

When a new letting of commercial property takes place, a market rent may be payable from day one, or alternatively, a landlord may grant a tenant a rent-free period

If, for example, the day one or 'equivalent' market rental value is £80,000 pa, a letting could be structured as a 15-year lease with rent reviews at years five and 10, and provide a rent-free period of one year, followed by a rent of £100,000 pa.

This £100,000 is known as a 'headline rent'. In simple terms, the deals can be considered equivalent, as in both cases £400,000 is paid over five years to the first rent review.

Pros and cons for the tenant

A rent-free period may benefit a tenant's cash flow position, particularly when starting up or relocating, and when capital costs are being incurred – especially for smaller businesses where cash flow is often at a premium.

A rent-free period also allows a tenant's costs or expenses to initially be lower, and profits or earnings to be higher.

This may be favourable for wider business reasons, including financial reporting, albeit only temporarily, until the headline rent is payable.

Some tenants incorrectly believe a rent-free period represents something for nothing – unaware that the rent payable at the expiry of the rent-free period will be higher than the day one market rent.

Tenants sometimes also fail to appreciate the potential longer-term effects of initially agreeing a rent-free period.

If, in the above, example, the market rent of £80,000 rises by 10% over the five years to the first rent review, the market rent would then be £88,000. With a rent-free period/headline rent arrangement, and an upwards-only rent review (as is typically the case), the tenant would continue paying £100,000 for another five years until the next rent review at year 10.

This represents £60,000 additional rent over five years as a result of taking a rent-free period initially. For the tenant to be in the equivalent position of paying the market rent of £100,000 after five years, the day one market rental value has to increase by 25%, from £80,000 to £100,000. Such scope for income above market rent to be secured beyond the next review is one of the benefits to a landlord of granting a rent-free period.

Investment property pricing

Another benefit to a landlord is the increase in capital or investment value that can result from the headline rent structure. In the above example, one year's lost rent is £80,000, but the extra £20,000 pa (headline rent less market rent) may be capitalised at a yield of, say, 8% in perpetuity (multiplier of 12.5), to produce a capital increase of £250,000.

In theory the market should recognise the artificially high rent emanating from a rent-free period, and should also acknowledge term and reversion/growth situations.

However, in many investment sub-markets, investment property pricing by investors and valuers does not necessarily work like this, with investors (as well as lenders) focusing disproportionately on the income actually received (which will be the headline rent once the rent-free period has expired).

It needs to be noted, however, that a too substantial headline rent may make the investment considerably over-rented, and therefore relatively unattractive to investors, thus having a disproportionately depressive effect on capital or investment value.

Investment strategy

Whether and how a rent-free period or headline rent structure benefits an investor also depends on their overall strategy. The above one-year rent-free arrangement may, for example, be beneficial for an investor wishing to sell and realise capital gains, or raise new finance on a higher valuation figure, between, say, one and two years after the initial letting.

If not selling or refinancing, the rent-free/headline rent structure may serve to inflate capital value only temporarily (and this may not be beneficial for the investor in terms of asset values and accounting issues).

Note also that a property not producing any rent may be relatively unattractive to the investment market, especially when investors draw on finance, and interest repayments among other costs have to be covered by rental income.

The effect of rent-free periods is, of course, most pronounced with single lettings, as against multilet interests.

Impact on rental levels

In multilet and/or portfolio situations, the terms of an individual letting will create comparable evidence for the benefit of other transactions in the same building, or in nearby properties – mainly rent reviews and lease renewals, but also lettings, assignments and sub-lettings.

Here, the treatment of rent-free periods, as with any other incentives, can have a substantial impact. And any practice by landlords of hiding or minimising the apparent extent of rent-free periods can become contentious.

Landlords' approaches vary but could include covering a rent-free period with a side letter agreeing not to collect rent; granting the rent-free period through a prior agreement so that the main lease has a day one rent commencement date; making an off-lease capital payment in exchange for a higher rent; or juggling any other terms of the transaction.

Where a rent-free period covers the cost of a tenant undertaking certain works in addition to providing an element of rent-free incentive, the landlord may try to structure the deal so that the period for works is relatively long, and the incentive rent-free period is relatively short.

This means that only the incentive rent-free, and not the works allowance rent-free, is discounted (see p478) – provided the works are for the landlord's benefit, such as would be the case if the new tenant was putting right the previous tenant's dilapidations, or if improvements were made, that were instantly rentalised.

The second of the two-part *Mainly for Students* feature on dilapidations (28 July 2001, p104 and 25 August 2001, p90) covers this in more detail.

Even when a rent-free period is transparent, there may be benefit to the landlord in clouding the reasons for its grant, and minimising the effect of the rent-free period when devaluing it.

Although relatively uncommon in this form, rent-free incentives may also be effective after a number of years have passed, or a break is not exercised (despite a day one rent appearing in the lease).

Commercial agents, rent review and lease renewal surveyors, and valuers need to be alert to hidden rent-free periods, and the potential misrepresentation of comparable evidence, even inadvertently, by landlords.

Surveyors structuring headline rented deals for their favourable wider effects need to be aware that misrepresentation in connection with a rent-free period (including the omission of facts) could carry severe personal and professional consequences.

Surveyors also need to be aware that headline rented deals can be planted in the property press by landlords in a way that raises perceptions of value and market sentiment.

Other factors

Before granting a rent-free period, the landlord does, of course, have to be satisfied that the tenant is of sufficient covenant strength to not reap the benefit of the rent-free period, and then disappear without trace or go bust.

The investor must also be able to afford to forgo rent for the period. Although rent-free periods of one year have been examined above, shorter periods of three or six months are also common.

Landlords also need to be careful about undertaking deals mid-term (including at assignment or rent review), such as paying reverse premiums for higher rents, and thereby endangering potential future claims against guarantors or former tenants.

For tenants, a rent-free period/headline rent arrangement can create an over-rented interest and a negative lease liability that would require a reverse premium in the case of disposal, and may also have to be stated as a liability in company accounts.

Lease conditions on alienation can cause particular problems with the sub-letting of over-rented interests, such as where sub-lettings must be at the passing rent, and the payment of a premium is not permitted.

For purchasers of investment property, care must be taken that incentives granted at the start of a letting have not led the property to be over-rented, thereby restricting the potential for rental growth, and perhaps adding to the overall risks of the investment.

Another example of the pitfalls for purchasers and valuers is that a property may still be over-rented despite a relatively recent rent review (in theory to a market rent) being recently agreed. This is because for over-rented interests, landlords may look to freshen the investment profile by seeking only a small increase in order to avoid the impression of over-renting and create a market-rented profile.

Only a small increase needed

Using the figures from the initial example, if at the first rent review, the rent passing/former headline rent is £100,000 and the market rent is £88,000, the landlord may propose a new rent at a small margin above £100,000, say at £103,000, with a view to securing anything possible above £100,000. Where the landlord has more than one tenant, the first deal struck with one can then be drawn on as evidence for others.

This is a good example of why it is important for tenants to liaise with each other. It also illustrates why tenants should always secure professional advice, and not agree small increases because expense would otherwise be incurred on fees. Likewise, surveyors need to research evidence thoroughly.

Tactical opportunities at rent review will be considered in future *Mainly for Students* features, but note, for example, how a landlord's triggering of a rent review of an already over-rented property may, under the terms of the lease and third party determination provisions, still lead to a market rental value actually being determined, because a tenant pursues the point for wider benefit, despite the rent not actually having to fall because of upward-only rent review provisions.

Tenants also need to give attention to the drafting of rent review provisions, and ensure that the basis of valuation is to market rental value (£80,000 in the initial example), and not to the headline rent which follows the rent-free period (£100,000 in the example).

Raising the returns – The wide impact of extra rent

Multilet and/or portfolio situations provide a good illustration of the wider effects of a successful letting, rent review or lease renewal.

If, for example, a landlord has 10 tenants within a property, an extra £1,000 pa secured on the rent review against one of them may help an extra £1,000 to be secured on the others at rent review thereafter, thus producing an extra £10,000 rent pa in total.

At an 8% yield/12.5 mutiplier, the extra £1,000 rent on one property may therefore lead to an increase in capital value on all properties of £125,000.

There are, in fact, many other issues at play, including the timing of other rent reviews, but the above is one of many factors that influence the returns that can be made from property.

Securing a headline rent – How deals might come about

To create a rent-free period/headline rent structure, a landlord may seek a relatively high market rent as part of a marketing campaign, with negotiating flexibility being through a rent-free period or other incentives rather than a reduction in the rent.

Artificially-high asking rents may be essential in order to preserve (or enhance) the perceived tone of market rental values for a property. Evidence of low asking rents for vacant units that have been difficult to let may be presented as part of rent review and lease renewal negotiations (including submissions to a third party), and may also affect capital valuations.

When market conditions weaken, such factors often account for the greater availability of incentives, ahead of a rental reduction. And if larger incentives are granted in a worsening market, the extent of overrenting, once the incentive has expired, is even greater.

Analysing rent-free periods – Establishing the true market rent

When a letting has been undertaken on the basis of, say, a rent-free period of one year, followed by a headline rent of £100,000 within a 15-year lease having five-yearly rent reviews, the true, day one, market rent may need to be established for purposes such as comparable evidence for rent reviews and lease renewals.

There are no precise rules on how rent-free periods should be analysed, and consideration is given to a combination of factors, including the nature of the reversion (if a lease renewal, the rent can fall to market value, unlike an upwards-only rent review); the timing of the next rent review; whether the review is upwards-only; whether there are any break provisions and expected market movements.

In the above example, the most favourable approach for the tenant in analysing the above deal as comparable evidence for a rent review on his own property would be to discount the rent-free period over the shortest term – five years – and produce a market rent of £80,000. This could be appropriate where the market rent is expected to have reached the headline rent by the first review.

Another possibility is to spread the rent-free period over 10 years, producing a market rent of £90,000. This may be appropriate where the headline rent is expected to continue beyond the first rent review, and up to the second rent review.

The reasons for the grant of the rent-free period are also important, noting that if the normal market lease length was five years, and a one-year rent-free period was granted within a 15-year lease in exchange for such a tenant's commitment, the headline rent for a 15-year lease may equate to the market rent for a five-year lease, with further discounting analysis not being appropriate.

If more accurately reflecting the timing of income receipt than the simplified flat-rate basis initially adopted in this feature, the one-year rent-free/ £100,000 headline rent discounted over five years would produce a rent of £76,800, not £80,000, if a yield of 8% was adopted.

The calculation is £100,000 × YP 4 years 8% (3.312) × PV 1 year 8% (0.926), all divided by YP 5 years at 8% (3.993) = £76,800 (a worthwhile calculation for the tenant to make).

The choice of yield would be another valuation issue – market investment yield, or opportunity cost (cash deposit, or finance rates).

Although it cannot generally be argued that a headline rent is in some way equivalent to a market rent, there may be situations where a landlord was desperate to secure a tenant, or where a tenant of substantially greater covenant than the typical tenant market for the property commanded a favourable deal.

Here the same arguments would apply as with any deal considered unrepresentative of market value, and the extent of any rent-free period should not be seen as accounting only for such factors.

Contributed by Austen Imber

CHAPTER 71

Telecoms valuation

Published as 'How much is that rooftop worth', 23 February 2002

In our ongoing series on specialist valuation, we examine how practice is developing in a rapidly expanding sector: telecoms

Telecoms masts, towers and rooftop installations have been in existence in the UK for over 50 years, with the dominant occupants initially comprising TV broadcast and fixed-line telephone companies.

The huge expansion of these installations occurred after 1984 when the government issued the first mobile telecoms licences to Vodafone and BT Cellnet (now mmO2). One 2 One, Orange and Hutchison are the other major players who have since entered the market. All five have recently secured third-generation (3g) licences, auctioned by the government in 2000, which enable a wider range of services to be provided through mobile 'devices'.

Telecoms companies are quickly expanding their networks – involving more individual sites and increased site sharing – and therefore expanding the work of the specialist telecoms surveyor.

Types of installations

The main types of telecoms installations, collectively known as base stations, comprise:

- **Greenfield**: approximately 20m × 20m compounds, fenced, with a steel lattice tower with telecoms kit and equipment cabin;
- **Rooftop**: rights on a rooftop for telecoms kit and an equipment cabin;
- **Microcells**: small alarm-size boxes fixed to either a tower or a building with small cabinets, and also installations disguised as street furniture such as street lamps.

Market transactions comprise mainly mobile phone companies acquiring freehold or leasehold interests in order to transmit their services. The growth of the sector has also seen investors acquiring sites on both a freehold and leasehold basis to then lease space to the mobile phone companies, and also to other users such as broadcasters and the emergency services. Investors are principally specialist network providers rather than mainstream property investors, and include Crown Castle International, NTL, Spectra and Pinnacle. Mainstream investors are, however, becoming more aware of the potential within the sector.

Sales of telecoms businesses and/or their operational assets, in whole and part, take place usually for strategic operational reasons, but sometimes also because a telecoms company has gone bust, such as Ionica – a FTSE 100 company at the time.

Telecoms surveyors' work

Telecoms surveyors may work either for a mobile, broadcast or fixed-line phone company, an investor, the telecoms department of a larger surveying practice or for small practices specialising in telecoms.

Telecoms surveyors cover the same areas of commercial property practice as surveyors involved with other property types, although the work varies between types of employer. Capital valuations are a good example of work generally undertaken by the larger practices, in-house surveyors and investors, but not by smaller practices, which tend to be more transaction orientated.

Landlord and Tenant Act and lease terms

The need for case law to help establish certain principles for such unusual property types means that it is sometimes uncertain as to whether the protection of the Landlord and Tenant Act 1954 is afforded to tenants. A greenfield compound would typically be protected, but rooftop facilities tend not to be of a defined area providing exclusive possession, and are generally not protected. Microcells are similarly unprotected.

Some telecoms leases are contracted out of sections 24-28 of the 1954 Act, thus denying the right to a new tenancy at lease expiry. However, the Telecommunications Act 1984 and the Telecommunications Code provide certain rights of further occupation.

Lease terms are typically 10 years, with three- or five-yearly rent reviews to open-market value being common. Some reviews are by reference only to RPI, while others are on the basis of OMV or RPI, whichever the greater. Landlord and/or tenant breaks are also common.

Site sharing

Some leases of mobile phone sites incorporate 'pay away' provisions, which involve a tenant paying to the landlord a percentage of the income, say 25%, received by the tenant from sharing a site with third parties. This tends to occur for greenfield tower sites owing to their relatively high installation and maintenance costs, but site sharing is rare for rooftop installations as there is often no physical facility to share.

Sites/leases which permit sharing are typically of greater value than those with a restricted lease, as sharing both reduces the risk to the tenant and increases the income to both parties. Although towers have capacity constraints, telecoms operators can apply for permission to extend the facility.

As site sharing is by way of licence, it does not endanger the Landlord and Tenant Act protection afforded to the principal lease-holder, as may sometimes be the case with the subletting of other property types. Note that rates liability generally rests with the principle tenant/occupier, which then recovers amounts from sharers.

Site sharing is encouraged by the government and local planning authorities – with PPG 8 recognising the importance of telecoms to the economy.

Valuation practice

From an owners'/investors' perspective, telecoms installations have traditionally been covered by accompanying notes to valuations of property interests, rather than having their current and/or potential rental income capitalised. In most cases, however telecoms income should be valued in perpetuity, not least because it is rare for telecoms operators to wish to leave a site once they have established a presence.

The RICS appraisal and valuation manual, the Red Book, applies to telecoms in the same way that it does to other property types. The majority of capital valuations are for company accounts purposes, although valuations for lending purposes and in connection with mergers and takeovers are occasionally undertaken – noting also that telecoms valuations may be inputs into valuations of mainstream property interests.

Valuations, and also development/ investment appraisals, may additionally be undertaken in connection with acquisition, disposal and development/investment work. DCF methodology is particularly helpful for site share situations.

Telecoms installations are valued to open market value (OMV) where a market for disposal exists, and depreciated replacement cost (DRC) in the case of specialist facilities where there is no open market. When a business is sold as a going concern, existing use value (EUV) or DRC will be the appropriate method, and OMV or DRC if sold piecemeal.

Although telecoms installations comprise mainly technical equipment, the apparatus which would be included on sale is valued as a property interest, with any unusual and/or particularly extensive additions being effectively classed as plant and machinery, fixtures and fittings. The over-specification of some installations can see a substantial difference between their initial cost and their open market value. The valuer also needs to establish the extent of any tenant's improvements.

Capital valuation

Open-market valuations of telecoms installations are typically based on an investment approach, with a yield being applied to existing and/or potential income. The yield derives from comparison with other investment transactions, and as with rental valuation reflects principal factors such as location, income security, covenant strength, planning permission and lease terms – and also the scope to secure income growth. From an investment perspective, the market is still immature, and where comparable evidence is limited, the valuer has to take an intuitive approach to potential rental levels and to yield selection.

Rental valuation

As well as valuers drawing on comparable rental evidence, there are broad levels of value attributed to the different types of site and facilities by telecoms operators and landlords. This helps establish valuation ranges within which lettings, rent reviews and lease renewals are likely to be achieved.

Location is an important factor, with the best rents often being secured in urban areas, where more sites are required and supply is scarce, as against rural locations, where there may be a greater availability of alternative sites. Such factors need to be borne in mind when transactions are presented as comparable evidence at rent review and lease renewal – and indeed when capital valuations are undertaken.

Future trends
As the majority of landlords are now professionally represented, deals are being concluded more expediently, with an increasingly consistent base of comparable evidence helping to establish distinct criteria by which telecoms installations can be valued with greater accuracy. This will be furthered by the greater number of transactions taking place for letting and sale, and through clarity from arbitrators' and independent experts' decisions and landlord and tenant case law. Although valuation methodology is relatively straightforward, the requisite technical and market knowledge is essential for valuation accuracy.

Training support for the sector
The development of the telecoms sector has resulted in the emergence of specialist telecoms surveyors, who need to keep up-to-date with the market changes taking place.

In order to be successful with the RICS Assessment of Professional Competence (APC), in addition to their telecoms work, telecoms candidates require a broad appreciation of the work involved with other property types. In view of the difficulties sometimes incurred in achieving this, particularly for specialist telecoms firms, GVA Grimley is running open APC training events dedicated to candidates with experience in telecoms. This is part of a wider programme of APC and CPD events run mainly for clients, and of private study material made available to all telecoms surveyors.

RICS Telecoms Forum has recently been established in order for telecoms surveyors to meet on a regular basis to discuss current issues, and to help establish consistency in valuation and other areas. The Forum, together with the RICS's APC department, are also in the process of making refinements to the APC that reflect the increasing recognition of telecoms as a specialist field of surveying. Telecoms acquisition, disposal and leasing work will be more specifically embodied with existing competencies, and candidates will be able to select a specialist area of telecoms on their application form. This will ensure that specialist telecoms experience is represented on the panel, and that the interview accurately reflects candidates' overall experience.

Contributed by Kerry Bourne

Index

Access to Neighbouring Land Act 1992 271
Accounts
    client 7
    company 30
Accounts method 427
Adjudication 106, 261
Advantage West Midlands 364
Alienation 219, 232, 237
All risks yield 440
Alternative dispute resolution 255
Amount of £1 437
Antecedent valuation date 456
Anti-social behaviour orders 427
APC 142
Appeal – rating 461
Appraisal – investment 196
Arbitration
    international 123
    rent review 247, 378
    rule against bias 371
Arbitration Act 1996 249
Assessment of professional competence 142
Assignment 219, 237
Assured shorthold tenancy 423
Assured tenancy 423
Authorised guarantee agreement 220, 240

Bailiffs 282
Base rate (*See* interest rates)
Bias, rule against 369
Birkett, Norman (Lord Birkett) (1880–1960) 180, 377
Birmingham Property Services 149
Bonds 21, 230, 470
Break clause 229, 238
Business angels 21
Business consultancy 25, 206
Business finance 15
Business names 9
Business occupation 224
Business plan 3, 5
Buy to let 420

Calculation of worth 196
Calderbank letter................................. 253
Calendar (Law of) 164
Campbell, John (Lord Campbell) (1779–1861) 382
Carnwarth Report (1989)............................ 349
Civil Evidence Act 1995............................. 250
Civil Procedure Rules 255, 274
Client accounts..................................... 7
Code of Practice for Commercial Leases................ 258
Commercial periodic tenancy 213
Common mistake (doctrine of) 79
Company accounts................................. 30
Comparable evidence 215, 250
Compensation
  at lease expiry 229
  improvements 229, 270
Competent landlord 224
Compound interest 437
Concurrent liability (contract and tort) 99
Condition precedent break 230
Conservation areas................................ 337
Construction Law
  adjudication of disputes........................ 106
  concurrent liability (Contract and Tort) 99
  delay by contractors 117
  partnering 111
Consumer protection............................... 91
Continuing professional development 137, 144 152
Contract
  compensation for delay 117
  concurrent liability with tort law 99
  construction contracts......................... 99
  employment contracts......................... 85
  force majeure 73
  frustration of 73
  mistake 79
  rectification 79
  unfair contract terms 91
Contracted out tenancy........................ 229, 243
Contractor's method 459
Contractors....................................... 117
Corporation tax.................................... 12
Costs
  and Civil Procedure Rules 256
  at arbitration 251

Cottenham, 1st Earl of (1781–1851). 370
CPD. 137, 144, 152
CPR 255, 274
Credit vetting. 284, 420
Criminal Law
   anti-social behaviour orders. 427
   health and safety prosecutions 100
   listed buildings. 345
   murder by a landlord 179
   murder by a tenant 385
Cross-examination 181, 377

Damages (for delay) 117
Data protection. 57
DCF 468
Defective premises 171
Deflation. 44
Delay (by contractors). 117
Delegated Legislation 174
Demolition controls 339
Denning, Alfred Thompson, Lord (1899–1999) 169
Development
   commercial 189, 352
   residential 389
Dilapidations. 221, 264
Directorships. 9, 20
Discount rate. 197
Dispute resolution 247, 255
Distraint 282
Dividends 13, 20
Drafting (legal). 174

Economic policy 42
Employment Law. 85, 400
Empty rates. 462
English Partnerships 362
Equated yield 471
Equities. 471
Equivalent yields 468
Estate management systems. 269, 286
Estoppel, proprietary. 395
European Commission 363
European Union 362
Eviction, protection from 292
Evidence

    anti-social behaviour orders 427
    expert witnesses 374
    hearsay 430
    previous inconsistent statements 378
    similar fact evidence 385
Exchange rates 41
Expert witnesses 261, 374

Fair hearing, right to 176, 369
Family businesses 25
Feuhold 234
Finance
    business finance 15
    property finance 25, 192, 205
Financial Services Authority 68
Force majeure 73
Forfeiture 281, 288
FRI lease 266
Frustration of contract 73
Fund management 194

Gap funding 363
Gearing 15, 34, 208
Gilts 21, 436, 470
Golden shares 20
Goodwill 452
Gowers, Sir Ernest (1880–1966) 174
Gregorian calendar 166
GVA Grimley 148

Headline rent 473
Health and safety – residential 422
Hearsay evidence 430
Housing Acts 1988 and 1996 423
Housing market (*See* residential)
Human rights 174, 312
Hurdle rate 197
Hypothetical rent review provisions 216

Improvements 227, 229, 270, 447
Income tax 11, 62
Independent expert 252
Inflation 39
Inherent defects 266
Initial yields 470

Institutional lease 213
Institutional property investors............................ 187
Insurance (against terrorism) 128
Insurance companies 187
Interest
   compound... 437
   rates 19, 42, 415
   simple 436
Interim continuation....................................... 224
Interim rent 217, 225
Internal rate of return (IRR) 197
International arbitrations 123
Investment (*See* property investment)
Investment Property Forum 195, 465
Investment strategies 189
Investment valuation 435, 444, 465, 473
Investment worth 196
Investors (*See* property investors)
IRI lease 266
IRR 197
Isaacs, Sir Rufus, Lord Reading (1860–1935)................. 181
ISVA assignment submission............................... 352

Johnson, Dr Samuel (1709–1784) 382, 384
Joint and several liability 100
Julian Calendar... 165

Land Law
   proprietary estoppel................................. 395
   restrictive covenants 400
Landlord and tenant
   dispute resolution............................... 247, 255
   introduction 213
   Scottish... 231
   See also alienation, dilapidations, forfeiture, lease renewal,
   rent review, service charges, surrender of leases
Landlord and Tenant (Covenants) Act 1995 .... 220, 239, 270
Landlord and Tenant Act 1927 .... 230, 238, 239, 272
Landlord and Tenant Act 1954........................... 216, 223
Landlord and Tenant Act 1985........................... 423
Landlord and Tenant Act 1988........................... 245
Lands Tribunal.. 402
Law of Property Act 1925 .... 268, 281
Lease renewal 216, 223
Leasehold Property (Repairs) Act 1938 .... 268, 276

Leasehold valuation 441
Leasehold Valuation Tribunals 302
Leases 213
Licences 214
Licensed and leisure properties............................. 450
Lifelong learning 151
Limitation periods 101
Limited company 9
Liquidated damages 121
Listed buildings... 343
Loans 19
Loan-to-value ratio 17, 193, 203
Local Government and Finance Act 1988 456
London (definition of)..................................... 159
Lords, House of 370

Management buy-out 21
Management shares 20
Market value (price, market value, worth) 196
Mediation 258
Midlands Property Training Centre.......................... 148
Mistake (in contract law) 79
Mortgages (residential) 388

National insurance 12
Negligence (Tort of)....................................... 99
Negotiating skills... 47
Nelsonian blindness 401
Net initial yield.. 470
Net present value (NPV) 197
Noise nuisance 332
Nominal equivalent yield 468
Non-domestic rates... 456
NPV 197
Nuisance
    public and private 322
    statutory 327

Office of the Deputy Prime Minister........................ 362
Ordinary shares.. 23
Overdrafts... 19
Overseas investors 188

PACT 259
Part 36 offer 261

Partnering	111
Partnership	9
Party Walls Act 1996	271
Pension funds	187
Pensions	12
Phasing	460
Planning contravention notices	348
Pre-action protocols	256
Pre-assignment conditions	241
Preference shares	23
Premium	219, 238, 442, 446
Present value	437
Price (price, market value, worth)	196
Private investors	188
Private life, right to	313, 316
Privity of contract	220, 239
Privity of estate	239
Privy Council, Judicial Committee	403
Professional Arbitration on Court Terms (PACT)	259
Professional indemnity insurance	7
Profit rent	441
Profits method	453, 459
Programming	461
Pronouns (in legal texts)	174
Property companies	188
Property development (*See* development)	
Property finance	25, 192, 205
Property investment	
high yield/business issues	203
investment appraisal	196
sector overview	187
small investor illustrations	203
valuation	435, 444, 465, 473
Property investors	
institutional	187
overseas	188
property companies	188
private	188
strategies	189
Property, right to	313
Purchasers' costs	470
Pure economic loss	102
PV	437
Quarter days	164, 235

Quarterly in advance 465
Quoted companies 22

Rack rent 214
Raising finance 15
Rate of return 197
Rateable value 456
Rating. 456
Rating (Valuation) Act 1999 458
Rating list 456
Rating revaluation 456
Rebus sic stantibus. 457
Rectification of documents 79
Redemption yield 471
Redundancies. 85
Re-entry, rights of 288
Regeneration. 360
Regional development agencies 360
Relief against forfeiture 281
Rent Act 1977 423
Rent arrears 279
Rent default
   commercial 279
   residential 421
Rent free periods. 473
Rent notice 215
Rent passing. 435
Rent review. 214
Rent tribunals 369
Rental valuation 215
Repair. 221, 264
Repairs notice. 267
Research. 194
Residential
   buy-to-let. 417, 420
   development 415
   health and safety. 422
   housing market trends. 413
   legislation 423
   lettings. 418
   mortgages. 414
   rent default 421
   tenancies. 416, 423
Residual valuation. 355
Restrictive covenants 400

Reverse premium ... 219, 238
Reversion ... 435
Reversionary yields ... 470
RICS ... 7, 139, 151, 248, 259, 262
    Appraisal and Valuation Manual ... 450
    Dispute Resolution Service ... 262
    Policy Unit ... 364
    Regeneration Forum ... 363
Rights issue ... 23
Rules of conduct ... 7

Sale and leaseback ... 22
Schedule of condition ... 221, 266
Schedule of dilapidations ... 267
Scott schedule ... 267
Scottish landlord and tenant ... 231
Secret trusts ... 406
Section 17 notice ... 270
Section 18 damages ... 272
Section 25 notice ... 217, 224
Section 26 notice ... 217, 224
Section 27 notice ... 224
Section 40 notices ... 224
Section 146 notice ... 268, 281
Security for debts ... 179
Security of tenure ... 214, 216, 223,
Self employment ... 3, 9, 17, 62
Service charges ... 299
Set off ... 285
Sewers and sewage ... 310
Shares ... 22, 23
    Golden shares ... 20
    Management shares ... 20
    Ordinary shares ... 23
    Preference shares ... 23
    Rights issue ... 23
    Share buy-back ... 23
    Share options ... 23
Simple interest ... 437
Single joint expert ... 255
Small print regulations ... 91
Smeaton, John (1724–1792) ... 374
Sole trader ... 3, 9
Stagflation ... 43
Stamp duty ... 296

Statutory continuation 224
Statutory demand 283, 422
Statutory nuisances. 327
Stock market 22
Sub-letting 219, 243
Surrender and renewal valuation 444
Surrender of leases 295

Tacit relocation 232
Target rate. 197
Telecommunications Act 1984. 481
Tenancy agreements
   commercial 213
   residential 416, 423
Tenancy at will. 214
Term and reversion 439
Terrorism, insurance against 128
Tone of the list. 461
Tort (concurrent liability with contract) 99
Trade names 9
Trading properties 450
Transitional relief 460
Trees. 340
True equivalent yield 468
Trusts 406
Tyler, John (1790–1862) 174

Unfair contract terms 91
Uniform Business rate. 456
Upwards only rent review 217, 228
Urban regeneration 360
User clause 218, 238

Valuation
   capital/investment 435, 465
   leaseholds 441
   rating 456
   surrender and renewal 444
   telecoms 480
Valuation Office Agency 456
VAT 13
Venture capital 20
Void rates 462

Waiver 270, 281,

Waste disposal 317
Water pollution 307
Woolf Report.. 255
Worth 196

Years' purchase....................................... 437
Yields 197, 440
YP.. 437